The Balkans on Trial

AF695369

This book assesses the legacy of the International Criminal Tribunal for former Yugoslavia (ICTY) and examines the conflicting intersection of law and politics in the search for justice, both thematically and through close analysis of some of the major trials.

It analyses the related case brought against Serbia and Montenegro by Bosnia and Herzegovina at the International Court of Justice (ICJ), as well as the Ganic case in London where the ICTY and ICJ findings were challenged. The book addresses the following questions:

- To what extent the political climate in which the ICTY was conceived, and continues to operate, has affected the declared aims of its founders?
- Have political considerations and political correctness, and the perceived need for political stability and democratic transition, at times proved an obstacle to the administration of justice?
- Are some of the acknowledged failings of international policy in the 1990s finding some resonance in more recent court proceedings?

This highly relevant and comprehensive book will be of interest to students and scholars of political science, international relations, transitional justice, Balkan area studies, human rights law, international criminal and peace and conflict studies.

Carole Hodge is a former Research Fellow and Head of Research and Study at the South-East European Research Unit at the University of Glasgow, UK.

Routledge Advances in European Politics

Uncovering the Territorial Dimension of European Union Cohesion Policy
Cohesion, Development, Impact Assessment, and Cooperation
Edited by Eduardo Medeiros

The Crisis of the European Union
Challenges, Analyses, Solutions
Edited by Andreas Grimmel

Promoting National Priorities in EU Foreign Policy
Czech Republic and the EU
Tomáš Weiss

Italy from Crisis to Crisis
Political Economy, Security, and Society in the 21st Century
Matthew Evangelista

Lobbying Success in the European Union
The Role of Information and Frames
Daniel Rasch

Muslim Attitudes Towards the European Union
Bernd Schlipphak and Mujtaba Isani

The Populist Radical Left in Europe
Edited by Giorgos Katsambekis and Alexandros Kioupkiolis

External Energy Security in the European Union
Small Member States' Perspective
Matúš Mišík

The Balkans on Trial
Justice vs. Realpolitik
Carole Hodge

For more information about this series, please visit: www.routledge.com/

The Balkans on Trial

Justice vs. Realpolitik

Carole Hodge

Routledge
Taylor & Francis Group
LONDON AND NEW YORK

First published 2019
by Routledge
2 Park Square, Milton Park, Abingdon, Oxon OX14 4RN

and by Routledge
605 Third Avenue, New York, NY 10017

First issued in paperback 2020

Routledge is an imprint of the Taylor & Francis Group, an informa business

© 2019 Carole Hodge

The right of Carole Hodge to be identified as author of this work has been asserted by her in accordance with sections 77 and 78 of the Copyright, Designs and Patents Act 1988.

All rights reserved. No part of this book may be reprinted or reproduced or utilised in any form or by any electronic, mechanical, or other means, now known or hereafter invented, including photocopying and recording, or in any information storage or retrieval system, without permission in writing from the publishers.

Trademark notice: Product or corporate names may be trademarks or registered trademarks, and are used only for identification and explanation without intent to infringe.

British Library Cataloguing-in-Publication Data
A catalogue record for this book is available from the British Library

Library of Congress Cataloging-in-Publication Data
A catalog record for this book has been requested

ISBN 13: 978-0-367-72913-4 (pbk)
ISBN 13: 978-0-415-63870-8 (hbk)

Typeset in Times New Roman
by Apex CoVantage, LLC

To all the child war victims and their families

Contents

Preface

One of the challenges in bringing this book to a close was where to draw the line, with major trials still ongoing in late 2018, 25 years after the establishment of the ICTY. Close study of some of the more recent judgements and decisions, moreover, suggests that some trial and appeals chambers have become increasingly remote from the compelling testimony of numerous witnesses spanning more than two decades.

In 1995, people worldwide were seized by the horrendous events at Srebrenica and looked to the ICTY and the major world powers and institutions for justice. It was a time when the tribunal was buzzing with energy and hope, albeit with some trepidation, at the mammoth task it was facing. Yet 25 years on, the trials of some of the tribunal's most notorious defendants, Radovan Karadžić and Ratko Mladić, indicted as early as 1995 for crimes against humanity and genocide in Europe's first major war since the Holocaust, linger on at half-mast and mostly away from the public eye.

The Bosnian war, Europe's first serious challenge since World War II to what some like to call 'European values', was the catalyst which arguably cast those values into a quite different perspective.

The legacy of the ICTY is likely to be extensively analysed in legal terms over time. What follows here is primarily a political analysis of some aspects of the tribunal's work, and of the Mechanism which succeeded it, particularly in the context of international policy in the Balkans in the 1990s and the resultant restraints on the tribunal's development.

This work has benefited from many discussions with tribunal officials, as well as politicians, lawyers, regional and international, human rights activists and others over the years, some of whom have preferred to remain unnamed. My gratitude goes to them all.

Carole Hodge, PhD, LLM
19 December 2018

Introduction

In the Spring of 1993, with tens of thousands of civilians killed and over two million displaced, and amid increasingly fruitless negotiations with Serbian, Bosnian and Croatian leaders in Geneva, London, New York, Belgrade and elsewhere, the one glimmer of hope was the International Criminal Tribunal (ICTY) at The Hague, founded to bring to justice the main perpetrators of some of the worst crimes against humanity in Europe since World War II.

But for some time, it remained just a glimmer. The siege and slaughter continued for another two-and-a-half years, met by a series of abortive international peace plans, until the Srebrenica genocide in July 1995, captured by cameras worldwide, prompted some capitals finally to focus on a more meaningful attempt to end the war. Even then, despite the indictment of Bosnian Serb political and military leaders Radovan Karadžić and Ratko Mladić for genocide just days after the fall of Srebrenica, neither was arrested. Instead, they were brought secretly into the Dayton peace negotiations, in which the Serbian president had a leading role, while the ICTY was sidelined and implicitly snubbed. It was only due to a handful of dedicated people at The Hague and elsewhere that the tribunal, against all odds, survived and eventually indicted 161 individuals, including the Serbian president, Slobodan Milosevic, once he was no longer deemed useful to the international negotiating process.

*

The Croatian war in 1991, where over 10,000 were killed and the multi-cultural town of Vukovar fell to Serb-led forces, presaged the Bosnian genocide, where Sarajevo was laid to siege, hundreds of thousands of civilians were forcibly expelled or killed and concentration camps set up, and where the process of systematic rape and torture became the norm in numerous municipalities across Bosnia and Herzegovina. International institutions and major state powers were made aware at the time of the scale of the crimes but failed to act or to form a concerted international policy to end the slaughter. On the contrary, Slobodan Milosevic, who was pivotal in both wars, was courted for many years in the apparent hope that he would order an end to the rampant nationalism he had rekindled in 1987 at Kosovo Polje.

The Commission of Experts was established by the United Nations (UN) in late 1992, mainly as a sop to public outrage at the apparent inertia of their politicians, yet was starved of funding and otherwise thwarted by senior UN officials and (mainly British) politicians and diplomats, and wound down prematurely. Credit for the volume of material it was to produce during its short duration, laying the foundation for evidence in several ICTY cases, was due mainly to its chairman, M. Cherif Bassiouni, and a dedicated group of specialists working with him in challenging conditions.

The ICTY, established by the UN Security Council under Chapter VII of the UN Charter, met with similar difficulties but survived and became a fully fledged institution thanks to the commitment and enthusiasm of its pioneers. In the early stages of its existence, the opposition in some international circles was not the only issue to hinder the tribunal. Its officials were working from a virtual blank sheet, struggling to draw up rules without expert knowledge. The closest precedent was Nuremberg but, due to its reputation for 'victors' justice', it was rejected as a blueprint.

It was hoped after the Srebrenica genocide that the ICTY would gain momentum and secure more support from the UN, which had created it, and from major world powers in funding investigations and facilitating arrests. Yet the Dayton Peace Agreement, which brought hostilities to an end, offered little hope. The ICTY was excluded from the 'high table' at the implementation conferences, while Slobodan Milosevic and Franjo Tudjman, the Croatian president responsible for the war between Croats and Bosniaks, were amongst the main signatories. Reference to the ICTY was omitted from the Dayton final text due to pressure from Milosevic, signalling to perpetrators that they were unlikely to end up at The Hague.

Disagreements amongst major world powers on the configuration of post-war Bosnia's constitutional arrangement were also unhelpful and resulted in a lowest common denominator solution – a weak, ethnically divided state with two separate entities and little power to central government. North Atlantic Treaty Organization (NATO) forces were brought in to cement the ethnic borders, but not to arrest indicted war criminals, allegedly for fear of local reprisals. At this time, over 40 individuals had been indicted but very few were in custody, with implications for those intrepid enough to attempt to return to their homes.

Politicians who were later to be indicted for genocide enjoyed leading roles in Bosnia in the aftermath of Dayton, while military commanders, later convicted for genocide in Srebrenica, remained in powerful positions for several years. Instead, Dusko Tadić, a prison guard arrested in Germany and transferred to The Hague, became the first suspect to be tried at the ICTY in a legally significant but lacklustre trial. International initiatives to arrest indictees in 1997 turned out to be less promising than proclaimed at the time, as Karadžić and Mladić remained at large for another 13 and 16 years, respectively, despite the continuing presence of NATO troops on the ground in Bosnia.

The indictment of Milosevic in the midst of NATO action in Kosovo was a significant boost to the tribunal and led to further indictments of Serbian generals involved in the Kosovo war. The task before ICTY Chief Prosecutor Carla Del Ponte was demanding, but her efforts to demonstrate impartiality and secure arrests meant unacceptable compromises, including indictments which failed to stand up in court and weakened the tribunal's standing. Her fragile indictment of Kosovar leader Ramush Haradinaj, tried twice at The Hague for comparatively minor offences and acquitted both times, was compounded by the trial chamber acquittal of Milan Milutinović, a close confidante of Milosevic, and Serbia's president during the Kosovo war.

Self-representation tested ICTY credibility to its very core. The Milosevic experience might have indicated to the tribunal that, for egregious crimes against humanity committed on a massive scale, self-representation was not a viable option. The handling of the Šešelj case by the presiding judge is discussed in some detail, as it exemplifies the extent of abuse of process which can occur to the detriment of the victims whose justice the tribunal was committed to achieving. The case also raised questions about witness protection and the accountability and impartiality of appointed judges. This was to come to a head in 2018 at the Mechanism for International Criminal Tribunals in an unprecedented clash between judges, which also implicitly raised questions over the composition of previous ICTY trial and appeals chambers.

The ICJ case, whose task was to determine the responsibility of Serbia as a state for the genocide in Bosnia, was pivotal in establishing the nature of the war there and the question of reparations payable, if any. The ICJ, unlike the ICTY which focused on individual responsibility, was in a position to approach the issue holistically. Yet the Court did not make use of its position, nor did it seek disclosure of the crucial Serbian Defence Council documents critical to forming its judgement, but merely reflected ICTY jurisprudence in rejecting genocide in the Bosnian municipalities in 1992.

The cases of Florence Hartmann, former official spokesperson at the ICTY, and Frederik Harhoff, *ad litem* judge at the tribunal, raised legitimate concerns about tribunal practice, and both paid the price: one in a brief prison sentence and the other in unceremonious expulsion from the ICTY. The judges' handling of their respective cases is examined in some detail against the legal backdrop of freedom of expression.

The arrest of Ejup Ganic moves the trial of suspects in the Bosnian war from The Hague to London, where Dr Ganic, a former Bosnian president, was arrested in 2010 following an extradition request by Serbia for alleged crimes relating to the so-called Dobrovoljacka episode, where a number of Yugoslav National Army (JNA) troops were killed in Sarajevo in early May 1992. Ganic spent nearly five months in detention or house arrest before being acquitted. The case highlighted some of the irregularities in the Serbian war crimes court, not least in the Jurisic case, and raised questions over the 2003 Extradition Act, but also about the British government's motives in choosing to act on what was clearly a faulty request. The request did, however, reflect a renewed confidence on the part of Serbia to rewrite the history of the Bosnian war and was later followed by similar extradition requests for Jovan Divjak in Austria and Ramush Haradinaj in France for alleged war crimes in Kosovo.

ICTY indictment procedures have been questioned as much for significant omissions of senior political and military leaders as for their timing and scope in high-profile cases, while sentencing patterns were often viewed as inconsistent and in some cases based on controversial plea agreements, most notably that of Biljana Plavsic. Political pressure and claims of ethnic bias prompted indictments which attempted to demonstrate the impartiality of the ICTY. But they often lacked firm evidence and led to acquittals. In 2012 and 2013, a series of controversial acquittals of senior political and military defendants were denounced by international commentators and survivors on the ground alike, while also challenging aspects of established ICTY jurisprudence and raising wider political questions.

The first-instance judgements of Karadžić and Mladić in March 2016 and November 2017, respectively, were generally applauded internationally and seen as bringing closure to the ICTY as it handed over to the Mechanism. But closer scrutiny revealed some questionable legal reasoning which would be left to the appeals chamber to address.

In June 2018, in a dramatic turn of events at the Mechanism, both the Mladić and Karadžić defence teams secured the withdrawal of several judges from the appeals benches, including the president, Theodor Meron. In the short term, it led to the postponement of both convicts' final judgement, delaying their transfer to serve their sentences in the harsher conditions of national prisons. It also raised questions about judicial ethics and the adequacy of the Rules of Procedure. In the longer term, and most seriously, it opened new channels for rewriting the Bosnian war.

1 Genesis of the tribunal

In extreme situations, silence is culpability.

– Elie Wiesel[1]

Introduction

The proposal for an international tribunal had already been mooted as a preventive measure in 1991, and again in early 1992, with the aim of prosecuting war crimes.[2] It only gained momentum, however, in response to worldwide public outrage following the exposure of Serb-run detention camps in northern Bosnia in August 1992. The graphic news reports of camp conditions with video footage of emaciated inmates, combined with the tacitly acknowledged failure of Lord Carrington's yearlong peace conference, underscored the international failure to end the carnage.[3] A new initiative was called for to demonstrate that the crimes would not go unpunished.

Initially, there was considerable reluctance amongst leading international players to setting up a tribunal and as an interim measure a so-called Commission of Experts was established in its place. The Commission served to appease world public opinion, while creating the impression that something was being done to address the war crimes, but was beset by obstacles from the outset. It lacked both resources and funding, and there were disagreements as to its role and purpose within the UN and amongst major world powers. Also, the practical difficulties of collecting evidence in a war zone, where the priority was the protection of UN troops on the ground, were overwhelming.

One of the main difficulties faced by the Commission of Experts (and later the *ad hoc* tribunal) was the refusal of leading international players to recognize the true nature of the war and act accordingly. Instead, over a year into hostilities, major world powers led by Britain and France continued to characterize the conflict as a civil war, born of ancient ethnic hatreds, with atrocities on all sides. This assumption of equivalence of guilt between the parties deflected from Serb responsibility and allayed public concern while facilitating ongoing negotiations with the main perpetrators, in particular Slobodan Milosevic, the Serbian president, and Bosnian Serb leader Radovan Karadžić.

To view international policy in Bosnia in the summer of 1992 in its full perspective, it is worth noting the situation in the area prior to the discovery of the camps.

Yugoslavia 1991

Ironically, it was the Bosnian president, Alija Izetbegovic, who in the first half of 1991, together with the Macedonian president, Kiro Gligorov, made the greatest effort, through a series of 'Yu-summits', to hold Yugoslavia together in the knowledge that its disintegration would be likely to unleash violence in Bosnia and Herzegovina, and possibly Macedonia.[4] The declarations of independence by Slovenia and Croatia in June 1991, however, compounded by the collapse of Lord Carrington's plan for a loose confederation in mid-October 1991, prompted the Bosnian parliament to vote later that month to declare Bosnia a 'sovereign republic'. The aim, according to Izetbegovic, was to ensure equal status for Bosnia with the other republics in the event of the secession of Slovenia and Croatia.[5] During the conflict in Croatia in 1991, Bosnia proved a vital base for JNA operations, exacerbating the tension between the ethnic groups.[6]

Bosnian Muslim leaders at this time were also preparing for resistance in the case of escalation of the war to Bosnia, in part through the newly formed Patriotic League, which had a civilian and a military wing, the latter mainly comprising former JNA officers of Muslim ethnicity. In this, however, Bosnia was faced with almost insurmountable obstacles. A blanket arms embargo[7] imposed on Yugoslavia by the UN Security Council in September 1991 meant that Bosnia, virtually landlocked, had no access to the means of self-defence against the might of the JNA, then one of Europe's largest armies. Each republic also had its separate Territorial Defence (TO), but at the end of 1991, an order came from Belgrade to Bosnian TO staffs to surrender their heavy weapons. This was endorsed by President Izetbegovic to appease the JNA and only rescinded the following March.[8]

From early 1991, Serbian Autonomous Regions (SAOs) began to be established in both Croatia and Bosnia.[9] From late August, the JNA participated in attacks on majority-Croat areas, together with the SAO Krajina special police (MUP),[10] in order to connect Serb-held territory.[11] Systematic acts of violence and intimidation were carried out by the JNA, Serbian paramilitaries and police against the non-Serb population, with the objective of driving them out of SAO Krajina.[12] On 1 October 1991, Dubrovnik came under siege by the JNA, civilians came under attack and the city was cut off by land and sea till late December.[13] More serious still were the JNA operations in Eastern Slavonia. In August 1991, the multi-national town of Vukovar came under siege and fell in November, followed by a massacre of civilians in nearby Ovcara.[14]

Two days later, on 20 November, the Bosnian president appealed to the UN for peacekeeping troops.[15] Following the international recognition of Slovenia and Croatia in December 1991, the situation in Bosnia rapidly deteriorated. JNA tanks and artillery were withdrawn from Croatia to Bosnia, and heavy artillery positions were set up around Sarajevo and other large Bosnian towns in the winter of

1991–1992.[16] The JNA openly favoured Serbs in its personnel policy, with non-Serb officers heavily pressured to resign. More than 90% of all JNA officers were now Serb or Montenegrin.[17]

By this time, the JNA had some 90,000 troops in Bosnia, it controlled most armouries and munitions stockpiles and could call on over 40 fighter planes, 6 helicopters and hundreds of tanks and heavy artillery. Added to this were thousands more troops stationed in Serbia and a sizeable number of Serbian paramilitary groupings. The Bosnian territorial forces numbered about 50,000, but possessed mainly small arms and, until 1993, just a single tank.[18] At the Bosnian Serb Assembly session of 27 March 1992, Karadžić recommended that, where possible, territorial units formed by the crisis staffs should be placed under JNA command. Once the JNA formally withdrew from Bosnia and Herzegovina they all, including the Serb territorial units, became part of the Bosnian Serb army, or *Vojska Republika Srpska* (VRS).[19]

The international response consisted of a series of abortive ceasefire agreements and setting up an international peace conference as a basis for negotiating a peace deal acceptable to all sides. The blanket arms embargo imposed in September 1991 was extended to Yugoslavia's successor states.[20]

Bosnia, 1991–1992

By early May 1992, large swathes of territory in North-Western, North-Eastern and South-Eastern Bosnia, and around Sarajevo, had already been taken over by the JNA in coordination with Serbian paramilitaries and the special police forces. Attempts at resistance by civilians and forces loyal to the Bosnian government varied from municipality to municipality but were largely unsuccessful due mainly to the disparity in weaponry.

North-Western Bosnia

By the time Bosnia and Herzegovina gained independence in April 1992, a considerable amount of territory in North-Western Bosnia was already under the control of the JNA and Serb paramilitary groups, following the establishment of SAO *Bosanska Krajina*. There is also evidence of detention camps in existence by 30 April.[21]

The strategy of destruction in the Prijedor municipality (44% Muslim, 43% Serb, 6% Croat and over 6,000 Yugoslav) had begun over six months earlier, despite the absence of any threat against the Serb inhabitants.[22] Serb officials began building their own administration, parallel to the legitimate authorities, which included a Serb police force with secret service functions.[23] In the early hours of 30 April 1992, JNA forces and Serb police took control of Prijedor, setting up checkpoints, occupying its most important buildings and taking over municipal administration organs and large companies. Police officers were obliged to pledge loyalty to the new Serb authorities, and Muslim police commanders were replaced by Serbs. Non-Serbs were removed from functions in the municipal assembly and administration and prohibited from entering the building. Shortly afterwards, Serb soldiers and reserve police officers levelled the predominantly Muslim old town with heavy machinery and destroyed the local mosque.[24] On 31 May, Serb nationalists ordered all non-Serbs to mark their houses with white flags or sheets and to wear a white armband if they left their homes.[25]

The shifting demographic balance in favour of the ethnic Muslim population had become a central issue in the municipality's political life in the prelude to hostilities. After the declaration of independence in Croatia and Slovenia in June 1991, Serbian nationalist propaganda became increasingly visible, with Serbs being encouraged to arm themselves, allegedly to prevent a repetition of the massacres of Serbs which had occurred in World War II. A large simultaneous influx of Serbs from Croatia exacerbated the situation.[26] In August 1991, Serbian paramilitaries took over the Mt Kozara transmitter station, and TV Sarajevo was replaced by broadcasts from Banja Luka and Belgrade.[27] The economic situation began to deteriorate as a result of power cuts and a disruption of traditional ties to Croatia and Slovenia.[28] In September 1991, the Prijedor Territorial Defence was mobilized and deployed to support the JNA offensive in Croatia. At a second mobilization on 7 November 1991, it was declared that whoever did not wish to participate could go home, but would have to surrender their equipment and weapons, further contributing to divisions between the communities.[29]

On 19 December 1991, the main board of the Serbian Democratic Party (SDS) in Bosnia adopted 'Instructions for the Organisation and Activity of Organs of the Serbian People in Bosnia and Herzegovina in Extraordinary Circumstances', which involved the formation of Serb government bodies, assemblies, executive boards, administrative organs, courts, public security stations and Serb crisis staff in Bosnian municipalities.[30] On 7 January 1992, Serb members of the Prijedor Municipal Assembly and local SDS presidents voted to join the Autonomous Region of Krajina (ARK). Further decisions to reinforce the crisis staff and create a number of clandestine Serb police stations set the scene for the forcible takeover of power in Prijedor on 29–30 April 1992.[31] The non-Serb population responded by establishing checkpoints in Kozarac, Hambarine and Brdo.[32] The people of Kozarac (99% Muslim) tried to control the perimeter of their town and organized patrols of around ten residents armed with hunting rifles. Nonetheless, within three weeks, Kozarac was taken over by the JNA and Serbian paramilitaries.[33]

On 29 February and 1 March 1992, coinciding with the Bosnian referendum on independence, Serb paramilitaries blockaded the municipality building in Banja Luka and on 3 April set up checkpoints around the town.[34] Civilians were killed, frequent attacks were carried out against property and businesses owned by non-Serbs, with thousands arrested.[35] By the end of 1992, most non-Serbs had been expelled or fled the region, with those remaining exposed daily to dangerous tasks, such as digging at the front lines.[36]

In March 1992, the municipality of Bosanska Krupa (74% Muslim and 24% Serb) was divided into Serb and Muslim areas, with the areas claimed by Serbs required to pledge loyalty to the Bosnian Serb Republic. On 19 April, the Serbs unilaterally proclaimed Bosanska Krupa a Serb municipality. Two days later, as

Serb civilians were seen leaving the town, Serb forces attacked with mortars from surrounding hills. Resistance, organized by members of the police and Patriotic League, broke down after four days, during which time most civilians fled, and a number were killed.[37]

In Prnjavor (71% Serb, 15% Muslim, 4% Croat) in March 1992, 250–300 Muslim men were interrogated and beaten by Serb guards, police officers and soldiers.[38] During the same month, the municipality of Sanski Most (47% Muslim, 42% Serb, 7% Croat) was divided along ethnic lines. On 17 April, the Serbs took control of Donji Vakuf (55% Muslim, 39% Serb, 3% Croat), while in Ključ (49% Serb, 47% Muslim, 1% Croat), two paramilitary groups and a number of JNA units entered the municipality and organized a Serb territorial unit.[39] In Kotor Varoš (38% Serb, 30% Muslim, 29% Croat) during April and May 1992, public institutions, including health and social services, and financial and postal services, began receiving their instructions from Banja Luka.[40] On 3 April, the Serb assembly issued a statement that as of 20 April only Bosnian Serb Republic laws would be in effect in 'Serb' Sanski Most. That day, Muslims and Croats, including judges, company directors and directors of the local radio and health centre, were dismissed from their jobs, along with Serb managers who had allowed Croats and Muslims to work in their companies. On 11 April, the Muslim president of the municipal court was told that he should leave Sanski Most, or his family would be harmed. On 17 April, the police were divided on ethnic lines, with police officers ordered to wear the Bosnian Serb Republic insignia to demonstrate their loyalty and to sign a declaration that they would respect its laws. Following attacks and intimidation during March and April 1992, many non-Serbs left the municipality.[41] In April, Teslić (55% Serb, 21% Muslim, 16% Croat) was barricaded, road signs put up in Cyrillic and all non-Serb police officers fired,[42] while in Bosanski Novi (60% Serb and 34% Muslim), the newly appointed Serb police chief dismissed all non-Serb officers and sacked non-Serb employees in the municipality. Later that month in Suhaca, Muslims surrendered their arms, and the villagers were instructed to move to a nearby field while Serb forces burned houses and mosques in the village and surrounding hills.[43]

By May 1992, Serb-run concentration camps were established in Omarska, Trnopolje, Keraterm, Manjaca and elsewhere. On 15 May, Bosnia's UN ambassador informed UN Secretary General Boutros Boutros-Ghali, but no action was taken.[44]

North-Eastern Bosnia, late 1991/May 1992

Bijeljina (59% Serb, 31% Muslim, 1% Croat) was the first municipality to be overtaken by Serb forces, when Serb paramilitaries took control of the main town structures on 31 March 1992. On 1–2 April, armed JNA reservists surrounded the town, and journalists and European monitors were prevented from entering. At least 48 civilians were killed during the takeover, most of them shot at close range, and 3,000 were displaced.[45] The pattern established in Bijeljina was later repeated in other municipalities in the area. Firstly, paramilitaries would arrive from Serbia and intimidate local Muslims, Croats and 'disloyal' Serbs. Many non-Serbs would be killed and, as a result, those remaining would leave their towns and villages. The JNA would then move in, allegedly to restore peace.[46]

Bratunac (64% Serb, 34% Muslim) was taken over by Serb forces in early April 1992, with a deadline of 29 April issued by the Serb authorities for non-Serbs to sign oaths of loyalty to Serb rule in the municipality.[47] In May 1992, 385 non-Serb civilians were reportedly massacred.[48] In Brčko, the JNA began preparations for military operations in February 1992. By the end of April, they had dug trenches, set up machine-gun nests and moved artillery, weapons and ammunition stores outside the town. On 1 May, 1,000 Serb forces, including JNA units, launched an attack on Brčko (44% Muslim, 25% Croat, 20% Serb), using heavy weapons, tanks and artillery.[49] In January and February 1992, 500 'White Eagles' paramilitaries entered the Doboj municipality (41% Muslim, 39% Serb, 13% Croat), and in March and April, the JNA set up checkpoints there, taking control of the town on 3 May, aided by police and paramilitaries.[50] In Vlasenica (55% Muslim, 42% Serb), Muslims working in state-owned companies were dismissed from their jobs from late 1991. In late April 1992, JNA soldiers took over Vlasenica, and Muslims were subjected to various disciplinary measures.[51] From early June 1992, large numbers of non-Serbs were detained in the Susica camp.[52] In Zvornik (59% Muslim, 38% Serb), two days after a mass exodus of Serb civilians from the town, Serb paramilitaries arrived and erected barricades throughout the municipality. On 8 April, a combination of Serb forces, partly originating from Serbia, launched an attack against Zvornik where dozens of civilians were killed and thousands displaced.[53] On 10 April, BBC correspondent Martin Bell witnessed the rearguard of the forced migration of some 2,000 Muslims and Croats from Zvornik.[54] Žepa, Srebrenica, Konjevic Polje and Cerska were bombed by aircraft from Serbia on a regular basis from early June 1992.[55] By that summer, Bosnian Muslims in the Drina valley were corralled into four areas, Gorazde, Srebrenica, Žepa and Cerska, surrounded by heavily armed Serb forces and without access to humanitarian aid.[56]

South-Eastern Bosnia, late 1991–1992

A similar process was taking place in South-Eastern Bosnia. In Višegrad (64% Muslim, 32% Serb), between late 1991 and early 1992, on JNA orders, territorial units largely comprised of Muslims were ordered to surrender their weapons. During that period, the JNA organized military training for the Serbs supplied local Serbs with weapons brought in from Serbia and provided military training.[57] In early April 1992, the JNA Uzice Corps seized strategic locations in the municipality, resulting in many Muslim civilians fleeing their villages. The following week, there was a brief counter-attack, as Muslim police officers arrested 12 armed Serbs and seized control of the hydroelectric dam, but the following day, the Uzice Corps retook control of the dam and entered Višegrad. Soon afterwards, both Serbs and Muslims raised barricades around the town, which was followed by random acts of violence.[58] A joint media campaign between JNA officers and

Muslim leaders tried to persuade people to return to their homes, and set up negotiations between the sides to attempt to defuse tensions.[59] However, during the negotiations, a Serb JNA officer was heard to explain to other officers that the Uzice Corps had 'clean[ed]' areas along the Drina river and indicated that an area with 4,000 Muslims would be 'clean' the following day.[60] On 15 April, the JNA Uzice Corps organized convoys to drive out Muslims from the surrounding villages. On later returning, many found their houses burned or otherwise damaged, while Serb houses were untouched. The Uzice Corps set up checkpoints in and around Višegrad, manned by JNA soldiers and local Serbs.[61] In a matter of days, Višegrad went from being predominantly Muslim to almost exclusively Serb.[62] On withdrawing on 19 May 1992, the JNA left weapons and equipment behind for the Serbian paramilitaries.[63] On 14 June 1992, more than 60 Muslim civilians were locked up in a house in Pionirska Street by Serb paramilitaries, and the house was set on fire with all but six burned alive.[64] Many others who disappeared between April and June 1992 were thrown into the river Drina.[65]

In Bileća (80% Serb, 15% Muslim) in January 1992, all police officers were required to wear insignia showing their loyalty to the Bosnian Serb Republic, and those who refused to comply were dismissed from their jobs. Checkpoints were erected in the municipality in April and restrictions imposed on the movement of Muslims.[66] In March 1992 in Čajniče (53% Serb, 45% Muslim), the local SDS leader and municipal president, Dusko Kornjaca, gained control of the local armed forces, assumed the presidency of the Čajniče crisis staff and became SAO Herzegovina defence minister. In April, local Serb authorities dismissed Muslims from positions of public authority and erected barricades on the roads out of Čajniče, with Muslims required to have documents signed by Kornjaca in order to leave the town. In April 1992, the crisis staff in Čajniče ordered the arrest of prominent Muslims. In mid-April, several Muslim civilians were arrested and detained in a storage container near a Serb checkpoint operated by the Blue Eagles paramilitary group. In early May, Serb forces, some in JNA uniform, in conjunction with paramilitaries, occupied Muslim-majority towns in the area by force. Homes were looted and burned across Western and Central Čajniče.[67]

In Foča (51% Muslim, 45% Serb) from April 1992, Muslims were dismissed from their jobs and restrictions were placed on their movements. Just before the outbreak of conflict on 8 April 1992, Serbs began evacuating their families and children, mostly to Serbia or Montenegro. On 7 April, Serbs were mobilized and issued with weapons. On the night of 8 April, Serbs took over the Foča radio station, the warehouse of the regional medical centre and of the TO where weapons were stored, and deployed heavy artillery on elevated sites around Foča, controlling JNA heavy weapons, and also the weaponry of the TO. On 8 April 1992 between 8.30 am and 10.00 am, Serbs, including from Serbia and Montenegro, attacked predominantly Muslim neighbourhoods of Foča, with infantry fire and shelling, and proceeded to take over the town area by area, securing the town within a week and the whole municipality ten days later. Large numbers, mostly civilians, were wounded, and many left the town. Muslim neighbourhoods were destroyed systematically by Serb soldiers, even after the town had been secured.

Between 14 and 17 April, civilians were arrested, including several doctors and medical staff from Foča hospital, and some were severely beaten.[68] Muslim businesses were looted or burned and equipment confiscated. The destruction of monuments, including the Alazda mosque, began in April 1992. From 19 April 1992, large-scale arrests of Muslim civilian men and women took place throughout the municipality, with some killed, raped or severely beaten.[69]

In Gacko (62% Serb, 36% Muslim), in early 1992, Serb reservists and police erected barricades. Violence against non-Serbs began in March when members of a local Serb paramilitary unit killed two Muslims. Muslim houses and businesses were burned, property looted and the Muslim police chief replaced by a Serb. From April 1992, Serb forces detained Muslims and Croats in Gacko in at least six locations. In Kalinovik, harassment and physical intimidation of Muslims began in late 1991. On 20 April, Muslim police officers, including the chief of police, were dismissed from their jobs, and the following month, Muslim residents were required to surrender their weapons.[70] In Rogatica (60% Muslim, 38% Serb), a Serb paramilitary unit was formed, and the municipal SDS president, Sveto Veselinovic, sought the partition of the municipality and division of the police and territorial army, which Muslim negotiators agreed to in March 1992, in order to avoid war, which was then implemented. Yet it did not prevent, from March onwards, armed Serb locals and JNA soldiers, including the Uzice Corps of the JNA, from robbing, harassing and otherwise mistreating Muslims in the municipality.[71] In March 1992 in Sokolac (69% Serb, 30% Muslim), barricades were set up, and local Serbs appeared in JNA and camouflage uniforms carrying automatic weapons. All Muslim police officers were dismissed from their jobs, and several paramilitary units based themselves in Sokolac and the surrounding villages.[72]

Sarajevo municipalities, 1992

The siege of Sarajevo began on 5 April 1992, but the surrounding area came under threat much earlier.

In the Ilidža municipality (43% Muslim, 37% Serb, 10% Croat and over 5,000 declared Yugoslav) at the beginning of March 1992, a Serb crisis centre was created. Muslim police officers were dismissed from their positions, followed by the arrival of several paramilitary formations, including Arkan's men. In Novi Grad (51% Muslim, 28% Serb, 7% Croat), a Serb municipality was established around 22 February. In March, local Serb leaders threatened to attack Muslims who did not leave the village. In early May, Arkan's paramilitaries and the White Eagles arrived. In Novo Sarajevo (36% Muslim, 35% Serb, 9% Croat) on 1 March 1992, Serbs began organizing barricades at strategic points in Sarajevo and the surrounding municipalities. The following day, non-Serbs set up barricades. Many were detained at Lukavica, where detainees were regularly beaten.[73] By the end of April 1992, JNA heavy artillery, rocket launchers, anti-aircraft guns and tanks fired every evening on targets in Sarajevo. In Ilijaš (45% Serb, 42% Muslim, 7% Croat) in March 1992, Serb flags were hoisted on the municipal building and police station, and non-Serb police officers, school, bank and hospital workers were dismissed, while Serb crisis staff took over all major military and civilian institutions and facilities, including the media. In Hadžići (64% Muslim, 26% Serb, 3% Croat) from mid-April 1992, JNA reserve units were brought in from Serbia and Montenegro in liaison with JNA barracks commanders, where they occupied strategically important buildings and positions.[74] At the end of April, JNA forces shelled Sarajevo and its surrounds, including Bijelo Polje and Novo Sarajevo.

In Pale (69% Serb, 27% Muslim, 1% Croat), non-Serbs were dismissed from the police in early March 1992. In March and April 1992, Serb paramilitaries, local police and reserve soldiers set up checkpoints in Pale which severely restricted the movements of Muslims. Local armed Serbs assisted at the barricades. In late March, the Pale chief of police, Koroman, told a Muslim delegation that he could no longer guarantee the safety of non-Serbs in Pale. In Trnovo (69% Muslim, 29% Serb) in March and April 1992, Serbs and Muslims both erected checkpoints. By early April 1992, Serb police officers formed their own police force and hoisted a Serb flag on the local culture centre which they had taken over as their base. On 26 April, at an SDS municipal board session, the division of the municipal administration along ethnic lines was called for.[75]

In early March 1992, in Vogošća (51% Muslim, 36% Serb, 4% Croat and 1,730 declared Yugoslavs), SDS delegates established their own assembly, calling for the municipality to be divided along ethnic lines, with Serbs controlling the town centre, important communication links and all local industry The JNA set up roadblocks around important factories in Sarajevo, including the Pretis artillery and rocket manufacturing plant in Vogošća, one of the largest in Europe. The police were divided along ethnic lines and, between 4 and 17 April, a large part of Vogošća was brought under Serb control by military force. On 2 May 1992, Serbs surrounded and shelled surrounding villages.[76]

The city of Sarajevo, April 1992

The siege of Sarajevo began on the eve of the European Community recognition of Bosnia Herzegovina as an independent state. The Bosnian Assembly building, Sarajevo Airport and other buildings were seized by armed Serbs, following which President Alija Izetbegovic ordered the full mobilization of the Bosnian Territorial Defence and police reserve forces. As thousands of protestors took to the streets in spontaneous peace marches, heavy machine-gun fire was heard across the city, accompanied by explosions and shooting into crowds of demonstrators by unidentified gunmen. At least seven people were killed and ten injured.[77]

On 6 April, the Old Town (Stari Grad) and Bazaar Districts, the main television tower and the centre for social work were hit. At least 11 were killed and a hundred wounded. Fierce fighting ensued in the battle for control of the airport. The EC Monitoring Mission office in Sarajevo reported that Serb police had seized the Interior Ministry police training centre, holding a number of cadets and teachers hostage. The JNA was reported to have joined Serbian irregulars on two outlying hillsides in launching rocket, mortar and artillery strikes, with Bosnian forces returning small arms fire. A state of emergency was declared.[78] On 8 April, the bombardment of the Old Town began at 5.30 am, lasting two hours, following a warning from a senior JNA general.[79] Intermittent shelling continued throughout April.

On 2 May, the JNA and Serbian paramilitaries established a total blockade of Sarajevo, cutting off major access roads, and attempted to divide the city and destroy the Bosnian presidency building.[80] At that time, its six barracks were surrounded by the Bosnian Territorial Defence. Between 3.30 and 5.00 am, the JNA shelled the city in the largest single bombardment to date. Many government buildings were targeted and the post office and the main telephone exchange destroyed.[81] Forty thousand phone lines were knocked out, including all those serving the city centre, where the government buildings were located.[82]

The earlier events represent just a cross-section of war crimes in the Bosnian municipalities during that time and are confirmed in ICTY judgements. The UN already had UNPROFOR (United Nations Protection force) troops in Sarajevo at the onset of war, as their operational base for the UN mission in Croatia. When Sarajevo came under attack, they pulled out, leaving just a small contingent of 'peacekeepers'. The UN later struck a deal with the Serbs to control Sarajevo airport, but it remained de facto under Serb control throughout the war.

International policy, 1992

In Bosnia, the situation differed from some other countries where war crimes have occurred due to specific international policies which generally favoured the main aggressor. These policies persisted despite information about wide-scale atrocities and the existence of camps held at the time by the UN, the Red Cross and Western government officials and analysts.[83]

On 14 April 1992, a classified memorandum submitted by US Assistant Secretary of State for European and Canadian Affairs Thomas M.T. Niles to US Deputy Secretary of State Lawrence Eagleburger described the Serbs' 'clear pattern of use of force, intimidation, and provocation to violence aimed at forcibly partitioning [Bosnia] and effecting large transfers of population'.[84] US official Jon Western and his colleagues had been sifting through up to a thousand documents on Bosnia daily since the beginning of the war from a multitude of sources and, by early July, had acquired clear evidence of a vast network of concentration camps across Bosnia.[85] Through satellite imagery, they were often able to predict imminent attacks by Bosnian Serb forces.[86] But it was not until journalists' exposure of the camps in early August that Niles admitted publicly to prior knowledge of their existence. State Department spokesman Richard Boucher went further, confirming having received 'continuing reports of abuses, torture and killings' in the camps.[87] Charles Kirudja, a UN official stationed across the border in Topusko, wrote to his superiors based on information from refugees crossing into Croatia:

> We believe the football field detainees are only a tip of the iceberg involving the concerted action of local Serbian authorities in BH trying to establish a

> Serbian Republic of BH, free of Muslims. In that process, the mayors, the milicija and TDF of Bosanski Novi, acting in unison with their counterparts, not only in the UNPA (Dvor and Kostajnica), but also with Bosanska Dubica, Banja Luka, Prijedor, Sanski Most and Ključ. The Serbs appear to be engaged in a determined process of forcefully disarming Muslims where they are clearly a small encircled minority, such as in Bosanski Novi, or besieging their city totally, such as in Bihac. Apparently the football field is the holding ground where Muslim groups are detained while their houses are being 'searched,' the men isolated and transported to concentration camps.[88]

A confidential UN memorandum, dated 3 July 1992, followed a stream of earlier reports indicating attempts to establish 'a Serbian republic free of Muslims'. Concentration camps were reported at four localities where treatment of Muslims was described as atrocious. There was clear frustration at being confined to writing reports and standing by, as UNPROFOR had no operational responsibilities across the border. The memorandum was first published in a 158-page Helsinki Watch report the following month. The report, based on two trips between 19 March and 19 June 1992, called for an international tribunal charged with investigating, pursuing, judging and punishing without distinction those responsible.[89] The report alleged that the scope and brutality of abuses far exceeded those reported, and considered that the systematic executions, forcible expulsions and shelling attacks offered *prima facie* evidence of genocide in progress, and called on the UN to ensure those engaging in genocide be held accountable.[90] Milosevic, Karadžić, Arkan and Šešelj were included in the list, with the claim that there was sufficient evidence to warrant investigations of war crimes, as well as for crimes by Croatian forces in Gospic in 1991. Providing a breakdown of applicable international law, the report alleged that the UN, through the Security Council, was under an obligation to prevent genocide in Bosnia. It was the first organization to call on the UN to set up an international tribunal to prosecute those responsible for war crimes.

The Bosnian president, Alija Izetbegovic, also appealed to the international community. On 28 June 1992, when French President Francois Mitterand flew into Sarajevo, Izetbegovic handed him details of 94 places of detention, including several alleged concentration camps. He asked Mitterand for a human rights mission to investigate but received no response at the time.[91] On 9 July, Izetbegovic provided a list of suspected Serb detention centres to a Commission on Security and Cooperation in Europe (CSCE) meeting in Helsinki. On 19 July, he sent a letter to the US president, George Bush, concerning 57 Serb concentration camps and, on 29 July, the Bosnian delegation handed a list of camps to the US delegation at a humanitarian meeting in Geneva.[92] By this time, over two million people had been displaced.[93]

US journalist Roy Gutman had already published information on the Manjaca camp in July, the first outside journalist to do so, and wrote a further report on Omarska on 2 August.[94] That same week, foreign TV crews gained access to three major camps. Graphic coverage by an ITN news team, followed by massive international news coverage, propelled Western governments into belated action to justify their policies. The need to demonstrate at least a modicum of international will to investigate the crimes and bring the perpetrators to justice had become imperative.

On 7 August, the UNHCR headquarters in Geneva admitted that officials had known about the death camps the previous month and reported them in their bulletin on 27 July.[95] Three days later, the UN Human Rights Commission met at the request of the Bush administration, and in an emergency session (the first in its 45-year history), former Polish prime minister Tadeusz Mazowiecki was appointed as special rapporteur on former Yugoslavia, with a mandate to collect evidence of human rights abuses and war crimes, and report back in a month.[96] It was the first time that a UN representative had a specific mandate to look into war crimes. In late 1992, Mazowiecki attempted to visit Manjaca but was turned away by Serb officials. He also sent a team to investigate mass rape charges and authorized a lawyer to investigate mass graves.[97] His appointment was one of the few positive international measures to emerge at the time, but he was impeded by lack of funds, denied resources for field officers, and shunned for 'exceeding' his mandate. In July 1995, Mazowiecki resigned, considering himself to be little more than 'a stenographer of horror'.[98] He criticized the UN relief agencies and peace negotiators, commenting that human rights agencies appeared to be at odds with the tribunal and peace at odds with human rights.[99]

> The character of my mandate allows me only to describe further crimes and violations of human rights. But the present critical moment forces us to realise the true character of those crimes, and the responsibility of Europe and the international community for their own helplessness in addressing them.[100]

One of Mazowiecki's main difficulties was the tension between his office and negotiators Vance and Owen. Despite repeated attempts to develop closer ties with the negotiating team, neither Mazowiecki himself nor the UN Human Rights Commission were ever consulted about the human rights component of the Vance Owen plan. In his sixth report, he stated that 'peace negotiations should not have been conducted without ensuring the cessation of massive and gross human rights violations'.[101] This was fundamentally at odds with the Vance Owen strategy of separating human rights and negotiations. The rift between the institutions was to undermine efforts to identify war criminals and bring them to justice.

The Vance Owen 'peace' conference had been set up following Lord Carrington's resignation in August 1992, when it was decided to unify the EC and UN mediating efforts, under newly appointed leaders, Lord David Owen representing the European Community and Cyrus Vance the UN.[102] All attention was now diverted to the London Conference, held on 26 August 1992. There was a threat to criminalize the instigators, but Europe was divided, with no common foreign or defence policy. The German foreign minister Klaus Kinkel proposed creating a criminal tribunal, warning that 'it is not just a matter of denouncing these crimes; their perpetrators must know that such acts will not go unpunished and that they will be prosecuted'.[103] Strong words for public consumption, but no-one in Belgrade was fooled.

War crimes and peace plans

By Autumn 1992, women's and human rights groups had joined with the media to present a chilling picture of rapes, expulsions and detentions.[104] In October, the UN Security Council established a Commission of Experts, the first UN institution officially charged with gathering evidence of war crimes in the Balkans; its mandate gave it the broadest international investigative authority since the UN War Crimes Commission of World War II.

The Commission of Experts came into being largely due to US Secretary of State Madeleine Albright as a political substitute for a meaningful military response to the atrocities. It was to meet with similar difficulties to Mazowiecki's mission. Owen and Vance's peace plan, if it was to achieve any measure of success, had to demonstrate that all sides were morally equivalent. The investigation of war crimes and crimes against humanity, overwhelmingly committed by Serbs against non-Serbs, would inevitably compromise their negotiations. British foreign minister Douglas Hogg was aware of where the responsibility lay.

> If . . . the responsibility for those crimes goes as high as . . . I expect, we must ask ourselves what is the priority; is it to bring people to trial or is it to make peace?[105]

The Vance Owen Plan was to have a decisive impact on the UN handling of war crimes. The chairmen were unwilling to link war crimes with the peace process, confirming the widely held conviction that the pursuit of war criminals was incompatible with negotiations aimed at a political settlement.[106] Apart from it not being within the mandate, Owen claimed that linkage would make it impossible for them to remain neutral and work as credible negotiators. Owen's position became evident on the day of the first meeting of the Commission of Experts on 12 December 1992 in Geneva.[107] In the room next door, where a meeting of the International Conference for Former Yugoslavia was in progress, US Deputy Secretary of State Lawrence Eagleburger was delivering his bombshell speech, calling for a second Nuremberg tribunal and listing Karadžić, Mladić, Milosevic and other Serb leaders as war crimes suspects.[108] Eagleburger's speech was carefully worded, however, and already cleared by the Bush administration and lawyers.[109] Since the Democrats were due to take over the following month, the speech was generally viewed as opportunistic.[110] Nor did he pursue the matter with President Bush. According to the acting Yugoslav desk officer, George Kenney, whose briefing paper had been altered by Eagleburger's office to imply that all sides were equal, Eagleburger had earlier tried to deflect anything which focused blame on the Serbs.[111]

*

Reservations about the establishment and proposed agenda of the Commission of Experts were shared amongst all major world powers, but in different degrees and for different reasons. The difficulty in establishing a consistent international approach to the war was to frustrate the work of the Commission, and later the ICTY, from the outset.

In the early stages of the war Washington, preoccupied with Iraq and the fallout from the Soviet Union disintegration, took a back seat, while Britain and France sought a diplomatic solution.[112] When the idea for an *ad hoc* tribunal for Yugoslavia was raised, the United States faced several dilemmas. How could it be justified to indict the Serbian leadership when they had renounced judgement of Saddam Hussein? The United States also opposed even the principle of a permanent international court in view of its unilateral military operations in Panama, Grenada and elsewhere. And, in the Balkans, US foreign policy was guided by senior officials with long-standing links to the Serbian leadership, to the extent that the Bush administration favoured the Serbs even after the fall of Vukovar.[113] Also, with the US presidential election looming, the Bush administration sought to avoid involvement by dismissing stories of Serb atrocities and equating them with Muslim and Croat violations.[114] Then there was the fractious US/UN relationship. The United States owed the UN hundreds of millions of dollars in arrears and opposed the growth of the UN budget. US leaders also did not trust the UN sufficiently to invest it with international criminal jurisdiction. Moreover, while insisting on a clause in the resolution obliging governments to submit information concerning violations of human rights at regular intervals to the Commission of Experts, the United States did not welcome the establishment of a tribunal which could not be dismantled.

European policy in the Balkans was dominated by Britain and France, the only two European countries with permanent membership of the UN Security Council, and large standing armies, but it was Britain which took the lead there in opposing all measures aimed at establishing an effectual tribunal.[115] In early 1992, Robert Badinter, former justice minister under Mitterand and president of the French Constitutional Council, France's supreme judicial body, was one of the first to evoke the necessity to pursue war criminals.[116] Mitterand was initially very reluctant, viewing it as a complication to a negotiated settlement. Badinter mentioned his project to Carrington and Vance but got no reaction, and finally approached Roland Dumas, then France's foreign minister, who saw the political advantages of such a proposal.

> I did not want to find myself in the situation of post WW2, when the world discovers the death camps, and nothing was available for punishing those responsible. I wanted that at least . . . they would answer to justice, since we already did not want to intervene militarily in Bosnia. I did not want us to appear as accomplices to crimes that were still being committed.[117]

The British government, the most opposed amongst Western powers to an international war crimes commission, wielded influence at various levels from the outset to limit its scope. In 1991, British leaders had assumed a leading international role in introducing measures which effectively shored up Serb territorial gains in both Croatia and Bosnia, in suggesting a mandatory arms embargo in September 1991, in deflecting calls by other European leaders for military intervention, and in proposing and chairing an international peace conference which at best achieved temporary ceasefires.[118]

It soon became clear that the United States and Britain had differing views on the purpose of the Commission. Firstly, there was the issue of its name. The US State Department wanted a commission which would establish a link with the United Nations War Crimes Commission, set up in 1943 to prepare the way for Nuremberg, since this would be more likely to lead to prosecutions. The United States also wanted the Commission to conduct its own field investigations. Britain, wary of the impact such a commission could have on a negotiated settlement, argued successfully for the words 'war crimes' to be omitted from the title, hence the compromise solution – 'Commission of Experts'.[119] Britain also argued against the Commission having a mandate to investigate in the field and, while eventually agreeing, insisted that it should be funded from existing UN resources. Given the pressures on the UN budget, partly due to the United States' failure to pay its dues, compounded by UN bureaucracy, the Commission started out with no specific funds allocated to investigations. Apart from this, the working conditions in Geneva were Spartan – there was no office to work in, no personnel, no translators and no computers.[120] The British preference was for a passive committee which would collect and analyse information received, and thus present little challenge to the 'peace' process. The United States had also argued for governments to submit material to the Commission, the first within 30 days, then at regular intervals. In practice, America was initially the only country to hand over information. Britain submitted documents only in late 1993, following pressure from a BBC Panorama documentary, exposing Britain's non-cooperation.

For similar reasons, Britain also managed to block the appointment of M. Cherif Bassiouni as chairman of the Commission. Professor Bassiouni, a naturalized US citizen born in Egypt, was a specialist in the law of war, but he was a man of action and a Muslim, so his appointment was likely to be strongly opposed by Belgrade.[121] A 70-year-old retired Dutch academic, Frits Kalshoven, was eventually chosen. Bassiouni, relegated to second position, was nevertheless to carry the Commission. Kalshoven later admitted he had no idea why he was appointed.[122] In fact, he was the only one who actually banked a salary; others were paid on *per diem* basis, without finance for field investigations or to create a database. In the event, Kalshoven took medical leave in August 1993 and resigned the following month. He singled out Britain and France as providing little support for the Commission's work, commenting that Lord Owen had warned him not to name specific individuals in his report.[123] He also informed the press that 'authoritative persons' at the UN Legal Advisor's Office had instructed him not to pursue Serbian politicians, such as Milosevic and Karadžić.[124] He specifically noted that Britain had refused to supply a combat engineering unit to undertake the exhumation at the site where 200 hospital patients were believed to have been massacred and buried.[125]

The Commission (and later the ICTY) were denied access to adequate funding for nearly two years, and specifically for field investigations, at Britain's insistence.[126] Funding came from the UN regular budget, and later from its legal budget, and voluntary contributions. This was well below what was required, however, so in January 1993, Commission members requested a separate fund for voluntary contributions but were blocked by the UN Legal Affairs Office, which ruled that UN Resolution 780 made no provision for such a fund.

These were not the only problems. The mandate was ambiguous since the resolution did not refer to a tribunal, and the methodology was also confused. Resolution 780 called for evidence of 'grave breaches' of the Geneva Conventions, but this would apply to international armed conflict only, and there was considerable controversy as to the nature of the Bosnian war.

The Commission of Experts – aims and achievements

Considering the obstacles placed in its path, both on the ground and internationally, the Commission of Experts achieved remarkable results in a short space of time. A body of material was assembled which facilitated prosecution based on command responsibility; rape became more precisely defined as a crime of violence in international humanitarian law, and evidence was produced to indicate the possible commission of genocide in Bosnia. Crucially, in terms of international policy, the Commission concluded that there was no factual basis for arguing a 'moral equivalence'.[127]

The Commission commenced work in November 1992 and was forced to wind up prematurely in April 1994. Personnel and time constraints, along with limited financial resources, meant that Commission members were not in a position to perform exhaustive investigations, nor to verify all allegations pertaining to violations of international humanitarian law.[128]

Following the untimely resignation of Kalshoven, M. Cherif Bassiouni took his place and, despite Security Council opposition, managed to establish a comprehensive database at DePaul University, recording all reported grave breaches of the Geneva Conventions and international humanitarian law. He also assembled 50 lawyers and students from across the United States to work for the Commission on a *pro bono* basis. The Commission's database was financed exclusively through funds provided by DePaul University's International Human Rights Law Institute, amounting to over $1 million by 30 April 1994.[129] On 26 March 1993, a Trust Fund was established to assist the Commission, and governments were requested to contribute financial resources or personnel.[130] The total amount of contributions to the Trust Fund amounted to $1,320,631, but became effective only in July 1993.[131]

*

The Commission's 30-page Final Report is backed up by 300 hours of videotaped testimony and news footage, as well as a 3,200-page, 5-volume annex supporting its conclusions. One of the main projects of the Commission was an investigation into war crimes and crimes against humanity in the Prijedor region, which included extensive interviews with nearly 400 victims and witnesses of events. The investigators found that

> despite the absence of a real non-Serbian threat, the main objective of the concentration camps, especially Omarska but also Keraterm, seems to have been to eliminate the non-Serbian leadership. Political leaders, officials from the courts and administration, academics and other intellectuals, religious

> leaders, key business people and artists – the backbone of the Muslim and Croatian communities – were removed, apparently with the intention that the removal be permanent. Similarly, law enforcement and military personnel were targeted for destruction . . . non-Serbs were instructed to wear white arm bands to identify themselves [and] subjected to crimes without the new Serbian leaders attempting to redress the problem. Rape, for example, became a serious problem for many women who were left alone because their husbands had been detained.[132]
>
> (i)t is unquestionable that the events in Opština Prijedor since 30 April 1992 qualify as crimes against humanity. Furthermore, it is likely to be confirmed in court under due process of law that these events constitute genocide.[133]

The Commission emphasized that the pattern documented in Prijedor matched closely similar information received in other regions, including Banja Luka, Brčko, Zvornik and Foča. The report concluded,

> Based on the many reports describing the policy and practices conducted in the former Yugoslavia, 'ethnic cleansing' has been carried out by means of murder, torture, arbitrary arrest and detention, extra-judicial executions, rape and sexual assaults, confinement of civilian population in ghetto areas, forcible removal, displacement and deportation of civilian population, deliberate military attacks or threats of attacks on civilians and civilian areas, and wanton destruction of property. Those practices constitute crimes against humanity and can be assimilated to specific war crimes. Furthermore, such acts could also fall within the meaning of the Genocide Convention.[134]

There were, however, major concerns as to the implications of a genocide charge within the UN Security Council. This would have carried serious policy implications: a deliberately conceived plan, aimed at eliminating the group as opposed to random acts of warfare, placed an obligation on the international community to punish and prevent the killing and challenged members of the Genocide Convention to bring Serbia to answer before the ICJ.[135]

On 20 June 1993, the Commission sent an investigative mission to Sarajevo to undertake a study of a specific incident in the battle of Sarajevo and conduct a legal analysis.[136] The incident finally selected for in-depth investigation was the mortar shelling of a soccer game in the Dobrinja suburb of Sarajevo on 1 June 1993. As was the case in other aspects of the Commission's work, the survey of the Sarajevo siege was hampered by lack of resources and time. The mission included a group of Canadian military lawyers and police investigators led by William Fenrick, with the objective of identifying specific violations of the law of war, particularly where civilian casualties occurred, and to assess the feasibility of identifying and prosecuting alleged offenders, especially military commanders.[137] The study concluded that the Bosnian Serb forces were systematically targeting the civilian population of Sarajevo, either as a measure of retaliation or to weaken their political resolve,[138] and that it should be possible to develop a *prima facie* case against the commander of the Bosnian Serb forces surrounding Sarajevo under the principle that a commander, as a fundamental aspect of command, has a duty to control his troops and ensure that they comply with the law.[139] This focus on command responsibility anticipated the tribunal work, especially in indicting and convicting General Stanislav Galic, who had commanded 18,000 military personnel in 10 brigades during most of the Sarajevo siege. It was not until over six years later that Galic was arrested and a further seven years before his life imprisonment sentence was confirmed.

*

The Commission also investigated the Croat forces' attack on the Medak Pocket on 9 September 1993. This was a collection of small rural villages and hamlets in Serb-controlled land jutting into Croat territory, where Croat forces killed or routed the few Serb defenders and overran the area.[140] The Commission found 'exceptionally strong support' for the suggestion that *prima facie* cases could be developed against named Croatian senior officers for the wanton destruction of civilian property.[141]

*

The charge of rape had not been adequately addressed in international law enforcement. Although constituting a crime, rape, unlike most codified penal laws in the world, was not precisely defined under international humanitarian law. The Commission report gave the process special impetus, concluding that 'ethnic cleansing', sexual assault and rape had been carried out so systematically that they strongly appeared to be the product of a policy.[142]

The pattern of reported cases of rape and sexual assault correlated with the publication of the Warburton Report, commissioned by the European Council in December 1992. Based on two visits to Croatia and Bosnia, the report, commenting on the systematic nature of the rapes, concluded that

> a horrifying number of Muslim women had been raped and this was continuing. . . . Women are understandably reluctant to recall details of the atrocities done to them and many may refer to their own experiences in the third person. . . . The enormity of the suffering being inflicted on the civilian population in this conflict defies expression. Indications are that at least some of the rapes have been committed in particularly sadistic ways, so as to inflict maximum humiliation on the victims, on their family, and on the whole community. In many cases there seems little doubt that the intention is deliberately to make women pregnant and then to detain them until pregnancy is far enough advanced to make termination impossible, as an additional form of humiliation and constant reminder of the abuse done to them.[143]

*

The Commission had been intending to conduct a full-scale investigation of the Ovcara grave site, reported to contain the bodies of some 200 Croats taken from the Vukovar Hospital in November 1991, where they were summarily executed and left in a shallow mass grave. The Commission conducted several reconnaissance missions to the areas, discovered the existence of a large number of bodies, collected some evidence and began exhumation in October 1993. The investigation proposed carrying out an autopsy to establish identification and the cause and manner of death, and, in time, the collection of other evidence, including testimonies, so that criminal responsibility for the killings could be determined.[144] The Commission faced both political and logistical difficulties in preparing for the Ovcara investigation, and were prevented from continuing their work by representatives of the 'local Serbian administration'.[145] In an effort to obtain the necessary political assurances, the Commission made nine visits to Vukovar, Belgrade and Knin between March and November 1993.[146] Finally, following a meeting with the Krajina authorities on 5 September, the Commission believed it had obtained the necessary approvals in writing to conduct the Ovcara excavation, on the understanding that preliminary site and radiological surveys would be conducted at an alleged Serb mass grave site in the Pakracka Poljana area.[147] On 22 October, Commission representatives were informed that, despite earlier approval, the 'Serb Republic of Krajina' parliament had decided that all activity at Ovcara be postponed until a political solution was found to the situation in the former Yugoslavia. After consultation with UNPROFOR, it was decided that to continue the project would expose personnel to unacceptable risk.[148]

The agreed preliminary site investigation at Pakracka Poljana was, however, permitted to take place, with 'a particularly high level of support from UNPROFOR'.[149] The site was alleged to contain mass graves with up to 1,700 bodies. Despite being examined with considerable care, the Commission found only 19 bodies (16 males and 3 females) buried in nine separate graves south of Pakracka Poljana. Again, time and personnel resources did not permit the work required to conduct a criminal investigation and to gather the necessary information.[150] No-one was brought before the ICTY in connection with the Pakracka Poljana deaths.

Following further efforts and a meeting on 17 November 1993 with Goran Hadzic, the Serb Krajina president, and others, the Krajina authorities agreed to cooperate in the excavations at Ovcara, starting in March or April the following year, when the weather conditions improved.[151] Early in 1994, the US ambassador to the UN, Madeleine Albright, flew to the Ovcara site and warned the Serb authorities that they should allow exhumation. It was never started, however, since the Commission was unexpectedly instructed by the UN Office of Legal Affairs to terminate its work in April 1994.

Conclusion

By June 1992, there was overwhelming evidence on the ground to indicate that large-scale war crimes and crimes against humanity had taken place in Bosnia Herzegovina, as earlier in Croatia. Yet, even following global media exposure of the concentration camps, apart from the closure of some of them, there was no effective international action to end the slaughter. The international community not only failed to bring the war to an end but, despite full involvement on several levels – political, diplomatic, military and humanitarian – reinforced its failure through obstructing the work of the Commission of Experts. The UN had created a Commission with a crucial task, but without the means to carry it out. It was the only initiative aimed at recording and bringing the perpetrators to justice, but from the outset was prevented from functioning fully through lack of funding, lack of security on the ground and reluctance to forward documentary material. This sent a signal to the Serb(ian) leadership, as well as future potential aggressors, that major world powers and institutions prioritized even-handed negotiations with war criminals over accountability, even when that entailed turning a blind eye to crimes against humanity. The interests of state trumped those of justice. The UN image was becoming tarnished, and the Commission and tribunal were accordingly weakened.

Notes

1 Elie Wiesel, Letter to Antonio Cassese, 28 June 1996, in *The Path to The Hague*, ICTY, doc.18.
2 Before the war began, journalist Mirko Klarin proposed the establishment of a new tribunal as a preventive measure. 'Nuremberg Now', *Borba,* 16 May 1991. At the time, the article hardly made a ripple internationally. In Spring 1992, Robert Badinter, a former justice minister under French President Mitterand and president of the French Constitutional Council, France's supreme judicial body, was among the first to press for pursuing war criminals in the region.
3 *War Crimes in Bosnia-Hercegovina*, Helsinki Watch Report, August 1992, p. 15.
4 Warren Zimmermann, *Origins of a Catastrophe*, Warren Random House, 1996, p. 136.
5 Meeting Between President Izetbegovic and US Ambassador Warren Zimmermann, ibid., p. 173. In the event of Slovenian and Croatian secession, Bosnia and Herzegovina and Macedonia would have been in a minority within the Yugoslav Presidium, given that four of the remaining six republics were Serbian governed or controlled.
6 *Prosecutor v. Momcilo Krajisnik*, ICTY Judgement, 27 September 2006, para. 707. According to the testimony of Milan Babic, the JNA was by then under the control of Serbian President Slobodan Milosevic. *Prosecutor v Slobodan Milosevic*, 2 December 2002, T.13744.
7 UN Security Council Resolution 713 (1991), 25 September 1991.
8 See Marko Attila Hoare, *How Bosnia Armed*, Saqi, 2004, p. 23.
9 Robert J. Donia, *Bosnia and Hercegovina: A Tradition Betrayed*, Columbia University Press, 1995, p. 228, and Noel Malcolm, *Bosnia. A Short History*, Macmillan, 1994, p. 217.
10 Ministarstvo Unutrasnjih Poslova [Ministry of Internal Affairs].
11 *Prosecutor v. Milan Martic*, Judgement, 12 June 2007, para. 443.
12 Ibid., p. 428.
13 UN Commission of Experts, Part IV, J.
14 Two former JNA officers were convicted by the ICTY in 2007 for 'a widespread and systematic attack by the JNA and other Serb forces against the Croat and other non-Serb civilian population in the wider Vukovar area', and for their role in the Ovcara massacre where the remains of 200 bodies were later exhumed from a mass grave. See *Prosecutor v Mile Mrksic, Miroslav Radic & Veselin Sljivancanin,* Judgement, 27 September 2007. UN Under-Secretary General Marrack Goulding prevented the media from entering Vukovar during the route. As a consequence, the events on the ground were under-reported in the international media at the time. See Marrack Goulding, *Peacemonger*, John Hopkins University Press, 2003, p. 303.

15 Susan L. Woodward, *Balkan Tragedy: Chaos and Dissolution After the Cold War*, Brookings, 1995, p. 193.
16 Malcolm, op. cit., p. 230.
17 *Krajisnik*, p. 201.
18 Donia, op. cit., pp. 238–239.
19 *Krajisnik*, op. cit., p. 285.
20 See *Hansard*, 2 June 1992, for British Foreign Secretary Douglas Hurd's comment on maintaining the arms embargo, and *Hansard*, September 1992, c.123, for Hurd eschewing military intervention in Bosnia.
21 *Prosecutor v Milomir Stakic*, Judgement, 31 July 2003, para. 544.
22 UN Commission of Experts, Final Report, para. 151. Ethnic composition of Bosnia-Herzegovina population, by municipalities and settlements, 1991. census, Zavod za statistiku Bosne i Hercegovine – Bilten no.234, Sarajevo 1991.
23 By the end of March 1992, Serb police chief Simo Drljaca had a force of 1,175 security officials deployed in 13 police stations. Guest, *On Trial, The United Nations, war crimes and the former Yugoslavia*, Refugee Policy Group, 1995, p. 28, Commission of Experts Final Report, para. 155.
24 *Krajisnik*, p. 470. *Prosecutor v Radoslav Brdjanin*, Judgement, 1 September 2004, pp. 161–166.
25 Nidzara Ahmetasevic, 'Bosnia's Unending War', *The New Yorker*, 4 November 2015.
26 *Stakic*, pp. 51–52.
27 The following March, Serb paramilitaries took over the TV transmitter for the area and broke off reception from Sarajevo and Zagreb to broadcast disinformation about non-Serb aggression against Serbs. Commission of Experts Final Report, para. 55.
28 *Stakic*, p. 53.
29 Ibid., p. 56.
30 Ibid., pp. 59–60.
31 Ibid., pp. 65–66, 74, 82.
32 Ibid., p. 85.
33 Ibid., p. 146, *Brdjanin*, p. 161.
34 *Krajisnik*, op. cit., p. 376.
35 Margaret Tutwiler, *Regular State Department Briefing*, 8 June 1992, reported by Reuters.
36 Human Rights Watch Report, 1 June 1994.
37 *Krajisnik*, op. cit., p. 393.
38 Ibid., p. 501.
39 Ibid., pp. 438, 444.
40 Ibid., p. 458.
41 Ibid., pp. 509–510.
42 Ibid., p. 535.
43 Ibid., pp. 404–405.
44 See Ed Vulliamy, *The War Is Dead: Long Live the War*, Bodley Head, 2011, Chapter 4.
45 *Krajisnik*, pp. 297, 299–301.
46 Ibid., p. 298. See also *War Crimes in Bosnia-Hercegovina*, Human Rights Watch, August 1992, pp. 62–74.
47 Ibid., p. 310, and *Prosecutor v Miroslav Deronjic*, Judgement, 30 March 2004, para. 72.
48 Hasan Nuhanovic, *Under the UN Flag: The International Community and the Srebrenica Genocide*, DES, 2007, p. 28.
49 *Krajisnik*, pp. 323–324. Witness account of Serb troops entry into Brcko on 1 May 1992, Medicins du Monde, *L'Enfer Yougoslave: Les victimes de la guerre temoignent*, Belfond, 1994, pp. 185–186. See also *Prosecutor v Goran Jelisic*, Judgement, 14 December 1999, for crimes against humanity in Brcko.
50 *Krajisnik*, p. 328.

51 This included the requirement to use passes to move around the municipality, and to surrender their weapons.
52 *Krajisnik*, p. 347. Nuhanovic, pp. 29–30. See also *Prosecutor v Dragan Nikolic*, Third Amended Indictment.
53 Donia, op. cit., p. 242, *Krajisnik*, p. 359. See personal account of attempts by Muslim inhabitants to defend Zvornik, du Monde, op. cit., pp. 177–179.
54 Martin Bell, *In Harm's Way*, Hamish Hamilton, 1995, pp. 19–22.
55 Hasan Nuhanovic, then a UN interpreter, describes the bombing as a daily occurrence, engendering psychological intimidation and insecurity, and that not a single NATO aircraft was recorded as flying over the area to ensure the no-fly zone was respected. Nuhanovic, op. cit., p. 41.
56 See Edina Becirevic, *Na Drini Genocid*, Sarajevo, 2009 (Genocide on the River Drina, Yale University Press, 2014), for a description of the Serb strategic objective to abolish the Drina river boundary to Serbia., p. 144.
57 *Prosecutor v. Milan Lukic, Sredoje Lukic*, Judgement, 20 July 2009, pp. 41, 823, and *Krajisnik*, op. cit., pp. 695–697.
58 *Lukic*, p. 43.
59 *Krajisnik*, p. 695, *Lukic*, p. 43.
60 *Lukic*, p. 45.
61 Ibid., p. 47, and *New York Times*, 15 April 1992.
62 Ibid., p. 882.
63 Ibid., p. 64.
64 *Prosecutor v Mitar Vasiljevic*, Judgement, 50. According to an International Red Cross report, around 500, mainly civilian, Muslims disappeared in Visegrad in May and June 1992. ICRC, Change in the Ethnic Composition in the Municipality of Visegrad, 1991–1997, 17 August 2001, pp. 17–21, Annex B & Appendix A-B. Ibid., paras. 51–53.
65 Ibid.
66 *Krajisnik*, p. 608.
67 Ibid., p. 616.
68 Ibid., pp. 623, 628.
69 Ibid., p. 639. Fifteen Muslims were executed in Trnovac, near Foca, in June 1992. https://trialinternational.org/latest-post/novislav-djajic/
70 *Krajisnik*, pp. 655–656, 661.
71 Ibid., p. 675.
72 Ibid., p. 687.
73 Ibid., pp. 567, 575–578.
74 Ibid., p. 542.
75 Ibid., pp. 584, 590.
76 Ibid., pp. 595, 598–599.
77 UN Commission of Experts, II. Chronology of the battle and siege of Sarajevo, April 1992.
78 Ibid.
79 Ibid.
80 See Chapter 10.
81 RFE Interview with Jovan Divjak, Retired Bosnian Army General, RFE *Radio Slobodna Evropa*, 2 October 2009.
82 Laura Silber and Allan Little, 'The Death of Yugoslavia'. Gordana Knezevic, then deputy editor of the Sarajevo daily, *Oslobodjenje*, witnessed the first trucks in a convoy of 17 military vehicles, heavily laden with weapons and soldiers, heading towards Marshal Tito barracks. Carol Off, *The Lion, the Fox and the Eagle*, Vintage Canada, 2001, p. 144.

83 See Vulliamy, op. cit. Chapter 4, for the refusal of UNHCR and the ICRC to report on their knowledge of the camps from late May 1992.
84 'Bosnia-Herzegovina: Stabilization', confidential information memorandum from Thomas M.T. Niles, US Deputy Secretary of State for European and Canadian Affairs, 14 April 1992, quoted in Samantha Power, *A Problem from Hell: America and the Age of Genocide*, Basic Books, 2002, p. 264.
85 US President Bush had requested the CIA to analyse Serb activities as early as May 1992, Guest, op. cit., p. 31.
86 Power, op. cit., pp. 264–268. See also Guest, op. cit. The State Department's Annual 1992 Report on human rights wrote that abuses in Bosnia 'dwarf anything seen since the Nazis and borders on genocide'. But desk officers who tried to force the issue were rebuked by the State Department. By October 1992, the Bush administration started to interview refugees, but only inexperienced or junior officers were assigned to the task.
87 *New York Times*, 5 August 1992.
88 *Prosecutor v Slobodan Milosevic,* 3 February 2003, T.15424. Charles Kirudja testimony.
89 Annex to Helsinki Watch Report, *War Crimes in Bosnia-Herzegovina*, 31 July 1992, pp. 228–229. For fuller details of the camps see Smail Cekic, Dejtonski (mirovni) Sporazum, Legalizacija genocida u republici Bosni I Herzegovini, Vol.I., pp. 357–528.
90 Ibid. See also *Prosecutor v Radoslav Brdjanin*, 12 February 2003, for Charles Kirudja's testimony. See also IWPR Tribunal Update No.300, 10–15 February 2003.
91 'How Europe's Leaders Let Yugoslav Crisis Get Out of Control', *Wall Street Journal*, 1 July 1992.
92 *New York Times*, 3 August 1992, and Guest, op. cit., p. 32.
93 UN Information Notes, 25 March 1993.
94 Roy Gutman, Death Camps, *Newsday*, 19 July 1992, 3 August 1992. Gutman invited the State Department, the House intelligence committee and the White House to comment, but without success. He was later awarded the Pulitzer Prize for his book *Witness to Genocide*.
95 Guest, op. cit., pp. 42–43.
96 UN Human Rights Commission Resolution 1992/S-1/1, 14 August 1992.
97 Annex 1 of UN document E/CN.4/1993/50, 10 February 1993.
98 Letter to UN Secretary General Boutros Boutros-Ghali, 27 July 1995, doc. S/1995/625.
99 Guest, op. cit., p. 10.
100 Tadeusz Mazowiecki, Letter to the Chairman of the Commission on Human Rights of the United Nations, 27 July 1995, published in Bosnia Report, Issue 11.
101 'Situation of Human Rights in the Territory of the Former Yugoslavia'. Sixth report of T. Mazowiecki to the UN Human Rights Commission. UN document E/CN.4/1994, para. 345.
102 The UN and EC inflated the significance of the Sarajevo Airport relief effort and peace talks to justify their inertia in Bosnia.
103 The Hague, doc.9.
104 Medicins du Monde, for instance, compared Milosevic to Hitler. Hazan, op. cit., p. 19.
105 Douglas Hogg, *Hansard,* 10 February 1993.
106 As Vernon Bogdanor later commented in relation to British government policy at the time, 'It was the motif of appeasement, as in the 1930s, that if you put pressure on the weaker side, you can avoid a war or the fighting will end more quickly because the aggressor will win more rapidly, and wars can always be avoided if the weaker side gives way to the side making a threat. . . [John Major] was a dangerous Prime Minister for troubled times, though fortunately Milosevic did not threaten the peace of Europe as Hitler did'. Vernon Bogdanor, *Prime Ministers in the Post-War World–John Major*, Gresham Lecture, September 2007.

107 Owen, along with British and French officials present, was reportedly incensed, fearing the collapse of the peace plan virtually at its inception. See M. Cherif Bassiouni, *Investigating War Crimes in the Former Yugoslav War 1992–1994*, Intersentia, 2017, pp. 103–107.
108 Bassiouni, ibid. And Hazan, op. cit., p. 30.
109 Michael P. Scharf, *Balkan Justice*, Carolina Academic Press, 1997, p. 44.
110 Eagleburger evidently sought the grand exit. He was also possibly trying to reestablish peace with the Arab states following Operation Desert Storm.
111 Patrick Glynn, "No Evil: Clinton, Bush and the Truth about Bosnia", *The New Republic*, 25 October 1993, p. 23. Kenney, who at that time favoured lifting the arms embargo and taking military action against the Serbs, was the first US official to resign, on 25 August 1992, publicly denouncing the US administration's counterproductive handling of the war. See Power op. cit., p. 285.
112 See Carole Hodge, *Britain and the Balkans*, Routledge, 2006, 2010, for analysis of the British role in the Bosnian war.
113 US Deputy Secretary of State Lawrence Eagleburger was US ambassador to Belgrade in late 1970s and advised President Bush on Yugoslavia in 1991–2. National Security Advisor Brent Scowcroft had served as US air attaché in Belgrade in the 1950s. Both were members of Kissinger Associates, an international geopolitical consulting firm, founded in 1982. Lord Carrington was also a director.
114 Glynn, op. cit.
115 See Bassiouni, op. cit., pp. xv, 100, 107–108 on Owen's 'moral blameworthiness realpolitik proposition' and p. 112 for the role of Ralph Zacklin, at the UN's Office of Legal Affairs.
116 Badinter had presided over the arbitration committee in 1991, aimed at finding an institutional arrangement to defuse the conflict in Croatia.
117 Interview, 27 October 1999, cited in Hazan, op. cit., p. 15.
118 Britain proposed to the Yugoslav foreign minister, Budimir Loncar, to request an arms embargo on Yugoslavia at the UN Security Council in September 1991. Hodge, op. cit., p. 12, citing James Gow, in A. Danchev and T. Halverson (ed.) *International Perspectives on the Yugoslav Conflict*, St. Antony's Series, 1996.
119 Hazan, op. cit., p. 24.
120 Ralph Zacklin at the UN Office of Legal Affairs acknowledged this. 'We found a little bit of money that was in principle reserved for the Law of the Sea to give to the Commission, but it was insufficient'. Hazan, op. cit., p. 27.
121 Britain's ambassador to the UN, David Hannay, reportedly voted against Bassiouni at the Security Council, as did France and Russia. See Bassiouni, op. cit., p. 110.
122 Roy Gutman, *Witness to Genocide*, Element, 1993, p. 58.
123 Owen denied this. See Off, *The Lion, the Fox and the Eagle*, p. 264.
124 Hagan, op. cit., p. 41.
125 *Daily Telegraph*, 4 December 1993.
126 Guest, op. cit., p. 9.
127 UN Commission of Experts Final Report 1994, 149. www.icty.org/x/file/About/OTP/un_commission_of_experts_report1994_en.pdf
128 Ibid., p. 30.
129 Ibid. I. D. 17.
130 Ibid., p. 16.
131 The United States, the only UN Security Council P5 member to contribute, gave $500,000. Other contributing states included Austria, Canada, the Czech Republic, Denmark, Germany, Hungary, Iceland, Liechtenstein, Micronesia, Morocco, the Netherlands, New Zealand, Norway, Sweden, Switzerland and Turkey. Ibid. Conclusions.
132 Final Report, pp. 174–176.
133 Ibid., p. 182.

134 Final Report, III. B. 'Ethnic Cleansing' 129/56.
135 The US government was anxious to avoid labelling the war as genocidal, and it was ordered that the word 'genocide' be proscribed from diplomats' vocabulary when discussing Bosnia to avoid triggering implementation of the Genocide Convention. Richard Johnson, Pin-stripe Approach to Genocide, unpublished paper for National War College, Washington, DC, 1 January 1994.
136 Final Report, pp. 195–209.
137 Ibid., pp. 195, 197.
138 Ibid., p. 207, Annex VI.A.
139 Ibid., p. 209.
140 Ibid., p. 210.
141 Ibid., p. 214.
142 See Final Report, pp. 232–253, 230. The Commission's database identified close to 800 victims by name or number. An additional 1,673 victims were referred to, but not named. There were also some 500 reported cases which refer to an unspecified number of victims. On legal aspects of rape and other sexual assaults, see Commission of Experts Report, Annex II, pp. 102–109.
143 Warburton Mission II Report, February 1993, pp. 14, 15. The Report estimated the number of victims at around 20,000.
144 Commission of Experts Report, IV. Substantive Findings, 265.
145 Ibid., pp. 266, 267.
146 Ibid., p. 268.
147 Ibid., p. 269. Bassiouni, at a contentious meeting with Owen at UN HQ Geneva, was advised by Owen that he should investigate three mass graves of 200 each (Croats, Muslims and Serbians), a blatant example of the moral equivalency policy then prevailing. See Hagan pp. 34–35, for a fuller account of the meeting.
148 Ibid., p. 272.
149 Ibid., p. 280.
150 Ibid., pp. 281–283.
151 Ibid., pp. 273, 275.

2 Teething problems

A landmark of a particularly dubious kind was reached in February 1993 when the Security Council decided to create an international criminal tribunal for the Former Yugoslavia.

– Ralph Zacklin[1]

Introduction

On 22 February 1993, the UN Security Council asked the secretary general to produce options for the creation of an international tribunal.[2] The resultant draft statute was presented to the Security Council on 3 May, and three weeks later, formal agreement was reached to establish the tribunal.[3] It took a further two years, amid continuing bloodshed, rape and torture, before any of the perpetrators were indicted.

The tribunal was compromised from the outset by its association with a weak and discredited international response to the Bosnian war. The main issue in dispute was the nature of the organ to be established. There was resistance to an effective tribunal from both influential quarters within the UN and the major world powers. The UN Office for Legal Affairs, along with Britain and France, sought control over the personnel being recruited, and to treat the tribunal as a subsidiary of the UN, rather than as an independent entity where defendants would be put on trial.[4] Even US Secretary of State Madeleine Albright, who had fought hard for the tribunal, doubted that anyone would ever be arrested.[5] The evidence depended largely on victim testimonials which were increasingly hard to secure with the passing of time. The difficulties and delays in setting up the tribunal arose mostly from political factors, buying time for the main perpetrators, the Serbs, while also working in favour of the policies of those states which argued for a political solution, based on an agreement between perpetrators and victims.

International peace process, early 1993

The various international measures introduced in a lame attempt to end the war, including numerous UN Security Council resolutions, the despatch of thousands of UN troops to Bosnia in a non-combat role,[6] the introduction of an unenforced no-fly zone and economic sanctions against Serbia, had all proved largely ineffective. The sanctions hit mostly poorer Serbs and arguably led to a hardening of attitudes, fuelled by propaganda from the government-controlled media.

It was into this environment that the Vance Owen peace plan (VOPP), backed by Britain, France and Russia, was presented to the parties in January 1993.[7] The plan, in which the Serbian president, Slobodan Milosevic, was invited to participate, involved the division of Bosnia into ten semi-autonomous multi-ethnic cantons.[8] It was rejected by the Bosnian Serb leadership on 6 May but, for want of a plausible alternative, was not officially declared dead by Lord Owen till 18 June. Even had it been fully accepted by all sides, the plan would have been unworkable, since it would have required massive numbers of international troops to enforce and police the multiple boundaries, provoked further population shifts and still left Karadžić's regime dominant.[9]

Vying with the VOPP was the US administration's tentative 'lift-and-strike' proposition. The newly elected US president, Bill Clinton, had been vocal in opposition, proposing more bullish methods to bring the Serbs to heel.[10] On his arrival at the White House, Clinton initially attempted to persuade his NATO allies to agree to remove the arms embargo against the Bosnian government, accompanied by strategic air strikes on Bosnian Serb artillery positions.[11] The main drawback to this policy was the presence of neutral, lightly armed UN troops on the ground, most of them from NATO member states, including Britain, France and Canada (but not the United States), who would be rendered virtual hostages in a combat situation.

US Secretary of State Warren Christopher's tour of the European capitals, which began in London on 1 May 1993, scuppered any notion of the lift-and-strike option.[12] As the 'new kid' on the block, Christopher was left in no doubt that America's NATO allies would not look kindly on a policy which endangered their troops. He returned to the United States empty-handed, and soon thereafter began to redefine the war, ordering his office to begin seeking out 'Muslim' atrocities in Bosnia.[13] The British and French 'even-handed' policy had prevailed.

Now, though, with the surrender of the US initiative, and the demise of Owen and Vance's plan, there was a vacuum in the international Balkans policy. Meanwhile, things were heating up on the ground in Bosnia, the Commission of Experts was gradually being wound down, and the tribunal still existed in name only.

Bosnia, early 1993

By the end of 1992, the situation in Bosnia had become critical. In the Banja Luka region, 53,000 out of the 56,000 non-Serbs living there had been expelled or had fled.[14] Hundreds of thousands found temporary refuge abroad, with the rest mostly corralled into central Bosnia. Those that remained in Serb-held territory were discriminated against at all levels and exposed daily to dangerous tasks, such as digging at the front lines.

In late January 1993, the Bosnian Serbs began a major offensive in the Drina Valley, aimed at eradicating non-Serbs from the area, and taking over the enclaves of Konjevic Polje and Cerska. In Srebrenica conditions were 'abysmal and deteriorated by the day'.[15]

> Several tens of thousands of refugees arrived in and lived crammed inside the town of Srebrenica and its surrounding area. . . . There was a constant and acute shortage of food bordering on starvation and hygienic conditions were appalling. In the winter, people were living on the streets in freezing temperatures.[16]

On 12 April 1993, an artillery barrage killed 36 people outright, mostly women and children, and wounded a further 102, resulting in a massive increase in displaced civilians and those needing urgent support.[17] According to Sadako Ogata, UN Commissioner for Refugees,

> the desperate humanitarian situation in many parts of the former Yugoslavia continues, and in many instances has worsened. Bosnian Serb authorities have consistently delayed and often denied passage to UNHCR convoys bound for Bosnian government-held enclaves in Eastern Bosnia.[18]

The enclaves along the Drina Valley relied almost entirely on UN convoys from Belgrade via Zvornik,[19] which were consistently blocked by VRS forces, leaving many people in the Drina valley hungry, and without medical aid.

> In many locations there is virtually no capacity to deal with the problems growing out of the war – in particular the treatment of victims of rape, torture and conflict.[20]

On 16 April, the UN passed a resolution demanding an immediate end to hostilities and the establishment of a 'safe area' in Srebrenica.[21] Two days later, an agreement was signed between the Bosnian government and Bosnian Serb military leaders to demilitarize the town, and a company of Canadian UN soldiers moved into Srebrenica, where there was an estimated 30,000 people without adequate shelter.[22] The social situation was deteriorating, with tension between the majority refugee population and the minority locals.[23] VRS troops turned back UNHCR trucks carrying tents to Srebrenica, confiscating 98.[24] Relief supplies were only restored to the eastern enclaves following an agreement between UNHCR and the Pale authorities on 19 May.[25] The water supply had been cut off since 5 April. The source of Srebrenica's water in Zeleni Jadar was now in Serb-controlled territory, and there was no sanitation.[26]

Coinciding with the Srebrenica crisis was the outbreak of heavy fighting between Bosnian government and Croat (HVO) forces in Central Bosnia and Western Herzegovina. The HVO attacks began in Prozor in October 1992, but increased in mid-April 1993, as Bosnian Croat forces sought to establish military and political power in the cantons designated as 'Croat' under the Vance Owen plan. Multiple towns and villages came under prolonged military assault, including East Mostar, Capljina, Stolac, Gornji Vakuf, Jablanica and elsewhere, where men in many cases were separated from women, children and the elderly, resulting in numerous civilian deaths, and affecting the UN aid flow. On 16 April, over 100 Bosniaks were massacred in the village of Ahmići. In Mostar the following month, shelling by HVO forces began in earnest, with East Mostar remaining under siege till the following April. Thousands were deported to the infamous Dretelj concentration camp, and other detention centres.[27]

Apart from the sharp upsurge in casualties, the new hostilities between Croats and Bosniaks fudged the situation on the ground, as Serbs were now no longer seen as the sole aggressors. There were atrocities on all sides, as Douglas Hurd, Britain's foreign secretary who had a leading role in the international appeasement policy, was prompt to announce.[28] This was not simply a civil war, however, nor should a moral equivalence have been drawn. The reasons for this new front in Bosnia were complex, and in no small part exacerbated by the Vance Owen plan which politically and territorially favoured the Croats, prompting extremist elements, supported by the Croatian government, to claim power over territory allocated to 'Croat' designated areas.[29]

The impact of international sanctions policies on Serbia had seriously affected services and the prices of basic commodities, augmenting the number requiring aid, and therefore impeding the implementation of relief assistance to the traumatized victims of conflict.[30] Much of this was channeled, with UNPROFOR assistance, to the Serb-controlled areas of Bosnia, and to Serbia. Banja Luka, under the control of the authorities in Pale, had not undergone any shelling, and had no front line and few refugees to contend with, yet was being supplied with a steady flow of aid from the UN depot in Zagreb.[31] At the same time, the Bosnian Serb terror campaign against the non-Serb minority in the Banja Luka region continued unabated, with many killed, harassed or evicted by force, and UNHCR staff there had their movements restricted.[32]

The international community was forced to take stock of the situation and seek a fresh approach. Meanwhile, the newly established tribunal at The Hague was faring little better.

What kind of tribunal?

The creation of the ICTY in late May 1993 was announced with much aplomb.[33] The UN secretary general declared that 'for the first time since the Nuremberg Tribunal, war criminals will thus know the sanction of international law' but a European diplomat who preferred to remain anonymous had a less sanguine view: 'When we don't have the desire to make war, we find substitutes, which doesn't necessarily mean that we give these substitutes the means to really exist'.[34] The UN by now had a tarnished image and, as a result, the tribunal, like its predecessor, was severely compromised from the outset.[35]

Differences between the United States and other Permanent Five (P5) members of the Security Council soon began to emerge, compounded by divisions within the United States itself.[36] Some in the Clinton administration wanted to see justice done, but for many in the US the tribunal represented moral legitimacy and political authority, while avoiding putting troops on the ground.[37] In France, it was hoped that the tribunal would allay public rancour.[38] The British government, on the other hand, had difficulty in accepting the idea of a war crimes tribunal at all, viewing it as conflicting with achieving a negotiated solution between perpetrators and victims.

A more ominous complication was the bid by Russia, then president of the Security Council, to take over UN policy in Bosnia. Russia had demonstrated its support for the Bosnian Serbs and had the potential to paralyze the Security Council.[39] In early April 1993, Russia proposed that the tribunal be administered by a sub-group, including the CSCE and parties to the conflict, providing an opening for endless delay.[40] On 18 May Russia's foreign minister, Andrei Kozyrev, produced a plan which included the establishment of the war crimes tribunal and the creation of safe havens in Eastern Bosnia. This formed the basis of a 13-point plan adopted by the United States on 22 May, representing significant concessions to the Serbs.

Following Security Council resolution 808 of 22 February 1993, the Office of Legal Affairs under Ralph Zacklin, deputy UN Legal Counsel, was tasked with presenting options for the establishment of the tribunal. There were basically two options – either to draft a convention, or to create a tribunal under the peace enforcement provisions of Chapter VII of the Security Council. The second option might have less global appeal but would be binding on all governments and could be voted more quickly through the Security Council. On the other hand, it risked losing support from some of the non-aligned and Islamic states, consisting of over three-quarters of the General Assembly members.

Then there was the thorny question of funding. The United States, the UN's largest contributor, was committed to addressing the war crimes, but with considerable arrears of payments to the UN when Clinton took office in 1993, was not best placed to argue the tribunal's case. The Clinton administration's determination to cut costs at the UN also conflicted with its support for pursuing war criminals. The anomalous position of the United States in the process of establishing the tribunal entailed a number of concessions and trade-offs.[41] Another potential obstacle was the UN Advisory Committee on Administrative and Budgetary Questions (ACABQ), a General Assembly body which had earlier cut into the Commission of Experts' budget and would need to agree the proposed budget for the tribunal.[42]

British officials proved particularly obstructive. Having curbed the power of the Commission of Experts, the British delegation, although superficially endorsing the tribunal, began to undermine it behind the scenes from the outset. In March 1993, Britain submitted a confidential 'non-paper' to the UN Secretariat, questioning the Security Council's authority to set up the tribunal. It also argued that the cardinal principles of international law were not always clear and should be omitted from the tribunal statute.[43] The first principle denied immunity from prosecution to heads of state. The UK was alone in its concern that the tribunal would lead to the indictment of the Serbian president, Slobodan Milosevic, which would compromise British policy.[44] On the basis of ambiguity, Britain also attacked the second principle, which does not allow individuals to escape responsibility by claiming that they acted under the orders of a superior.[45] The British 'non-paper' also argued that it was preferable for war criminals to be prosecuted at national level, but without taking into account the suitability of the national courts to try their own defendants. The 'non-paper' had the potential not only to bog judges down in endless debating of legal finesses but also implicitly questioned how well certain crucial legal principles were grounded in customary law. The objective was clearly to marginalize the tribunal and ensure it was tied up in debating accepted principles of international law, and then rendered superfluous once national trials began. Britain was later accused by Human Rights Watch (HRW) of 'delaying and obstructing' the tribunal's ability to function.[46]

The international paralysis was evidently noted by Ratko Mladić and his forces. According to the ICTY president, Antonio Cassese, UNPROFOR reports in the first weeks of the tribunal's establishment noted Serb officers' anxiety over the creation of the tribunal. This was soon to recede.[47]

International peace efforts, May 1993–July 1994

Following the collapse of the Vance Owen Plan, the international negotiators made several abortive attempts to reach agreement on the way forward. In early May 1993, in a knee-jerk reaction to the VRS encroachment on the enclaves, Gorazde, Tuzla and Žepa were also declared 'safe areas' by the Security Council, as well as Sarajevo and Bihac, which continued to be shelled.[48]

David Owen and a former Norwegian foreign minister, Thorvald Stoltenberg, Cyrus Vance's successor as UN representative on the International Conference on the Former Yugoslavia (ICFY), began to promote a new plan to divide Bosnia into a confederation of three ethnic regions. Despite the first plan having been rejected by the Serbs, the co-chairmen conveyed the impression that the Bosnian government was the more intransigent, a cynical appeasement tactic, pressurizing the weaker side to accept an agreement which favoured the aggressors.[49]

To this end, Owen and Stoltenberg brought into negotiations Fikret Abdic, a Muslim who controlled the northern part of the Bihac enclave, and traded with the Karadžić regime in violation of UN sanctions. Later that year, Abdic was to sign an agreement with Karadžić in Belgrade, in Milosevic's presence, citing the authority of the London Conference, to declare that all war criminals would be prosecuted locally, that is to say, either in Republika Srpska or the Autonomous Province of Western Bosnia.[50] As well as weakening the Bosnian government and forcing Izetbegovic into signing the latest plan, the co-chairmen's support of Abdic undermined the tribunal.[51]

Despite voicing support for the tribunal in late 1992, Owen acted in other ways to impede its development, marginalizing both UN rapporteur Tadeusz Mazowiecki and the Commission of Experts, and refusing to press UNPROFOR for field support for the investigations. According to the UN special rapporteur for minorities, Asbjorn Eide, the whole tenor of the peace process, in its neutrality, had accelerated ethnic 'purity', elevating the role of the Bosnian Serbs and Croats, while undermining the Bosnian government.[52]

Election of judges

The election of tribunal judges took place on 17 September 1993, before the creation of a prosecution team, thereby reversing the Nuremberg process. This was potentially problematic since without prosecutions the judges were superfluous, as well as costly. Some of them lacked courtroom experience, and there was no Muslim, although four judges came from Muslim-majority states (Malaysia, Nigeria, Egypt and Pakistan).[53] It was informally agreed that no candidates from countries perceived as 'partial' in the Bosnian war, or individuals involved in the peace process, should be accepted. Britain did not put forward a candidate, ostensibly because it had already proposed a prosecutor (John Duncan Lowe) but possibly also because it feared rejection due its controversial role in the war. But former governor-general of Australia, Sir Ninian Stephen, was elected, although Australia's candidate was British born, a member of the Privy Council and held several British knighthoods.[54]

On 17 November 1993, at the first plenary session of the ICTY, Antonio Cassese was elected president of the tribunal. A professor, internationalist and activist, with a career in public service, Cassese unlike most of the judges viewed the tribunal as a precursor to an international criminal court and was prepared to confront the politicians. Co-architect of the European Convention on Torture (1987), Cassese viewed the law as a tool for social transformation and justice. Initially, he believed in the political will of international leaders. Later he was to call himself naïve.[55]

With no funding or resources, the judges were prepared to go home and wait till the tribunal was more fully established. As one judge commented, they had no offices, no statutes, no prison, no accused, no logistics, not even a prosecutor.[56] The tribunal's budget had not yet been approved by the UN, so the judges were paid per diem. Also, the fact that the tribunal was unable to engage anyone for more than three months seriously affected the ability to secure high calibre legal staff. The staff, meanwhile, worked in a meeting room and offices at the Palace of Peace in The Hague, which they were able to rent for just two weeks.[57]

At a conference at the University of Connecticut before US diplomats, Cassese made his position clear:

> If in one or two years there are still no accused in the dock, it would be better that the judges pack their bags and go home. Our duty will be to tell the UN, and the Security Council in particular, that our mission ended in failure and that we do not intend to be the alibi for the political impotence of the international community.[58]

Rules of procedure

In November 1993, the judges began work on drafting the rules. The challenge was to present a coherent set of procedures, incorporating the different world legal systems, while demonstrating a clear commitment to due process, thus distinguishing the tribunal from its predecessors in Nuremberg and Tokyo, which have often been criticized as 'victors' courts, providing few guarantees for defendants.[59] In essence, this meant achieving a fusion of two very different legal systems – the common law adversarial system and the civil law inquisitorial system, which would reflect not only the composition of the judiciary but also demonstrate the international nature of the tribunal.[60] Also, there was very little precedent for guidance, with the Nuremberg and Tokyo rules having been short on substance.[61]

Under the Anglo-Saxon common law system, the prosecutor and defence argue the case before a jury, with many guarantees provided to defendants who are assumed innocent until proven guilty, and given access to the evidence of the prosecution. In the civil law system generally prevailing in Europe, the judge leads the investigation and decides what evidence to include, and whether it will be made public. Witnesses may never need to appear in court, if the judge so decides. Many Europeans consider that, under the common law system, the accused are provided with so many guarantees that a conviction is often virtually impossible to achieve. On the other hand, common law lawyers often argue that due process and the rights of the accused are paramount, even if this involves a protracted trial. This position is also supported by fundamental human rights law as laid down, for instance, in the International Covenant on the Protection of Civil Rights. Overshadowing this, however, is the pervasive problem of obtaining state cooperation.[62]

In practice, it was the adversarial approach which the judges mainly adopted, possibly reflecting the dominant influence of the United States at that stage, although trial by jury had been dispensed with.

One of the issues seen as a test case for the tribunal was the handling of rape cases. Here, context was imperative. The definition of rape in many legal systems as the absence of consent, backed by a witness statement and corroboration, was inappropriate in the circumstances prevailing in the former Yugoslavia, where coercion and violence were the norm. Rape was accordingly omitted from the first draft of the rules but, in response to claims that this would fail to safeguard defendants' rights sufficiently, the judges later amended the rules to allow for a limited admission of consent.[63] It was also important to confirm the legal principle of command responsibility.

Plea bargaining was initially not included but, after much debate, with the United States opposing Cassese, a compromise was reached, and the tribunal agreed that cooperation should be taken into account in deciding sentence.[64] This was critical in the case of Drazen Erdemovic who received a reduced sentence in return for testimony against Mladić and Karadžić in Srebrenica.

Thc contumacy debate also raged, with a clamour for the provision of *in absentia* trials, in light of the unlikely prospect of arresting suspects in an ongoing conflict and extraditing them to The Hague.[65] In some civil law systems, trials *in absentia* are permitted. The continental judges saw this as an essential element in stigmatizing war criminals, especially in view of the difficulty in issuing indictments and arresting high political and military officials. The contumacy doctrine would allow them to try and convict criminals in their absence, which would be effective politically in discrediting an indictee's status as a respectable negotiator in the peace process. The common law judges feared a trial without a defendant would conflict with the notion of due process and turn the court into a legal circus. In the event, it was the presence of some of the major indictees in court which did just that. Judges on both sides feared the court being discredited, but for different reasons.

In 1999, a Committee of Experts, engaged by the UN to assess the record of the tribunal, concluded that the civil law system may have been more appropriate in the Balkans context.[66]

> The Statutes are largely, although not entirely, reflective of the common law adversarial system, and the future evolution of the Tribunals' procedural jurisprudence, while necessarily complying with their Statues, is apt to adopt aspects of the civil law model . . . some civil law models can doubtless deal with criminal law cases more expeditiously than the common law adversarial system. Since all the accused before the Tribunals are from civil law backgrounds, it could hardly be objectionable to them.[67]

Another problem was that judges knew little or nothing of the Balkans when they arrived at The Hague and, in focusing on the fairness of the rules, tended to lose sight of the context, namely, an ongoing war with mounting atrocities, resulting in a focus on procedure, almost impenetrable to the uninitiated, and therefore difficult to communicate. 'The ICTY is being crushed under a slab of narrow legalism', according to one judge.[68] Another judge from a common law background opined that, in the unique circumstances of the ICTY, the civil law model might have been better suited to its work.

The judges were also under the misapprehension that UNPROFOR would be policing the arrests. 'Naively we thought that if the Security Council had created a tribunal it would provide us the means to work'.[69] Since the tribunal was created under Chapter VII of the UN Charter, which authorizes the use of force in the interests of international security, this was an understandable assumption. Five years later, when judges were interviewed by a UN panel of experts, they agreed that the single most important obstacle to effective functioning of the tribunal was the lack of cooperation by Republika Srpska and Serbia. With few exceptions, indictees in custody were relatively low-level miscreants whose alleged crimes, although serious, might have been better tried in national courts. Lack of state cooperation (unlike at the Rwanda tribunal) impeded the availability of evidence and witnesses, affecting the length of investigations and trials. Unavoidable early political pressures on the Office of the Prosecutor (OTP) to act against perpetrators of war crimes led to the first trials being against relatively minor figures, comparing unfavourably with the Rwanda court where senior figures were more promptly arrested and brought to trial.[70] Trials of low-level figures failed to demonstrate the resolve of the international community and did not draw world attention sufficiently to the command structure governing the crimes.

Eleven judges in search of a prosecutor

The two most burning issues in getting the tribunal working, however, were the election of a chief prosecutor and the budget.

UN Secretary General Boutros Boutros-Ghali had initially nominated the Commission of Experts chairman, M. Cherif Bassiouni, as ICTY prosecutor in August 1993. But the UK led a strenuous opposition, arguing that Bassiouni lacked prosecutorial experience and administrative skills, and was too victim-oriented and biased, as he was a Muslim.[71] The British also reportedly blocked Bassiouni because they feared he would 'quickly bring charges against the Serbs' and so complicate Owen's efforts to negotiate a peace agreement.[72] An informal Security Council vote was divided 7–7, with one abstention. The United States then tried to broker a deal for Bassiouni to be appointed deputy prosecutor, but the other permanent members of the Security Council opposed him.[73] The United States, which had voted in Bassiouni's favour in the first round, deferred to the UK. The British had, in the meantime, succeeded in persuading council members that the choice of prosecutor should be by consensus rather than election. This decision was primarily responsible for the subsequent delays in appointing the prosecutor.[74]

Eventually, in Autumn 1993, Ramon Escovar-Salom, the attorney general of Venezuela, was chosen as the tribunal's first chief prosecutor. In late January 1994, however, Escovar-Salom announced that he would not be taking up the post after all. His timing was unfortunate, coming as it did just a month after the decision to wind up the Commission of Experts. It was to take a further five months for the Security Council to agree on Escovar-Salom's replacement. Meanwhile, just days after his withdrawal, on 5 February 1994, one of the worst atrocities of the Bosnian war occurred when a mortar shell killed 68 people at the Markale market in Sarajevo.

By June 1994, there was still no chief prosecutor, and the acting deputy prosecutor, Graham Blewitt, had little job security and faced bureaucratic obstruction in his attempts to create a prosecution team. He recalled the period as 'one of the worst experiences of my life'.[75]

The world by now was becoming distracted by events in Rwanda.

It was perhaps at this point that the United States realized the potential political mileage of the tribunal, both in marginalizing ultra-national politicians in the peace process through indictments and in being involved without having to put in troops. It decided, therefore, to despatch 22 high-level functionaries, Pentagon military analysts, CIA intelligence specialists and lawyers, to the tribunal for two years, from 13 June 1994, forming the core of the OTP, the effectiveness of which, in the common-law adversarial system, was essential to the tribunal. While this move was welcomed by the interim prosecutor, Graham Blewitt, the UN headquarters in New York regarded their arrival with dismay and insultingly forced them to sign a document respecting ICTY confidentiality. The move was not appreciated in European capitals either. The United States also offered $3 million computer equipment. This equalled the voluntary contributions so far, 90% of which were from Malaysia and Pakistan, two Islamic states. In Europe, there was little or no support, apart from the Netherlands. But there was now a perceived American dominance within the tribunal, risking its impartiality.

The tribunal had remained without a prosecutor for 15 months. This meant that the objectives and penal strategy could not be defined, blocking the way to indictments and prosecution, a situation welcomed by the tribunal's detractors. The impasse was finally broken when Nelson Mandela agreed to release Richard Goldstone to the tribunal for a limited period. Goldstone's credentials, experience and background seemed custom made. The nomination of a white South African lawyer who had a seat on the Supreme Court of Transvaal and had worked to establish the truth about the apartheid system there would be a powerful symbol.[76] A country with few interests in the Balkans, South Africa in the early 1990s was at the height of its prestige. Goldstone was also Jewish, which gave him equal credibility with Catholics, Orthodox and Muslims alike. Tough enough for America, his moderate reputation was also acceptable to France and Britain, and the fact that he, a white South African, opposed apartheid suited Russia and China, too. Goldstone assumed his post in the summer of 1994.

Goldstone later noted that, on his arrival, the credibility of the tribunal was worse than zero.[77] The media criticized its inaction, the judges clamoured for defendants and even the UN was looking for results. Goldstone promptly indicted two suspects, one of whom, Dusko Tadić, who had run the notorious Omarska camp, had already been arrested in Germany. The other, Dragan Nikolic, had been the Serb commander of the Susica camp. But in the broader scale, both were relatively small fry. The main suspects, Karadžić, Mladić, Milosevic, Šešelj and Arkan, were not indicted. Some of the judges felt Goldstone had succumbed to political pressure and that he lacked a penal strategy. Indeed, his main focus seemed to be on his relations with the major governments and the media, rather than on indicting leading suspects.[78] Meanwhile, Karadžić travelled to Geneva for talks with the co-chairmen of the international peace conference, Lord Owen and Thorvald Stoltenberg, where he continued to be regarded as a credible interlocutor.

The scepticism, official and unofficial, demonstrated regarding the tribunal's establishment, both at government and institutional levels, was tantamount to a no-confidence vote and a signal to the perpetrators that they were unlikely to be brought to book for their crimes.

Financing

The failure on the part of the UN Secretariat and member states to secure adequate funding for the tribunal from the outset mirrored the collective international failure to bring an end to the war.

The crucial question of financing seriously impacted on the establishment and operation of the tribunal in the early years. It meant that personnel could only be recruited on short-term contracts, considerably narrowing the choice; technical equipment needed to start investigations could not be purchased; nor could a formal lease for premises be entered into.

At the member-state level, a variety of reasons accounted for the lack of support. Permanent Security Council members, Britain, France and Russia, viewed an effective tribunal, which would issue indictments against the main perpetrators, as a threat to the ongoing peace process, which entailed negotiations with those same perpetrators. The position of the United States was more complex. As the main contributor to the UN, the United States had for years sought its reform and to curb its expenditure, partly through the powerful ACABQ which has to reach a consensus before the General Assembly can adopt the UN budget.[79] This, along with payment arrears amounting to $435 million in early 1993 when President Clinton assumed office, made it difficult for US officials to argue for the substantial budget required to render the tribunal functional. Non-aligned countries and developing states, on the other hand, were reluctant to agree to large sums of money being allocated to address European war crimes.[80]

At UN level, the problem stemmed from a fundamental disagreement between the General Assembly and the Security Council over the source of funding. The Security Council, on the recommendation of the UN Secretariat, proposed that the tribunal should be financed from the UN regular budget, administered by a small committee set up under the Security Council. At first glance, this seemed reasonable, since it would guarantee the tribunal funding for two years, since the UN budget operated on a two-year cycle and was tightly controlled by the Security Council, as opposed to the General Assembly or UN Secretariat. The General Assembly, which had authority in budgetary matters, was not consulted, however, and some of the poorer states and non-aligned governments, who formed a majority on the General Assembly, including India, Mexico and Brazil, protested vigorously, alleging arrogance on the part of major world powers. Also, since, under UN rules, peacekeeping is funded mostly by the P5, with developing countries paying just a fifth of the amount to peacekeeping than to the UN regular budget, this proposal meant that the General Assembly would be required to pay proportionately more than the P5.[81]

The tensions within the UN were exacerbated by the UN Secretariat's controversial handling of the proposed budget. In view of its track record with the Commission of Experts, it was perhaps surprising that the Office of Legal Affairs (OLA) should have been assigned to administer the tribunal's funding.[82] On 19 May 1993, the OLA proposed a one-page budget for the tribunal, following discussions with the UN Controller's office, representing a ballpark sum of $31.2 million for the first year of operation, which included funding for 373 new posts. This was a large sum of money and the proposal, couched in vague terms, was predictably rejected by the ACABQ, on the basis of its size and vagueness. On 14 September 1993, the UN Secretariat was required by the General Assembly to present more details. The Secretariat's response, on 8 December, was to cut the figure in half – i.e. $33.2 million for two years – with the number of staff reduced from 373 to 108. The ACABQ was still dissatisfied, and queried the amount allocated for judges' salaries when there were no indictments. The ACABQ refused to authorize the two-year sum, allocating only $5.6 million for first six months of 1994 and $11 million for the rest of the year, with contracts of up to a year. The

UN Secretariat also proposed that virtually the entire budget allocation should go to the prosecution, which meant hardly any funding for translation, post-mortems, witnesses' travelling expenses or protection, betraying 'extraordinary ignorance' of the task facing the prosecution.[83] What may have seemed pragmatic to the UN gave the appearance of a tribunal on probation and appeared from outside as if the UN had no confidence in its own creation. The ICTY president, Antonio Cassese, warned publicly that the tribunal could be prevented from starting work in the summer of 1994 since it lacked, amongst other things, funding for defence lawyers. Cassese later commented that it was like operating with one hand tied behind the back.[84]

There was also a dispute between the UN and the Netherlands government over the financing of the premises, the Secretariat assuming the Dutch would offer premises at a nominal rent, as well as covering additional costs. But the Dutch were concerned about the lack of Security Council support, the United States' desire to save money and the opposition from the non-aligned countries.[85] Then there was the question of security, with the potential risks increasingly outweighing the prestige of hosting the first international war crimes tribunal since World War II.[86]

In a speech that month, even Cassese was moved to comment that the tribunal was seen as a substitute for a more robust approach. Governments did little to change that view.

Meanwhile, in Bosnia

During the 14 months that it took to appoint a prosecutor for the tribunal, the humanitarian operation in Bosnia and Herzegovina went from severe to critical. According to a UNHCR field report issued on 1 September 1993,

> Our operation has now evolved in such a manner that we believe that our original objective has become unattainable and therefore obscured. Our raison d'être has become staff security and how to stay operational in an increasingly impossible situation . . . and the suffering continues unabated.[87]

A further report issued a month later suggested that the whole United Nations High Commissioner for Refugees (UNHCR) Operation might be even counter-productive:

> UNHCR humanitarian operations are potentially helping aggressors . . . fuel has a high military value. However well-controlled, its supply in a war zone for any purpose other than direct use by humanitarian aid workers may not be a neutral act because it may release other fuel for military purposes.[88]

Meanwhile, the siege of Sarajevo continued. On 1 June 1993, 2 mortars were fired from Serb-held positions onto a football pitch in Dobrinja, a Sarajevo suburb surrounded by VRS forces, where 12 were killed and 133 wounded.[89] On 1 July, the Bosnian Serb authorities introduced taxes for all aid convoys crossing 'their' territory. That month, shelling from Bosnian Serb positions surrounding Sarajevo were reported as exceeding 3,000 shells a day.[90] In a VRS attack on a water queue in Dobrinja on 12 July 1993, 12 civilians were killed and 15 wounded. Hundreds of new cases of typhus and dysentery were reported, and the city remained without a regular supply of water or electricity.[91]

The UN Commissioner for Refugees, Sadako Ogata, stressed that 'access to the Eastern Bosnia enclaves for vitally needed shelter and other winterization materials remains effectively blocked, with the Bosnian Serb authorities in practice insisting on reciprocity of assistance'.[92] Also, 'never have the obstacles and risks been so dreadful and unacceptable as during the last two months . . . the international relief effort has little access, little mobility and little security'.[93]

The situation was greatly exacerbated by the HVO who were blocking crucial energy engineering parts to Central Bosnia, and food supplies to Tuzla.[94] Only 13% of Tuzla's food requirements were delivered in September 1993, a dire situation which lasted till the US-initiated Washington Agreement in March 1994, signed by representatives of the Republic of Bosnia and Herzegovina and the Croat Republic of Herceg-Bosna, one of the few successful (albeit uneasy) peace initiatives of the war.[95]

In July 1993, a major VRS offensive was launched on Mt. Igman, the only high ground around Sarajevo not held by Serb forces, and the only significant supply road into the city, part of which was captured on 4 August. The VRS advance was halted following the US threat of NATO air strikes and declared a demilitarized zone by the UN, although over a thousand VRS troops remained on Igman.[96] The US-led threat of military force worked, and the Igman route remained the main supply route into Sarajevo till the end of the war.

On 24 November 1993, the Bosnian government charged Britain with genocide before the ICJ, for having opposed the lifting of the arms embargo on Bosnia. Ostensibly, Britain had made the largest contribution to Bosnia, with £141 million of aid, 4,000 troops serving with UNPROFOR, £10 million towards restoring Sarajevo's electricity and £14 million to the health system. Britain promptly threatened to suspend the aid if Bosnia carried out its threat, and Bosnia subsequently withdrew its charge.

In early 1994, assaults on Sarajevo by Mladić's forces intensified. On 1 February, UNICEF released the results of a survey carried out in Sarajevo which identified children at risk of war trauma, and revealed that 97% had been exposed to shelling and shooting at close range, 37% had family members wounded or killed, and 55% had been shot at by snipers.[97] On 22 January, an attack on Alipasino polje killed six people and wounded another five, including children.[98] On 4 February, a humanitarian aid queue in Dobrinja was shelled. On 5 February, just after midday, a 120 millimetre mortar shell landed in the centre of the crowded Markale marketplace in Sarajevo, killing 68 people and wounding 144.[99]

The UNHCR interviewed families on 29 January 1994 to check on living conditions and food availability, and found that out of four families in Goradze, three were completely out of food.[100] On 30 March 1994, VRS forces launched a major offensive on another UN 'safe area', Gorazde. After air strikes against Serb tanks and a NATO ultimatum, Serb forces agreed to withdraw their artillery to 20 kilometre from the town.

On 1 June 1994 HRW published a report on the situation in Banja Luka, where it recorded

> the scene of much of the most severe and systematic 'ethnic cleansing': torture, murder, rape, beatings, harassment, de jure discrimination, intimidation, expulsion from homes, confiscation of property, bombing of businesses, dismissal from work, outlawing of all scripts except the Cyrillic in public institutions, and the destruction of cultural objects such as mosques and Catholic churches.[101]

In November 1994, the UN 'safe area' of Bihac, under siege for over three years by VRS forces, was again attacked and a third of the zone taken. The UN Security Council failed to reach an agreement on a statement condemning the Serb shelling of and entry into Bihac, and the US plan to use NATO airpower was rejected by Britain and France.

The largest number of people killed was during the early stages of the war in 1992, but, as evidenced earlier, the siege of major cities and assaults on UN allegedly safe areas continued unabated until the end of the war.

The tribunal continues at half mast

In early January 1995, six months after Richard Goldstone's appointment, the judges revolted, accusing Goldstone of failing to run an effective public relations campaign.[102] The judges could also not accept that Goldstone had not indicted the Serbian president through the legal doctrine of 'command responsibility', using the Yamashita case, to limit atrocities.[103] Goldstone regarded this as conquerors' justice, which risked the reputation of the tribunal. But the judges, led by Antonio Cassese, Georges Abi-Saab and Claude Jorda, all representing civil law, required Goldstone to explain his position.[104] Goldstone expanded on his 'pyramid' strategy, starting from the bottom up, a strategy which may have been effective against organized crime, but was considerably less so in a wartime context. The judges prepared a public communiqué and were eventually joined by the Anglo-American judges. Goldstone initially faced down the judges, but finally capitulated, adding his support, once a few minor changes were made.

On 24 April 1995, Goldstone announced that Radovan Karadžić and Ratko Mladić were being investigated for criminal responsibility but were not accused and had the right to the presumption of innocence. He argued that the tribunal had only the Commission of Experts report and not enough to indict Milosevic and other major players. But this argument did not hold.[105] Goldstone's pragmatism evidently led him to judge that it was necessary to work within the prevailing framework and not close the door on a chance of a peace deal through Belgrade. Significantly, there was no team of investigators building a case against the main players.

Goldstone's warning to the Bosnian Serb leaders apparently fell on deaf ears. On 25 May 1995, the Serbs ignored a UN order to surrender their heavy weapons around Sarajevo and proceeded to bomb the UN 'safe areas', including Tuzla, killing 71 young people and wounding 240. On 26 May, UNPROFOR Commander Lt. General Rupert Smith called for NATO air strikes on VRS munitions depots. The Serbs responded by taking 370 UN staff hostage.

On 4 July, Serb forces shelled Srebrenica, using heavy artillery. On 9 July, Izetbegovic warned UNPROFOR of a possible massacre if the enclave fell. Two days later, VRS forces moved into the enclave and, during the week that followed, over 8,000 men and boys were massacred. As the enclave fell, several of the main international interlocutors, diplomatic and military, were absent from their posts.[106]

Srebrenica demonstrated the ineffectiveness of the tribunal, its credibility forfeited to the warlords. By the summer 1995, only 12 governments had passed laws to recognize its jurisdiction and surrender suspects. Britain was not amongst them. David Owen, in a later interview, put the situation in a nutshell, implicitly also recognizing the failure of European Union policy which he fronted:

> By 1995, Karadžić and Mladić had an incommensurable contempt for the West and the international community, going so far as refusing the peace plan of the Contact Group formed by the most powerful countries on the planet. As for the tribunal, they didn't give a damn.[107]

Richard Goldstone was finally obliged to reconsider his strategy and, on 25 July, indicted Karadžić and Mladić for genocide and crimes against humanity in the municipalities in 1992.[108]

Conclusion

The establishment of the tribunal followed a similar trajectory to that of the Commission of Experts in the absence of financial and other essential support from international institutions and states.

That the tribunal survived these difficulties was down mainly to a handful of committed individuals, including M. Cherif Bassiouni who produced material evidence when no-one else did, UN Secretary of State Madeleine Albright who argued for the tribunal at the Security Council, Antonio Cassese who refused to bow to international pressure, Graham Blewitt who filled the needed complementary role as deputy prosecutor, Richard Goldstone with his ability to raise funds and negotiate with international players and those lawyers and others who worked in difficult conditions with little job security or financial recompense. Support was also forthcoming from the host country – the Netherlands, from the UN secretary general, and donors, such as George Soros. Against these, there were the concerted efforts of major world powers Britain, France and Russia, as well as the UN Secretariat, to put the brakes on the tribunal's development, along with the fluctuating position of the US government.

In the time between the establishment of the tribunal in early 1993 and the fall of Srebrenica to VRS forces in July 1995, the six UN-proclaimed 'safe' areas remained under siege, a NATO ultimatum following the Markale market massacre in February 1994 was foiled due to British/Russian intervention and, in May 1995, hundreds of UN personnel were taken hostage by Serb forces with no effective international mechanism in place for their release. During much of this time, the ICTY was starved of resources and without a prosecutor, with the consequence that no indictments were raised.

In light of this massive international deficit both on the ground and at The Hague, where peace plans hinging on ethnic division took precedence over addressing four years of the most heinous crimes in Europe since 1945, it is perhaps not surprising that the Srebrenica genocide occurred.

Notes

1 Ralph Zacklin CMG, Hersch Lauterpacht Memorial Lectures 2008, Lecture 2, para. 19. British lawyer Ralph Zacklin was deputy legal counsel at the UN Office of Legal Affairs during the Bosnian war. He was described by both UN Commission of Experts Chairman M. Cherif Bassiouni and ICTY Chief Prosecutor Richard Goldstone, as obstructive to the work of the Commission and tribunal. See M. Cherif Bassiouni, *Investigating War Crimes in the Former Yugoslav War 1992–1994*, Intersentia, 2017, pp. 108, 405–407.

2 Security Council Resolution 808, 22 February 1993.

3 Security Council Resolution 827, 25 May 1993.

4 Hazan, op. cit., p. 50. See Bassiouni, op. cit., pp. 109–112. As Bassiouni later commented, 'Zacklin Wanted to Bury the Work of the Commission of Experts and He Succeeded', p. 407.

5 Gary Jonathan Bass, *Stay the Hand of Vengeance: The Politics of War Crimes Tribunals*, Princeton University Press, 2000, p. 215.

6 Some observers nearly 20 years on were still apparently deluded as to the role of UNPROFOR into Bosnia. 'I do not agree with all the criticisms of Bosnia. I think it is true that Britain probably did too little and too late, but we did after all join the UN force which eventually went there and we made a contribution to the peacekeeping, and indeed still do, in that country'. Lord Butler, *Bogdanor lecture, Prime Ministers in the Post-War World-John Major*, Gresham Lecture, September 2007.

7 The peace plan emerged from the International Conference for the Former Yugoslavia. founded in 1991 to seek a political settlement in the Yugoslav wars, chaired by former British foreign secretary David Owen and Cyrus Vance, former US Secretary of State.

8 The plan proposed that Bosniaks and Serbs would each have a majority in three cantons, the Croats in two and one would be mixed Serb and Croat, with Sarajevo as an open city.

9 For further on the Vance Owen peace plan, see Guest, op. cit., pp. 99–100, Hodge, Chapter 3, pp. 52–56.

10 'If the horrors of the Holocaust taught us anything, it is the high cost of remaining silent and paralyzed in the face of genocide. I will strongly support urgent and appropriate action to stop the killing'. Bill Clinton, 4 August 1992, quoted in Guest, op. cit., p. 106.

11 US Secretary of State Warren Christopher gave a speech on 10 February 1993, in which he signalled a new approach to check Serb aggression.
12 See Hodge, op. cit., pp. 55–56, for Christopher's visit to London.
13 This apparently surprised State Department officials who pointed out that any atrocities committed by Bosnian government soldiers were dwarfed by those for which Serb and Croat troops were responsible and, unlike the Serb war crimes, could not be tied to official Bosnian government policy. Guest, op. cit., p. 110.
14 See Human Rights Watch Report, op. cit. for crimes in BiH in 1992–4.
15 *Prosecutor v Naser Oric*, Judgement Summary, ICTY, 20 June 2006.
16 Ibid.
17 Beneficiaries in the region increased from 500,000 in December 1991 to 3,820,000 in March 1993. From December 1992 to March 1993 the total of refugees and displaced persons increased by 765,000. UN Information Notes, March and April 1993.
18 UN High Commissioner for Refugees Sadako Ogata and Under-Secretary for Humanitarian Affairs Jan Eliasson. Ibid. UN Information Notes, 25 April 1993.
19 UN Information Notes, 25 March 1993.
20 Ibid. Brief Summary of the UN Revised Consolidated Inter-Agency Appeal for Former Yugoslavia.
21 UN Security Council Resolution 819.
22 UNHCR reported around 250 persons living in caves. UN Information Notes, May 1993.
23 Ibid.
24 Ibid., April 1993.
25 Ibid., May 1993.
26 Ibid., April 1993. See Edina Becirevic, *Na Drini Genocid*, Buybook, 2009, for genocide in the Drina Valley, 1992–1993, from p. 95.
27 See *Prosecutor v Jadranko Prlic, Bruno Stojic, Slobodan Praljak, Milivoj Petkovic, Valentin Coric & Berislav Pusic*, ICTY Judgement, 29 May 2013, and *Prosecutor v Dario Kordic & Mario Cerkez*, Judgement, 26 February 2001.
28 House of Commons, 12 May 1993. On Hurd's policy, see also Hodge, op. cit. and 'The Hurd Mentality', *The New Republic*, June 1995, and Brendan Simms, *Unfinest Hour: Britain and the Destruction of Bosnia*, Penguin Press, 2002.
29 See Hodge, Chapter 3 for a fuller analysis of the Bosnian/Croat outbreak of hostilities. See also evidence Captain Dundas-Whatley, at the Blaskic trial, 29 October 1998, T.14072, where he refers to the build-up of tension between the Bosnian Army and Croat forces resulting from the Vance Owen plan.
30 Ibid. And UN Information Notes, October 1993.
31 See Carole Hodge, 'Slimey Limeys', *The New Republic*, January 1995.
32 Ibid. And UN Information Notes, January 1994. The UN High Commissioner noted her 'particular outrage at the treatment of Muslims and ethnic Croats in the Banja Luka region, where intimidation is now further increasing'. UN Information Notes, February 1994.
33 The tribunal is 'to bring to justice the persons who are responsible . . . will contribute to ensuring that such violations [of international humanitarian law] are halted and effectively redressed' UNSCR 827 (1993) paras. 12–13.
34 *Le Monde*, 24 April 1993.
35 Zlatko Dizdarevic, editor of Oslobodjenje, voiced the increasing sentiment of Bosnians: 'We, the people of BiH, we know that the proud glass house on the banks of the East River (UN) far from being the fortress of brave horsemen quick to defend the rights of nations, houses only mediocre bureaucrats, blind, greedy and cowardly. [They] who gargle grand words while genocide goes on'. J'accuse l'ONU' Pris Calmann-Levy, 1995, p. 14.
36 Bass, p. 277 'vietmalia'.

37 See Power, op. cit. for US desk officers' opposition to the Clinton administration police.
38 Hazan, op. cit., p. 45.
39 Russia's foreign minister, Andrei Kozyrev, delivered a speech in Stockholm in December 1992 in which he circuitously warned of a possible change of Russian policy in the Balkans in post-Yeltsin times, shocking the Western establishment. See William Safire, 'Essay: Kozyrev's Wake-up Slap', *New York Times*, 17 December 1992.
40 See Security Council doc. S/2537, 6 April 1993. The Russian proposal was rejected.
41 At the World Conference on Human Rights in Vienna in June 1993, the United States was constrained in speaking out about the atrocities in Bosnia because country-specific allegations would risk losing the support of Asian governments in creating a UN High Commissioner for Human Rights. In the event, the Islamic governments forced the issue and a resolution on Bosnia was passed.
42 See Guest, op. cit., pp. 61–63 for more detail on funding.
43 Ibid., pp. 181–185.
44 Commentary on Article 6 of the Tribunal Statute, S/25704, p. 14.
45 This principle was enshrined in the Charter of the Nuremberg Tribunal (Art.8) and ensured the prosecution of several defendants. In 1950, it was endorsed by the International Law Commission.
46 'The War Crimes Tribunal: One Year Later', *Human Rights Watch/Helsinki Watch*, Vol.6, Issue 3, February 1994, quoted in Guest, op. cit., p. 122. The report provoked an angry response from the British Ambassador to Belgrade, Sir David Hannay. Letter to Human Rights Watch, 7 March 1994. Hannay had directed, according to UN diplomats, a long campaign to weaken the pursuit of war criminals in Bosnia.
47 Hazan, op. cit., p. 47.
48 The VRS shelling of the Sarajevo and Bihac 'safe areas' continued until late summer of 1995, in defiance of the Security Council resolution.
49 Commenting on British policy in the Bosnian war, British historian Vernon Bogdanor observed, 'It was the motif of appeasement, as in the 1930s, that if you put pressure on the weaker side, you can avoid a war or the fighting will end more quickly because the aggressor will win more rapidly, and wars can always be avoided if the weaker side gives way to the side making a threat . . . He (John Major) was a dangerous Prime Minister for troubled times', Bogdanor, 21 June 2007.
50 See Guest, op. cit., p. 103.
51 Abdic's forces were defeated by the Bosnian Army in the summer of 1994 but continued to present a threat to the authority of the Bosnian government in the Bihac enclave. Abdic was later put on trial and imprisoned.
52 Guest, op. cit., p. 104. Eide commented that even the description of the Bosnian government as 'Muslims' denigrated its authority in implying that it was merely one of three ethnic factions.
53 Michael Scharf who had helped draft the Statutes had a slightly different view. Characterising the war in Bosnia as 'in large measure a religious war between Bosnian Muslims and Bosnian Serbs', Scharf commented that since there were four judges from predominantly Muslim populations, while the Russian nominee was defeated, 'not surprisingly, the Tribunal proved unacceptable to the government of Serbia!' Scharf, op. cit., p. 72.
54 These include the Order of the Garter, the highest order of chivalry in England, Knight Commander of the British Empire (KBE), and the Most Distinguished Order of Saint Michael and Saint George (KCMG). Stephen was to have a crucial role in the first trial to be held at the ICTY.
55 Hazan, op. cit., p. 49.
56 Only six governments offered prison space, none of them from the P5 at the Security Council. See ICTY Yearbook 1994, paras. 29 and 35 for early tribunal difficulties.

57 The owner, the secretary general of the Carnegie Foundation, refused point blank to extend the contract for more than two weeks, reportedly fearing that the poor international standing of the ICTY would damage the reputation of Carnegie. Off, p. 263. See also Hazan, op. cit., p. 49.
58 Cassese quoted in Hazan, op. cit., p. 50.
59 Scharf, op. cit., pp. 11–13.
60 Antonio Cassese (Italy), Odio-Benito (Costa Rica), Karibi White (Nigeria), Kirk MacDonald (America), Sir Ninian Stephens (Australia), Haopei Li (China), Deschenes (Canada), Sidhwa (Pakistan), Abi-Saab (Egypt), Lal Vohrah (Malaysia), Jordan (France).
61 The Nuremberg Tribunal Rules covered barely three-and-a-half pages, and the Tokyo Tribunal had only nine rules. By February 1994, the judges had adopted 125 rules.
62 UN Document A/54/436 (1999) (h) 91.
63 Cassese had argued vigorously that rape in the context of intimidation and violence took on a different meaning, but Sir Ninian Stephen insisted on a degree of admission of consent, which reasserted the balance in favour of the defendant. Guest, op. cit., p. 133.
64 Rules of Procedure & Evidence, Rule 101.
65 See Scharf, op. cit., p. 68 for discussion of '*in absentia*' Rule 61.
66 UN Document (1999) 82g.
67 Ibid.
68 Ibid., p. 51.
69 Interview with judge under condition of anonymity, quoted in Hazan, op. cit., p. 44.
70 At the ICTR, one prime minister, ten former cabinet ministers, six other senior political appointees, four senior military officers, three former provincial governors and five mayors of provincial capitals were indicted. This had the added effect of attracting greater attention in Rwanda itself to the tribunal proceedings.
71 Guest, op. cit., p. 146, Hazan, op. cit., p. 54.
72 *The Times*, UN correspondent, 4 September 1993. The British campaign against Bassiouni provoked Boutros-Ghali into instructing Britain to 'put up or shut up'. Guest, op. cit., p. 146. Bassiouni pointed to Britain's Ambassador to the UN, David Hannay, as having blocked his appointment. Bassiouni, op. cit., pp. 109–113.
73 Scharf comments that, had the United States lobbied more aggressively for Bassiouni, other members may have followed. Hungary and Brazil later let it be known that they would have followed the United States' lead. Scharf, op. cit., p. 77.
74 Ibid.
75 Guest, op. cit., p. 154.
76 Goldstone enjoyed a liberal reputation as an anti-apartheid activist and had worked his way to the Transvaal Supreme Court and the appellate division of South Africa's Supreme Court. On the other hand, as Bassiouni remarked, Goldstone was not familiar with the background to the war. Orr, p. 270.
77 Hazan, op. cit., p. 57.
78 Ibid., p. 62.
79 The ACABQ, a 16-member body, which operates behind closed doors, had cut deep into the funding of the UN Commission of Experts.
80 India and Brazil's support for Tito's Yugoslavia through the Non-Aligned Movement was initially transferred to Serbia.
81 M. Cherif Bassiouni commented that this was a 'knee-jerk reaction' which would undermine the tribunal's appeal to Third World countries.
82 'In light of the problems encountered by the 780 Commission, we frankly did not trust the UN Secretariat on its own to provide the necessary budget and staff'. Scharf, p. 58. Michael Scharf had been part of the team drawing up the tribunal's Rules and Procedure.

83 For instance, witnesses from five European countries required to be questioned by the prosecution before Dusko Tadic, the first indictee to be delivered to The Hague, could be extradited from Germany. Guest, op. cit., p. 139.
84 ICTY Annual Report, 1994.
85 Guest, op. cit., p. 138.
86 The Serbian warlord, Arkan, was wanted for robbery in Holland, his followers being heavily involved with the drug trade in Amsterdam.
87 UN Information Notes, September 1993.
88 Ibid. October 1993. See also Hodge, op. cit.
89 Chuck Sudetic, 'Mortar Fire Kills 12 at Soccer Game in Bosnian Capital', *New York Times*, 2 June 1993, and Kurt Schork, *Guardian*, 2 June 1993.
90 UN Information Notes, 8/93, 1 August 1993.
91 UN Information Notes, 28 June 1993. 'Bosnia attack adds tension to peace talks', *New York Times*, 13 July 1993.
92 Ibid. On 28 September 1993, Dragan Kekic, 'president' of the Pale coordinating body for humanitarian aid denied authorisation for six UNHCR trucks to travel to Srebrenica.
93 UN Information Notes, 28 June 1993.
94 UN Information Notes, November 1993.
95 Under the Agreement, the combined territory held by Croatian and Bosnian government forces was divided into autonomous cantons, establishing the Federation of Bosnia and Herzegovina, a precursor to the Dayton Agreement. www.usip.org/files/file/resources/collections/peace_agreements/washagree_03011994.pdf
96 *Independent*, 13 August 1993.
97 Ibid.
98 Mladic trial: Witness recalls Sarajevo shelling, Balkan Transitional Justice, 31 October 2012.
99 See Hodge, Chapter 5, pp. 83–87 for international handling of the crisis.
100 One UNHCR field officer reported 'I have seen people gather wheat flour from air-drops with spoons from the mud. This is a mixture of mud and flour but it is still precious'. UN Information Notes, No.2/94, February 1994.
101 www.unhcr.org/refworld/country'HRW"BIH"45cb0ca52'0.ht
102 Hazan, op. cit., p. 58.
103 Cassese pointed at length to the Yamashita example of 7 December 1945, when the command responsibility principle was established. Paul Stuebner, Goldstone's deputy, however, viewed that judgement as the quintessence of conqueror's justice.
104 The judges decided to issue a public communiqué, expressing their concerns about the penal strategy. Theoretically, however, the judges had no right to question the prosecutor who is sovereign in raising indictments. Fifth plenary session, 16–30 January 1995, and La Grogne des Juges du Tribunal de la Haye, *Le Monde*, 2 February 1995.
105 M. Cherif Bassiouni believed Milosevic could probably have been indicted for command responsibility for the murder of 200 patients and personnel at Ovcara but considered that the United States wanted to use the ICTY strategically as a weapon to encourage the military to challenge the Milosevic regime. Cited in Hazan, op. cit., p. 62.
106 See Hodge, op. cit., p. 119.
107 Owen quoted in Hazan, op. cit., p. 65.
108 Ibid.

3 Srebrenica

A catalyst for change?

One issue hangs like a sword of Damocles above the peace process, namely that of the continued freedom and impunity of persons indicted by the Tribunal.[1]

Introduction

By the summer of 1995, there was a noticeable shift in the balance of military power in the area with the consolidation of the Bosnian/Croat federation and the partial lifting of the arms embargo, benefiting the Bosnian government forces. In the meantime, as the Croatian army (HV) was reinforced, the Serb forces (VRS) in Bosnia and Croatia, always short on manpower, now also began losing strategic ground.

The VRS takeover of the UN 'safe' areas, Srebrenica and Žepa, represented a victory not only over the Bosnian government forces but also in successfully flouting UN Security Council resolutions. But it was a short-lived triumph as, just weeks later, the Croatian army regained control of the Krajina region and, together with the Bosnian army (AbiH), lifted the siege of the 'safe area' of Bihac.[2]

On 25 July, the chief prosecutor of the ICTY, Richard Goldstone, brought indictments against Radovan Karadžić and Ratko Mladić for genocide and crimes against humanity in the municipalities in 1992, and issued warrants for their arrest.[3] The Bosnian Serb leaders remained in power, however, while the ongoing hostilities continued to compound logistical difficulties for the tribunal, still not in a position to call witnesses, execute arrest warrants or conduct field investigations.[4]

A second 120 milimetre mortar attack on the Markale marketplace in Sarajevo in September 1995, killing 34 civilians, finally triggered NATO action against the Serb defence bases surrounding the city, creating the conditions for ending the three-and-a-half-year siege. As the dust gradually began to settle, world leaders strove to establish a longer-term ceasefire in the form of an internationally brokered agreement which would be broadly acceptable to all sides. The Dayton Agreement which ensued from this finally signalled an end to the bloodshed, although the optimism felt by the tribunal in face of the NATO action was short-lived.

Preamble to Dayton: politics trumps justice

The international policy in Bosnia which had prevailed through the war continued in the wake of Srebrenica. Slobodan Milosevic was still viewed as an indispensable element in bringing about a settlement in the region based on the ethnic partition of Bosnia and Herzegovina. The tribunal, meanwhile, despite the indictments of the Bosnian Serb leaders, was used primarily as a negotiating tool, rather than a means of bringing indicted war criminals to justice. This favoured nationalist politicians, while seriously impeding the functioning and reputation of the tribunal.[5] The ICTY indictments meant that Karadžić and Mladić were prevented from taking up official office, or from travelling abroad where they would be subject to international arrest warrants, strengthening Milosevic's bid to negotiate on behalf of the Bosnian Serbs. Milosevic used this power to shape Bosnia's political future, bringing both genocide indictees into the pre-Dayton negotiations with international representatives and supporting their unofficial infiltration into Bosnian politics in the critical post-Dayton months.

The fact that Milosevic had not been indicted along with his Bosnian Serb counterparts, contributed to the misconception that he was a suitable negotiating partner at international level. His flouting of the ICTY arrest warrants reinforced his apparent exemption from international sanction, while reaffirming the general impression of the tribunal as a 'paper tiger'.[6] The decision not to build a case against Milosevic at the time had clear political overtones. Interviewed years later, David Owen, the EU envoy to former Yugoslavia till June 1995, outlined the *realpolitik* governing international thinking:

> When I met Goldstone . . . I did not recommend against indicting Milosevic or the others. . . [it] would not have been wise . . . I explained to them the detail of the negotiations, showed him the difficulties. . . . The conclusion that they could easily draw was that it would not be very wise to indict the heads of state if we wanted to arrive at a negotiated peace between them and with them. I believe that Goldstone and Arbour had this pragmatic attitude, this judgment of good sense, and that the tribunal only indicted Milosevic when the prosecutor understood that he was no longer an obstacle politically. Because after Kosovo there were no more means to negotiate with Milosevic.[7]

Long after Milosevic was indicted for genocide, Owen still appeared to view this position as tenable. It was not until years later that the major world powers released sufficient evidence to indict Milosevic. Yet, international players were by no means deluded as to the Serbian president's role in the Srebrenica events, as two international diplomats, who worked closely with Milosevic at the time, were later to testify. In his memoir, published in 1998, Carl Bildt, the EU envoy to Bosnia at the time, reflected,

> I find it – as a minimum – extremely difficult to believe that the General Staff [Perišić] of the . . . JNA (*sic*) in Belgrade would not have been aware of the

> evolving attack, and that they would not have told Milosevic . . . he should at the very least have been able to stop the attack, had he so chosen. This was the minimum. The maximum was that he was aware of it all and saw it as a useful operation to start to sort out the map in anticipation of the peace negotiations. [8]

The chief US negotiator, Richard Holbrooke, writing at the same time, was more specific about Milosevic's involvement.

> I told [Milosevic] that we knew that Mladić, who considered himself an officer of the Yugoslav Army, had received support from their units situated just across the Serbian border from Srebrenica, from an army under Milosevic's command.[9]

As Srebrenica was being shelled, and just days before the massacres, Carl Bildt shared a lavish ten-hour lunch with Milosevic, during which issues other than Srebrenica dominated the agenda.[10] The day after the enclave fell to Mladić's forces, Bildt was advised that talks with Mladić were 'important'.[11] Accordingly, three days later, as genocide was taking place around Srebrenica, Mladić was present at a secret meeting hosted by Milosevic at Dobanovci, just outside Belgrade, also attended by senior international diplomatic and military officials, including UN Civil Affairs Chief Yasushi Akashi, UN representative Thorvald Stoltenberg, UN General Rupert Smith and Carl Bildt. The meeting, aimed at reaching a deal on access to the enclave was, in the circumstances, little more than a charade, although Bildt described it as 'achieving results'.[12]

The international courting of the Serbian president, which had prevailed throughout the war, continued to dominate peace efforts in the misguided belief that, through Milosevic, negotiators could drive a wedge between the Serb leaders – somewhat in the spirit of the imperial 'divide and rule' era, a tactic which proved less effective in the late twentieth-century Balkans. During the negotiations leading up to Dayton, Richard Holbrooke went along with the Serbian president's game-play, while the latter assumed the role of consummate host, providing lavish spreads on his home grounds in allegedly even-handed negotiations.

The bombing by Serb forces of the Markale marketplace in Sarajevo on 28 August 1995 provided the pretext for NATO air strikes against Serb air defences to break the siege of Sarajevo. Just 3 days later, at a 12-hour meeting hosted by Milosevic at Dobanovci, Richard Holbrooke, having been wined and dined, was presented with a paper proposed by Milosevic and witnessed by the Serbian Patriarch.[13] The proposal was for a joint Yugoslav-*Republika Srpska* delegation for all future peace talks, headed by Milosevic, which Holbrooke declared to be 'a real breakthrough'. The proposal was adopted the following week at Geneva, where a 'set of basic principles' was agreed.[14] While the internationally recognized borders of a 'sovereign' Bosnia were confirmed, *Republika Srpska* became recognized for the first time as one of two self-governing entities. Crucially, the right (of Serbs and Croats) to establish 'parallel special relationships with neighbouring countries' was also recognized.[15] Bildt viewed the Geneva meeting as 'an important success . . . the most important meeting in the process that led to the peace'. Karadžić also reportedly professed his satisfaction.[16] This agreement was to seal the fate of Bosnia and Herzegovina for decades.

The timing of the Dobanovci proposal coincided with the increasing demoralization of the Bosnian Serb forces, who were rapidly losing in strength and momentum. Milosevic had long been ready to settle on such a peace plan which would ensure Serb control over a substantial area of Bosnia, provided the deal included the removal of sanctions over Serbia. The NATO strikes over Sarajevo, meanwhile, diverted the attention of the VRS forces, while facilitating the seizure by the Bosnian and Croatian armies of large swathes of North-Western Bosnia, held by Mladić's forces since 1992. Carl Bildt recalled Mladić's 'war-weariness' and that Karadžić in Pale expressed a 'new flexibility' in his meeting with UN officials.[17]

Now was the best opportunity since the war began for a settlement based on criteria other than ethnic division. Yet there emerged significant disagreement between US and European leaders over the NATO campaign which was opposed by many European states and British leaders in particular.[18] After a temporary pause for negotiation, British UN Commander Rupert Smith, who had led the campaign, was reluctant to resume bombing, to the surprise of US negotiators.[19] Also, world leaders and diplomats still looked to Milosevic and, concerned that the recent gains would affect the Contact Group plan, warned Bosnian and Croatian leaders that Banja Luka was out of bounds.[20] This was a momentous move at a time when the Bosnian and Croatian forces had arrived within 15 miles of the Serb-controlled city.[21] Holbrooke recalled urging Tudjman to take Sanski Most, Prijedor and Bosanski Novi, but opined that 'Banja Luka was a different matter. The city was unquestionably within the Serb portion of Bosnia. Even if it were captured, it would have to be given back to the Serbs in any peace negotiation'.[22]

The fact that Banja Luka had been a multi-cultural city with 45% non-Serbs before the war appeared immaterial to Holbrooke.[23] His instruction, accepted by Tudjman, cemented many of the gains achieved by crimes against humanity, while reassuring Serb leaders (under indictment for genocide) that the international community stood behind the Contact Group plan, irrespective of any changes on the ground.[24] Contrary to progressive trends elsewhere in the world, Bosnia was to remain ethnically divided for the foreseeable future.[25] In his memoirs, Holbrooke belatedly questioned the necessity to hold onto that ratio.

> Given that the Serbs had conquered so much territory through infamous methods, it would have been just for the Federation to control more than 51 per cent of the land.[26]

The international insistence on retaining the 51:49 per cent ratio began, according to Holbrooke,

> with a flawed intelligence assessment . . . 'experts' predicted that the more successful the Croatian-Bosnian offensive, the greater the chance that the

> regular VJ would re-enter the war. These opinions were based not on secret intelligence of Yugoslav plans, but on a long-standing belief in the intelligence community about the military superiority of the Serbs and their cohesiveness.[27]

Yet, this 'flawed intelligence assessment' which helped govern the British-led international policy throughout the war was to prevail over the post-war peace settlement and beyond, as negotiations continued in Belgrade under the tutelage of Slobodan Milosevic.

On 13 September, Milosevic cajoled Holbrooke into negotiating with the Bosnian Serb leaders.[28] Although Holbrooke was later to express regret that he had not taken a firmer stance on a number of issues, at the time, he apparently felt it 'justifiable under the circumstances' to sit down and negotiate with indicted war criminals, handing the Serbs concessions they had ceased to expect.[29] He seemed unaware of the irony, or of how his conduct might be interpreted in Belgrade and Sarajevo. Drawn ever closer into Milosevic's fold, Holbrooke became increasingly critical of the Bosnian leaders who objected to negotiating on equal terms with genocide indictees.[30] Carl Bildt, by his own admission, was equally dismissive of the Bosnian leaders.[31] And, as a measure of further reassurance, a former US president, Jimmy Carter, who had earlier in the year volunteered his services as negotiator with Karadžić, now kept in regular phone contact with him.[32]

At a subsequent meeting on 16 September, lasting some seven hours, to which Milosevic invited the Yugoslav Army Commander, General Momčilo Perišić, Perišić offered General Dragomir Milosevic (later indicted by the ICTY) for talks with General Smith on breaking the Sarajevo siege.[33] Subsequent meetings were held between UNPROFOR commandeer General Janvier and Mladić, during which Mladić combined 'peace offerings and threats'.[34] NATO action had now been suspended, yet the roads to Sarajevo remained closed, violating one of the guarantees obtained from the Serb leaders.[35] Holbrooke only later admitted that a further two weeks' bombing would have strengthened his negotiating position with Milosevic.[36]

In a constitutional accord, fleshed out on 26 September in New York, the Serb(ian) war leaders won the day on virtually all the main points at dispute: the ethnic division of territory, the post-war institutions, the entities' names, sanctions and, most significantly, the status of the Serb leaders indicted by the ICTY.[37] For Bosnia to function as a state, it was essential to establish strong internal institutional structures. Yet in the pre-Dayton discussions, international divisions prevalent during the war once again rose to the surface. Whereas the United States in general favoured a solid upper constitutional layer, well defended by an international police force, the Europeans, led by Britain, argued for weak central institutions and a limited police force with no powers of arrest.[38] At a 16-hour meeting with Milosevic on 23 September, US officials Chris Hill and Roberts Owen agreed to soften language on central government functions, which was to result in two separate 'states' within the one country, with a massive bureaucratic structure managed by nationalists on all sides.[39] It also meant that there was no external authority to ensure that war crimes indictees would be delivered for trial at The Hague.

Thirdly was the issue of the names of the entities. Milosevic insisted on calling the Serb entity '*Republika Srpska*' and that Bosnia Herzegovina renounce the title 'republic'. Holbrooke again caved in to Milosevic, insisting to Izetbegovic that the arrangement should stand.[40] Only later did he acknowledge his error:

> I regret that we did not make a stronger effort to drop the name Republika Srpska. We underestimated the value to Pale of retaining their blood-soaked name. We may also have underestimated the strength of our negotiating hand on that day, when the bombing had resumed. . . . To permit Karadžić to keep the name he had invented was more of a concession than we realized.[41]

A central issue on which Milosevic took a stand was the international sanctions against Serbia, which had affected Serbia's economic position, cutting industrial output by two-thirds.[42] They also threatened Milosevic's survival as leader. Here, again, there was a divide between the US and European positions.[43] The US administration was adamant that sanctions should remain in place until a settlement to end the war had been reached. Senior European officials, however, wanted sanctions lifted regardless of any concessions from Belgrade, a position which they had held since the previous year.[44] Most important of all, however, was the question of how to respond to the ICTY indictments of the Bosnian Serb leaders, and once more, Milosevic managed to relegate the ICTY to the background in the Dayton talks and secured an important concession in the final agreement which was to have long-term consequences, as discussed next. The significance of Milosevic's success was again reflected in Holbrooke's memoirs, where he acknowledged he could have secured a better deal.

On 29 September, the ICTY, learning that Mladić was in Belgrade, sent a formal request to Milosevic for his extradition.[45] Ignoring this, Milosevic hosted a meeting in Belgrade with Holbrooke and his team the following week, allocating them a room where they could type a proposed ceasefire agreement while outside lingered Karadžić and Mladić, waiting to be invited into the talks.[46] With Holbrooke's agreement, the two genocide indictees joined the discussions. Holbrooke later admitted to putting heavy pressure on the Bosnian president, Izebegovic, to accept the Serb proposals.[47]

On 9 October, the ICTY sought an international warrant for Dragan Nikolic, the first suspect to be indicted by the ICTY for war crimes. At a press conference on the same day, tribunal judges argued strenuously against a decrease in the ICTY spending budget which would have prevented investigations from continuing. By October 1995, the ICTY had indicted over 50 suspects, although notorious Serb paramilitary leaders, such as Zeljko Raznatovic (Arkan) and Vojislav Šešelj, were not amongst them. Neither were RS leader Rajko Kasagic, the Croatian president Franjo Tudjman, Croatian defence minister Gojko Susak nor Bosnian Croat leader Mate Boban indicted.[48] Arkan at this time was launching an attack on non-Serbs remaining behind Serb lines in Prijedor and Sanski Most, with the full support of Milosevic.[49]

The weakness displayed by international players over the weeks following the NATO air strikes encouraged the Serbs in their negotiating stand and confirmed the Bosnian Serb leaders' role in the process.[50] The scene was set for negotiations at Dayton.

Dayton: pragmatism before principles

Bosnia and Herzegovina was restructured under the Dayton Peace Agreement (DPA) with no clear winners or losers, amounting to a compromise reflecting the differing objectives of the P5 members of the UN Security Council during the war.[51] The Agreement compounded existing ethnic divisions, in ratifying the Serb-held territory as a republic, led by war criminals and brought about by genocide and the forcible expulsion of hundreds of thousands of civilians.[52] While the overall objectives of the United States and Europe were at one in wishing to end hostilities in Bosnia, the terms on which they were prepared to do so differed. There were also differences within the United States, both at the administration level and in the Pentagon, and, not surprisingly, between the various European states, which largely echoed positions taken during the war years. While Britain and Russia backed a solution which effectively left Serbia as a leading regional player, the United States was mainly concerned to exercise its political leadership in a major European war and to bring it to an end well before the looming US elections through the introduction of a US-led NATO force. The US military was against assuming any responsibilities beyond security, however, which in practice meant separating the parties to the conflict. Some within the US administration and elsewhere argued for a more just solution, albeit with little success.

The cessation of hostilities brought about by the Dayton Agreement meant, in theory, that ICTY officials would be facilitated easier access to crime sites and mass graves.[53] Yet the Agreement proved to be a double-edged sword for the tribunal. ICTY president Cassese had wanted to secure the establishment of a NATO police force mandated to arrest indictees, seize documents and participate in the tribunal's investigations. Chief Prosecutor Richard Goldstone, meanwhile, spent two days in mid-November meeting with top officials from the White House, Pentagon, State Department and CIA, but later acknowledged that he had failed to secure assurance that the Dayton Agreement would require the handover of indictees.[54] It was becoming increasingly clear that the focus at Dayton was more on ending the conflict than on any international commitment to bring war criminals to justice.

Britain, which had assumed a leading international role during the Bosnian and Croatian wars in appeasing the Belgrade regime and looking to Milosevic for solutions, now also took the European lead at Dayton. France, under its newly elected president, Jacques Chirac, had displayed a more militant stance against the Serb leaders following the fall of Srebrenica but at Dayton was handicapped by the need to ensure the safe return of two French pilots missing in Bosnia.[55] Pauline Neville-Jones, appointed by the Foreign Office to head the British team, used her position to argue strongly for a limited role for the NATO implementation force (IFOR) and a small international police force (IPTF) in Bosnia, along with a weak 'roof' over the central government authorities, and correspondingly strengthened powers for the entities.[56] In this, she had an important ally. According to EU envoy, Carl Bildt,

> It had . . . become clear that there was a difference in the approach to the role that policing was to play in peace implementation . . . the US argued strongly for an extremely robust force 4–5,000 strong which would not only act as monitors and instructors for the local police, but would also have concrete powers to intervene, make arrests, and generally enforce the law of the land. The Europeans were sceptical . . . how would we handle a situation in which our police made arrests but then the local courts released the prisoner because they did not accept police intervention?[57]

The Neville-Jones/Bildt position coincided with that of Milosevic also in regard to keeping the question of the arrest of Karadžić and Mladić off the agenda.[58] As Neville-Jones saw it, there was no mechanism in the Dayton Accords for sanction or the arrest of war criminals due to the fear that the local population would be provoked into reprisals.[59] Neville-Jones evidently won the day at Dayton since, despite the indictments for genocide and the large-scale presence of NATO troops on the ground, there were no clear instructions for the arrest or removal from power of either genocide indictee, a calculated omission that was to prolong their pervasive influence on Bosnian politics into the crucial months following Dayton.[60]

Holbrooke, who had spent more time than most outsiders in Milosevic's company, later summed up the Serbian leader's aims at Dayton.

> Milosevic's first priority was lifting sanctions. He then wanted an early international conference where the 3 presidents would sign an agreement of 2–3 pages, freezing armies in place, that political provisions be ambiguous and limited, and central government functions and authority restricted. To create a similar situation to Cyprus – where a temporary dividing line became a permanent one.[61]

Apart from the length of the final agreement, Milosevic achieved his aims, although Holbrooke omitted to mention Milosevic's equally successful bid to marginalize the tribunal at Dayton, apparently with the acquiescence of the US Secretary of State. As Carl Bildt later wrote,

> the Serbs did not want any mention of the Tribunal in the framework agreement – a battle which they eventually won in a direct session with [US Secretary of State Warren] Christopher. The Tribunal disappeared from the text, to be replaced by a general reference to international undertakings.[62]

Holbrooke, according to his own account, argued for a more active role, including arresting powers for the proposed NATO IFOR, a large international police force and funding directed to the Sarajevo government to strengthen central institutions, but he clearly did not argue strongly enough. He appeared, on the contrary, to be charmed by Milosevic, while bringing increasing pressure to bear on the Bosnian delegation.[63] He may well also have been influenced by the fact that none of the major world powers had passed on information to indict the Serbian president.[64] Carl Bildt, also seemingly impressed by Milosevic, threatened the Bosnian delegation that he would close the talks, keep the arms embargo and have the UN withdrawn.[65] His proclivity towards the Serb camp was clear:

> Once again, the internal divisions amongst the Bosnian Muslims had complicated our work. . . . It was crucially important to try to persuade the Bosnian delegation to get its act together and be prepared to take the statesmanlike step that would be inevitable, sooner or later . . . everything was now about to collapse because the Muslims were unable to make the transition from war to peace.[66]

The rumour that Richard Holbrooke had made a deal with Milosevic, guaranteeing immunity in return for his cooperation at Dayton, did not help the reputation of the tribunal.[67] Following the genocide indictments, the chief prosecutor, Richard Goldstone, along with many ICTY judges who felt they had been used by the international community, threatened to resign en masse if the rumour of a deal was proved correct, or if Karadžić and Mladić were granted amnesty as part of a peace deal or allowed to appear at Dayton.[68]

*

The Accords were signed by the Federal Republic of Yugoslavia (FRY), Bosnia and Herzegovina and Croatia. Their leaders also endorsed the various annexes, undertaking to 'respect and promote fulfilment' of their provisions. Third States, namely, France, the United States, Britain, Germany and Russia, and EU envoy Carl Bildt, initialled the General Framework Agreement (GFA) merely as 'witnesses'. There were precedents in this, although in the other cases, the United States had assumed the legal obligation to ensure compliance.[69] At Dayton, the Third States, in confining themselves to merely witnessing the GFA, avoided assuming any technical obligation to safeguard compliance with it.[70] This point was raised frequently thereafter by internationals seeking to make the 'parties' solely responsible for upholding the Agreement. Also, and crucially for the ICTY, there was no mention of the tribunal in the GFA. Instead, it was relegated to the annexes, which were not signed by the international heads of state.[71] President Clinton's news conference at the end of the Dayton talks was indicative of US priorities, with his only direct reference to war criminals being that they would be excluded from political life.[72]

The tribunal was by now concerned not only about its poor representation in the Dayton Agreement but also for its actual survival.[73] Although over 40 individuals had been indicted, very few were in custody. On 16 November, as the Dayton talks were drawing to a close, Mladić and Karadžić were again indicted by the ICTY, this time for genocide and crimes against humanity in Srebrenica. This followed an indictment on 7 November against Milan Mrksic, Miroslav Radic and Veselin Sljivancanin, officers of the Yugoslav People's Army (JNA) Belgrade-based 1st Guards Motorised Brigade, for the mass killing of 264 non-Serbs removed by force from Vukovar hospital and later executed and buried in a mass grave at Ovcara.[74] Had the tribunal played a major role in the Dayton negotiations – as its establishment under Chapter VII of the UN Charter would imply it should have – the Vukovar indictments would have had a radical impact, since the crimes were committed under Milosevic's watch. But this irony international leaders evidently chose to ignore. In marked contrast to the pivotal role assigned to it by the UN Security Council, the tribunal was barely a player in the Dayton proceedings. The leading role at the negotiating table was tacitly accorded to Milosevic, who represented both the FRY and the Bosnian Serb entity (RS), thus placing Serbia in a powerful position to influence both the terms of the DPA and post-war developments.[75]

Another consequence of the partition of Bosnia and Herzegovina was that it left Serbia in exclusive control of the Serbian/Bosnian border and Bosnia with neither an integrated army to protect its international frontiers nor a police force to secure order throughout its territory. As the Dayton talks progressed, Serbian army technicians were already busy restructuring the Bosnian Serb army's communication systems destroyed by NATO air strikes and routinely sending helicopters and fixed-wing aircraft with supplies to Banja Luka.[76]

Yet one of the most serious implications of ethnically partitioning Bosnia was that it would render the return home of refugees and displaced people highly dangerous if their homes were in the Serb entity.[77] The lack of freedom of movement across inter-entity boundaries meant that Bosniaks still could not enter RS, or visit many of the Croat-held areas in the Federation, as politicians responsible for the genocide and crimes against humanity throughout the war remained in a position to influence the political situation and the public mindset, either from leadership positions (Krajisnik, Drljaća) or from behind the scenes.[78] The Dayton Agreement was also ambivalent on the penalizing of political leaders who might seek to prevent repatriation and reintegration. These ambiguities were to have long-term consequences, as nearly two decades later, few non-Serbs were able to vote in their places of residence in 1992.[79]

The genocide indictments did have the immediate effect of preventing Karadžić and Mladić from travelling to Dayton for the negotiations. On the other hand, had they travelled to the United States, the US administration would have been in a position under United Nations Security Council resolution (UNSCR)827 to arrest them on arrival. In which case, the tribunal would have been greatly strengthened and subsequent developments in Bosnia probably very different.[80]

*

On the day after the conference ended, a UN Security Council resolution conferred on the commander of the international force and the civilian 'high representative' the power to report to the Security Council significant noncompliance by any of the parties to the Agreement.[81] The resolution also noted that 'compliance with the requests and orders of the International Tribunal for the former Yugoslavia constitutes an essential aspect of implementing the Peace Agreement'.[82] In contrast to the spirit of the resolution, and despite the Serbian government's failure to comply with an essential aspect of the Dayton Agreement, sanctions on the FRY were suspended indefinitely, thus surrendering a powerful weapon for ensuring cooperation with the tribunal. In October 1996, sanctions were lifted permanently from the FRY, despite Serbia's failure – and that of the RS government for which the FRY was a guarantor – to deliver any war crimes indictees to The Hague.[83]

On 22 November, almost the entire Bosnian Serb leadership gathered at Dobanovci with Milosevic, including Radovan Karadžić, Momcilo Krajisnik, Biljana Plavsic, Aleksa Buha, Nikola Koljevic, Rajko Kasagic and General Zdravko Tolimir (representing Ratko Mladić). Days later, Karadžić threatened that Sarajevo could become the Beirut of Europe if Serbs were forced to accept 'Muslim' rule and that any attempt to arrest him would jeopardize the final signing of the Dayton Agreement due to take place in Paris in early December.[84] Yet, for several weeks after this, Karadžić and Mladić were conspicuously absent from the political scene. In the immediate aftermath of Dayton, Karadžić had less support in RS than he had earlier enjoyed, and his arrest at that time would have sent a clear signal to other indictees and been unlikely to engender large-scale opposition in RS.[85]

Much was to hang on implementing the Accords on the ground, which was mainly in the hands of the international military and civilian designated leaders, IFOR Commander Admiral Leighton-Smith and High Representative Carl Bildt, respectively.[86]

Conclusion

It might have been assumed that the Srebrenica genocide would prove a catalyst in bringing the ICTY to the forefront of international efforts to address the war in Bosnia. Yet, while the significance of the Bosnian Serb political and military leaders' indictment just two weeks after the fall of Srebrenica should not be underestimated, the charges did not extend to the main driver behind the wars in Croatia and Bosnia, the Serbian president, Slobodan Milosevic. The NATO campaign which opened up an opportunity for a settlement based on other than ethnic criteria was lost, and Milosevic continued to be courted by international diplomats and negotiators. Indeed, the negotiations depended on Milosevic's promotion and legitimization, as he became a key player at Dayton. The Bosnian delegation, on the other hand, was compelled, under threat of continued warfare and the withdrawal of EU and US support, to sign the Accords alongside Milosevic and the Croatian president, Franjo Tudjman, both of whom had apparently been exonerated of all responsibility for crimes committed under their command. The failure to indict the Serbian and Croatian presidents at this crucial time, and the international clout they enjoyed in their leading roles at Dayton, was to skew any understanding of the war externally and to affect implementation of the Accords for decades.

The Dayton Accords were drawn up hastily in a last-ditch attempt to end the war, with a consequent lack of clarity and many ambiguities. This was partly a result of the need to reconcile different international perspectives and objectives but was also a reflection of a peace dishonourably secured through international collusion with the instigators of the crimes. As during the war, the main message conveyed at Dayton to major indictees was one of probable impunity, as Karadžić and Mladić remained free to influence events, fostering partition and justifying injustice, and Serbia was rewarded with the lifting of sanctions.

An agreement which failed to address adequately the crimes committed, or to fully recognize the mechanism set up to bring the perpetrators to justice – the International Criminal Tribunal – could not be anything but flawed. But the Dayton Peace Agreement, albeit temporary in nature and contradictory in simultaneously advocating military separation and political unity, did contain the rudiments of an interim solution. It confirmed Bosnia as a sovereign state; it enhanced the role of the tribunal in restating and specifying the obligation of *all* states to cooperate fully and it granted the right to freedom of movement throughout the country and for refugees and displaced persons to return home safely, and regain lost property or obtain just compensation.

All of this, however, depended on the provisions being rigorously implemented on the ground which, given the circumstances, required the active combined and cohesive commitment of the key international players – the commander of the NATO IFOR and the civilian high representative, and those under their command. The months following the close of the Dayton Conference would prove to be a crucial testing time.

Notes

1. Aid and Accountability: Dayton Implementation, International Crisis Group, Bosnia Report No.17, 24 November 1996.
2. Bihac had been surrounded by VRS forces, with part of it under the fiefdom of renegade Bosnian leader Fikret Abdic, who enjoyed the backing of Belgrade.
3. There were 46 indictments by this time. As UNPROFOR refused to transmit the warrants to the Bosnian Serb authorities, the 'Office of the Serb Republic' situated in Belgrade accepted them but did not transmit them to the accused or respond to further requests by the Registry to do so. ICTY Annual Report, 23 August 1995, paras. 91–92.
4. Ibid., para. 92.
5. According to Richard Holbrooke, 'The tribunal at the start was regarded as little more than a public relations device . . . During our negotiations, the tribunal emerged as a valuable instrument of policy that allowed us, for example, to bar Karadzic and all other indictees from public office. Yet no mechanism existed for their arrest'. Richard Holbrooke, *To End A War*, Random House, 1998, p. 190.
6. ICTY Annual Report, 23 August 1995, paras. 175–178.
7. David Owen, interview with Pierre Hazan, Hazan, op. cit., p. 61. Many judges felt privately that Goldstone had succumbed to outside political pressure.
8. Carl Bildt, *Peace Journey: The Struggle for Peace in Bosnia*, Weidenfeld and Nicolson, 1998, p. 61.
9. This in itself should have been reason enough to indict Milosevic and VJ Commander Momcilo Perisic. It was significant that Milosevic, while denying involvement in

Srebrenica, agreed 'to allow international investigators to travel to the enclaves to gather on-site information on what had happened'. Holbrooke apparently regarded this as 'a significant concession if he meant it'. Holbrooke, p. 108. Holbrooke did not comment on the implication of the 'concession', i.e. that Milosevic had ultimate control over the enclaves.

10 Bildt, pp. 51–52.

11 Ibid., p. 59. Reportedly, UN Lt-General Bernard Janvier had called for a withdrawal from all the enclaves in a confidential briefing on 24 May 1995, in New York. *Independent*, 30 October 1995.

12 Bildt, p. 63. For the international position leading up to the genocide, see Sylvie Matton, *Srebrenica: Un Genocide Annonce*, Flammarion, 2005.

13 Holbrooke, p. 107. 'The meal was, as usual, several different preparations of lamb, accompanied by potatoes and vegetables, and for variety some pork . . . fuelled by . . . scotch, wine and plum brandy . . . We sat . . . eating and drinking almost continually (*sic*)'. Holbrooke, op. cit., pp. 107–108, 113.

14 *Guardian* leader, 6 September 1995.

15 *Guardian*, 9 September 1995. See a critique of the Geneva accord by Ivo Banac, 'Shotgun Wedding in the Balkans', *The Nation*, 23 October 1995.

16 Bildt, op. cit., p. 100.

17 Following a meeting with Momcilo Krajisnik, Bildt comments, 'Krajisnik knew they were losing the war. The ABIH was growing stronger every month and the VRS was exhausted, defeated and increasingly thin on the ground'. Bildt, p. 91.

18 Holbrooke notes the firm support of NATO Secretary General, Willy Claes 'amidst a notable lack of enthusiasm from most of his fellow Europeans, Claes made one of those bureaucratic decisions whose importance is lost to most outside observers . . . I have no doubt the Europeans would have blocked or minimized the bombing were it not for Washington's new resolve'. Holbrooke, pp. 99, 104. Meeting Ivor Roberts, the British Ambassador to Belgrade, on 31 August, Holbrooke found him 'erudite and charming . . . although he seemed excessively pro-Serb. Don't put them in a corner, Roberts urged, or they will lash back. The clear subtext was that the bombing was a mistake'. Holbrooke, p. 110.

19 'General Rupert Smith was now recommending that the bombing not resume–an astonishing and dismaying change of position' Holbrooke, p. 132.

20 'The point is to avoid an attack on Banja Luka'. British Foreign Secretary Malcolm Rifkind, *Guardian*, 19 September 1995. Rifkind was having dinner with Milosevic as the deadline for the Serb withdrawal of artillery from around Sarajevo approached. British officials accompanying Rifkind indicated that if 50% of the guns were withdrawn by the deadline, it would be 'encouraging'. *Times*, 15 September 1995. US officials involved in the talks in New York on the future of Bosnia had not been briefed in detail on Rifkind's visit to Belgrade. Roy Gutman, *Newsday*, September 1995. See also John Sweeney's article on the British disinformation campaign following the fall of Srebrenica. 'UN Cover-up of Srebrenica Massacre', *Observer*, 10 September 1995.

21 *Daily Telegraph*, 22 September 1995.

22 Holbrooke, op. cit., pp. 160, 166.

23 In 1991, Banja Luka was a multi-national town where the Serbs constituted just over 54%. During the war, over 60,000 non-Serbs were forced to leave the city, and Banja Luka became overwhelmingly Serb populated. United Nations High Commissioner for Refugees and OSCE Regional Centre Banja Luka Fact Sheet.

24 Holbrooke later referred to the 'ineffectiveness' of the contact group. Holbrooke, p. 137.

25 Apartheid in South Africa officially ended in 1994, although the system still defines the country at the time of writing.

26 Holbrooke, p. 295.

27 Ibid., p. 158. According to the UK foreign secretary, Malcolm Rifkind, 'There must always be a risk that Yugoslavia may feel the need to be drawn in'. He also warned the Croatians that if they opened a new front, close ties with the EU would be jeopardized. *Guardian*, 20 September 1995.
28 *Independent*, 16 September 1995. When Milosevic invited Karadzic and Mladic to join the negotiations, Holbrooke asked the ABC crew outside to leave. He later recalled, 'we waited nervously and reviewed our strategy'. In his memoirs, Holrooke described Mladic as 'a charismatic murderer', while Karadzic had 'surprisingly gentle eyes'. Holbrooke, pp. 148–149.
29 *Times* editorial, 16 September 1995.
30 Holbrooke, p. 195.
31 Bildt, op. cit., p. 103.
32 *Times*, 5 September 1995.
33 Holbrooke, pp. 156–157. Momcilo Perisic was sentenced to 27 years at the ICTY, but acquitted on appeal. Dragomir Milosevic is currently serving a 29-year sentence in Estonia for crimes against humanity and war crimes in Bosnia.
34 Holbrooke, p. 128.
35 Ibid., p. 187. The Serb proposal defined heavy weapons as any artillery greater than 100 milimetre and any mortar with a calibre greater than 82 milimetre, which meant that a great deal of the lighter artillery could be retained. But the document was enough to stop the bombing. Bildt, p. 104.
36 Holbrooke, p. 153. Within the United States, there was support for the European position from the Pentagon which was wary of being drawn into a conflict indefinitely. Holbrooke, Albright at the UN and some others in the US administration argued for more sustained bombing to assist negotiations.
37 Negotiators conceded that the accord was full of holes. *Times*, 28 September 1995.
38 According to Holbrooke, dealing with the Europeans was 'delicate and nettlesome throughout the Bosnia crisis, and put an unprecedented strain on NATO and the Atlantic Alliance just when the Cold War ties that had held us together had also disappeared'. Holbrooke, op. cit., p. 83.
39 Holbrooke, p. 177.
40 Holbrooke told Izetbegovic, 'We do not believe the name RS . . . means much . . . we can't get RS out of the draft. I'm sorry', Holbrooke, p. 131.
41 Holbrooke, pp. 135, 361.
42 *Guardian*, 8 September 1995.
43 Holbrooke noted that 'Milosevic hated the sanctions. . . . This gave us a potential lever over him, but by the fall of 1994, London, Paris, and Moscow wanted to lift all or most of the sanctions in return for almost nothing. Washington had a different view . . . not held unanimously . . . I . . . opposed giving Milosevic relief without getting something tangible in return', Holbrooke, p. 88.
44 'Fewer issues have caused greater tension with our major European allies and Russia than sanctions'. Ibid.
45 See ICTY Yearbook, 1996, 181–185, for the tribunal's requests for states' support in surrendering and arresting indictees, in line with their obligations under Security Council Resolution 827.
46 Holbrooke, p. 196.
47 Ibid., p. 195. During the same week, Mladic received a delegation from the Russian defence ministry in Bijeljina. SRNA Review of Daily News, 30 September 1995.
48 Rajko Kasagic was president of the executive board of SO Banja Luka. Mate Boban was named in the *Prlic et al* first-instance judgement as a member of the joint criminal enterprise. He died in 1998. Susak had a leading role in the Croat aggression against Bosniaks in 1993–1994. He died in 1997.
49 *New York Times*, 12 October 1995. According to Holbrooke, Milosevic expressed annoyance when he raised Arkan's name, referring to him as a mere 'peanut issue'. Holbrooke, pp. 189–190. See also pp. 211–212.

50 In mid-October, nine independent members of the Bosnian Serb assembly called for a 'government of national salvation' to replace the Karadzic administration, but this was not acted on by international negotiators. *Independent*, 16 October 1995.

51 China, although a P5 member at the Security Council, did not participate Security Council voting at that time.

52 As former ICTY judge Patricia Wald commented, 'many conclude their testimony on the atrocities they suffered by focusing on the injustice of deportation or expulsion from their communities, of being made refugees with no way to return to their ancestral homes and villages. In that sense, many of the perpetrators of the worst war crimes won their war, regardless of the ICTY verdicts'. For further discussion, see Patricia Wald, 'Dealing with Witnesses in War Crimes Trials: Lessons from the Yugoslav Tribunal', *Yale Human Rights & Development Journal*, Vol.5, Issue 1, 18 February 2014, and Diane F Orentlicher, *That Someone Guilty be Punished: The Impact of the ICTY in Bosnia*, Open Society Justice Initiative, 2010.

53 Article II(4) of Annex 1-A and Annex 4 and 6, undertook to facilitate 'unimpeded access and movement' to international personnel.

54 *New York Times*, 14 and 15 November 1995, and Hazan interview with Cassese, Hazan, op. cit., p. 68. Goldstone also pressed for some punitive sanctions to be retained against Serbia until Milosevic surrendered the Bosnian Serb leaders.

55 In the concluding statement at Dayton, all signatories to the Agreement undertook to assist in locating the two French pilots missing in Bosnia and to ensure their safe return. UN Security Council Resolution 1022, 22 November 1995.

56 *Pauline Neville-Jones*, Political Director at the Foreign Office, was a key player in ensuring Britain's perceived interests were well represented. According to someone who had read her confidential telegrams to the FCO, they would make 'vintage reading in 30 years' time', reflecting a continuous tension between the Europeans and the US negotiators. 'Nobody who has attempted to marginalize the formidable Miss Neville-Jones has previously escaped unscathed'. Michael Sheridan, *Independent*, 25 November 1995.

57 Bildt, op, cit., p. 132. Bildt was soon to change his view on the importance of a strong role for the international police force (see Chapter 4).

58 'The question of justice was absolutely not a priority. Our hypothesis . . . was that Karadzic and the others would capitulate. Or, at least, we expected to isolate Karadzic and Mladic . . . to reduce their political influence, rather than arrest them'. *Pauline Neville-Jones*, Interview with Pierre Hazan, 9 November 1999. Hazan, op. cit., p. 70.

59 Neville-Jones was to participate later that year with former foreign secretary Douglas Hurd in an initiative which was to result in strengthening the financial reserves of the Milosevic regime See Hodge, op. cit., pp. 127–128, for the so-called breakfast deal.

60 See International Crisis Group, Report, June 1996.

61 Holbrooke, p. 169.

62 Bildt, p. 139.

63 Holbrooke socialized freely with Milosevic at Dayton, and on one occasion pressurized the Bosnian Prime Minister, Haris Silajdzic, to join Milosevic at his dinnertable at Dayton, rather than seek a neutral venue for talks. Holbrooke, pp. 280–281.

64 According to Goldstone's deputy, Paul Stuebner: 'Neither the US, nor France, nor GB, nor any of the other countries aided us in building an indictment against Milosevic'. Stuebner interview with Pierre Hazan, Hazan, op. cit., p. 67.

65 'Milosevic offered us a stage show in which he mimicked the various negotiators and mediators . . . Carrington, Owen' Bildt, pp. 145–146, 156.

66 Bildt, p. 152.

67 Judge Georges Abi-Saab, Hazan, op. cit., p. 68.

68 *Guardian*, 17 November 1995. Arguably, amnesty for those accused of genocide would be contrary to *jus cogens* under Article 33 of the Vienna Convention on the Law of Treaties, and therefore void. See Jones, op. cit., p. 234, on this.

69 The Camp David Agreement in 1978 and the 1979 Washington Peace Treaty between Egypt and Israel.
70 For a fuller discussion of the implications of this, see Paola Gaeta, 'Symposium: The Dayton Agreements: A Breakthrough for Peace and Justice', *The European Journal of International Law*, Vol.7, 1996, pp. 153–156. Gaeta concludes that from the vantage point of legal logic, it might have been more appropriate for the annexes which enumerated the detailed conditions for peace to constitute the main treaty.
71 Article X of Annex 1-A of the Dayton Peace Agreement. See Gaeta, ibid. on this.
72 Also, the Agreement on Military Aspects of the Peace Settlement and the Agreement on Inter-Entity Boundary Line and Related Issue designed to ensure the cessation of hostilities, were accorded pride of place, with less importance to the future of BiH as a sovereign state within its present international boundaries. Gaeta, ibid.156.
73 The lifespan of the tribunal under UNSC Resolution 827 was open ended and could have been ended by the Security Council once peace in Bosnia was secured.
74 The indictment alleged that, after the fall of Vukovar to Serb forces, following a 3-month siege, JNA officers removed about 400 non-Serbs from the Vukovar hospital where they had sought shelter, and transported them to a farm building at Ovcara, where they were beaten and at least 261 killed and buried by bulldozer in a mass grave. On 3 April 1996, the Trial Chamber issued an arrest warrant for the three JNA officers to all states and to IFOR. In a later Rule 61 Proceeding, the Trial Chamber concluded that the failure to arrest the men could be ascribed to the refusal of Serbia to cooperate with the ICTY. Following a letter to this effect by President Cassese on 24 April 1996, the UN Security Council issued a number of resolutions urging compliance with the tribunal. *Prosecutor v Mrksic et al.*, 'Vukovar hospital', ICTY Case Information Sheet.
75 As Milosevic arrived at Dayton, Lawrence Eagleburger repeated allegations made three years previously as US secretary of state that Milosevic had command responsibility for crimes against humanity. Senate Republican leader Robert Dole and former US ambassador to Belgrade Walter Zimmerman expressed similar reservations. *Times*, 2 November 1995.
76 Confidential UN report dated 30 October 1995, reported by *New York Times*, 16 November 1995.
77 A Zone of Separation was established (Annex 1A, Art.IV, 2a), separating the entities, which would seem to confuse the purpose of Annex VII, Art.1 of the Dayton Agreement, where it is stated that an important objective of the DPA is that refugees and displaced persons have the right return home in safety.
78 For a fuller analysis of the Dayton Agreement, see Branka Magas, *Dubious Deal in Dayton: A Nation Betrayed*, the Tablet, 2 December 1995.
79 In the October 2014 elections, attempts by the Democratic Front party to reverse this trend were only partially successful, the nationalists once again winning the majority of seats. In May 2012, the Prijedor police banned a public gathering commemorating the brutal murder of 266 women and children in Prijedor in 1992. On December 10, 2012, as the international community commemorated the 64th International Human Rights Day, the Prijedor police placed itself above Republika Srpska law and banned a peaceful march that aimed to mark the anniversary.
80 UNSCR 827, 25 May 1993 (4), 'decides that all States shall co-operate fully with the ICTY' including requests or orders issued under Art.29 of the ICTY Statute. The United States signed a specific Agreement with the tribunal to surrender indictees to The Hague, although the Agreement still awaited implementing legislation. ICTY Annual Report, 23 August 1995.
81 UN Security Council Resolution 1022 (1995), 22 November 1995.
82 Ibid.
83 'UN Formally Ends Sanctions on Yugoslavia', *New York Times*, 2 October 1996.

84 *The Times*, 27 November 1995.
85 See Hodge, op. cit., p. 133.
86 UNSCR 1031 (1995) 15 December 1995. Following the Paris Peace Conference on 15 December 1995, the Security Council confirmed that the IFOR commander and high representative had the final authority to interpret the military and civilian aspects of the DPA, representing a partial delegation of power to them by the Council. Jones, op. cit.

4 Post Dayton

Genocide and impunity

We must rid this planet of the obscenity that a person stands a better chance of being tried and judged for killing one human being than for killing 100,000.

– Jose Ayala Lasso[1]

Introduction

The failure to arrest the Bosnian Serb leaders was to haunt the implementation of the Dayton Agreement, reconciliation within the communities and the economic recovery of Bosnia and Herzegovina for decades. It was also to have a lasting impact on the work of the ICTY.

In the immediate aftermath of Dayton, there was a clear opportunity to isolate Karadžić, as prominent figures even from his own party began to denounce the war and its political leaders.[2] A number of ex-soldiers rejected the notion of a Serb Republic and (rightly) feared the emergence of Momčilo Krajisnik, a key player in the war crimes, as a post-war leader.[3] According to one ICTY official, it would have been possible after Dayton 'to arrest Karadžić and Mladić with little consequence because the Bosnian Serbs were so demoralised. The failure to arrest them allowed them to once again consolidate their power'.[4] This opportunity was lost and, encouraged by statements from the international military and civilian heads, IFOR Commander Admiral Leighton-Smith and High Representative Carl Bildt, Radovan Karadžić not only remained free but also gained a new political momentum, while Mladić issued veiled threats of what might happen if he were to be arrested.[5] Slobodan Milosevic remained unindicted, and only one suspect had been delivered to The Hague, sending signals to the perpetrators that their crimes would be met largely with impunity and to potential dissenters within RS that they would enjoy little support internationally.

The crucial months following the peace agreement were marked by continued violations of human rights, and the obstruction of refugee returns to Republika Srpska, a massive exodus of Serb civilians from Sarajevo, enforced by their own leaders, and a consequent strengthening of nationalist positions on all sides.

Meanwhile, with just one indictee at The Hague, the ICTY prosecutor, Richard Goldstone, decided to hold an 'in abstentia' hearing. In mid-1996, he also opened the trial of Dusan Tadić, a relatively small fish in the scale of the Bosnian atrocities. As the first ICTY trial, it attracted worldwide attention yet, both in its handling and verdict, fell well short of expectations internationally and in Bosnia.

Job description issues

IFOR implementation

The ink was hardly dry on the Dayton Accords when the military and civilian heads of mission in Bosnia and other dignitaries made their understanding of NATO's role in Bosnia and their respective duties public.

US Secretary of State Warren Christopher was amongst the first to clarify his understanding of the NATO mission when, on 5 December 1995 at NATO headquarters, he announced that

> it is not part of the NATO obligation – not part of IFOR's responsibility – to hunt down or to seek out war criminals . . . that is not part of NATO's mission.[6]

It was election year in the United States, and President Clinton, fearing reprisals, was evidently not prepared to take risks. Christopher's statement was underlined by a spokesperson for the multi-national military IFOR, who explained that IFOR would arrest suspects only if they encountered them.[7] Yet, in practice, IFOR seemed unprepared to go even that far. In early 1996, Italian IFOR troops holding a checkpoint near Pale ignored the arrival of Karadžić at the Serb headquarters, while Mladić was known to be in the American zone, and journalists met with indictees.[8] The fact that the Agreement places the primary responsibility on the parties to cooperate with the tribunal was often cited by senior international politicians and diplomats, NATO officials[9] and even ICTY sources.[10] Richard Holbrooke, who had brokered the Dayton Agreement, also appeared to misunderstand the obligations of IFOR.[11]

Yet probably the most damaging comment to the peace process at that point came from the IFOR commander himself, Admiral Leighton-Smith, during his first local media appearance in a live call-in on Pale television on 18 January 1996, when he made it clear that he intended to take a minimalist approach to all aspects of implementation, apart from the protection of his forces.[12] Asked if he intended to arrest Serbs in the Serb-populated provinces of Sarajevo, Leighton-Smith declared he did not have the authority to arrest anybody.[13] The IFOR commander had effectively sent a message of reassurance to Karadžić, over his own network.[14] The following month, this was to have crucial consequences for Sarajevo, and for the peace process generally.

On 1 March 1996, in an open letter to IFOR commanders and troop-contributing states, Amnesty International stressed that the refusal to search for ICTY indictees was a clear violation of international law.

> All the states contributing troops to IFOR are state parties or successor-state parties to the Geneva Conventions and each is therefore obliged 'to search for persons alleged to have committed, or to have ordered to be committed, such grave breaches, or shall bring such persons, regardless of their nationality, before its own courts', the courts of another state or an international criminal court.[15]

This obligation, Amnesty underlined, was independent of any action taken by the ICTY or a national court, and 'states parties to the Geneva Conventions may not absolve themselves of any liability which they or other states parties have incurred in respect of grave breaches'.[16] Amnesty also pointed out that the refusal to search for ICTY suspects violated troop-contributing states' legal obligations under UN Security Council Resolution 827, which required all states to contribute fully with the tribunal and to take all measures necessary to implement the resolution.[17] The failure to search for and arrest indictees was also inconsistent with the principles of the Dayton Agreement which required IFOR 'to take such actions as required' to ensure compliance with Annex I of the Agreement.[18] Amnesty also reminded IFOR of its responsibility under the Dayton Agreement to ensure that the parties 'cooperate fully with any international personnel, including investigators . . . facilitating free and unimpeded access and movement'.[19]

A number of international lawyers writing at the time arrived at similar conclusions to Amnesty. John Jones pointed to the importance of the context of the Dayton Agreement in relation to the Security Council resolutions.[20] The Security Council, under the UN Charter, has 'primary responsibility for the maintenance of international peace and security', and the Charter prevails over member states' obligations under any other international agreement.[21] Niccolo Figa-Talamanca, discussing the legal implications of the role of NATO, stressed that

> the issue of co-operation with the ICTY is an example of where the pre-existing obligations under international law of each contributing State to IFOR take precedence over NATO's perception of its role in the implementation of the Peace Agreement, and even NATO member States' obligations towards the Organisation.[22]

The obligation of individual States to comply with the requests for assistance or orders issued by the tribunal is independent of the Dayton Agreement, deriving directly from UNSCR 827, which takes precedence over any obligations owed by member States to a particular Organization and, as UNSCR 1031 reiterates, the duty to cooperate is incumbent on *all* States.[23] John Jones argued that IFOR had not only the right but the duty to execute the tribunal's arrest warrants, under the obligation of all States to comply with the ICTY's orders pursuant to UNSCR 827 (1993). The IFOR US contingent, for instance, had responsibility for an area which included Srebrenica. The registrar of the ICTY could therefore send an arrest warrant to the appropriate authorities of the United States, which would then have the duty to execute it. Under the Dayton Agreement, Jones argued, IFOR enjoyed rights analogous to an occupying force:

> The IFOR shall have complete and unimpeded freedom of movement by ground, air and water throughout Bosnia and Herzegovina . . . to bivouac, manoeuvre, billet, and use any area or facilities to carry out its responsibilities as required, for its support, training and operations.[24]

Jones, like Amnesty, recalled troop-contributing states' duty under the Geneva Convention to search for persons charged under Art.2 of the ICTY Statute for grave breaches and to bring such persons, regardless of their nationality, before the courts.[25]

In his response to Amnesty, on 12 March 1996, Max S Johnson Jr., the legal advisor to the Supreme Allied Command in Europe (SACEUR), stated that IFOR is not bound by the Geneva Conventions or Additional Protocol I and that it 'should not be equated to a State in terms of international obligations'.[26] Amnesty responded that the contention was

> not only wrong as a matter of law, but contrary to the interpretation of these treaties by the International Committee of the Red Cross (ICRC), the collective opinion of states parties and recent practice of the UN in peacekeeping operations. . . . There are no exceptions to the duties in the Geneva Conventions or Additional Protocol I when 'political realities' make implementing humanitarian law inconvenient . . . any other interpretation would lead to absurd results. All any state would have to do to escape from its solemn treaty obligations under the Geneva Conventions . . . would be to participate in a multilateral force and say that the multilateral force was not a party to these treaties.[27]

The SACEUR legal advisor also wrote that IFOR was not yet prepared to provide adequate security for all 3,000 mass grave sites, to which Amnesty responded that 'IFOR regards the protection of mass grave sites as a diversion from its "principal tasks" '.[28] IFOR had agreed to provide 'area security' for forensic excavators during the day, but did not provide round-the-clock security for most grave sites, with the result that much of the evidence was destroyed over time.[29] Initially, there were not enough forces to commit, but, confronted by the ICTY, Madeleine Albright, the US ambassador to the UN and John Shattuck, Leighton-Smith made his position publicly clear: 'NATO is not, I repeat, NATO is not going to provide specific security, or in other words guarantee security, for teams investigating these grave sites'.[30]

*

IFOR's declared reluctance to act against alleged war criminals might presuppose that the Bosnian authorities would have the right of arrest, but this was apparently not so. On 30 January 1996, Bosnian Serb generals Djordje Djukic and

Aleksa Krsmanovic were arrested by the Bosnian government army along with half-a-dozen other Bosnian Serb soldiers. Djukic had been a member of the Main Staff and head of logistics for the Bosnian Serb Army from 19 May 1992, and Krsmanovic for the Sarajevo area. Although not indicted by the ICTY, on 7 February, the tribunal instigated proceedings against them, and five days later, they were transferred to The Hague. Yet Goldstone received little international support. IFOR was reportedly scandalized and, as Mladić publicly ordered the VRS to end cooperation with IFOR, there was concern at the Pentagon over the safety of US troops.[31] Milosevic, referring to them as 'simple soldiers', promptly ordered their release. On 2 February, Holbrooke returned to the region with Warren Christopher and, on 3 February, both had lunch with Milosevic. Following a frantic round of negotiations led by Holbrooke, the other soldiers were released, and the Bosnian army pledged not to make any further arrests of unindicted individuals.[32] Holbrooke later commented that Goldstone had 'complicated matters considerably'.[33] Krsmanovic was never charged, and Djukic was released two months later on grounds of ill health and died in May 1996. At his funeral, Ratko Mladić, in full military uniform, paraded before the world cameras at the graveside.[34]

On 18 February, the Dayton signatories established new 'Rules of the Road', which stipulated that suspects could only be apprehended if the ICTY had already reviewed a warrant. This raised an interesting point as to the legitimacy and constitutionality of denying Bosnia the right to arrest those suspected of having committed grave crimes on Bosnian territory.[35]

By the end of February 1996, over 50 individuals had been indicted by the ICTY, yet only one indictee, arrested in Germany, had been transferred to the Hague.[36] Most of the suspects were believed to have remained in the former Yugoslavia, yet none of the arrest warrants issued by the tribunal had been served.[37]

Civilian implementation: the role of the high representative

At the outset of the Dayton negotiations, the job that later became termed 'high representative' was regarded as a largely ceremonial post, overseeing aid and reconstruction.[38] Yet UN Security Council resolution 1022, adopted at the end of the Dayton conference, was to make the high representative the most powerful civilian in Bosnia.[39] A policy document from the Clinton Presidential Libraries, released in 2014, stressed the importance of the role.

> The High Representative can, by himself, pull the trigger on restoring economic sanctions. This gives the High Representative the power to decide if the FRY and the Bosnian Serbs are complying with their obligations to the War Crimes Tribunal. The High Representative is the only person who can use the threat of re-imposing sanctions to help the Tribunal apprehend indicted war criminals.[40]

In the view of the White House, the choice of high representative was 'as important to the success of the ICTY as was the right choice of Chief Prosecutor'. The high representative had the power, with US support in vetoing sanctions removal, to force compliance with the tribunal's indictments.[41]

The British and French (and, to a lesser extent, the Germans) backed Carl Bildt's appointment, but it was opposed in varying degrees by the United States and smaller European states, including the Netherlands, Austria and Sweden. The United States initially worked to secure an American candidate, or a more suitably qualified European.[42]

> The High Representative must share the vision that justice is the key to breaking the cycle of violence in the former Yugoslavia. The US should insist upon an alternative to Carl Bildt from among a number of excellent European candidates with both human rights stature and practical experience. . . . The right choice for High Representative is the best opportunity the US will have to ensure the Tribunal's success.[43]

American resistance to the appointment of Bildt stemmed from an analysis of his performance as EU mediator, where he was viewed as

> a 'trimmer' working to level out the moral ground by raising some and knocking down others so that all parties can negotiate together. With respect to the way Bildt would deal with war crimes, there is reason to believe Bildt will not pursue war criminals aggressively. This will frustrate US policy on the vigorous prosecution of genocide, crimes against humanity and war crimes.[44]

The White House document stressed that Bildt had made no significant public condemnation of Srebrenica and, after the capture of over 6,000 men, had argued that the moral duty was to negotiate.[45] On 16 July 1995, Bildt had announced a deal with the Bosnian Serbs that the International Red Cross could have access to the prisoners at a time when most had already been killed. Bildt's one major peace initiative, his effort to agree to lift sanctions in exchange for Milosevic's written agreement to recognize Bosnia's international boundaries was dismissed by the United States and Germany as being 'far too generous to Serbia'.[46]

Britain and France won the day, however, and Carl Bildt was appointed, a possible concession by the United States to shore up the faltering US/UK alliance.[47]

Yet US misgivings were proved well-founded from the outset. As soon as he assumed office, Bildt sought to downplay his capacity to ensure compliance by the parties. In response to an editorial in the *New York Times* of 17 December 1995, he wrote,

> You seem to overestimate the powers of the High Representative. His powers are not to execute or enforce but to monitor and coordinate. In contrast to the military implementation with its distinct chain of command and single-key approach, the civilian implementation structures have numerous chains of command and multiple keys.

In his memoirs, Bildt wrote that he was not entirely happy with UNSCR 1022 about the provision, 'largely because I was convinced that none of the parties would voluntarily hand people over to The Hague in the immediate future'.[48] Not merely overlooking his powers to reactivate sanctions on the FRY and RS, the high representative travelled frequently to Belgrade as supplicant.

Bildt admittedly faced a number of hurdles upon taking office, not least the lack of resources and conflicting international policies and disputes – both between and within the United States and European states – over the respective responsibilities of IFOR and the IPTF in regard to arresting war criminals.[49] His personal approach to his job, however, contributed significantly to the failure of key aspects of the Dayton Accords, especially human rights abuse affecting minorities, displaced people and refugees and to the increasing power wielded by indicted war criminals in RS, which often appeared to disrespect the high representative.[50] Bildt appeared to eschew conditionality, arguing for equal financial assistance to both entities, regardless of the failure to implement the Accords.[51] He also demonstrated scant knowledge of the background to the Bosnian war.

> With the outbreak of war the Muslims had virtually taken over the state, with all its assets and institutions . . . the Serbs had established their own state 'Republika Srpska' as best they could.[52]

Bildt later reflected that

> there was a deep gulf between European and US perceptions on what peace implementation really meant . . . we had a more coherent European view than Washington could still show . . . they were militarily muscular and time-limited; we had put far greater stress on the qualitative aspects of all the political, economic, humanitarian and other aspects of the enormous task of building a true and lasting peace.[53]

The record of Bildt's tenure as high representative makes it difficult to see what he meant. According to Richard Holbrooke, the civilian implementation of the Dayton Accords was almost a year behind schedule.[54] A US government report assessed that of the estimated two million people who were forced or fled from their homes during the war, in 1996, only 252,000 had returned home, almost all of them to areas in which they would be in the majority ethnic group, while at the same time, 80,000 others fled or were driven from their homes. Reasons hindering returns included fear stemming from lack of personal security and violence triggered by attempted cross-ethnic returns.[55]

UNHCR conceded that by mid-1997, most of the 'easy' returns had taken place and that it would be increasingly difficult for the 800,000 remaining internally displaced people and the 700,000 Bosnians abroad to return home. About 27,000 Serbs had returned to the Federation and fewer than 1,600 non-Serbs to RS.[56] In 51 group visits across the inter-entity boundaries between 17 April and 15 May, 22 were cancelled or aborted, as IFOR preferred to prevent visits going ahead to avoid violence. In some cases, displaced people trying to visit their homes were beaten up and killed.[57] Non-Serbs in Doboj and Teslić continued to be subjected to the psychological and physical terror which existed at the height of the war.[58]

A report by HRW, published 11 months after Dayton, documented evidence that the RS leadership and the state organs and agencies under its control, were responsible for directing, aiding and abetting continuing human rights abuses on an RS-wide scale against non-Serb minorities and moderate Serbs involved in opposition movements, including premeditated murder, expulsions, obstruction of freedom of movement, beatings and torture in detention, threats and intimidation and looting and destruction of property, in 'a highly organized fashion'.[59] The report revealed evidence of underground Bosnian Serb paramilitary organizations led by the SDS which planned to destabilize the peace process, stir up animosity towards the Federation and destroy moderate-line Serb elements not affiliated with the SDS. 'Liquidation units' had been formed to eliminate specific high-ranking moderate Serb leaders and non-Serb minorities still living in RS. HRW judged that the absence of 'robust' and proactive protection of these people had emboldened hard-line Serb authorities, and urged transparency and proactive engagement on the part of the high representative and the Organization for Security and Co-operation in Europe (OSCE) chairman, who should make it clear that non-compliance with the DPA would lead to immediate punitive measures, such as withholding aid and re-imposing sanctions. HRW recommended a time limit for compliance, failing which UNHSC 1074 would be implemented.

> By opting to remain silent about many of the abuses and the identity of the abusers, the international community has become complicit in the continuation of serious human rights abuses and the final stages of 'ethnic cleansing'.[60]

*

The first major challenge for the implementing authorities, however, was meeting the Dayton target date for the withdrawal of Bosnian Serb forces from Sarajevo which, under the Dayton Agreement, was to remain the undivided capital of Bosnia.

The Serb mass exodus from Sarajevo in the weeks preceding the deadline was foreseeable and a joint failure on the part of IFOR, which chose not to use its powers of arrest, and the Office of the High Representative (OHR), which took no punitive measures against those generating fear and forcibly expelling Serb civilians from their homes. Bildt blamed IFOR for not intervening, along with the 'Muslim leaders in general and Izetbegovic in particular' for a betrayal of multi-ethnic Sarajevo.[61] The Bosnian Serb media, controlled by Karadžić, broadcast repeated warnings that it was dangerous for Serbs to remain in the Sarajevo suburbs, as the vast majority were terrorized by their own authorities into leaving in the weeks preceding the handover; extremists burned apartments and forcibly expelled those who resisted leaving, destroyed or withdrew utilities and services and contributed to an atmosphere of panic and fear.[62] According to UN press officer Alexander

Ivanko, everything necessary for the people of Ilidža and neighbouring settlements disappeared, machines, medicine, office equipment, banks, while IFOR troops stood idly by. He called the Serb leadership 'the masters of manipulation', saying they had made it impossible for their people to stay, even while publicly urging them to do so.[63] Federation firefighters who belatedly attempted to stop the burning of houses were driven back by Serb grenade assaults, while NATO, the IPTF and the high representative tried to counter the onslaught. But their efforts were slow, disorganized and unconvincing. Officials did little beyond distributing leaflets to dissuade Bosnian Serbs from leaving the Sarajevo area.[64]

The strategy was clearly spelt out by Momčilo Krajisnik, the Serb member of the Bosnian tripartite presidency:

> The mission of this republic and its first strategic goal is for us to divide from Muslims and Croats . . . nobody is allowed now to create a new solution to stay together . . . at the end of it all the best solution is that people leave Sarajevo.

The events were witnessed by a number of international observers. UNHRC spokesperson Kris Janowski estimated that before the exodus there were 70,000 Serbs in Sarajevo, of whom at least 30,000 wanted to stay. After Pale tactics, fewer than 10,000 remained. Many of these left soon after.

> Most were ready to stay had they not been forced to leave . . .
>
> What the [Bosnian Serb] radio and TV are doing is portraying the international community as the enemy of the Serbs of Sarajevo, and the people seem to be listening . . . We're seeing a multi-ethnic Bosnia flushed down the toilet.[65]

Holbrooke saw the disaster as ending the sense of hope and momentum begun in late November. Bosnians in general read the events as evidence that multi-ethnic cooperation would not be encouraged by NATO. And, crucially, the lack of international will to play its part in assisting Dayton implementation set the scene for the return of Karadžić to the forefront. World leaders, fronted by Bildt, now began pursuing a policy which made it harder for refugees and displaced people to return home safely, cementing the ethnic divide for decades to come.

'In absentia' – the Rule 61 hearing

Meanwhile, as Richard Goldstone's tenure as ICTY chief prosecutor was drawing to an end, the likelihood of the two Bosnian Serb leaders indicted for genocide being brought to justice receded into the distance.

By mid-1996, Goldstone had issued over 50 indictments, but the arrest warrants for Karadžić and Mladić had not been executed. With the tribunal under-utilized, Goldstone decided to go ahead with a Rule 61 '*in absentia*' hearing, a controversial move since it was prohibited under the ICTY Statute on the grounds that it would be inconsistent with Article 14 of the International Covenant on Civil and Political Rights (ICCPR).[66] The ICTY Statute even qualifies this right as a minimum guarantee.[67] Unlike the ICCPR, however, under the European Convention, the right of an accused to be present at trial is only implicit, not unambiguous.[68] ICTY president, Antonio Cassese, was keen to have an *in absentia* capability, and, despite the strong reservations of some in the tribunal, Goldstone also felt that a Rule 61 hearing on Karadžić and Mladić would assist ongoing investigations and enable prosecutors to press judges to issue an international arrest warrant where national authorities were uncooperative, as well as putting pressure on NATO to arrest indictees. The hearing was convened on 27 June 1996, in the absence of Karadžić and Mladić. It had no legal effect but did shed further light on the crimes committed in Srebrenica and on international responsibility for failing to prevent them.[69] It was also an opportunity for wider debate on the international role in the war, although, in the event, that failed to materialize. US prosecution lawyer Mark Harmon ended the hearing, commenting,

> What should be remembered . . . is that the world had the ability to bring these two alleged architects of genocide to justice and did nothing. It will haunt the victims and it will shame us all.[70]

The hearing served one purpose, however, in helping to remove Karadžić from elective office.[71]

Two weeks later, the judges named Milosevic for the first time, confirming his role in RAM, a plan designed in Serbia at the highest military and political levels to set up a new state through the use of violence.[72] However, due to international diplomatic and political reaction, the judges withdrew the press communiqué, and in a new press release merely confirmed the indictment of the Bosnian Serb leaders issued the previous year, omitting the name of Milosevic. The Serbian leader was evidently too useful to ongoing negotiations to be brought to justice at The Hague.

Much hope at this time was placed on the trial of Dusko Tadić, the first to be held at the ICTY and therefore of crucial importance, both in legal and publicity terms.

The Tadić trial

The trial of Dusko Tadić began on 7 May 1996 and has since been frequently cited for landmark legal decisions yet, in political and international terms, it failed to achieve its potential. Richard Goldstone had been under pressure from the ACABQ committee since Autumn 1994 to utilize tribunal resources, and issue indictments, and decided to focus on Tadić rather than Romania corps commanders as M. Cherif Bassiouni had suggested, not least because Tadić had already been apprehended in Germany. Also, trying a more marginal player in the war would make fewer political waves in international negotiating circles. The decision to go ahead with the trial of a relatively minor indictee also led to fierce debate amongst international lawyers.[73]

Much of the groundwork had been laid by the Commission of Experts' work in Prijedor, and the trial had the potential of being the first in international criminal law since World War II to find an indictee guilty of acts of political or racial persecution constituting a crime against humanity. Yet the difficulties the Tadić prosecution team faced, and the danger to potential witnesses, soon became clear. Conditions in the Prijedor region were appalling. In the initial stages of the investigation, the war was still in progress; the infrastructure had virtually collapsed; food, water and heating were unreliable; and interpreters, vital to the mission, were often unpaid. Also, although it was ruled that rape victims could testify anonymously, Simo Drljaća, the Prijedor police chief consistently mentioned in the testimonies of witnesses, was still in total command in the town and had not been publicly indicted. The key rape witness, despite being placed in a witness protection programme, withdrew in fear, and the opportunity for distinguishing the Tadić case as the first conviction for rape as a war crime was lost.

On the first day of the trial, TV and print journalists covering the trial spilt out onto the lawn outside the tribunal building and set up several tents. Broadcast live by interviews on satellite, with edited programmes re-broadcast on Bosnian state television, it was alleged to be more important than any trial since 1945, especially in its potential deterrent effect.[74] The presentation of evidence by the first witnesses, however, created a somnambulant atmosphere which drove all but the hardiest of reporters away. Five weeks into the trial, there was no eyewitness evidence presented of Tadić's personal connection with the crimes. A key witness, H, questioned about the castration episode described holding down the victim, and on cross-examination revealed that Tadić had not been present at the event. Drago Opacic, a star witness, referred to in closed session as L, a guard at Trnopolje, was exposed as a liar and recanted his story, claiming that the Bosnian authorities had threatened him to present the story to the tribunal. From there followed the tortuous legal argument on which the case eventually turned about the difference between a 'significant' presence and a 'mere' presence at the camps.

In November 1996, following 82 days in court, 115 witnesses and over 6,000 pages of transcripts, the case concluded. The verdict was delivered six months later, followed by an appeal. Initially, Tadić was convicted on 9 counts, including persecution, and partially on a further 2. Acquitted on 20 counts, he was sentenced to 20 years. The most significant Trial Chamber decision in legal terms, and for an understanding of the nature of the Bosnian war (with Presiding Judge Gabrielle Kirk McDonald strongly dissenting), was that the conflict was not international in nature, since the VRS could not be regarded as an extension of the Yugoslav Army. Four years later, the appeals chamber reversed that decision, ruling that the Bosnian conflict was international, with close organizational, personal and logistic interconnections between the two armies.[75] The verdict was to be revisited in future cases, with surprising and contradictory consequences.[76] The provision that Tadić should serve at least ten years from the time of his detention in Germany made him available for release as early as 2008, just six years after the final verdict, despite his lack of remorse, a sentence which may have signalled to future potential witnesses that it would be unsafe to testify.

As the first case to be tried for war crimes in Bosnia, the Tadić trial initially attracted considerable world media attention. But this fast fizzled out, as the first prosecution witness to take the stand, James Gow, launched into a long-winded account of the background to the conflict, turgid in style and lacklustre in delivery. The crimes Tadić was charged with were brutal, and in some respects grotesque, and represented in microcosm the numerous atrocities committed throughout Bosnia. Yet the impact was lost, media interest quickly faded and human rights and other pressure groups turned elsewhere. The prosecutor's choice of James Gow as the first prosecution witness was, in hindsight, a mistake. Early decline of media interest meant that the impact of the first indictee to be tried at The Hague was lost.

However, while the preparation and handling of the Tadić case by the prosecution team merited some criticism, the main responsibility for the failure to make a more global impact lay with the continuing international policy of appeasement to Belgrade. Both in issuing orders to NATO troops not to arrest the wartime leaders, Mladić and Karadžić, and in failing to provide the tribunal with adequate means to conduct their investigation at The Hague and in the field, the international powers, including P5 Security Council members and the High Representative, Carl Bildt, sent signals to the world at large that the case, and by inference the war in Bosnia, was of relatively minor relevance in the wider scale of things.

*

By late 1996, Goldstone had brought over 70 indictments, a number of which were considered to be insufficiently grounded, risking the credibility of the ICTY. There was also criticism about the amount of time Goldstone was spending away from The Hague, mostly in the United States, although he argued that these visits were essential in establishing the tribunal, both financially and as an institution.

As the wartime conditions which had held communities together in many parts of Bosnia gave way to an uneasy peace, Bosnians gradually began to take stock and, faced with grim economic prospects and often personal loss, rifts arose within the communities, especially in the Federation which, through Dayton, had forced former foes to work together.

War criminals in power

By mid-1996, at least 50 indicted war criminals remained at large in Bosnia, with just six (three Muslims, one Serb and two Croats) in custody.[77] Most of them held positions of authority across Republika Srpska. The Bosnian Federation was the most cooperative party, executing arrest warrants against Delic and Landzo while, at the other end of the spectrum, RS ignored requirements to execute any of the arrest warrants for the scores of indictees in that entity.[78] Croatia enacted a law on cooperation with the ICTY and arrested Aleksovski, while Tihomir Blaskic surrendered voluntarily to the tribunal. But Croatia failed to arrest other indictees, or to investigate and prosecute violations of international law committed during and after Operation Storm.[79] Meanwhile, in August 1997, Franjo Tudjman was sworn in for a second five-year term as president, amid Croatia's increasing international isolation.

Politicians who would later be indicted by the ICTY continued to occupy leading positions in post-Dayton Bosnia. Momčilo Krajisnik won the Serb seat in the three-person co-presidency of Bosnia by an overwhelming majority, and Plavsic secured the presidency of RS with ease while, in the Federation, Jadranko Prlic (later convicted for war crimes and crimes against humanity) replaced Muhamed Sacirbey as foreign minister.

Karadžić regains momentum

Karadžić had been making a gradual comeback for over two months and would have been encouraged by the lack of international action to prevent the Serb exodus from Sarajevo. On 1 April 1996, in a long speech at the RS assembly, he sent the clear message that he wanted to see a united state of all Serbs and a national programme for Serbs to be formulated by representatives from RS, Serbia and Montenegro.[80] On 13 May, the day after Bildt had attended a meeting in Brussels, Karadžić counter-attacked in a TV appearance lasting several hours, which included a staged Q&A with the public, emphasizing the perilous position of RS and rejecting any idea of a cohesive Bosnia. On 15 May, he dismissed the more moderate Kasagic as prime minister and set up a committee through which all positions for future talks would be channelled, headed by the RS foreign minister, Aleksa Buha – and so, effectively, by Karadžić himself.

Bildt acknowledged that Karadžić's position and political influence was posing an increasing strain on the peace process, blaming the United States and IFOR alternately for not acting to arrest him. Yet he was reluctant to call for the reimposition of sanctions, as the United States proposed.[81]

In mid-1996, the International Crisis Group (ICG) carried out interviews with IFOR, UNHCR, OSCE and European Community Monitor Mission (ECMM) representatives, as well as members of political parties and journalists across RS. It assessed that the likelihood of violence if Karadžić were arrested would be minimal and that so long as he was at liberty, the power structure in RS would remain the same, effectively leaving him in office.[82] Power in RS continued to lie with a small clique of about 15 people in Pale, including Karadžić, Krajisnik and Plavsic. The report concluded that the entire clique in Pale posed a significant threat to the Dayton Agreement since, having compromised themselves beyond reprieve during the war, it was against their interests to reintegrate Bosnia in any way. They should therefore be considered as a whole.[83] International leaders instead began promoting Plavsic as RS president.

The ICG interestingly viewed one of the greatest obstacles to Karadzic's arrest to be the international community which, the report alleged, had 'gone local' in RS. Apart from claiming that his arrest would be counterproductive and possibly trigger a violent reaction, many international troops and civilian staff arriving in RS for the first time were unaware that some 50,000 non-Serbs had been killed or expelled by the Serb authorities that they were attempting to win over.[84] The situation in post-Dayton Prijedor, analysed by Human Rights Watch, bears out the conclusions of the report.[85]

Political alternatives to the Pale clique were many, but nearly all of them opposed reintegration with the Federation. None had the financial basis to present a serious challenge to the SDS, and would anyway have difficulty in getting their message across, since Karadzic controlled the media.[86]

In mid-July, agreement was reached with Milosevic through Holbrooke that Karadzic would withdraw from public office. The fact that he was not arrested was later ascribed by some to the fact that Holbrooke had promised him immunity from prosecution. Aleksa Buha, who was present at the talks with Milosevic, later commented,

> It was in fact an understood part of the agreement that The Hague would not pursue Karadzic after he had resigned. It is true that there is no documentary evidence but, since the talks were begun on that premise, Holbrooke, once he had got the text, assured me personally that, after this agreement, The Hague was in the past for Karadzic.[87]

But a year later, it became increasingly clear that Karadzic's arrest was critically important to the success of the Dayton Agreement. A US government report stressed that Karadzic, unaccountable to the electorate, dominated Bosnian Serb political leaders through a 'reign of terror', blocked international efforts to work with more 'moderate' Bosnian Serb political leaders and had not allowed other political leaders to hold to agreements made with the international community on small-scale attempts to link the ethnic groups politically or economically.

According to an IFOR source, who preferred to remain anonymous,

> It doesn't even matter that Karadzic was publicly banned from political office by Holbrooke and the Americans; he still continues to exercise complete control over all events in RS. . . . Karadzic has made sure his political party, the SDS, runs, controls and owns the entity's police, court system, media, major industries and local NGOs such as the Red Cross . . . he has exclusively employed the power of the entity's Ministry of Internal Affairs (MUP) to keep all internal problems in check, and this underground paramilitary organization has emerged from within its very ranks. [88]

As the elections approached, only 7 of the 75 indictees had been arrested or surrendered to the ICTY. The rest remained at large, mainly in RS, but also in the FRY, Croat-controlled parts of the Federation and Croatia.[89] OSCE Chairman-in-Office Cotti reiterated concerns already expressed by representatives of other organizations:

> Co-operation with the tribunal . . . must become a fact. . . . If no actions are taken right now against the indicted war criminals, it can be taken for granted

> that the elections will very quickly give way to developments diametrically opposed to those which they were expected to yield. There exists the most serious danger that they then degenerate into a pseudo-democratic legitimisation of extreme nationalist power structures and ethnic cleansing.[90]

His words were prescient.

The International Crisis Group called on IFOR to make arrests if the local authorities failed to do so, stressing that responsibility lay first and foremost with the governments of the United States, France and the United Kingdom, as parties to the Genocide and Geneva Conventions, and as the powers that led the IFOR command and the North Atlantic Council.[91]

Amnesty International similarly stressed that

> on almost every front, significant barriers block further progress. . . . Unless Western governments take bold and resolute action to remove existing barriers, the integration process will simply not take place. . . . The continuation of indicted war criminals in positions of power remains the biggest obstacle to a successful peace process in Bosnia.[92]

Western governments differed on the issue of arrests. While Canada pressed hard for the new NATO force to become involved in tracking down war criminals, the British foreign secretary, Malcolm Rifkind, predictably disagreed, pointing to the risk to troops of becoming embroiled in a nationwide hunt for war criminals.[93] Just weeks before the Bosnian elections, a programme entitled 'Karadzic's Women' was broadcast on BBC in which a skewed picture of the situation was presented, with no counterargument. Interviewees claimed that the Serbs didn't start the war, a Muslim fundamentalist state was being created in Sarajevo and that Radovan Karadzic, a medical doctor supported by many who would even die for him, 'cannot be such a bad guy'. The programme inferred that the arrest of Karadzic would not make much difference anyway. There was little other coverage of the lead-up to such momentous elections in the British media.[94]

Under considerable pressure, Karadzic formally resigned from the RS presidency and the SDS on 18 July 1996, but continued to exercise real power, with the SDS persisting with the view that he was a Serb hero, unfairly vilified by the West. In the lead-up to the 1996 elections, Karadzic remained 'an omnipresent campaign force', as RS towns proliferated with his posters and SDS politicians introduced themselves on behalf of their 'closest associate' while opposition parties faced harassment, intimidation and physical violence.[95]

Since the ICTY and the IPTF had no arresting powers, however, IFOR were not prepared to risk reprisals, and the high representative eschewed the reimposition of sanctions on Serbia which would have propelled Milosevic into surrendering the Bosnian Serb leader, an impasse arose which, by default, reconfirmed Milosevic's dominance in international policy in Bosnia.

The Plavsic era: plus ça change . . .

Biljana Plavsic was a leading politician in the Pale clique. Initially, she was an acting president of the so-called Serb republic, following which she became its vice-president, and from November 1992 was a member of the Supreme Command of the RS army. At the Milošević trial, Vojislav Šešelj described Karadžić's motives for nominating her. 'She held very extremist positions during the war, insufferably extremist, even for me. . . . Radovan Karadzic believed her to be more extreme than himself in every way'.[96] During the Bosnian war, Plavsic declared that the 'ethnic cleansing' of non-Serbs was a 'natural phenomenon', that Bosnian Serbs were ethnically racially superior to Bosnian Muslims and that negotiations with whom was impossible due to genetics.[97]

Such was the person in whom the international community placed trust. Had the tribunal been supported effectively from the outset, Biljana Plavsic would probably have been indicted along with the other Bosnian Serb leaders responsible for orchestrating Bosnian war crimes. But Plavsic was seen as a more compliant leader than Karadzic, one with whom international negotiators could work. In practice, though, it meant that one war criminal had effectively been replaced by another.

In the United States, the main concern was to meet the Dayton deadline for holding elections which, it was believed, would bring a measure of stability to Bosnia before the US presidential elections that November. US Ambassador to the UN Bill Richardson misguidedly believed that the implementation of Dayton depended on the outcome of the political struggle between Plavsic and Karadzic,

> The key question now facing all of us is how to support President Plavsic while simultaneously preventing her removal. . . . We in the United States are going to give her some help . . . she is a strong woman.[98]

Britain also brought its weight behind Plavsic, both from London and on the ground, with Carl Bildt at the forefront. In this he solicited the assistance of Milosevic, who negotiated a deal to make Plavsic president using methods reminiscent of wartime Bosnia.[99] As Bildt put it, Plavsic gradually formed closer contacts 'with key representatives of the international community, myself the most prominent of these'.[100] Bildt and others apparently believed that the way to diminish the power centre of Pale was to concentrate efforts in strengthening Banja Luka as the RS capital.[101]

But Plavsic's loyalties were never really in doubt. Emboldened by Western support, she began to demonstrate ultranationalist traits.[102] And, as supreme commander of the RS army, she announced in late 1996,

> I am exceptionally sorry that, owing to the well-known view of part of the international community, I cannot appoint General Ratko Mladić as chief of the General Staff.

Plavsic went on to thank Mladić personally for all he and other Main HQ members had done for the Serb people during the war.[103] On 2 January 1997, she wrote to the UN Security Council, claiming that

> the present position of Republika Srpska is that we are unwilling to hand over Dr Karadzic and General Mladić for trial in The Hague, as we believe that any such trial now falls outside the scope of the Tribunal's constitutional framework.[104]

Meanwhile, on 30 October 1996, the newly appointed ICTY prosecutor, Louise Arbour, attempted to secure a mandate for IFOR to arrest indictees, but was rebuffed by NATO military and diplomatic leaders.

At the 54-nation Dayton Implementation Conference in London on 4–5 December 1996, John Major vowed to pursue Bosnia's war criminals and commented that the events in Serbia were 'very much on our minds'.[105] Yet, although Britain assigned a number of police officers to assist in investigating war crimes and other abuses committed by local police, they were not mandated to make arrests.[106] Nor did the British government invite the ICTY to the conference as a participant. After considerable pressure from Cassese, its delegates were admitted not as a participant but as a mere observer,[107] provoking an unprecedented declaration from the 11 judges at the ICTY who accused the conference of downgrading their attempt to bring indictees to trial, expressing 'deep concern' that the London Conference organizers had dropped the crucial question of cooperation with the tribunal from the agenda. Reference to States' obligation to cooperate with the tribunal in arresting indictees was erased in the communiqué, in effect violating UN Security Council resolution 922.

A month after Labour was elected to power, the newly appointed foreign secretary, Robin Cook, announced Britain's firm commitment to human rights, and the Labour government opened its files to the tribunal.[108] The vast majority of the material had been provided 'on the same basis as it would have been made available to British prosecuting authorities', but some was withheld in order not to compromise sources. Allegedly, nothing in the possession of the British authorities implicated Milosevic in the crimes, although considering Britain's major role at all levels in international involvement in the Bosnian war, this seems hardly credible.

Holbrooke later commented on the 'new generation of leaders willing to reach out to one another', citing RS Prime Minister Milorad Dodik as an example.[109]

At the end of June 1997, Plavsic visited Britain, where the Foreign Office under the New Labour government honoured her with an official greeting from foreign minister Tony Lloyd, viewing her as a 'moderate' who was willing to deliver on the Dayton Agreement, which was particularly ironic when Plavsic had considered Karadzic a 'weak-kneed moderate' during the Bosnian war.[110]

Days later, Cook announced Britain's veto of an International Monetary Fund (IMF) loan to Croatia.

The US threat to withdraw a $10 billion loan promised by the World Bank concentrated the Croatian president's mind and, in early October 1997, Dario Kordic and nine other indicted Bosnian Croats 'voluntarily' surrendered under pressure from Zagreb and left for The Hague.[111]

Prijedor and Drljača

In January 1997, HRW published an excoriating 67-page report, exposing the channelling of public funds to those who had committed atrocities in the war, continued to be involved in other criminal activities in Prijedor, and now had complete control over the police and military, allowing them a stranglehold over the whole community where British IFOR troops were stationed. Leading figures included Simo Drljača, Milan Kovačević and Momir Stakic. In February 1997, following the report, plans evolved for a series of 'snatch operations' designed to abduct indictees and deliver them to The Hague.[112] Simo Drljača, then under sealed indictment for genocide by the ICTY, was the first to be targeted. On 10 July 1997, British Special Air Service (SAS) commandos shot Drljača dead in the process of arresting him. Milan Kovačević, Prijedor hospital director, was also arrested in the same operation on charges of complicity in genocide against non-Serbs during the war.[113] The day after the SAS operation, Downing Street announced that it was part of a more proactive international stance, stressing the operation had the support of NATO Secretary General Javier Solana, General George Joulwan Supreme Allied Commander Europe and the North Atlantic Council.[114]

There was now speculation that the net was closing in on Karadzic and Mladić.[115] But General Klaus Naumann of Germany, chairman of NATO's military committee, declared that NATO troops would not 'fall into the trap of fulfilling police tasks and would only go after war criminals if they cross our path'.[116] Robin Cook promptly echoed Naumann's message, confirming that it was 'highly unlikely' that any attempt in the near future would be made to arrest Karadzic or Mladić.[117] After talks with Krajisnik, Cook, totally misunderstanding the situation, called for the Karadzic trial to be moved to Bosnia.[118] During Cook's visit to Bosnia, he made a point of praising Plavsic, while criticizing Bosnian government politicians for corruption, as UK press reports suggested a symmetry of guilt.[119] Plavsic, meanwhile, denounced the SAS operation in a press release, condemning Drljača's killing.[120] She also demanded Kovačević's release, an irony considering both men were involved in the local mafia, protection rackets, expropriating businesses, homes and the assets of 50,000 people, and controlling organized crime, issues Plavsic purportedly condemned, and for which she was receiving international support.[121]

Drljača, a newfound martyr, meanwhile, was accorded a full state funeral three days later, televised live, with a turnout of over 3,000 people, carrying placards of Karadzic.[122] Rhetoric whipped up Serb emotion against their non-Serb neighbours, and support for Karadzic grew. But, as Holbrooke remarked, 'The Bosnian

Serbs . . . would have offered little resistance had IFOR enforced tough guidelines. . . . Rallying, [they] began to resist on almost every non-military issue, while avoiding clashes with NATO almost as if they had an implicit understanding with the IFOR command'.[123]

On 2 September 1997, a Stabilization Force (SFOR) commander signed an agreement with hard-line Pale leaders loyal to Karadzic to surrender to Karadzic loyalists the Udrigovo TV transmission tower which SFOR had secured on 28 August, encouraging Karadzic's supporters to believe that mob violence and terrorism against international forces paid off.[124]

Searching for an alternative strategy: the Milosevic role

In a cynical replay of wartime tactics, Slobodan Milosevic, yet to be indicted, continued to be perceived internationally as the lynchpin to maintaining peace in Bosnia. Milosevic's main focus, as always, was his own position in Serbia. Sanctions had been lifted from the FRY, despite non-compliance with Security Council resolutions, the ICTY or its obligations under Dayton. This, along with clear international reluctance to arrest war crimes suspects, placed Milosevic in a powerful negotiating position.

In spring and early summer 1996, a number of meetings took place in Belgrade between Milosevic and Karadzic, and with international negotiators, as the Serbian president sought to ensure Karadzic's position at the helm in Bosnia.[125] During several meetings with Bildt, Milosevic blatantly denied that Karadzic's position as RS president constituted a breach of the Dayton Agreement.[126] Agreement was reached that Karadzic should be no longer seen or heard, but not that he would step down as president.[127] Bildt did not press the fact that the FRY was violating the Dayton Agreement on several counts, including failing to enact legislation to allow it to cooperate with the tribunal.[128] The prime American concern, to meet the Dayton timetable for holding elections, coincided with that of Milosevic who was keen to legitimize existing structures so they would acquire permanence.[129] On 17–18 July, Holbrooke travelled to Belgrade where Milosevic finally conceded that a genocide indictee would be unacceptable as president of RS, and clinched a deal with Holbrooke that Karadzic would resign as RS president and Biljana Plavsic takeover.[130] That Plavsic was equally compromised as a result of her wartime activities, and committed to a separate state for Serbs in Bosnia, was balanced in the international view by the fact that she had not been indicted and was therefore technically eligible to stand for election.[131] Plavsic stood on an anti-corruption ticket, appealing to the international community, as the fight against corruption by now rife in both Bosnian entities eclipsed the imperative to bring war criminals to justice.

The deal relieved pressure for a military operation to arrest Karadzic, and allowed the elections to go ahead, albeit with SDS participation, while Milosevic continued covert support for Karadzic.[132] On Krajisnik's insistence, Karadzic remained at large in Bosnia. Although there were many parties contending for power in RS, none had the charisma or clout of Karadzic who continued to control the security services and media. The plight of the internationally supported Kasagic illustrated the difficulties faced by anyone assuming power who was not an insider at Pale.[133]

The 1996 municipal elections in Serbia offered an opportunity for the international community to support the removal of Milosevic who was facing a major challenge to his presidency, as Zajedno, the opposition coalition to Milosevic's Socialist Party (SPS), won the majority of seats.[134] When the SPS annulled the results, widespread daily demonstrations, reaching 50,000 in Belgrade, spread to other cities. There was no outside intervention until late December when the OSCE sent a delegation to review the election results, which concluded that Zajedno had won. But they had no enforcement powers. According to Holbrooke, the United States was unable to support the protests due to the transitional period in the Clinton administration.[135]

Milosevic then turned to nationalists, including Karadzic, for support.[136] On 8 December, Karadzic, unchallenged by the military, gave on-the-record interviews to European journalists.[137] The protests lasted till 11 February 1997 when Milosevic accepted the opposition victory without acknowledging wrongdoing. But by then, the Zajedno movement was no longer united, its leaders split amongst themselves.[138]

Initially, the demonstrations received little attention from Kosovo. But by January 1997, as the protests seemed to threaten Milosevic's control, the Albanian leadership saw the potential for Kosovo's independence drive and sent supportive statements to Serbian opposition politicians. But in late January 1997, there were rumours that Milosevic might be fomenting violent confrontation in Kosovo, creating a crisis that would distract from the Serbian protests, and allow him to declare martial law.

*

Meanwhile, the tribunal continued to struggle with the consequences of international policy. As discussed earlier, Britain had soft-pedalled the war crimes issue since the establishment of the tribunal. The British ambassador, Ivor Roberts, in Belgrade since March 1994, had more access than any other Western diplomat to the Serbian president, and was widely regarded in Belgrade as Milosevic's 'handmaiden'.[139] On 24 July 1996, former British foreign secretary Douglas Hurd and former Foreign Office political director Pauline Neville-Jones visited Milosevic in Belgrade where a $10 million deal was signed between Serbia and NatWest Markets to assist in privatizing Serbian Telecom.[140] This was to prove crucial to funding the Kosovo war two years later.

In December 1998, Gabrielle Kirk McDonald, the new tribunal president, having written five times to the UN General Assembly, addressed 50 heads of state at a Dayton implementation conference in Madrid, pointing out that the FRY was blatantly violating international law and its obligations under Dayton:

> The problem of non-cooperation looms larger than ever. . . . [The FRY's] conduct and statements are an affront to the Security Council that established the

> tribunal, and to this Council that is charged with overseeing the implementation of the Dayton Agreement. I urge you: end this obstruction now. Failure to do so will imperil all of the tribunal's work to date. One state must not be allowed to dictate the agenda of the international community.[141]

Her speech apparently fell on deaf ears, for no measures were taken to sanction the FRY's lack of cooperation. The conflict had by then spread to Kosovo, while international leaders continued to negotiate with Milosevic until he was finally indicted the following May, several weeks into the NATO action.

Conclusion

The Dayton Agreement was an expedient solution to end the Bosnian war through appeasement of the main aggressors. It rewarded Republika Srpska with its own republic, and territory well in access of its population ratio, and cemented ethnic divisions driven by genocide and crimes against humanity. It was underpinned, however, by UN Security Council resolutions which spelt out clearly the responsibilities of the parties – local and international – including the obligation to arrest war crimes suspects indicted by the ICTY. The high representative was given the power to call for the reimposition of sanctions against any signatory violating the Dayton provisions, including the obstruction of free and safe movement between the entities. The failure to meet those obligations in the early post-Dayton period meant that suspects, some of them indicted for genocide, were free to wield power in Republika Srpska, obstruct the Agreement and prevent the reintegration of the communities. After the signing of the Dayton Agreement, Radovan Karadzic, still officially RS president, made inflammatory speeches, gave interviews to foreign journalists, appeared on TV, and passed with impunity through NATO checkpoints. For at least two years afterwards, Karadzic and Mladić were living openly in Bosnia and/or Serbia. Both were to remain at large for more than a decade.

The culture of impunity which prevailed resulted in a missed opportunity to bring the main perpetrators to justice. The handling of the Tadić trial unwittingly confirmed this, in opening with a long-winded historical overview, rather than bringing to immediate public and media attention the crimes themselves. This left an opening for Karadzic and Mladić, when they finally came to trial, to attempt to rewrite history in the course of their defence and examination of witnesses, an exercise which would have been denied them in the early days following the war, when memories were fresh and journalists eager to report proceedings.

The imperative to remove Karadzic from power prompted the international community, concerned to meet the Dayton implementation deadline for elections, to promote Biljana Plavsic as president of RS. What international decision makers ignored, or chose not to address, was that it was not in the interests of any of the Pale leaders, including Plavsic, seriously compromised by their wartime activities, for Bosnia and Herzegovina to be reintegrated.

The fact that the two main indictees had managed to evade arrest for so long was due not least to the message spelt out by international negotiators that the

ICTY was marginal to the peace process. This, as discussed earlier, was a position which had beleaguered the tribunal from its conception, yet, without the powers of arrest, and with limited investigative powers, its hands were tied.

Differences arising between the United States and major European powers during the war continued to prevail in the post-Dayton period, as illustrated in the separate memoirs of Richard Holbrooke and Carl Bildt, the main international interlocutors. Britain's continuing focus on a policy which appeased the Milosevic regime included, in Bosnia, channelling reconstruction aid to war criminals where BritBat were based and attempting to exclude the ICTY from the Dayton implementation conference in December 1996. Washington was compromised by the forthcoming elections in America, with the result that US officials insisted on meeting the deadline for the Bosnian elections even where conditions regarding returnees had clearly not been met. The US government also failed to support legitimate protests following the local Serbian elections which, if successful in the early stages, could have significantly weakened the Milosevic regime and, arguably, prevented another Balkans war.

Notes

1 Jose Ayala Lasso, quoted in ICTY Annual Report, 16 August 1996(5), was the first UN High Commissioner for Human Rights, serving from 1994–1997.

2 'Our main goal now is to take these war criminals, like Karadzic, and put them on trial. The Bosnian Serbs must punish those who carried out these crimes, otherwise, in the eyes of the world, we will bear the guilt for the atrocities they committed in our name'. Miodrag Zivanovic, president of the opposition Liberal Party. 'Top Leader of the Bosnian Serbs Now Under Attack from Within', *New York Times*, 4 January 1996. Carl Bildt also records Karadzic as having been 'pushed into the background . . . unsure of himself and frightened during the first month of the peace-implementation process' Bildt, op. cit., p. 189.

3 In Ljubinje, near Trebinje, veterans of the Bosnian Serb Army were reported as wanting no part of RS. 'I don't remember what we were trying to do with this war, and now I don't care . . . our town suffered for something that is worthless . . . the good people here never supported what happened to our neighbours'. *New York Times,* 15 January 1996. See also Hodge, op. cit., p. 133, for Bosnian Serb attitudes in the immediate post-war period.

4 Payam Akhavan, legal adviser, ICTY. Interview quoted in Michael Scharf, 'The Tools for Enforcing International Criminal Justice in the New Millennium. Lessons from the Yugoslav Tribunal', *De Paul Law Review,* Vol.49, Issue 4, Summer 2000, pp. 957–958.

5 'They can't arrest me and they should not even think of that. I am going to travel whenever I feel the need to travel'. Quoted in Hagan, p. 75.

6 Federal News Service, 5 December 1995, quoted in John R. W. D. Jones, 'The Implications of the Peace Agreement for the International Criminal Tribunal for the former Yugoslavia', *The European Journal of International Law*, Vol.7, Issue 48, 1996, p. 239.

7 On 12 February 1996, Lt. Col. Mark Raynor stated that IFOR troops 'have the authority, but not the obligation, to detain indicted war criminals', cited in An Open Letter from Amnesty International to IFOR Commanders and Contributing Governments, 1 March 1996, AI Index EUR 63/08/96.

8 Paul Stuebner, interviewed by Pierre Hazan, Hazan, op. cit., p. 95. See also US Assistant Secretary of State John Shattuck's description of US IFOR commanders going

out of their way to avoid indicted war criminals, and on the lack of support of IFOR Commander Leighton-Smith. John Shattuck, 'Freedom on Fire: Human Rights Wars and America's Response', Harvard University Press, 2003, pp. 213–216.

9 *New York Times*, 20 January 1996, p. 6.

10 ICTY Bulletin, No.2, 22 January 1996: 'The Tribunal stresses that the burden of co-operation rests upon the governments which are parties to the Peace Agreement. This is their obligation . . . to apprehend and turn over the accused sought by the Tribunal. This is their duty, and not IFOR's'. See also Weekly Press Briefing of the Spokesman for the ICTY, 9 January 1996 'IFOR soldiers have no authority for chasing, hunting down the accused'.

11 Holbrooke, p. 222.

12 Leighton-Smith's British deputy, General Michael Walker, reportedly shared this view. See Holbrooke, pp. 327–329.

13 Holbrooke later distanced himself from Leighton-Smith's approach: 'Based on Shalikashvili's statements at White House meetings, Christopher and I had assumed that the IFOR commander would use his authority to do substantially more than he was *obligated* to do'. Holbrooke, p. 328.

14 Ibid. Admiral Leighton-Smith resigned from the Navy later that year, before his term of duty expired. The following year, he was awarded an honorary knighthood by Queen Elizabeth II for his work in Bosnia.

15 Geneva Convention No.I, Art.49; Geneva Convention No.II, Art.50; Geneva Convention No.III, Art 129; Geneva Convention No.IV, Art.146. Open Letter from Amnesty International to IFOR Commanders and Contributing Governments, 1 March 1996.

16 Ibid. Art.51; Geneva Convention No.II, Art.52; Geneva Convention No.III, Art.131; Geneva Convention No.IV, Art.148.

17 As the UN secretary general pointed out, 'An order by a Trial Chamber . . . shall be considered to be the application of an enforcement measure under chapter VII of the UN Charter'. Report of the UN Secretary General pursuant to SCR 808 (1993) UN Doc. S/25704, para. 126.

18 UN Security Council Resolution 1031, 15 December 1995, gave IFOR the authority to detain and transfer indictees to The Hague. Open Letter from Amnesty International to IFOR Commanders and Contributing Governments, 1 March 1996.

19 Open Letter, ibid. Dayton Peace Agreement, Annex I-A, Art.II.

20 Jones, p. 228. John Jones was a member of the Bar of England and Wales.

21 United Nations Charter, Articles 24(1) and 103.

22 See Niccolo Figa-Talamanca, 'The Role of NATO in the Peace Agreement for Bosnia and Herzegovina', *The European Journal of International Law*, Vol.7, Issue 2, 1996, pp. 171–172.

23 'From the point of view of international law, it is IFOR contributing States that are authorized to take military action in . . . Bosnia and Herzegovina under SCR 1031, not NATO as an organization, despite the fact that NATO has negotiated, in IFOR'S name, the Agreements on the Status of Forces in Bosnia and Herzegovina . . . Hence, the obligation to co-operate with the Tribunal is not conditional upon NATO's Rules of Engagement, in the same way that it is not conditional to States' domestic legislation. 'Figa-Talamanca', ibid., pp. 173–174. For further discussion, see also Paola Gaeta, 'The Dayton Agreements and International Law', *The European Journal of International Law*, Vol.7, Issue 2, 1996, p. 157.

24 Dayton Agreement, Art.6(9)a of Annex IA. John Jones, ibid.

25 Jones, op. cit., 1996, p. 239.

26 Amnesty International renews calls for IFOR to comply with international law, Amnesty International, April 1996. AI Index EUR 63/11/96.

27 Amnesty stressed that the Geneva Conventions 'are now generally accepted as reflecting customary international law binding on all states, and, therefore, binding on intergovernmental organisations which are established by and composed of states'. Amnesty

International renews calls for IFOR to comply with international law, Amnesty International, April 1996. Ibid.

28 'IFOR has an authorized strength of 60,000 and has extensive intelligence gathering capabilities . . . It operates at will throughout the country'. Amnesty International, April 1996. Ibid.

29 According to one IFOR commander, Major Daniel Zajac, there was already evidence of disturbance and partial destruction of mass graves near Srebrenica. Amnesty International, April 1996. Ibid.

30 Bass, op. cit., pp. 250–253. John Shattuck was US Assistant Secretary of State for Democracy and Human Rights.

31 Bass, op. cit., p. 250.

32 *Washington Post*, 7 April 1996.

33 'Christopher and I were greatly disturbed by this incident. The seizure of the two men, neither of whom was ever indicted, had disrupted the implementation process and set a bad precedent for the future. We determined to try to prevent any repetition of such an incident before it became a pattern'. Holbrooke, pp. 332–333.

34 Hagan, op. cit., p. 74.

35 See Jones, op. cit., p. 236, n.40.

36 The home of one of Bosnia's most wanted war criminals, Milan Martic, was barely 50 yards away from a house occupied by 8 NATO soldiers. *Telegraph*, 27 December 1996.

37 While Bosnia and Herzegovina had enacted legislation, deferring prosecutions at the request of the tribunal, Croatia and the Bosnian Serb authorities merely permitted tribunal investigators to operate in Croatia without legislating. The Federal Republic of Yugoslavia (Serbia and Montenegro), the Bosnian Serb authorities, the Croatian and Bosnian Croat authorities all failed to transfer indictees to the tribunal.

38 Clinton Presidential Libraries, FOIA 2006-0647-F – Genocide in the Former Yugoslavia. http://clinton.presidentiallibraries.us/items/show/14581

39 Article 3 of Resolution 1022 stipulated that if the High Representative informed the Security Council that the authorities were failing significantly to meet their obligations under Dayton, sanctions should be reimposed.

40 Warren Christopher. Statement, Geneva, 2 June 1996. Clinton Presidential Library, Case No. 2006-0459-F Civilian Implementation: The Role of the High Representative, https://docs.google.com/viewerng/viewer?url=http://clinton.presidentiallibraries.us/files/original/5c1fe224e8217fee60eab3b438daea32.pdf

41 The White House considered that had the British choice, John Duncan Lowe, been made chief prosecutor, Karadzic and Mladic would not have been indicted in July 1995. Civilian Implementation: The Role of the High Representative, ibid.

42 The Role of the High Representative, ibid.

43 Ibid.

44 Ibid. See also 'Bildt in a Day', *Foreign Policy*, 8 May 2014.

45 In his memoirs published in 1998, Bildt refers merely to 'massacres' at Srebrenica, in contrast to his strong condemnation of the Croatian offensive on Krajina. Bildt, pp. 75, 382. See also Marko Hoare, 'Swedish Foreign Minister Carl Bildt Denies Over Half the Srebrenica Massacre'. https://greatersurbiton.wordpress.com/2009/07/21/swedish-foreign-minister-carl-bildt-denies-over-half-the-srebrenica-massacre/

46 1995-07-31A BTF Report re Impact of Bildt's Position on Serbian Sanctions, Clinton Presidential Library, op. cit.

47 'In September 1994, the strains in the Anglo-American alliance had been at a level that was nearly intolerable, and rebuilding the relationship . . . had been a high priority' Holbrooke, p. 333.

48 Bildt, p. 253.

49 Pauline Neville-Jones led the argument that the IPTF should not have arresting powers, citing the Northern Ireland experience. NATO was also opposed on the grounds that the military would have to bail them out if they got into difficulties. Holbrooke, p. 251.

According to Holbrooke, however, when the Bosnian Serbs defied Dayton, the United States urged Bildt to interpret his authority under Dayton broadly, but that the Europeans 'reined him in'. Ibid., p. 362. See also James Sloan, 'The Dayton Peace Agreement: Human Rights Guarantees and Their Implementation', *The European Journal of International Law*, Vol.7, Issue 2, 1996, pp. 221–222.

50 On one occasion Krajisnik presented Bildt with a pistol and a paper illustration of a man riddled with bullet holes, to demonstrate the gun's effectiveness. 'It was difficult to know how I should react to the gift', Bildt, p. 233.

51 Bildt justified this by arguing that 'Bosnia was the victim not only of five years of war – but of fifty years of socialism. This called for a major programme of reforms', Bildt, p. 258.

52 Ibid., p. 249.

53 Ibid., p. 118.

54 Reuters, Banja Luka, 12 September 1997.

55 'Bosnia Peace Operation: Progress towards the Dayton Agreement's Goals -An Update'. United States Government Accountability Office, National Security and International Affairs Division, 17 July 1997.

56 Pamela O'Toole, UNHCR spokesperson, Reuter report, Geneva, 5 August 1997.

57 'The Dayton Peace Accords: A Six Month Review', International Crisis Group, June 1996.

58 Human Rights Watch, 'Bosnia-Hercegovina: The Continuing Influence of Bosnia's Warlords', *Human Rights Watch*, Vol.8, Issue 17 (D), December 1996.

59 Ibid.

60 Ibid.

61 Bildt acknowledged that Izetbegovic had intervened against the worst of the violations but claimed he did not show signs of statesmanship. Bildt, pp. 187, 196, 198.

62 US Balkans envoy Robert Gelbard, in Sarajevo at the time, witnessed IFOR and the IPTF as they refused to arrest the arsonists. 'Desperate, the Muslims sent their antiquated fire-fighting equipment into the Serb area, but were attacked with rocks by Serb arsonists. Gelbard watched buildings burn as IFOR troops stood by less than 150 metres away, and observed . . . (British IFOR Commander Michael) Walker . . . coolly reject the pleas of (deputy High Representative, Michael) Steiner for IFOR intervention. I was ashamed to be associated with it'. Holbrooke, pp. 336–337.

63 *USA Today*, The War in Bosnia, 29 February 1996.

64 *Los Angeles Times*, 22 February 1996.

65 Holbrooke, pp. 336–337.

66 International Covenant for Civil and Political Rights, quoted in UN Doc. S/25704, 3 May 1993. French law permits trials in absentia for those charged with crimes against humanity, however. Also, Martin Bormann was tried in absentia at Nuremberg.

67 Updated Statute of the International Criminal Tribunal for the Former Yugoslavia, September 2009, Art.21(4). The International Criminal Tribunal for Rwanda, the statute of which mirrors that of the ICTY, completed a trial without the accused present, when he refused to appear in court. *Prosecutor v. Barayagwiza*, ICTR 99-52-T, Judgement, 3 December 2003.

68 See European Convention on Human Rights, art.6 (1) and (3)c. The Special Tribunal for Lebanon allows for trials in absentia in its statute, art.22.

69 See Hazan, op. cit., pp. 76–85 for a fuller account of the hearing.

70 See 'Procedure in case of failure to execute a warrant', Rule 61 of Rules of Procedure and Evidence, ICTY.

71 Richard Holbrooke acknowledged this in paying tribute to the tribunal. Holbrooke, p. 190.

72 'Bosnian Serb chiefs face new warrants', Marlise Simons, *New York Times*, 12 July 1996.

73 Michael Scharf considered the Tadic case extremely important, 'inaugurating a new age of human rights enforcement'. Scharf, pp. 214–215. Geoffrey Robertson, on the other hand, voiced the majority view that the Tadic case took on 'a symbolic capacity,

a scapegoat almost, for the community of which he was part'. Goeffrey Robertson, *Crimes Against Humanity: The Struggle for Global Justice*, Allen Lane, 1999, p. 310.
74 Hagan, p. 81. Bosniaks were reported as finding the coverage therapeutic. The trial was not broadcast in RS or in Croat-controlled parts of the Federation, however. ICG, 'The Dayton Peace Accords: A Six Month Review'. June 1996, p. 7.
75 For analysis of this, see Antonio Cassese, 'The Nicaragua and Tadic Tests Revisited in Light of the ICJ Judgment on Bosnia', *The European Journal of International Law*, Vol.18, 2007, pp. 649–668.
76 See Chapters 8 and 11.
77 'Report of the High Representative for Implementation of the Bosnian Peace Agreement to the Secretary General of the United Nations', 10 July 1996, para. 78. IFOR, fearing 'mission creep', had left responsibility for arresting indictees to the civilian authorities.
78 For instance, Zelenovic, Kunarac, Kovac and Vukovic from Foca were indicted in June 1996, but remained at large for many years. RS cooperated only so far as to allow investigators to mass grave sites, although most of these had been tampered with, or emptied. ICTY Annual Report 1996, paras. 167–168.
79 Ibid., para. 171.
80 Bildt, p. 207.
81 Ibid., pp. 208, 209, 215.
82 'Power Struggle in Republika Srpska', ICG Bosnia Report, 11 July 1996.
83 Ibid.
84 Ibid.
85 See 'The Unindicted: Reaping the Rewards of "Ethnic Cleansing"', *Human Rights Watch Report*, Vol.9, Issue 1, January 1997 (D), discussed next.
86 Ibid. The one exception was Miodrag Zivanovic's Social Liberals who consistently opposed the war, and openly supported reintegration, but he was under personal threat and his anti-war stance gained few votes in RS.
87 Aleksa Buha. www.srpskadijaspora.info/akademik-prof-dr-aleksa-buha-ko-se-plasi-obelodanjivanja-sporazuma-karadzic-holbruk/ (Author's translation).
88 The report was based on Human Rights Watch interviews conducted with representatives of a number of organizations involved in implementing the Dayton Agreement, including the OSCE, ECCC, UNCA. UNHCR, OHR and IFOR. Sources asked that their names and the areas where they were based not be disclosed since their own organizations were not publicly exposing the activities of local political leaders.
89 ICG Bosnia Report No.16, 22 September 1996.
90 Ibid., No.14, 14 August 1996.
91 Ibid., 22 November 1996.
92 Amnesty International Report 1997 – Bosnia and Herzegovina, 1 January 1997. See also ICG Report, 'Dayton: Make or Break', 11 June 1996.
93 *The Herald*, 5 December 1996.
94 BBC Radio 4 Woman's Hour, 22 August 1996. In response to this author, the BBC argued that programme makers were obliged to remain impartial and allow audiences to decide for themselves, and that it was felt 'appropriate to allow an opportunity for all views to be heard'. Letter to Carole Hodge from the BBC, 16 September 1996.
95 ICG Report, op. cit.
96 *Prosecutor v Slobodan Milosevic*, Šešelj testimony, 30 August 2005.
97 Michael Mann, *The Dark Side of Democracy: Explaining Ethnic Cleansing*, Cambridge University Press, 2004, p. 389, Franke Wilmer, *The Social Construction of Man, the State and War: Identity, Conflict, and Violence in Former Yugoslavia*, Routledge, 2002, p. 217, and Maya Shatzmiller, *Islam and Bosnia: Conflict Resolution and Foreign Policy in Multi-Ethnic States*, McGill-Queen's University Press, 2002, p. 58.
98 *Reuters*, Rome, 23 July 1997.
99 Bildt, p. 230.

100 Cheryl Plumridge, recruited from the British Ministry of Defence, was appointed the head of Bildt's office in Banja Luka and formed a close relationship with Plavsic. Bildt, p. 335.
101 Bildt, pp. 219, 356.
102 'Serbs are united east and west. This is all Serb land' Biljana Plavsic, quoted in *The Times*, 26 August 1997.
103 SRNA (Bosnian Serb news agency), 9 November 1996, published in translation. EE/2766 A/1.
104 Note from the UN secretary general to the UN Security Council, quoted in A/52/375/S/1997/729, 18 September 1997, para. 134.
105 *Times*, 6 December 1996.
106 *Independent*, 6 December 1996. The communiqué at the end of conference made it clear that the responsibility for arresting indictees lay with the local police. *The Times*, 6 December 1996. See also Hazan, op. cit., p. 93.
107 *Guardian*, 5 December 1996.
108 Britain continued, however, to sell Hawk aircraft valued at 160 million pounds to Indonesia, despite its internal repression and aggression in East Timor. *Guardian*, 12 June 1997.
109 Holbrooke, p. 364. 'Dodik announced that he would honor Dayton and build a multi-ethnic Bosnia . . . The US then began releasing funds. By March the US was sufficiently pleased with the situation that it began to "reward" Belgrade for supporting Dodik by removing some of the remaining economic restrictions of Yugoslavia . . . The American effort in Bosnia was paying off'. Holbrooke, p. 357.
110 *Independent on Sunday*, 29 June 1997.
111 Holbrooke, p. 351. A poll by the Croatian daily, *Tjednik*, revealed that only 18.7% of those polled believed the Croatian army committed crimes in the war.
112 *Daily Telegraph*, 10 February 1997.
113 See Hodge, pp. 135–137, for conflicting UK media coverage of this.
114 *Independent*, 11 July 1997.
115 Ibid.
116 *Reuters*, London, 12 September 1997.
117 *Sunday Telegraph*, 13 July 1997.
118 *Observer*, 24 August 1997.
119 *Times* editorial, 'Benighted Balkans', 28 July 1997.
120 *Times*, 14 July 1997.
121 *Guardian*, 11 July 1997.
122 *Guardian*, 14 July 1997. Mladic at this time was spotted in a Belgrade shopping centre. He travelled unhindered through the region, attending his son's wedding at a Belgrade hotel and holidaying in Montenegro. *Times*, 6 August 1997.
123 Holbrooke, p. 338.
124 'Statement on SFOR Agreement with Karadzic Loyalists', ICG Bosnia Project, 4 September 1997.
125 Bildt, p. 337, Holbrooke, pp. 343, 354.
126 Ibid., pp. 210, 220.
127 Ibid., p. 347.
128 ICTY Annual Report, 1996, para. 169.
129 Bildt, 254.
130 The meeting was eerily reminiscent of pre-Dayton negotiations. Holbrooke described the ten-hour negotiating session over 'the best [dinner] he had ever offered us', with 'Krajisnik & Buha . . . upstairs' waiting to play their part in the deal. Holbrooke, p. 341.
131 At the time, Nikola Koljevic was deemed to be the obvious choice for the RS presidency, especially because his command of English would have helped in dealings with international negotiators, but Milosevic considered Plavsic, an extremist even in Pale terms, less likely to surrender Karadzic to The Hague.

132 Bildt, p. 354.
133 Bildt later recorded, 'On Wednesday of election week, I was due to have lunch with Milosevic in Belgrade . . . to get support for efforts to persuade Krajisnik to accept a meeting in Sarajevo', ibid., p. 276.
134 The one common denominator in Zajedno, an otherwise disparate mixture of nationalists, moderates and those who simply wanted change, was the specific goal of removing Milosevic and his party from power, and working towards a multi-party democracy.
135 Holbrooke, p. 245.
136 Ivica Dacic, Serbian Socialist Party spokesman (and currently Serbia's foreign minister) rejected Western charges of election rigging. *Independent*, 5 December 1996.
137 Holbrooke, p. 346.
138 Ibid., p. 345.
139 *Guardian*, 6 December 1996. See also *Financial Times*, 5 December 1996, for views of Serbia's opposition coalition leaders. Ivor Roberts joined the Foreign Office in 1968 and was knighted in 2000.
140 In October 1995, Hurd accepted a part-time position at NatWest bank at an annual salary of 250,000, for services of a promotional or ambassadorial nature, 'as well as acting as a senior adviser to NatWest Markets on world-wide political and economic issues'. *Guardian*, 17 October 1995. Pauline Neville-Jones became head of NatWest Markets global business strategy. George Monbiot interview with Pauline Neville-Jones, BBC Talking Point, 16 July 2001. See also Francis Wheen's satirical rendering, *Guardian*, 4 September 1996 and, for further discussion, Hodge, pp. 127–128.
141 Tribunal Update, 106, 19 December 1998.

5 Kosovo indictments and sentencing

An exercise in equalization?

The primary responsibility for gross government abuses lies with Slobodan Milošević, who rode to power in the late eighties by inciting Serbian nationalist chauvinism around the Kosovo issue. Now, after wars in Bosnia and Croatia, he has returned to the place where his post-communist career began.[1]

Introduction

Just 15 people were indicted by the ICTY in the aftermath of the Kosovo war: nine Serbians, including politicians, military and police officers (two of whom died before conviction) and six Kosovo Albanians, all members of the Kosovo Liberation Army (KLA). The KLA members' indictments were all for war crimes committed in 1998, yet no Serbian officials were called to account for crimes committed during that year. The Prosecution's choice of indictments failed to reflect fully the nature of the war and the context in which it was fought. This, combined with the questionable, and at times deleterious, international response to the numerous post-war issues in Kosovo, was to have an indelible impact on subsequent developments in the region.

*

Full-scale war in Kosovo was not inevitable. Yet, the continuing international perception that Milosevic was the key to peace in the Balkans, along with the belief that the passive resistance of Rugova's government would keep Kosovo in check, increased the likelihood that the persistent repression and discrimination by the Serbian police and armed forces against the majority Albanian population would eventually lead to some form of armed rebellion.

Equally, in light of the Bosnian war, and particularly the Srebrenica genocide, the reaction of the Serbian war machine, firstly to the KLA which gained momentum in the late 1990s, and later to the NATO air strikes, was not difficult to predict. The distinctive pattern of aggression and oppression, which started in Croatia and continued with a vengeance in Bosnia and Herzegovina, came into play once more in Kosovo in 1998 shortly after the first display of KLA active resistance, and only subsided after nearly three months of wide-scale NATO bombing in Kosovo and Serbia.

Kosovo gained its independence in 2007, yet over a decade later the new state was still struggling both in political and economic terms, while issues with Serbia remained substantially unresolved.

Historical context

The 1974 Constitution defined Kosovo as an autonomous province of Serbia, one of the constituent entities of the SFRY, granting it a status nearly equivalent to that of the republics, but without the right to secede. Following the death of Tito in 1980, Kosovo Albanians started to demand republic status.

During the 1980s, the Serbian media spread allegations of epidemics of rape perpetrated by Kosovo Albanian men against Kosovo Serb women. An independent committee of Serbian lawyers and human rights experts, however, found a markedly lower incidence of rape in Kosovo than in other regions of Yugoslavia.[2] In 1986, the infamous 'Memorandum' was produced by the Serbian Academy of Sciences and Arts, containing highly inflammatory allegations against Kosovo's Albanians.

On 3 March 1989, the Serbian Assembly revoked the province's autonomous status, and amended the constitution, granting Serbia control over Kosovo's internal affairs. A series of measures were introduced which led to the dismissal of Albanians from political and economic institutions and large commercial enterprises. Albanian language teaching in secondary schools ended, and the Albanian language media was closed. Albanians responded by setting up a parallel system of education. A number of political parties and movements emerged, including the Lidhja Demokratike e Kosovës (LDK) under Ibrahim Rugova in 1989, which advocated a peaceful solution through dialogue.

*

The dire situation for the ethnic Albanian majority population in Kosovo in the 1990s, resulting in the formation of the KLA and subsequent armed conflict, has been recorded in some detail by human rights organizations and others.[3] Amnesty International, in several reports published in June 1998, noted that

> Recent Serbian police and military operations, although ostensibly directed at the armed opposition Kosovo Liberation Army, have led to hundreds of civilian deaths, many apparently a result of deliberate or indiscriminate attacks.[4]

According to HRW,

> Despite its obligations under international law, the Serbian government has blatantly and systematically violated the most basic tenets set forth in international human rights documents. Serbian authorities in Kosovo are responsible for the torture and killing of ethnic Albanians in detention. Adequate investigation, prosecution or punishment of those responsible for the murder, torture or mistreatment of Albanians in Kosovo is rarely undertaken. Albanians are

> arrested, detained, prosecuted and imprisoned solely on the basis of their ethnic affiliation, political beliefs or membership in organizations or institutions which are banned or looked upon with disfavour by the Serbian government. The Serbian government has promulgated laws which, either expressly or through implementation, discriminate against Albanians in Kosovo.[5]

HRW pointed to the distribution of weapons to Serbian civilians in Kosovo from 1990, while Serbian paramilitary groups recruited members and increased their presence in Kosovo with the apparent knowledge of the Serbian authorities.[6] With the withdrawal of the JNA from Macedonia, much of its personnel and materiel were moved to Kosovo.[7] The legal system was manipulated as human rights abuses against ethnic Albanians in Kosovo became legalized, laws restricting the sale and rental of property in Kosovo by or to Albanians were introduced, and all public administration and publicly funded enterprises and institutions in Kosovo came under the direct control of the Serbian authorities, with Albanians purged from their positions. Restrictions were imposed on freedom of association and expression. When 5,000–6,000 Albanian professors and students at the University of Pristina demonstrated in July 1991, protesting the new laws on 'special measures', many were dismissed from their jobs. Journalists were persecuted, with severe restrictions imposed on the freedom of the press and use of the Albanian language. The Albanian language Pristina Radio and TV was closed by Serbian police units, and later became a subsidiary of the Milosevic-controlled Serbian Radio and Television. Discrimination against ethnic Albanians in health and education led to the dismissal of doctors, technicians, nurses and teaching staff, particularly in the Pristina area; a new Serbian curriculum was introduced in schools while thousands of teachers who refused to teach the new curriculum were dismissed from their posts.[8]

In 1997, in the FRY, approximately 34 ethnic Albanian political prisoners were convicted, often after unfair trials and detention conditions where they were routinely tortured.[9] At least three died in police custody, allegedly following torture.[10]

> Incidents in which police beat and ill-treated ethnic Albanians, including women, children and elderly people, took place daily throughout the year. Victims were often beaten in their homes during searches for arms.[11]

The international response, 1991–1997

The 1991 European Community conference on Yugoslavia and the subsequent international conference in London in August 1992 barely touched on the Kosovo crisis. Neither did the Dayton conference ending the Bosnian war in 1995. To many Kosovo Albanians it appeared that the United States had abandoned their cause and had settled for Kosovo remaining part of Serbia. Disappointed, the more radical elements in Kosovo and parts of the Diaspora began to abandon the tactics of non-violent resistance. This led gradually to the formation of the KLA which, in 1997, began hit-and-run attacks, responded to with excess force by the

Yugoslav Army (VJ), regular Serbian police and three special police forces from the Ministry of the Interior of Serbia (MUP).

The Saint'Egidio conflict resolution organization under the control of the Vatican Diplomatic corps became involved in peace efforts. The Vatican was anxious to prevent an Islamic state from being established but would have had little influence without the Catholic British Ambassador in Belgrade, Ivor Roberts, a close confidante of Milosevic, who worked to draw the Serbian president into the peace process.[12] Milosevic prepared to cooperate in order to get UN sanctions lifted and improve Serbia's position internationally. Yet the resultant Education Accord, signed in 1996 with the support of the Contact Group, changed little on the ground.[13]

In 1997, the pyramid bank crisis in Albania resulted in a state awash with arms, from which the KLA was soon to benefit. Yet the situation in Albania was *sui generis*. Large numbers of people had a grievance against the Berisha government, whereas in Kosovo the insurgents had to overcome an organized and well-armed Serbian security apparatus, which had repressed the majority Albanian population for decades.

1998: civilian slaughter and international paralysis

In 1998, full armed conflict erupted between the KLA and Serb forces, as more than 200,000 Albanians were driven from their homes.[14] The first attack by Serb special forces on Donji Prekaz on 22 January focused on the Jashari compound. On 28 February and 1 March, Serbian forces launched an attack on two Albanian villages, Likosane and Cirez, in the Drenica area, without warning, where at least 24 women and children died.[15] On 5 March, Serbian security forces again attacked the family compound of Jashari in Prekaz, with fighting lasting 36 hours. Over 80 people were killed, including at least 24 women and children, many shot at close range, and some while in police custody.[16] The Serbian police blocked aid deliveries during the attacks, and doctors were prevented from entering the villages to perform autopsies.[17]

The events in Drenica were a watershed. Tens of thousands attended the funerals, and many Kosovars living abroad returned at that time, while thousands, formerly committed to non-violent activity as propagated by Rugova, joined the KLA. On 7 March in Pristina, a march of over 100,000 took place. The fighting intensified and widened as Milosevic decided to implement the 'Operation Horseshoe' plan in full, which involved an attack on the Kosovo population.[18] The Yugoslav army (VJ) began taking over from the police in Kosovo, moving heavy armour to secure major strategic roads.[19]

*

The international approach to the armed conflict in Kosovo in 1998 was conditioned by several factors, resulting in a containment policy which tolerated serious human rights violations and contributed to keeping Milosevic in power for a further year.

Considerations such as the fear of regional destabilization if the conflict spread to neighbouring countries, coupled with overwhelming opposition to an independent Kosovo and reluctance to commit resources to preserve peace there, were compounded by international divisions within the Security Council and NATO. The ensuing paralysis resulted in the weakness and ambivalence which had dogged international policy during the Croatian and Bosnian wars. In the initial stages of the conflict, a number of senior international officials, including Robert Gelbard, condemned the KLA for terrorist actions.[20] These impressions were fuelled by Belgrade.[21]

The first international move following the massacre at Drenica was the Contact Group statement of 9 March, calling for a number of measures, including ten days to withdraw the special police units and cease action by security forces affecting civilian access to Kosovo for aid organizations and diplomats, and a moratorium on government-financed export credit support for investment in Serbia, which Russia refused to endorse.[22] The 10 days became 15, during which Milosevic only briefly reduced the police attacks and promised to implement the moribund St. Egidio education agreement. This bought Milosevic time and held off further sanctions.

It was not until 29 April that the Contact Group next met, when the Kosovo violence was played down. NATO also displayed little appetite for intervention. The earlier demand to withdraw the special police units was now watered down to 'cessation of repression'. The demand for access for aid organizations was dropped altogether.

The only measure adopted with any teeth was a Security Council resolution on 31 March, imposing an arms embargo on the FRY, although this was only marginally effective in view of the quantity of arms in the area already.[23] Also, Russia and China, both permanent Security Council members with veto power, maintained that the conflict was an internal matter. Within the Contact Group, Russia was again the spoiler, opposing a moratorium on support for trade and investment in Serbia. Russia was often used as an excuse for inaction, however. Statements and actions in response to the growing conflict were weak, and watered down to lowest common denominator. Condemnation, threats and sanctions, as in Bosnia, were often empty, and deadlines broken, with limited or no repercussions.

As the tensions escalated in Kosovo, Milosevic continued to be appeased internationally, and considered key to a negotiated solution. In a move brokered by Richard Holbrooke, and considered at the time an international triumph, Milosevic agreed to meet the Kosovo leader, Ibrahim Rugova on 15 May. Contrary to all previous conditions set by both the international community and the Kosovo leadership, and in a major concession to Milosevic, the meeting took place without the presence of foreign mediators. It was a public relations disaster, losing Rugova popularity in Kosovo and strengthening support for the KLA. As a reward to Milosevic, international pressure was once again eased as, on 25 May, a European Union General Affairs Council meeting agreed that, in light of the Milosevic/Rugova meeting, the proposed measures to halt new investment in Serbia would not go forward. Milosevic's hand was strengthened, and the decade-long peaceful approach Rugova's party had advocated discredited.

In mid-May, Milosevic launched a major new scorched earth offensive along the border with Albania, involving serious breaches in international humanitarian law, as the combined forces of the VJ and Serbian police attacked, looted and then systematically destroyed, towns and villages along the Albanian border from Pec to the north of Djakove. Non-combatants were systematically attacked during indiscriminate shelling in their villages, or deliberately targeted as they were fleeing, contrary to Article 3 of the Geneva Conventions.[24] In Ljubenic, a number of ethnic Albanians were summarily executed by the Serbian special police.[25] Landmines were strategically placed and livestock shot to ensure no-one returned in the short term. An estimated 30,000 people fled to Montenegro and 15,000 to Albania.[26]

Belgrade's continued refusal to take the steps necessary to stabilize the situation combined with the rapid growth of the KLA led ICTY Chief Prosecutor Louise Arbour to announce that the situation in Kosovo met the definition of armed conflict under relevant international law. Various meetings from 9 and 12 June between EU foreign ministers, NATO defence ministers and the Contact Group stepped up pressure on Belgrade, confirming the investment ban, and discussing options for possible military action, prompting Milosevic to make minor concessions, such as agreement to meet the Russian president, Boris Yeltsin, and permission for diplomatic observers to monitor throughout Kosovo. Pressure on NATO was mounting, but action confined to a virtually useless NATO flyover.

At the US House of Representatives, Serbia's responsibility was clearly spelt out, however.[27]

> Although we are concerned about the actions of the KLA . . . we mustn't lose sight of the fact that Belgrade initiated the confrontation in Kosovo, and President Milosevic and his government have primary responsibility for taking the steps necessary to bring an end to the violence.
>
> Milosevic must: first, pull back the security forces engaged in repressive actions in Kosovo; second initiate meaningful dialogue with KLA leadership to produce political settlement; third, reach agreement with UNHCR and ICRC on programme for refugee return; ensure freedom of access to international personnel; support international efforts to monitor events 'with complete and unfettered access'.[28]

The first major KLA offensive began in July 1998 in the attempted capture of Orahovec, but its achievements were short-lived as, within two days, the Serbian police recaptured the town and 42 were killed, some of them in summary executions.[29] No international presence was allowed as the offensive extended over the summer to September, in an attempt to crush civilian support to the KLA. According to Human Rights Watch, most of those killed during the Serb offensive were civilians, with 250,000, mostly women and children, displaced.[30] The use of torture of detainees was widespread, and at times fatal.[31]

In late July, the Serbs also defeated the KLA at Lapusnik and Carraleve, with large-scale Serbian armoured forces now deployed, including 140 tanks and 220 metre cannon, as against KLA mortars.[32] On 24 August, Serbian police attacked a humanitarian aid convoy, killing three Albanians working with the Mother Theresa Society.[33] First-hand evidence of a massacre in late September, in Gornje Obrinje, was witnessed by BBC journalists, when 18 Kosovar civilians, mostly women and children, were killed with shots to the head or knives, some of them mutilated, and two decapitated. A further 14 corpses were located in Vucitern.[34] Two days later, four ethnic Albanians were slaughtered when a refugee convoy was ambushed in South-West Kosovo.[35]

During this time, there were many symbolic missions and tough-sounding declarations, but little effective international action. By September 1998, the UNHCR reported a total of 241,700 displaced persons, most of them within Kosovo, with about 50,000 trying to survive in the open. Even though most returned to their homes later, their crops had not been harvested and their livestock were scattered or dead.[36]

Meanwhile, the international community dithered and remained conflicted in its approach to Milosevic. With no US intelligence presence on the ground, NATO relied on European material, which involved contact, even collaboration, with Belgrade. International concern to preserve international borders continued to take priority over the need to stem the atrocities, due partly to the potential for regional destabilization, but also the fear of setting a precedent for secessionist movements elsewhere in Europe.

With so many displaced, the Security Council, on 23 September 1998, declared the conflict a threat to regional peace, and demanded the withdrawal of Serbian forces.[37] The following day, an 'Activation Warning' for a limited air campaign was issued to pressure Milosevic, followed by an attempt by Richard Holbrooke to broker an agreement. In mid-October, under threat of NATO action, Milosevic agreed to withdraw his troops and allow the deployment of an OSCE Kosovo Verification Mission (KVM) and, on 13 October, NATO withdrew the threat of air strikes. But most of the displaced remained in hiding, and the KVM became increasingly dependent for information on the VJ officers, as the harsh winter prevented free movement. But at least the ceasefire held for a while.[38] But by late December, the KVM still only numbered a few hundred out of the proposed 2,000.[39] Finally, the Security Council adopted a resolution under Chapter VII of the UN Charter, confirming its authority.[40] But Milosevic's continued international support was reflected at a NATO foreign ministers' meeting on 16 December which, while calling on the KLA to disarm, required the VJ merely to reduce its numbers and refrain from further intimidation, causing outrage amongst Kosovo's Albanians.

Some in the United States and UK began looking to the KLA as a potential 'anti-Milosevic' force, with the UK government setting up a framework for 'Operation Horn', an undercover operation for the KLA which would not destabilize the Milosevic regime.[41] British Prime Minister Tony Blair, who wielded considerable influence internationally and favoured NATO action, gradually began to take over policy from the foreign secretary, Robin Cook, splitting the British establishment.[42] US president Clinton at this time was distracted by impeachment charges and Operation Desert Fox against Saddam Hussein.

Throughout 1998, the Serbian authorities refused access to ICTY investigators to investigate crime scenes.[43] This was to prove crucial to the whole tribunal approach to the Kosovo war. It took the massacre of Kosovo Albanian civilians at Racak to trigger a more focused international approach to the increasing tensions in the province.

Racak-Rambouillet, January–March 1999

> US and European policymakers are repeating in Kosovo many of the same mistakes they made before during and after the wars in Croatia and Bosnia. . . . After neglecting the Kosovo issue for nearly a decade, US and European policymakers only began considering it when large numbers of dead Albanians began appearing on their television screens.[44]

On 15 January 1999, in the village of Racak, 45 Albanian civilians were killed in a massacre. The victims included three women, several elderly men and a 12-year-old boy.[45] The facts as verified by the KVM included evidence of arbitrary detentions, extra-judicial killings and the mutilation of unarmed civilians by the Serbian security forces. It brought the situation back to international notice, prompting world leaders to lay the foundations for a peace settlement.

The KVM called on the ICTY to commence an immediate investigation into the crimes committed in Racak. On 18 January, Chief Prosecutor Louise Arbour was prevented at the border between Macedonia and the FRY from entering the country. The FRY had denied tribunal investigators access for the previous ten months, claiming that it had no jurisdiction over its territory. Over 2,000 people had died since February 1998, many of them executed or deliberately and arbitrarily killed. Some 700 people, the majority ethnic Albanians, but also over a hundred Serbs, remained unaccounted for. At least 1,000 ethnic Albanians were detained by the Serbian authorities in 1998.

The international peace talks at Rambouillet in February 1999 were a last-ditch attempt to prevent a descent into full-scale war.[46] Ironically, the protracted negotiations allowed the Yugoslav Army (VJ) to reinforce. By 5 March, the number of VJ troops in Kosovo was over 5 times the limit set by the October Agreement, with 15 VJ units in the field as against the permitted 3.[47] Although violence on the ground in Kosovo had abated, the Serbian authorities were now developing extensive coordinated plans for a large spring offensive.[48] Convoys of armoured military vehicles and tanks arrived in Kosovo in February and early March, along with special police forces.

NATO action: the question of legality

The decision to conduct NATO air strikes in Kosovo and Serbia was controversial both legally and politically. It followed months of negotiations, culminating in the failed international conferences at Rambouillet and in Paris. Detractors alleged that NATO intervention was a violation of international law, lacking the authorization of the UN Security Council, and that NATO, in acting outside its treaty area against a country which posed no threat to member states, had set a precedent.[49] Former ICTY chief prosecutor Antonio Cassese argued that the intervention, although illegal under international law, might herald a new doctrine allowing the use of force to prevent large-scale atrocities within a state.[50] The Independent International Commission on Kosovo termed the intervention as an illegal but legitimate action.[51] The issue continues to engage international lawyers and others, especially in the context of its implications for subsequent wars.

It was not the first time that NATO had threatened to intervene in Kosovo, and the action took place against the backdrop of several UN Security Council resolutions passed the previous year, recognizing an impending humanitarian crisis.[52] NATO action was consistent with the stated purposes of the UN Charter (Article 1). A primary justification offered by NATO states for intervention was the threat to European peace and stability, given the conflict's potential to spill over into neighbouring countries. Additionally, the Security Council was itself unable to act to maintain regional peace and security due to political deadlock.[53] NATO member states were also acting to fulfil their legal obligations to prevent genocide, and the Kosovo Albanians' inability to exercise their right to self-determination arguably superseded the FRY's right to territorial integrity.[54]

The right to self-defence includes the right to call on other states to engage in collective self-defence against an oppressive regime only in certain circumstances. In the case of Nicaragua, for instance, the ICJ rejected the Reagan Administration's attempt to intervene in 1985 on the grounds that adoption of a particular ideology or political doctrine on the side of the oppressive state is insufficient to create a new rule. NATO did not intend to impose a democratic government in the FRY, however, but to protect Kosovo Albanians from gross abuse of human rights, which is not prohibited by Article 2(4) of the Charter. The multilateral nature of the NATO states' intervention lent further legitimacy.[55]

On the other hand, the concern that justifying NATO intervention in Kosovo would encourage international intervention in less altruistic circumstances was, as later events demonstrated, not without foundation.

ICTY indictments

Following the Kosovo war, the ICTY indicted nine Serbs and six Kosovo Albanians for war crimes and crimes against humanity committed in 1998 and 1999 in Kosovo. The respective judgements resulted in convictions for six of the Serbs and one Kosovo Albanian.[56]

Despite overwhelming evidence from human rights and other organizations of breaches of humanitarian law by the Yugoslav Army (VJ) and Serbian police (MUP) against non-Serb civilians in Kosovo in 1998, the only indictments brought by the ICTY for that year were against Kosovo Albanians. This may partly be explained by the fact that ICTY investigators were barred by the

Serbian authorities from entering Kosovo in 1998, and the court relied on evidence obtained from mostly Serbian sources. The witnesses called by the prosecution were often unreliable and included disaffected Kosovars who testified against former colleagues. Added to this was the considerable pressure on the ICTY, both from Belgrade and internationally to indict non-Serbs.[57]

On 9 October 2000, just days after Milosevic's downfall, the European Union decided to ease economic sanctions on the FRY, unconditionally. UN officials and Western leaders offered full backing to President Kostunica, despite his continuing support for incorporating parts of Bosnia into Serbia, and his declared opposition to the tribunal.[58] Carl Bildt referred to Kostunica as a moderate, a man of peace,[59] while the French Foreign Minister, Hubert Vedrine, and Defence Minister Alain Richard regarded him as 'the key to transforming Yugoslavia'.[60] Additionally, Kostunica was assured in a visit to the neo-conservative US Cato Institute that the Bush administration would eventually dump the tribunal which it regarded as a Trojan horse of international justice.[61] Even the discovery on 28 May 2001, of 80 Albanian corpses transported by the Serbian police in refrigerator trucks from Kosovo to Batajnica, a military airfield outside Belgrade, did not appear to galvanize international support for the tribunal.[62]

The tribunal had no powers of arrest. Nor did it have the means to press the FRY to hand over its indictees. But when Del Ponte pressed Western leaders to impose conditionality on financial aid to the FRY, she was accused of political interference. Hans Corell, the UN under-secretary for legal affairs warned, 'You cannot go around criticizing Kostunica', while UN Secretary General Kofi Annan cautioned her that she should not engage in political matters.[63] In her memoirs, Del Ponte recalls that US Secretary of State Madeleine Albright appealed to her not to call for Milosevic's transferral to the tribunal and to remain silent about Karadzic. As if to prove a point, Mladić later openly attended a wedding in Belgrade.[64]

In an attempt to persuade the Belgrade authorities to hand over indicted war criminals sheltered in Serbia, Del Ponte met a number of times with Kostunica, Prime Minister Zoran Djindjic and other Serbian politicians in Belgrade and at The Hague, but with relatively little success. On 18 April 2002, visiting Belgrade, she requested the arrest of 23 indictees, and the release of documentary evidence. Djindjic anxious not to jeopardize Serbia's position at the international donors' conference on 29 June, promised Washington Milosevic would be delivered before then. Yet Del Ponte secured limited cooperation from the Djindjic government on requests for access to relevant archives, noting that only 1 out of 77 requests for interviews with prospective witnesses was granted.[65] When she informed Djindjic that indictments against four Serbians involved in the Kosovo war would be issued, including Sreten Lukić, Djindjic, who had made compromises with Lukić and others in the overthrow of Milosevic, warned that the indictments would pose grave political problems.[66] On 3 October, Del Ponte informed the Belgrade government about the sealed indictments which Serbian prime minister Zoran Zivkovic refused to accept. The United States issued conflicting signals, Ambassador William Montgomery reportedly advising Del Ponte to go public with the indictments, yet later stating that she had been insensitive to the political realities in Serbia, while the US war crimes ambassador, Pierre-Richard Prosper, asked Del Ponte not to make the indictments public.[67] On 30 October, Del Ponte complained to the UN Security Council about Serbia's lack of cooperation over access to archives, whereupon Serbia applied for protective measures under ICTY Rule 54 *bis* on the basis of 'national security interests' which were granted by the Trial Chamber on 5 June 2003.[68]

The Serbian authorities had correctly read the signal that international leaders were not proposing to impose conditionality to compel Serbia to cooperate with the tribunal. How was Del Ponte to respond? Meeting an impasse which affected both the record of the ICTY and her personal reputation, she decided to cut a deal – non-Serbs would be indicted in exchange for surrenders of Serbian indictees, an insidious decision which bore little relation to culpability and tainted the ICTY's reputation.

On 17 February 2003, anticipating that FRY foreign minister Goran Svilanovic would make a pre-emptive demand for 'balance', Del Ponte informed him that indictments against KLA members, were forthcoming. She also agreed to the provisional release of the Serbian president, Milan Milutinović, in order to 'build confidence' and create a 'positive climate'.[69]

Del Ponte proved true to her word. Fatmir Limaj, a former KLA commander, along with another KLA commander, Isak Musliu, and a guard at Llapushnik camp, Haradin Bala, were indicted on 27 January 2003 for crimes against humanity and war crimes in Kosovo between May and July 1998. The case was ill-prepared. Limaj pleaded not guilty to all charges, and was acquitted by the trial chamber, and again on appeal. Musliu was also acquitted, while Bala was convicted for war crimes and sentenced to 13 years imprisonment.[70]

The Limaj indictments did not lead to an immediate change of position in Belgrade. When Del Ponte met with Svilanovic on 2 April 2003, he stated that Belgrade would not accept any tribunal documents based on 'command responsibility' nor consider handing over Lukić, Perišić or Lazarevic, and also that it was important to preserve Pavkovic to retain army support.[71] He also warned that indictments would derail scheduled Kosovo negotiations in Vienna.

The Limaj case should never have gone to The Hague. Apart from the lack of substantive evidence and unreliable witnesses, the charges themselves were relatively minor in relation to alleged crimes by Serbian officers. While Toplica Miladinovic, the Serbian military commander in Pec/Peja was tried by the Serbian War Crimes Chamber (and acquitted on appeal) for killing 119 people, for instance, Fatmir Limaj and other former KLA members were tried for less heinous crimes, mostly referred to the national courts.[72] The Belgrade Appeals Court annulled the first-instance verdict without justification and ordered a retrial.[73] Established in 2003, the Serbian War Crimes Chamber, by 2008, was considered to have established a working relationship with the ICTY.[74] The overall record of the Serbian courts, however, leaves much room for improvement.

The Milutinovic judgement

The initial indictment against Milan Milutinović for crimes against humanity and war crimes under Article 7 of the ICTY Statute was confirmed on 22 May (together with Milosevic and other Serbian officials), and made public on 27 May 1999.[75] Milutinović under pressure surrendered on 20 January 2003, and was acquitted of all charges in February 2009. In contrast, Sreten Lukić, head of the Ministry of Internal Affairs (MUP) from May 1998, for which Milutinović, as head of state, was *de jure* responsible, was found guilty and sentenced to 22 years. Several arguments by the Trial Chamber in support of Milutinović's acquittal merit closer examination.

Milutinović's powers as Serbian president and within the Supreme Defence Council (SDC)

The powers Milan Milutinović was able to exercise by virtue of his position proved to be a highly contentious issue. The prosecution claimed that, as president of Serbia from December 1997 till 2002, active in the Socialist Party of Serbia (SPS) and a close confidante of Milosevic, Milutinović was one of the most powerful political figures in Serbia, representing the country before foreign states and international organizations and having *de jure* authority over the Serbian police (MUP). He was one of just three members of the Supreme Defence Council (SDC) of the FRY with full voting rights, participating in decisions over the use of the VJ, and able to utilize certain powers over the Ministry of the Interior under the Serbian Constitution.[76]

The fact that the prosecution called no witnesses on constitutional law issues to support its case was cited by the Trial Chamber as relevant to the judgement. The defence, on the other hand, presented evidence from Ratko Marković, Serbian deputy prime minister at the time, and a professor with some 40 years' experience in constitutional law, who had drafted the 1990 and 1992 Serbian and FRY constitutions, respectively. While the Trial Chamber acknowledged that Marković was not an independent witness, being a close confidante of Milosevic, he was nonetheless deemed to be 'credible on certain issues but not on others'.[77] Marković's evidence in the Milutinović case, on the crucial issue of presidential powers, conflicted with that given at the Milosevic trial in 2005. This was apparently not considered relevant, however, since Marković's evidence weighed heavily on constitutional and other issues raised in the trial, including the Rambouillet negotiations, where Marković had led the Serbian delegation.[78]

According to Marković, despite the fact that Milutinović's mandate came from the electorate, his powers were considerably narrower than those of a head of state in a 'regular' presidential system. He argued that, while the Serbian constitution (Article 83(5)) provided that the Serbian president was to 'lead the armed forces', in the absence of Serbian forces that article was devoid of meaning.[79] In cross-examination, however, Marković conceded that the Serbian president could suspend a law until the next session of the national assembly, but there was no evidence of Milutinović exercising a 'suspensive veto' prior to the war.[80]

Although, as Marković stressed, the FRY president, Slobodan Milosevic, was the ultimate commander of the VJ, he conceded on cross-examination that, according to the 1992 SDC Rules of Procedure, the president's proposals could be outvoted by the other two members (Milutinović and Djukanovic) until the change to the rules on 23 March 1999. The significance of this became evident in the pivotal military and police appointments made in late 1998 with Milutinović's full support.

The Chamber concluded that

> there existed provisions in the Serbian Constitution which could have been used by a President who had charisma and popular support to exert influence over the Government Ministries and policies. For example, the power in article 85, as conceded by Marković himself, was ultimately dependent on the popular and political support of a particular President and had potential therefore to be of great significance. Indeed, Slobodan Milošević, who was President of Serbia until 1997, the leader of a major political party in Serbia at the time of his Presidency, and also considered a highly charismatic individual, was able to exert much influence over various Republican, and even Federal, organs and institutions.[81]

In other words, according to the judges, a charismatic and 'popular' Serbian president like Milosevic could use provisions in the Serbian constitution to exert influence, while Milutinović could not. This conclusion set aside the fact that Milutinović, elected by the Serbian people, was, arguably, far more 'popular' at that time than Milosevic during much of his term as Serbian president.[82] He could, therefore, have used this popularity to confront Milosevic, especially within the SDC where he would have had Djukanovic's support. That he did not do so when the opportunity arose points to his full collusion in the criminal enterprise led by Milosevic.

It should also be noted, however, that all defendants were indicted under Article 7 (1) and (3) of the ICTY Statute, for individual criminal responsibility. Had the indictment included Article 7 (2), the prosecution would arguably have stood a better chance of convicting Milutinović.[83]

Controversial appointments made in late 1998

The prosecution alleged that, through the Supreme Defence Council, Milosevic and Milutinović systematically removed those opposing the use of the VJ outside the established chain of command, and instead appointed officers willing to further the criminal plan.[84] The defence countered that SDC members met to receive information and adopt conclusions or political standpoints, not decisions.[85]

In an SDC meeting in late 1998, Milosevic proposed that those opposed to the use of the VJ outside the established chain of command, including Yugoslav Army

Chief of Staff General Momčilo Perišić, be removed and replaced by Dragoljub Ojdanic. Nebojsa Pavkovic and Vladimir Lazarevic were also to be promoted to senior military posts. Milo Djukanovic, the Montenegrin president and the third member of the SDC, argued strongly against Milosevic's proposal but was outnumbered, as Milutinović gave Milosevic full support.

Although the Trial Chamber conceded that the SDC made decisions, it nonetheless concluded that

> Milutinović could be said to have been demonstrating loyalty to Milosevic rather than exercising independent judgement. . . . However, even if Milutinović had sided with Djukanovic . . . the outcome would not have been any different since the appointments and promotions of VJ Generals were exclusively within Milosevic's jurisdiction, pursuant to article 136 of the FRY Constitution.[86]

Article 136, arguably, would not supersede an SDC decision. Milutinović had the constitutional power, together with Djukanovic, to outvote Milosevic's proposal, and not only failed to do so but voiced his strong support, with fatal consequences for thousands of Kosovo Albanian civilians. The Trial Chamber's conclusion on this issue, heavily influenced by Marković's evidence, more or less sums up the judges' position overall, namely, that Milosevic had full and final control over all decisions, while Milutinović's powers were negligible by comparison.

Milutinović's role in the MUP and his promotion of Sreten Lukić

Using his presidential powers, Milutinović issued an ordinance promoting Sreten Lukić to the rank of Lieutenant General in May 1999 on the recommendation of the MUP minister. In the period leading up to and during the NATO air campaign, the MUP had played a central role in planning, organizing, controlling, and directing the work of the various MUP units active in Kosovo, as well as coordinating and planning joint operations with the VJ.[87]

The prosecution alleged that Milutinović, as Serbian president, failed to use the powers available to him to make it 'significantly more difficult for the crimes charged' to occur, instead using them to empower and encourage Sreten Lukić.[88] The Trial Chamber noted that the prosecution had provided no evidence to counter the argument that the Serbian president's role was a formal one, and again accepted the Defence argument that 'the extent to which [the powers and responsibilities] were used to their full potential depended on the person holding the post',[89] concluding,

> Accordingly, taken altogether, the evidence does not establish extensive interaction between Milutinović and the Serbian Government, and the MUP in particular. It therefore partly confirms the evidence of Ratko Marković . . . that the President of Serbia did not have extensive executive powers. Indeed, the President's de jure powers over the MUP were not extensive and the

> evidence led does not indicate that significant de facto powers resided in the hands of Milutinović.[90]

As Serbian president, however, Milutinović did have *de jure* powers over the Serbian police force (MUP). He simply chose not to use them to prevent Lukić's promotion.

Decrees issued by Milutinović

Milutinović issued 16 decrees during the war, two of which, according to the prosecution, were designed to contribute to altering the ethnic balance in Kosovo: the Decree on Identification Cards in Time of War and the Decree on Citizens' Domicile and Residence During the State of War. These two decrees, drafted by the Ministry of the Interior, set impossible conditions for the Kosovo Albanians who were expelled, in that they obliged everyone over 14 to register changes of residence or address within 24 hours, changes of domicile within 12 hours, and deregistration of a residence or domicile had to take place immediately prior to departure. Failure to do so could result in 30 days in prison.[91]

On 2 May 1999, Sreten Lukić issued directions to the SUPs in Kosovo, referring to the Domicile Decree, and requiring them to

> (a) organise a residence registration service in all places 'accommodating refugees who had left their domicile due to bombing by NATO forces', (b) make it possible for all persons to register their residence on the established form and then issue certificates of residence registration, (c) provide protection for persons with registered residence, and (d) ensure that they turn over weapons (without any consequences), that they do not receive 'terrorists or armed persons in their place of residence', that they do not obstruct the police and the army in their movements, that they designate representatives who will carry out local police work and make contact with government organs for the purpose of resolving humanitarian matters, and that they carry with them a residence registration certificate, which will give them freedom of movement except in the zones of 'combat and anti-terrorist operations'.[92]

As for the decree on ID cards, an expert witness for the Lukić defence, Branislav Simonovic, conceded that it would have been easier for a returnee to prove identity and citizenship, with a Yugoslav identification card.[93] Interestingly, it was Ratko Marković, as deputy prime minister, who signed four of the letters to Milutinović, recommending that he adopt the decrees in question.[94] The other 12 decrees, according to Marković, were signed by another deputy prime minister, Vojislav Šešelj![95]

The prosecution contended that Milutinović failed to use Article 83(7) to intervene to prevent or impede crimes committed by MUP, instead using his power to issue decrees with the purpose of altering the ethnic balance of Kosovo.[96] The

Trial Chamber, as on other occasions, faulted the prosecution for not having produced evidence to disprove the defence claim.

> The Chamber is satisfied that the Kosovo Albanian citizens of the FRY whose identity documents were seized did not lose their citizenship as a result. The Chamber notes, as acknowledged by Simonović, that proving identity and thus citizenship would be easier for a person in possession of a Yugoslav identity document. However, this would have been the case regardless of whether or not the ID Decree was in force at the time, especially if the person trying to prove his or her citizenship had been out of Kosovo for more than 15 days. In addition, the Chamber received no evidence of Kosovo Albanians encountering problems on their return to Kosovo because of the loss of the identity documents. Accordingly, the Chamber is of the view that the Prosecution failed to explain and show how the ID Decree actually worked in practice in order to achieve the aim of the joint criminal enterprise.[97]

Yet, as the judges presumably knew, the reason Kosovo Albanians returning to Kosovo without identity documents did not encounter any problems was because after the NATO campaign there were no longer Serb forces around to impede their re-entry! A demonstration of how the ID Decree 'actually worked in practice' was therefore redundant.

The judges further concluded,

> In addition, the purpose behind all four decrees described in detail above, is open to an interpretation other than the one suggested by the Prosecution, namely that, rather than encouraging expulsions, they appeared to have been ensuring increased police control over the whereabouts of the population within Kosovo, as well as increased control over the younger members of that population. Indeed, all four decrees were issued around about the same time Lukić instructed the SUPs to prevent civilians from leaving their place of residence. Accordingly, for all these reasons, the Chamber is unable to draw an inference adverse to Milutinović from the evidence surrounding the decrees.[98]

In the circumstances prevailing in Kosovo at that time, it requires a good stretch of the imagination to conclude, as the Trial Chamber did, that the decrees were to ensure increased police control over the whereabouts of the Kosovo population, especially as large numbers of civilians had already been forcibly driven out of Kosovo by early May 1999 when the decrees came into force.

The Racak massacre

The judgement refers to a meeting which took place between US General Wesley Clark, General Naumann, FRY President Milosevic, Serbian President Milutinovic and Deputy Prime Minister Nikola Sainovic on 19 January 1999, days after the Racak 'incident', to warn Milosevic 'that there should be no repetition of this kind of action, to persuade him to return to the terms of the October Agreements', and to agree to allow access to Kosovo to Louise Arbour, the ICTY chief prosecutor, to investigate the 'incident'.[99] On considering evidence of Milutinović's meetings with foreign officials, the Trial Chamber concluded that

> [t]he evidence summarised above of the meetings Milutinović had with the representatives of NATO and the KVM shows that he did not take an active role during the same and never stood out as somebody who had much influence or involvement in the discussions.[100]

Leaving aside the Trial Chamber's choice of term for the Racak massacre, Milutinović's presence at the meeting four days after Racak signified his seniority in the Serbian/FRY political hierarchy and ensured that he was fully informed of the massacre. The fact that Milutinović and Šainović 'never interrupted or corrected Milosevic' in this and other meetings, is open to interpretation, but suggests acquiescence, as confirmed in the testimony of several foreign representatives.[101] This position is also supported by Milutinović's conduct at SDC meetings, as discussed earlier. There is no record, moreover, of any independent investigation by the Serbian authorities of MUP in the massacre,[102] an investigation which Milutinović could, and arguably was bound to, authorize.

The Rambouillet/Paris negotiations

Milutinović's leading role in the Rambouillet conference and the subsequent talks in Paris also came under scrutiny during his trial, the prosecution alleging that Milutinović displayed an obstructionist attitude.[103]

Yet again, the judges gave greater weight to the evidence of Ratko Marković, who headed the Serbian delegation to the conference, than to the prosecution or the testimony of former Austrian Ambassador to Belgrade and EU Special Envoy to Kosovo, Wolfgang Petritsch.[104] This was particularly surprising given that the presiding judge, Iain Bonomy, had also sat on the Trial Chamber bench in the Milosevic trial in 2005 when Marković had given conflicting evidence for the Defence as to the respective roles of Milosevic and Milutinović. At that time, Marković claimed that it was *his* decision to refuse to sign the Rambouillet agreement on the political settlement for Kosovo, pointing out it would be tantamount to the occupation of the FRY. He stated that Slobodan Milosevic, then president of the FRY, was in no way involved and that the decision to reject the Agreement was taken independently and unanimously by all members of the delegation, which was headed by him and the then president of Serbia, Milan Milutinović, without 'any instructions from Belgrade'.[105] At the Milutinović trial, on the other hand, Marković testified that Milutinović never obstructed the negotiations in Rambouillet or Paris, but rather tried to enhance the process, supporting political dialogue between the two sides.[106] When asked if Milutinović misled the National Assembly on 23 March 1999, Marković responded that his speech simply reflected what had happened at the talks.[107] The Trial Chamber noted that, on 18 February 1999, Milutinović met with US ambassador Christopher Hill in Paris, a meeting recorded as having a negative outcome and being 'absolutely unproductive', because the most contentious issues, such as the military aspects of the Agreement, remained open.[108] Marković wrote a letter on 23 February 1999 to the international negotiators, indicating that the talks had failed.[109] Marković evidently tailored his responses according to the person in the dock. In other words, he lied on oath, which should have been sufficient to have him dismissed as a serious witness.

Milutinović's obstructionist attitude at Rambouillet and Paris is documented in contemporaneous reports of the events, as well as by Petritsch and other prosecution witnesses. Petritsch testified that 'Milutinović proved more intransigent than his delegation on the political part. Bombing Serbia would lead to massacres'.[110] He opined that after Milošević, he considered Milutinović to be the most to blame for the events in Kosovo, as he was the most supportive of Milošević's policies and 'most vociferous in defending those policies', a view also held by the OSCE chairman in Kosovo, Knut Vollabaek.[111]

Milutinović reiterated his government's opposition to the proposed NATO implementation mission. His team were prepared to sign a political deal, guaranteeing Kosovo autonomy over a transitional three-year period but implacably opposed to a NATO force to implement the deal.[112] In a press conference on 20 February, the 'suave but menacing Mr Milutinović' questioned the logic of 'so many foreign troops to chase terrorists'. He banked on international divisions regarding NATO involvement. As the Rambouillet talks ended without agreement, fighting continued on the ground, with monitors and diplomats reporting that much of the military activity issued from special police units 'with every kind of weapon up to tanks', while OSCE monitors also came under attack.[113]

As the talks resumed in Paris on 15 March, Milutinović reneged on the political deal agreed by the Serbs in February, now insisting on substantial amendments to the autonomy deal he had agreed on at Rambouillet and warned that a bloodbath reminiscent of Vietnam would engulf Yugoslavia if NATO were to bomb, with 'blood up to the knees'.[114] By this time, large-scale offensives were already under way. During the week preceding the NATO bombing, according to UNHCR, at least 20,000 more Kosovo Albanians were forced to abandon their villages, bringing the total to an estimated 230,000 displaced people before NATO action had even begun.[115]

Under pressure of US withdrawal, the Kosovo Albanian delegation reluctantly signed a peace agreement at Paris which fell far short of their hopes, leaving the province firmly in Serbian hands, with no guarantee of protection. But the Serbian side remained intransigent, rendering the Agreement worthless, and the Paris talks were suspended, the British foreign secretary, Robin Cook, and his French counterpart, Hubert Vedrine, concluding that the Serbs were not acting in good faith.[116] In the days before NATO acted, and OSCE verifiers departed, the situation in Kosovo, according to the head of UNHCR in Kosovo, Joe Hegenauer, accelerated out of control.[117]

The Trial Chamber saw things differently.

> Particularly in light of the refusal of the Kosovo Albanians to negotiate . . . it cannot be concluded that Milutinović, who participated so actively in the negotiation process and appeared to be willing to meet the leading representatives of the Kosovo Albanians, was obstructing any genuine attempt at a solution.[118]
>
> The Chamber recalls here its earlier finding that all sides were ultimately to blame for the failure of the negotiations at Rambouillet. Thus, the evidence of Milutinović's criticisms of the process in the later stage of the negotiations does not necessarily lead to the conclusion that he did not want to achieve an agreement and avoid the NATO threat. The evidence above, especially when combined with the evidence discussed earlier in Section V, also indicates that the decision on whether to accept the Agreement was ultimately in Milošević's hands and that, therefore, neither Milutinović nor Šainović had the power to make a decision to the contrary. Accordingly, the Chamber is not satisfied that the evidence led shows that Milutinović personally exhibited an obstructive attitude aimed at ensuring their failure. The evidence is equally open to the interpretation that he was endeavouring to secure a deal that would be accepted by the FRY/Serbian authorities.[119]

A tortuous conclusion which bore little relation to the situation on the ground and in Belgrade in early 1999. Milutinović was acquitted on all charges.

The trial and retrial of Ramush Haradinaj

The Haradinaj trial arguably altered the course of Kosovo's political development at a crucial time in its history.

On the eve of his election by the Kosovo Assembly to become prime minister, Ramush Haradinaj wrote,

> I am proud of the part that I played in protecting my people from Slobodan Milosevic and his henchmen, and I am ready to defend my actions against criticism and innuendo. I therefore welcome the scrutiny of my war record by the International Criminal Tribunal for the Former Yugoslavia . . . and am confident that truth and justice will prevail. However, any attempt – be it by the ICTY with the best of motives, or others with the worst – to morally equate Milosevic's state-sponsored terror with the actions of the Kosova Liberation Army in defense of Kosovar Albanians will only make the task [that lies ahead for Kosova] more difficult. For the need now is to look forward rather than back, to create an inclusive, democratic independent state in Kosova that respects the rights of all of its citizens and is both just and tolerant.[120]

Haradinaj's comment was prescient. Within weeks, he was indicted by the ICTY, immediately resigned as prime minister and voluntarily surrendered to the tribunal to defend himself in what was to become a landmark trial, and retrial, spanning over seven years.

The shock indictment of the Kosovo prime minister followed a number of meetings in the preceding months between Del Ponte and Serbian leaders. In early October 2004, Serbian President Kostunica complained that the tribunal had not indicted any leader of the Kosovo militia, and Del Ponte reassured him that the prosecution would present an indictment against a high-level commander of the KLA.[121]

Haradinaj had been prime minister for just 100 days. He was indicted as commander in most of Western Kosovo where he allegedly had command authority over Balaj and Brahimaj and other KLA personnel. The three were indicted on 37 counts under Articles 3, 5 and 7(1) of the Statute, for charges including murder, torture, and cruel treatment, in a joint criminal enterprise (JCE) to consolidate control over the Dukagjin Operational Zone by removal of Serb civilians and mistreatment of collaborators with Serbian forces.

During his brief term in office, Haradinaj had impressed senior international officials, especially over his endeavours to build bridges between the Serbian and Albanian communities, and his indictment was criticized by a number of leaders with whom he had come into close contact. Soren Jessen-Petersen, the Danish head of the United Nations Mission in Kosovo (UNMIK) at the level of UN under-secretary general, made no secret of his opposition to the indictment. Jessen-Petersen had enjoyed a distinguished service within the UN since 1972, and held many senior positions.[122] Former Kosovo Force (KFOR) commander General Klaus Reinhardt also vouched for Haradinaj, commenting that he trusted him wholeheartedly and actively sought his advice.[123] Robin Cook, the British foreign secretary at the time, commented that Kosovo had made more progress under Haradinaj on key standards such as minority rights and conditions for the return of Serb refugees than anyone in the previous five years.[124] The negative response from senior international figures to Haradinaj's indictment was confirmed by Del Ponte herself in her opening statement in court and later in her memoir.[125]

The evidence on which Haradinaj had been indicted met with criticism from a number of senior international lawyers, including the lead prosecutor in the Milosevic trial, Sir Geoffrey Nice, QC, and another ICTY prosecutor, Andrew Cayley, QC. Cayley was asked to take charge of the indictment but declined. In a later interview in *The Observer*, Cayley said that, having reviewed the evidence, he wrote an extensive report to the prosecutor stating that he could not proceed on the evidence available. He charged that the report was suppressed within the OTP, and that he had been reprimanded.[126] In a subsequent article in *Jutarnji List*, Sir Geoffrey Nice wrote that Del Ponte had eventually instructed three managers 'who had some qualifications as lawyers' to write an indictment against Haradinaj, which they did, apparently under some pressure.[127] Nice, together with another senior ICTY prosecutor, Mark Harmon, wrote to Del Ponte on 22 December 2004, stressing the importance of a peer review in such contentious cases, in the interests of transparency and collective responsibility.[128] Yet no independent peer review took place.

Niccolo Figa-Talamanca, project director of No Peace without Justice and former ICTY law clerk, voiced the views of many:

> We are witnessing a misguided attempt by the ICTY to prosecute all groups – Serbs, Croatians, Bosniaks, and Kosovars – even-handedly, irrespective of the scale of the crimes committed [and the result is] an attempt to rewrite history and to negate the true measure of responsibility for the horrors of the Balkan wars.[129]

In the course of the controversial 113-day trial which began in March 2007, the prosecution presented 81 witnesses and 1,044 prosecution exhibits, against the defence with 145 exhibits and no witnesses. Detailed comments concerning witness intimidation made by Del Ponte in her opening statement were objected to by Defence Counsel, Guy-Smith, as being both prejudicial and well outside the purpose of the opening statement, and received a caution from the presiding judge, Alphons Orie.[130] In his summing up, Judge Orie commented that 'the Trial Chamber gained a strong impression that the trial was being held in an atmosphere where witnesses felt unsafe'.[131]

Allegations of witness intimidation by the prosecution proved a major issue during the trial. There was no proof that it had taken place, but it cast a long shadow over both the Limaj and Haradinaj trials. Del Ponte complained about UNMIK's handling of witness protection issues, arguing in her memoir that Kosovo was an extremely difficult place for testifying witnesses.[132] Yet, significantly, she admitted that 'the prosecution did not possess information that witnesses had been intimidated, much less intimidated by Haradinaj, something that it is extremely difficult to show'.[133]

On the other hand, the degree of intimidation evident in other trials has been less emphasized. In the Milosevic trial, for instance, K–12, a truck driver in the transport of bodies from Kosovo to Serbia, refused to give evidence against Milosevic on the grounds that he would leak his identity. Others claiming death threats and similar included Dragan Karleusa and Serbian police officer, Zoran Stijovic, as Milosevic's power reached well beyond his cell. Prosecution witnesses were also up against the FRY government, which refused to waive prosecution in cases where 'state secrets' were deemed to have been revealed. And if they finally came to court, they faced intimidating questioning from Milosevic, backed by threatening calls to their families.[134] There was also alleged intimidation in the Stanisic and Simatovic trial, where a potential witness for the prosecution told the investigator that they were the most powerful persons in the country and annoying them could have dangerous consequences for him.[135] Undoubtedly, though, the most blatant intimidation of witnesses occurred, mostly with impunity, in the trial of Vojislav Šešelj.

The prosecution's overall presentation also came in for considerable criticism by the judges:

> The Trial Chamber has heard evidence on a relatively small number of incidents. Moreover, the evidence is often insufficiently precise to conclude who

> was or were responsible for the incidents and whether they formed part of a larger attack against a civilian population. The evidence that has been presented with regard to the allegation in the Indictment that the KLA abducted 60 civilians, and subsequently killed many of them, is not nearly sufficient to establish that this number of civilians were abducted, that many of them were killed, and that the KLA bear responsibility for the alleged acts. . . . The Trial Chamber can therefore not draw any general conclusion with regard to the alleged attack against a civilian population from the mere fact that many Serbian civilians left their homes during this period.[136]

Faced with a collapsing trial, the Trial Chamber, on 3 April 2008, acquitted Haradinaj on all counts of being involved in unlawful conduct while he was a commander in the Kosovo Liberation Army.[137] Although finding a large number of crimes had been committed by KLA soldiers, the judges ruled that there was insufficient evidence to establish the existence of a JCE and acquitted Haradinaj, Balaj and Brahimaj of any criminal liability through such an enterprise. Brahimaj was found individually guilty of cruel and inhumane treatment of civilians at the Jablanica camp and sentenced to six years' imprisonment. Haradinaj's acquittal provoked angry reaction in Belgrade, with many Serbian politicians pressing for appeal.[138]

*

On 19 July 2010, the Appeals Chamber, with Judge Robinson partially dissenting, quashed the Trial Chamber's decision to acquit Haradinaj and Balaj, and ordered a partial retrial relating to alleged crimes at the KLA compound at Jablanice, noting that the Trial Chamber 'had failed to take sufficient steps to facilitate the Prosecution's requests to secure the testimony of the two witnesses'. The Appeals Chamber decision came after the prosecution convinced the judges that Shefket Kabashi and 'Witness X' had been intimidated during the original trial. Unusually, the Chamber also allowed the prosecution new witnesses to testify, and to permit allegations to remain in the indictment that had no bearing on the six counts.

The Appeal turned on the reasonableness of the Trial Chamber's exercise of its discretionary powers. In dissenting, Judge Robinson referred to the Majority as creating 'a dangerous precedent which militates against the proper discharge by the Tribunal of its mandate to try persons for serious breaches of international humanitarian law'. The Appeals Chamber, according to Judge Robinson, practically substituted its own discretion for the discretion of the Trial Chamber in concluding that the Trial Chamber had erred in failing to take sufficient steps 'to counter the witness intimidation that permeated the trial'. The Trial Chamber had allowed three time extensions in order to facilitate the testimony of important witnesses. Robinson argued that, since the issues on appeal related to trial management, the Trial Chamber should have been accorded 'a reasonable measure of deference' based on the recognition by the Appeals Chamber of 'the Trial Chamber's organic familiarity with the day-to-day conduct of the parties and practical demands of the case', a standard not applied by the Majority. According to Judge Robinson,

> The findings of the Majority in respect of ground 1 of the Prosecution's Appeal bring into question the limits of the trial and appellate functions. When the Appeals Chamber gets it wrong, as I, respectfully, submit it has in this case, the relationship between the two functions, the proper discharge by the Tribunal of its mandate to try persons for serious breaches of international humanitarian law, is gravely compromised.[139]

Robinson cited, amongst others, a decision in the Milosevic case which found that '[p]rovided that the Trial Chamber has properly exercised its discretion, its discretion will not be disturbed on appeal, even though the Appeals Chamber itself may have exercised the discretion differently. That is fundamental to any discretionary decision'.[140] Robinson questioned how many opportunities a Trial Chamber should give a party to produce a witness. His main criticism, however, was that the Appeals Chamber conclusion lent to fair trial rights a hierarchical structure not supported by the Statute, Article 21(4), which placed the securing of a witness's testimony above the rights of the accused to an expeditious trial.

*

The first retrial in the history of the tribunal began on 18 August 2011, with evidence from 56 witnesses, including the two in respect of whom it was ordered. The new prosecutor, Paul Rogers, asserted that the KLA was a legitimate force when it fought for Kosovo's independence from Serbia in 1998 and 1999, but that it had used illegal means against its Serbian, Roma and Albanian opponents. In support of this, he called Shefqet Kabashi, allegedly a former prison guard in the Jablanica camp, to the stand. But Kabashi, whose testimony was said to be crucial, repeatedly refused to testify, as he had done twice during the original trial, and contradicted his previous statements to ICTY investigators. Pleading guilty to contempt of court, he was sentenced on 16 September 2011 to two months in jail.

Allegations that Shefqet Kabashi and a protected witness had been intimidated were never confirmed. Kabashi not only repeatedly refused to answer the prosecutor's questions but also cast doubt on the truth of his previous statements to the investigators. Those statements, he suggested, were elicited by the investigators 'who draw your blood slowly [through a] straw'.[141] In a further blow to the prosecution's case against Haradinaj, Witness X, whose testimony was also supposed to be the justification for the partial retrial, failed to show up in court in February 2012. This resulted in the temporary suspension of proceedings.

Ben Emmerson, representing Haradinaj, in his opening statement described the case as 'limpingly and appallingly put together'. Emmerson alleged that both the original case and the retrial were based 'primarily' on an investigation conducted by Serbian intelligence officials, known to engage in the 'basest methods of evidence manipulation'. Emmerson also pointed out that Carla Del Ponte had been advised that there was 'no sustainable case' against Haradinaj at the start, but went ahead with it anyway.[142]

Some of the witnesses unwittingly assisted the defence case. A former head of the Serbian State Security Service, Zoran Stijovic testified under cross-examination how informers from the KLA were recruited, being 'given a choice' to cooperate or risk criminal prosecution or disclosure of details from their private life. Stijovic testified that the police had obtained information that the Kosovo Liberation Army had lists of Albanians collaborating with the Serbian authorities who were slated for execution. Stijovic alleged that the Albanian 'collaborators' were killed, and Serbian police officers and civilians were attacked by the KLA members from Jablanice. Under cross-examination, it emerged that the information collected was not reliable as the police had collected it illegally through coercion. Presiding judge Bakone Moloto observed that Stijovic's explanation was too long and asked him to describe the police approach in one word. 'Blackmail. I cannot think of any other word', the witness replied.[143]

Prosecution witness, former chief of the KLA Main Staff Bislim Zyrapi, had testified that, in the summer of 1998, Ramush Haradinaj was the commander of the Dukagjin Operational Zone, which included the KLA camp in Jablanica. The prosecution alleged that many crimes were committed there against Albanian, Serb and Roma prisoners. Zyrapi stated that his first visit, in the presence of Haradinaj, occurred in mid-July and the second in late August or early September. On cross-examination, however, he conceded that he had not gone into the camp itself, but only visited the units deployed around it. Zyrapi confirmed that the situation during his second visit was similar. He had not visited the camp and was not told by anyone that there was a prison there.[144] He also agreed with defence counsel Emmerson that the KLA was an embryonic army without a strict chain of command. This was confirmed by prosecution witness and former KLA commander Skender Rexhahmetaj in cross-examination.[145]

Another prosecution witness, Witness 75, testifying under anonymity, had his testimony interrupted when it was alleged by defence counsel that he had agreed to testify in The Hague as a prosecution witness in order to improve his chances in the procedure of obtaining asylum or refugee documents in a foreign country. Two documents were disclosed that day, including an email between the witness's lawyer and an OTP investigator, indicating, according to the defence counsel, 'Prosecutor Rodgers deliberately and knowingly intervened to assist the witness in his asylum application'. The defence teams demanded that Rogers be sanctioned and called for the trial to be adjourned, pending on the disclosure of the remaining material about the asylum proceedings. Presiding Judge Moloto agreed to the second request, and the trial continued later in closed session.[146]

Emmerson voiced concern that some prosecution witnesses came to The Hague later than previously scheduled. The testimony for Witness 81 was postponed without any explanation from the prosecution. 'In the interest of justice and the rights of the accused', the defence argued that the prosecution should rest its case by the end of 2011. Emmerson noted that Witness 81 had changed the statements he gave to the prosecution several times 'under the influence of the officials in the country of his residence'.[147]

Many doubted the wisdom of calling for a retrial. The decision was unprecedented in ICTY history, and raised the question of *ne bis in idem*, or double jeopardy. According to Robert Churcher, a post-conflict specialist who testified at the ICTY trial for KLA Commander Fatmir Limaj: 'Serbian officials have been spoon feeding the Prosecution with spurious evidence from the beginning. . . . As a sop to Belgrade, the Prosecution is attempting to retry the Haradinaj case from scratch'.[148] Churcher claimed that, to some extent, the ICTY was a willing accomplice because of Serbia's successful propaganda campaign against the KLA after the war ended.

> To satisfy a need to be seen as ethnically balanced, the ICTY has ended up casting all parties in the Balkan wars as equally responsible, even though Serbia started all of the wars and Milosevic's military and paramilitary forces were responsible for 90 percent of the atrocities that were committed. To be sure, sporadic, terrible incidents occurred on the Kosovar side, but nothing amounting to moral equivalence between the KLA and Serbia.[149]

Roland Gjoni held a similar view, alleging that the Appeals Chamber's recent rulings about the Haradinaj case had heightened concerns that the ICTY might be bending fundamental legal principles in favour of prosecution.

> The Chamber's decision appears to represent a departure from the fundamental principles of international criminal law, the incarceration and retrial of the three accused merits closer scrutiny and analysis. The decision undermines two key principles of criminal law mentioned above – *ne bis in idem* and *res judicata*. It also does not reflect the principle of finality in criminal proceedings. *Ne bis in idem* was previously interpreted by the ICTY in its decisions for Dusko Tadić (1993) and Naser Oric (2009) to bar the prosecution from putting an accused at risk of being retried for a crime for which he had been acquitted.[150]

Gjoni alleged that by allowing allegations unrelated to six crimes to remain in the indictment, the Appeals Chamber is giving the prosecution, at least theoretically, much greater scope to assert that Haradinaj and his co-defendants were responsible for crimes not only in Jablanica but also throughout the Dukagjini Operational Zone and to call new witnesses who would testify about crimes for which the accused had already been acquitted, and with statements which had not been disclosed to the defence.[151]

The acquittals of Fatmir Limaj or Ramush Haradinaj were not the only failed attempts on the part of the ICTY chief prosecutor to hold senior Kosovo Albanian figures responsible for war crimes. In 2002, the Prosecution Office continued to find difficulty in amassing enough evidence for indictments against Kosovo

Albanians. In her memoir published in 2008, Del Ponte recounted a visit by the tribunal, together with UNMIK investigators, to Albania to visit a 'yellow house' identified as the place where captives had been killed for their organs. Investigators found pieces of gauze, a used syringe, two empty plastic drip bags and spent medicine vials, but no evidence of any linkage with the Kosovo higher authorities.[152] Two years later, based on Del Ponte's claims, Rapporteur Dick Marty wrote a controversial report to the Council of Europe, alleging the existence of a large-scale enterprise involving crimes, including kidnapping, torture and organ harvesting committed by KLA members during and after the conflict, but neither Marty nor a subsequent investigation by the EU Special Investigative Task Force found evidence to proceed.[153]

On 29 July 2014, a report by the EU Special Investigative Task Force declared that senior officials of the former KLA would face indictments for crimes against humanity in 1999 but that there was still insufficient evidence for organ-trafficking indictments.

Conclusion

The Kosovo war was in some ways pivotal to the reputation of the ICTY. The negotiations in Rambouillet and Paris eventually convinced international leaders that Milosevic was no longer a viable bargaining partner. His political survival was firmly rooted in the destiny of Kosovo and negotiations, such as in Dayton for Bosnia's future, were not an option for the Serbian leader. It was this new intransigence which finally led to the NATO invasion, and to Milosevic's later indictment at The Hague, the first time an acting head of state had been indicted in an international court. A combination of Serbian Prime Minister Zoran Djindjic's need for economic investment and Western (primarily US) imposition of conditionality persuaded Djindjic to surrender Milosevic to The Hague. It also resulted over succeeding years in the arrest of political and military leaders from Serbia proper, and their eventual conviction.

The decision to use NATO in the first full-scale operation in Europe followed months of negotiations, conferences and broken agreements, and was not taken lightly by the North Atlantic member states. The massacre at Racak in January 1999 focused international attention on the need for a firm resolution, yet it was not the first massacre by Serbian forces against the majority Kosovo Albanian civilian population, but simply the culmination of years of segregation and other human rights abuse, flouting international law, to which international players largely turned a blind eye.

Yet international appeasement of the Belgrade authorities did not end with Milosevic's indictment and transference to The Hague. The new Serbian leader, Vojislav Kostunica, was wooed, especially by European heads and UN leaders, in an effort to secure stability in the largest and most powerful Balkan state, to the point of attempting to establish a measure of symmetry of guilt before the ICTY. The chief prosecutor, Carla Del Ponte, initially railed against this, challenging NATO leaders to act to arrest indictees, but eventually succumbed, both because the tribunal had limited powers and in order to persuade the Serbian leaders to arrest indictees who continued to be sheltered by the Serbian state. To an extent this worked, but at a cost, including the indictment of the Kosovo prime minster, Ramush Haradinaj, on charges which the ICTY prosecutors were unable to sustain. In his short time in power, Haradinaj had proved a conciliator who reached out to incorporate the Serbian communities into the new Kosovo structures, an initiative which was welcomed neither in Belgrade nor in sectors of the international community, which resisted any move which might strengthen Kosovo and lead to its future independence.

The trial and retrial of Haradinaj led to decisions reached by the ICTY being received with increasing scepticism in Kosovo, as Kosovo Albanians began to see the court as often politically influenced, although the tribunal had been widely held in high esteem in the years immediately after the Kosovo war. Even the convictions against several of Milosevic's closest allies for their role in the conflict in Kosovo failed to quell the dissatisfaction. The acquittal of the Serbian president, Milan Milutinović, was viewed in Kosovo as incomprehensible, and raises the question of command responsibility which the Trial Chamber failed to address adequately.

The seven years Haradinaj spent excluded from the Kosovo political scene led to internal divisions, which continue at the time of writing, and had an indelible impact on the embryonic state's development, despite its declaration of independence, partly upheld at the ICJ. The lingering suspicion of organ trafficking also cast a dark cloud over Kosovo's future.

Aside from the prioritizing, and the persistent suspicions in Kosovo that trials like Haradinaj's were motivated by outside parties (in this case Serbia), the slow-moving nature of the ICTY's work was another cause for frustration. Many prosecutions had to be abandoned, more often than not after key witnesses had disappeared.[154]

Notes

1 Human Rights Watch Report, October 1998.

2 Between 1982 and 1989, a total of 31 cases of rape, committed or attempted were reported in Kosovo, which also had the lowest murder rate in Yugoslavia. *Prosecutor v Djordjevic*, Judgement, paras. 626–628. See also Eliott Behar, *Tell it to the World: International Justice and the Secret Campaign to Hide Mass Murder in Kosovo*, Dundurn, 2014, p. 87.

3 For a detailed overview of the situation in Kosovo leading up to the 1999 war, see James Pettifer, *Kosova Express: A Journey in Wartime*, Hurst, 2005.

4 Amnesty International, AI Index: EUR 70/32-35/98.

5 Yugoslavia: Human Rights Abuses in Kosovo 1990–1992. Human Rights Watch. www.hrw.org/legacy/reports/1992/yugoslavia/

6 The International Helsinki Federation reported the establishment of a registration centre for volunteers to join the Srpska Dobrovoljacka Garda (Serbian National Guard) and Beli Orlovi (White Eagles) paramilitary groups in Pristina.

7 According to the Conference on Security and Cooperation in Europe (CSCE) the JNA stationed its 52nd corps of approximately 4,000 men in Kosovo. Human Rights Watch, op. cit.

8 It was estimated that 300,000 to 450,000 Albanian children had not attended school for two years. Human Rights Watch, op. cit. See also Helsinki Committee for Human Rights in Serbia, for attempts to establish a Serbian/Albanian dialogue, 'Untying the Kosovo Knot' Files. No.20, www.helsinki.org.rs.
9 Avni Klinaku and 19 other ethnic Albanians were sentenced in May 1997, following an unfair trial based on statements extracted under torture. In July and December 1997, over 30 ethnic Albanians were similarly convicted. Amnesty International, Annual Report, 1998, p. 362.
10 Ibid., p. 364.
11 Ibid., p. 362.
12 Pettifer, p. 90.
13 On events leading up to the Kosovo war, see Sonja Biserko, *Yugoslavia's Implosion: The Fatal Attraction of Serbian Nationalism*, Norwegian Helsinki Committee, 2012.
14 Amnesty International, 'A Human Rights Crisis in Kosovo Province, Document Series A: Violence in Drenica', February–April 1998.
15 'Under Orders', Human Rights Watch Report, 2000.
16 Humanitarian Law: Violations in Kosovo. Human Rights Watch, October 1998, pp. 18–26. See also Humanitarian Law Centre, Spotlight Report, No.26, 'Kosovo: Human Rights in Terms of Armed Conflict', May 1998.
17 Humanitarian Law: Violations in Kosovo. Human Rights Watch, October 1998, p. 65.
18 James Gow, *The Serbian Project and its Adversaries; A Strategy of War Crimes*, Hurst, 2003.
19 James Pettifer, *The Kosova Liberation Army: Underground War to Balkan Insurgency, 1948–2001*, Hurst, 2012, p. 120, and *Prosecutor v Limaj et al.*, Transcripts, 13 January 2005.
20 Robert Gelbard, Press Conference, Pristina, 22 February 1998. US Department of State Archive.
21 Radovan Radinovic, Analyst at Centre for Military/Strategic Research at Economic Institute in Belgrade referred to the KLA as a classic terroristic organization. 'It is not an army but an organization carrying out terrorist activities . . . no system of command'. *Nasa Borba*, 9 April 1998.
22 The following day in the House of Commons, British foreign secretary Robin Cook announced that military intervention was not contemplated. *Hansard*, 10 March 1998, 322.
23 UNSCR 1160 1998, China abstaining.
24 *Humanitarian Law: Violations in Kosovo*, Human Rights Watch (HRW), October 1998, p. 42.
25 Estimates from six different organizations vary. See, for instance, Human Rights Watch report, October 1998, pp. 38–44, Amnesty International, 'A Human Rights Crisis in Kosovo Province, Doc. Series A: Events to June 1998, July 1998, Roy Gutman, *Newsday*, 22 June 1998, Helsinki Committee for Human Rights in Serbia, Belgrade, 18 June 1998, Council for the Defense of Human Rights and Freedoms, "Human Rights Violations in the Curse of June-July 1998" '.
26 HRW, op. cit., October 1998, p. 4.
27 Support for the KLA had been growing in the United States. See Kosovo Spring, International Crisis Group, 20 March 1998. Holbrooke visiting around 24 June, had seen the KLA as mainly defensive, not a terrorist conspiracy. Christopher Hill, US ambassador to Macedonia, joined Milosevic's call to Kosovars for talks.
28 Robert Gelbard, *Kosovo: Current Situation and Future Options, Hearing Before the Committee on International Relations*, House of Representatives, 23 July 1998 http://commdocs.house.gov/committees/intlrel/hfa50674.000/hfa50674_0f.htm
29 The KLA was heavily defeated in the attempt to take over the town, suffering serious reverses. The inhabitants were subjected to 'three days of terror, with many homes burnt to the ground' by Serbian forces [p. 138].

30 HRW, October 1998, op. cit.
31 ICRC Position on the Crisis in Kosovo. International Committee of the Red Cross, September 1998.
32 Witness Statement, John Crosland, *Prosecutor v Fatmir Limaj*, 5 December 2000.
33 Three days later, a Serbian police checkpoint at Slatina, as on numerous previous occasions, turned back an 8-truck UNHCR convoy carrying supplies to over 30,000 families AFP, 27 August 1998.
34 BBC News, Massacre in Kosovo, 30 September 1998.
35 *BBC News*, 1 October 1998.
36 'Kosovo's Long Hot Summer', ICG, Report No.41, 2 September 1998. The UN estimated the VJ had 29,000 army troops in Kosovo, and 14,000 after KVM deployment. See also Violations in Kosovo. Human Rights Watch, October 1998, p. 61.
37 UNSCR 1199. See also Judith Armatta, *Twilight of Impunity: The War Crimes Trial of Slobodan Milosevic*, Duke University Press, 2010, p. 51.
38 Pettifer, ibid., pp. 159–161.
39 Ibid., p. 45. See also House of Commons Foreign Affairs Committee, 4th Report, 7 June 2000, 51.
40 UNSCR 1203, 24 October 1998.
41 See Pettifer, op. cit, for British relations with Serbia at this time.
42 The British were the most influential Western nation in Belgrade under Milosevic and wished to protect that traditional 'special relationship', which pinnacled between 1993–1996 when Ivor Roberts was ambassador. The British Defence Intelligence Service (with old Yugoslav assumptions) clashed with the US Defence Intelligence Agency, which had been centrally involved in Bosnia NATO air strikes in September 1995. See Hodge, op. cit. Chapter 9.
43 ICTY Annual Report, 1999.
44 International Crisis Group Report, 'Bite the Bullet', 22 January 1999.
45 Amnesty International, EUR 70/005/1999, 18 January 1999, Human Rights Watch, Government War Crimes in Racak, January 1999. Racak had been attacked twice in 1998 by Serbian forces. It was essential to control the village, and roads through it, to protect KLA communications channels. Armatta, op. cit., p. 59.
46 Biserko, op. cit., pp. 238–239.
47 Pettifer, The Kosova Liberation Army, op. cit., p. 199.
48 Behar, p. 125.
49 Article 2(4) of the UN Charter prohibits 'the threat or use of force against the territorial integrity or political independence of any state, or in any other manner inconsistent with the Purposes of the United Nations'. Chapter VII of the Charter provides two exceptions to Article 2(4). Article 39 permits the Security Council to authorize the use of force to maintain or restore international peace and security, and Article 51 recognizes the 'inherent right of individual or collective self-defence'.
50 Antonio Cassese, 'Ex iniuria ius Oritur: Are We Moving Towards International Legitimation of Forcible Humanitarian Countermeasures in the World Community?' *The European Journal of International Law*, Vol.10, 1999, pp. 23–30.
51 The Kosovo Report, available on http://www/oxfordscholarship.com/oso/public/content/politicalscience/0199243093/toc.html
52 UNSCR 1199, 23 September 1998, UNSCR 1160, 31 March 1998 and UNSCR 1203, 24 October 1998.
53 Madeleine Albright pointed out that the FRY had flouted the three resolutions imposing mandatory obligations on the FRY. Press conference, on Kosovo, Washington, 25 March 1999.
54 Paul Williams and Michael Scharf, 'NATO Intervention on Trial: The Legal Case That Was Never Made', *Human Right Review*, Vol.103, 2000. Parties to the Genocide Convention have an obligation to intervene to prevent genocide, which has attained the level of a preemptory norm of international law (*jus cogens*) superseding other

treaty rights and obligations. See also Antonio Cassese, *Self-Determination of Peoples: A Legal Reappraisal*, Cambridge University Press, 1995, p. 515.

55 For further analysis of the legality of the NATO intervention, see 'The Kosovo Conflict and International Law: An Analytical Documentation 1974–1999', ed. Heike Krieger.

56 Milosevic died before his trial ended, Stoljkovic committed suicide, and Milutinovic was acquitted. Fatmir Limaj and Isak Musliu were acquitted in 2005, and again on appeal in 2007. Ramush Haradinaj and Idris Balaj were acquitted by the Trial Chamber in 2008, and again on retrial in 2012. Lahi Brahimaj was sentenced to six years in 2008 and acquitted on retrial in 2012. Haradin Bala was sentenced to 13 years and affirmed on appeal.

57 On 20 October, the tribunal lifted the seal on the four generals' indictments. On 31 October, US career prosecutor Pierre-Richard Prosper visited The Hague, informing Del Ponte that it was 'inappropriate' to lift the seal. 'You know you had an open door in Washington. Now you will have to knock'. Carla Del Ponte and Chuck Sudetic, *Madam Prosecutor: Confrontations With Humanity's Worst Criminals and the Culture of Impunity – A Memoir*, Other Press, 2011, p. 216.

58 For Kostunica's role in the lead-up to the Kosovo war, see Biserko, op. cit., pp. 236–239.

59 Del Ponte, op. cit., p. 100.

60 Ibid., pp. 111–112, 148.

61 Ibid. In fact, one of the first acts of the new Bush administration was to withdraw the signature of his predecessor on the Rome Statute, rescinding US commitment to the International Criminal Court.

62 For details of the Batajnica operation, see *Prosecutor v Vlastimir Djordjevic,* Judgement, 23 February 2011.

63 Del Ponte, op. cit., p. 105.

64 Ibid., p. 91.

65 Ibid., pp. 148–149.

66 Ibid., p. 175. Vlajko Stojiljkovic, the former interior minister linked by documentary evidence as the key leader in transportation of corpses to mass graves in Serbia, committed suicide on the day the Serbian parliament approved a law on cooperation with the tribunal.

67 Ibid., p. 214.

68 Ibid., p. 164. See Chapter 9.

69 Ibid., p. 173.

70 For analysis of the acquittals, see SENSE www.sense-agency.com/icty/why-have-limaj-and-musliu-been-acquitted.29.html?news_id=9407

71 Del Ponte, p. 195.

72 Trial International, 23 April 2016, See Chapter 11 for discussion of ICTY sentencing and indictments, and Chapter 10 for the Serbian courts.

73 For analysis of the annulment see, www.balkaninsight.com/en/article/kosovo-massacres-trial-understanding-the-acquittal, 14 May 2015. Apart from the issue of the will of witnesses to testify again, the evidence against Miladinovic, if found guilty, would connect the Yugoslav Army directly with the crime, and implicate other Serbian officers, including Miladinovic's superior, Major-General Dragan Zivanovic.

74 Diane Orentlicher, *Shrinking the Space for Denial, The Impact of the ICTY in Serbia*, Open Society Justice Initiative, May 2008, p. 6.

75 *Prosecutor v Šainović et al.*, Judgement, 26 February 2009.

76 Ibid., Vol.4, paras. 99–103.

77 Ibid., Vol.I, para. 262. Markovic was also a leading witness for the defence in the Milosevic trial. *Milosevic*, transcripts, 13–19 January 2005, p. 35021.

78 At the beginning of the cross-examination in *Prosecutor v Milosevic*, Prosecutor Geoffrey Nice, QC, quoted a text written by the witness at the time of the so-called anti-bureaucratic revolution and the campaign to amend the Serbian constitution, in which Markovic advocated that 'all attributes of statehood be stripped' off the provinces and

that any 'direct links of the provinces and the federation' be discontinued. As Milosevic's defence witness, Markovic stated that he had participated in drafting the constitutions of 'four states'. He named three of them (Serbia, Montenegro and FRY) and stated that he could not reveal the name of the fourth one as it was a 'professional secret'. Reminding him that the day before the witness had categorically stated that he 'had not taken part in the drafting of the constitutions of Republika Srpska and of the Republic of Serbian Krajina', the prosecutor accused the witness of a 'deliberate attempt to mislead this court' and went on to Markovic's participation in the Serb-Croat working group, established after the Karadjordjevo meeting between Milosevic and Tudjman in March 1991. The prosecutor's argument, corroborated by several prosecution witnesses, including Stipe Mesic and Ante Markovic, was that the working group was drafting maps for the division of Bosnia Herzegovina, as agreed in principle in Karadjordjevo. 'Prosecutor challenges Professor Markovic's credibility', SENSE, 20 January 2005.

79 *Šainović et al.*, Judgement, Vol.I., para. 263. This was a moot point, however, since Article 83(5) was never amended to bring the Serbian Constitution in line with the FRY Constitution. Ibid., p. 265.

80 Ibid., para. 269. Despite the Trial Chamber's qualified reliance on Markovic's testimony, it contained elements of semantic disingenuity, such as Markovic's assertion (to exonerate Milutinovic) that Serbia did not have its own army. Ibid., para. 265. For fuller Trial Chamber conclusions on Markovic's testimony, see paras. 260–286.

81 *Šainović et al.*, Judgement, 26 February 2009.

82 See Chapter 4 for anti-Milosevic demonstrations.

83 'The official position of any accused person, whether as Head of State or Government or as a responsible Government official, shall not relieve such person of criminal responsibility nor mitigate punishment'. ICTY Statute, Article 7 (2).

84 *Šainović et al.*, Judgement, Vol.III., para. 106.

85 Ibid.

86 Ibid., p. 126. Article 136 of the FRY Constitution states, 'The President of the Republic shall appoint, promote and dismiss from service officers of the Army of Yugoslavia stipulated by federal law; shall appoint and dismiss the president, judges and judge assessors of military tribunals and military prosecutors'.

87 *Šainović et al.*, Judgement, Vol.III., para. 144.

88 Ibid.

89 Ibid., p. 147.

90 Ibid., p. 160.

91 For Milutinovic's power to issue decrees, *s*ee paras. 161–173.

92 Ibid., p. 167.

93 Branislav Simonovic, T.25638-9, 17 April 2008.

94 *Šainović et al.*, Judgement, Vol.III, ibid., p. 169.

95 Ibid., p. 162. In the Milosevic trial, the prosecutor showed a video recording of Vojislav Šešelj saying in March 1998 that 'there will be many casualties among Serbs if NATO launches an aggression, but there will be no Albanians in Kosovo'. Markovic confirmed that he had participated in the appointment of Šešelj as a full professor at the Law School and that he considered him to be an 'excellent lecturer and professor'. SENSE, 20 January 2005.

96 Ibid., p. 162.

97 Ibid., p. 172.

98 Ibid., p. 173. There was some discrepancy over the signing of the decrees, which was not clarified at the trial. The decrees had a signature date of 31 March or 1 April and were later signed by Milutinovic, implying that the signature came before the recommendation. In any case, the mass expulsion of the Albanian population began with the start of the NATO campaign, on 24 March.

99 Ibid., p. 195.

100 Ibid., p. 200.
101 Ibid., p. 196. According to Knut Vollebaek, the OSCE chairman-in-office in 1999, Milutinović would generally be very supportive of Milošević in the meetings. Ibid., p. 199.
102 Armatta, op. cit., p. 66.
103 *Šainović et al.*, Judgement, Vol.III, ibid., p. 202.
104 Wolfgang Petritsch testified that, during the Rambouillet and Paris talks, Milutinović was the fiercest critic of the negotiation process, someone who was very negative and very cynical during the negotiations, *Prosecutor v. Milošević*, T.2793.
105 See SENSE, 9 January 2005.
106 *Šainović et al.*, Ratko Marković, T.13225-6 (9 August 2007).
107 Ibid. T.13229-13230.
108 Ibid. Judgement, Vol.III. See paras. 191–203 for Milutinovic's meetings with internationals.
109 *Šainović et al.*, 1 March 2007, T.10747.
110 Ibid., 28 February 2007, T.10727. Petritsch repeated several times that the Yugoslav side refused to sign the Rambouillet document, although it was just a draft of the agreement that was subject to further negotiations and changes. He saw Milutinovic as 'a less flexible negotiator' who, at one meeting, warned that there 'would be a massacre in Kosovo' if NATO were to intervene. SENSE, 28 February 2007.
111 Wolfgang Petritsch, P2792 (witness statement dated 9 June 1999), p. 5, and Knut Vollebaek, T.9509 (31 January 2007), P2634 (witness statement dated 8 January), paras. 23 and 39.
112 *The Times,* 16 February 1999. A 28,000-strong NATO peace implementation force was a key element of the peace deal.
113 *Guardian,* 23 and 26 February 1999, *Sunday Telegraph,* 28 February 1999, and *Sunday Herald*, 14 March 1999. For a report on the main obstacles to agreement, and continued attacks in Stimje, Podujevo and Mitrovica, see *Le Monde,* 25 February 1999.
114 *Independent,* 20 March 1999.
115 *Guardian,* 20 March 1999, and *The Sunday Herald,* 21 March 1999.
116 *Times,* 22 March 1999.
117 *The Times,* 22 March 1999, and *Guardian,* 22 March 1999.
118 *Šainović et al.*, Judgement, Vol.III, Judgement, para. 190.
119 Ibid., para. 213.
120 Ramush Haradinaj, op-ed, *The Wall Street Journal Europe*, 1 December 2004.
121 Vladan Batic, Serbia's justice minister, had provided numerous documents for investigating the KLA but they had turned out to be unhelpful. Del Ponte, op. cit., p. 313.
122 For Jessen-Petersen's comments on Haradinaj's indictment, see Michael O'Reilly, *The Kosovo Indictment: How Politics Subverted Justice in the War Crimes Prosecution of Prime Minister Ramush Haradinaj*, European University of Tirana Press, 2015. O'Reilly worked with Haradinaj's defence team at the tribunal.
123 O'Reilly, ibid.
124 Ibid., pp. 80–81.
125 I make no apology; this will not be an easy prosecution. It is a prosecution, frankly, that some did not want to see brought and that few supported by their cooperation at both international and local level. Carla del Ponte, Opening Statement, *Prosecutor v Ramush Haradinaj, Idriz Balaj & Lahi Brahimaj,* 5 March 2007, p. 359.
126 *Observer*, 2 December 2012, cited in O'Reilly, p. 109.
127 *Jutarnji List*, 12 April 2007. See also Geoffrey Nice, 'Justice for All and How to Achieve it. Citizens, lawyers and the Law in the Age of Human Rights', *Scala,* 2017, p. 306.
128 O'Reilly, op. cit., pp. 109–110.
129 www.aacl.us/Cloyes_DioGuardi_Haradinaj_ENG.htm. Niccolo Figa-Salamanca is secretary general of the NGO, No Peace without Justice.

130 *Haradinaj*, op. cit., pp. 358–361.
131 Ibid., Judgment, para. 6.
132 Del Ponte, pp. 300–301.
133 Ibid., p. 297.
134 Armatta, op. cit., pp. 106–107.
135 Del Ponte, p. 310.
136 *Haradinaj,* Judgment, paras. 118 and 120.
137 O'Reilly points out that the closing comments of Judge Orie and his colleagues 'avoided any criticism of a thoroughly undermined prosecution case . . . and never alluded to the fact that Serb "civilian" witnesses turned out to be combatants or in the pay of the Serbian state or that evidence provided by Begrade was taken under torture, or was the outcome of blackmail'. O'Reilly, op. cit., pp. 172–173.
138 See O'Reilly, pp. 174–175 for Serbian reactions to the judgement.
139 *Prosecutor v Ramush Haradinaj, Idriz Balaj & Lahi Brahimaj* Appeals Chamber Judgment, 19 July 2010, Partially Dissenting Opinion of Judge Patrick Robinson, VI, pp. 116–119.
140 *Prosecutor v Slobodan Milosevic*, Decision of 18 April 2002, para. 4.
141 *International Justice Tribune*, 31 August 2011.
142 *Institute of War and Peace Reporting,* 19 August 2011.
143 'Blackmail Used to Obtain Intelligence on KLA'. SENSE, 28 August 2011.
144 SENSE, 26 August 2011.
145 Ibid., 1 September 2011.
146 Ibid.
147 Will the Retrial be Repeated, SENSE, 3 November 2011.
148 Robert Churcher, 'Justice Delayed is Justice Denied', Op. Ed. *Eurasia Review*, 27 May 2012.
149 Churcher, ibid.
150 Roland Gjoni, *ICTY, Favouring Prosecution over Justice*, Open Democracy, 9 August 2011.
151 Ibid. Ramush Haradinaj's Retrial: Is the ICTY Favouring the Prosecution at the Expense of Justice?
152 Del Ponte, op. cit., pp. 284–285.
153 www.assembly.coe.int/CommitteeDocs/2010/ajdoc462010prov.pdf In May 2010, EULEX chief war crimes investigator Matti Raatikainen said, 'The fact is that there is no evidence whatsoever in this case. No bodies. No witnesses. All the reports and media attention to this issue have not been helpful to us. In fact they have not been helpful to anyone'. According to BBC News, Raatikainen said that 'the main problem' was that 'the scandal created by the allegations has distracted attention from the real work of finding the remains of 1,861 people still missing from the war and its aftermath.'
154 *Deutsche Presse*, 17 August 2011, www.dw-world.de/dw/article/0,15323973,00.html

6 Self-representation

Balancing the rights

I stress that it would be wrong for the Chamber to impose counsel on the accused because that would be in breach of the position under customary international law.[1]

Introduction

Self-representation has proved one of the more challenging questions to face the ICTY and, arguably, the most contentious. Few defendants have chosen to represent themselves in legal history, resulting in an absence of substantial case law on self-representation. In this, as in other areas, the tribunal was forced into creating legal precedent and on-the-hoof, and often costly, decision making which at times permitted abuse of process and afforded defendants the opportunity to place on record an alternative version of the Bosnian war.

As well as the challenges presented to judges, self-representation also exacerbated the difficulties in attempting to fuse common and civil law practice within court procedures, civil law being traditionally relatively inflexible in permitting the exercise of defendants' rights to represent themselves in court. The fact that many senior judges came from common law tradition, and the United States, a common law country, had a major hand in the initial stages of establishing the tribunal and drawing up its statute, meant that common law had the upper hand, and self-representing defendants in practice had virtual free rein in influencing and delaying court proceedings. Their role carried special privileges and responsibilities. They enjoyed enhanced trust in access to files and confidential information, and the right to make binding declarations.[2] They also became elevated to the role of defending counsel, sitting in the main court as opposed to being isolated 'in the dock', even though some were without any legal training. This psychologically boosted their legal standing and morale, and sent misleading messages to both witnesses and outside observers.

In practice, few indictees at the ICTY opted for self-representation and those that did were mostly Serbs who had been in leading political or military positions during the Bosnian war.

Precedent

In drawing up the Statute, tribunal judges followed the human rights norms guaranteed in the ICCPR, both to self-representation and legal assistance.[3] The European Convention on Human Rights (ECHR) states simply that

> Everyone charged with a criminal offence has the following minimum rights . . . to defend himself in person or through level assistance of his own choosing or, if he has not sufficient means to pay for legal assistance, to be given it free when the interests of justice so require.[4]

The European Court on Human Rights (EctHR), however, has not declared self-representation to be a fundamental right.[5] In determining whether the interests of justice justify the appointment of defence counsel to an indigent accused, the seriousness and complexity of the offence are considered, along with the particularity of the proceedings and of the accused. Any of these criteria can, in itself, trigger the right to counsel.[6] In international criminal tribunals, these conditions are mostly met. So, if the spirit of the EctHR practice is respected, counsel must always be assigned to a defendant who has not opted for counsel of his choosing. The ICTY clearly went 'beyond the case-law of the EctHR in accommodating the wish of an accused to defend himself without the assistance of counsel of his own choosing or legal aid counsel', according to Stefan Treschel, a practice he referred to as 'a dangerous experiment'.[7]

In the civil law tradition, defence counsel is usually assigned as a mandatory measure, especially in serious cases. The Criminal Procedure Act of the FRY provides that 'the defendant shall have the right to defend himself in person'.[8] It also states, however, that for offences where the sentence is expected to exceed ten years, the accused must have a defence counsel from the outset, regardless of the accused's legal training and qualifications.[9] The accused is entitled to question witnesses only when authorized by the presiding judge.[10] Similar terms apply in the Criminal Procedure Code for the Federation of Bosnia and Herzegovina.[11] In Germany, defence counsel is also generally assigned as a mandatory measure.[12] The French Code of Criminal Procedure similarly provides that a person accused of a serious crime must be represented by counsel at hearings.[13] In Bulgaria, an accused must be represented in cases where imprisonment is expected to exceed ten years.[14] The Belgian and Danish codes contain similar provisions.

Human rights case law regarding these provisions on mandatory defence counsel is limited and inconsistent. In *Michael and Brian Hill v Spain*, the Human Rights Committee found that the accused had the right to defend himself, even where assistance was required by statute.[15] In *Croissant v Germany*, on the other hand, the EctHR considered the Convention in a broader context and found that Article 140 of the German Code was not incompatible with Article 6(3) of the ECHR.[16] A similar conclusion was reached in *Philis v Greece*.[17]

In contrast to civil law tradition, common law jurisdictions entitle an accused to conduct his own defence regardless of the seriousness of the case. In English case law, the accused is allowed to represent himself, or to dismiss his counsel at any stage in the trial. The American Convention on Human Rights protects 'the right of the accused to defend himself personally or to be assisted by legal counsel of his own choosing'.[18] And the UN Body of Principles for the Protection of All Persons Under Any Form of Detention or Imprisonment states, '[A] detained person shall have the right to defend himself or to be assisted by counsel as prescribed by law' (Principle 11). At least 33 national constitutions recognize the right to self-representation and more than 65 contain language implying this right.[19]

In the United States, the case of *Moussaoui* exemplifies the difficulties caused by self-representation in US courts.[20] In *Faretta v California*, the Supreme Court held that forcing a lawyer on an accused who is competent to conduct his own defence is a breach of the accuser's constitutional right to conduct his own defence.[21] The only exception where self-representation could be terminated was in the case of deliberate 'serious obstructionist misconduct'. In *McCaskey v Wiggins*,[22] the standby counsel notion was developed to ensure that the *pro se* defendant maintained actual control of his case and, secondly, that the standby counsel's actions should preserve the jury's perception that the accused is conducting his own defence. Defendants cannot object to the appointment of standby counsel, but case law is not clear on how active a standby counsel may be. There is a fine line between an active standby counsel and 'hybrid representation' where a defendant represents himself but is also represented by counsel, the two effectively becoming co-counsel, but it can cause problems, as it goes against the typical lawyer-client relationship.[23] *Faretta* still represents the law at the trial level, however. The right to self-representation in the United States does not apply in appeal cases. In *Martinez v Court of Appeal of California*, the Supreme Court observed that 'even at the trial level . . . the government's interest in ensuring the integrity and efficiency of the trial at times outweighs the defendant's interest in acting as his own lawyer'.[24]

The former Serbian president was the first defendant to declare his right to self-representation at the ICTY, although it was in the later trial of Vojislav Šešelj that matters came to a head.

Milosevic: the first experiment in self-representation

Slobodan Milosevic, on his arrival at The Hague, would have been regarded in a somewhat different light from, say, Saddam Hussein, hunted down and captured in a bunker following the coalition invasion of Iraq, or Gaddafi and Osama bin Laden, perennial enemies of the West, had they lived to be tried in court. Although often grouped together with these in terms of criminality, Milosevic, unlike other international leaders who end up in the dock, had enjoyed a rather different international reputation.

In bringing major war crimes indictees to book, the ICTY approach was still relatively fresh and untested when Milosevic arrived at The Hague, and mainly concerned to be seen to be conducting a fair trial. The former Serbian leader, on the other hand, was a seasoned politician with years of experience in interacting directly with senior international diplomats and politicians, not merely in negotiating, but ostensibly contributing to the international peace effort in Bosnia, and trusted internationally as representing the Bosnian Serbs at Dayton. At The Hague, bolstered by his legal training, Milosevic interacted easily with court officials. His main motivation in directing war operations had always been the exercise of power, and this he could also do within the adversarial structures in place at the tribunal, in control of his own defence. Sufficiently canny to realize the extent to which he could abuse court proceedings, court officers and witnesses with impunity, he determined to exploit his position to the full, refusing to recognize the legitimacy of the tribunal or to abide by the rules of the Court, while grasping the opportunity to air his political views to the Serbian public, and beyond.[25] In this, Milosevic was aided initially by a judge steeped in the adversarial tradition, and later by an inefficient Appeals Chamber which blocked the Trial Chamber's bid to impose defence counsel.

When Milosevic first appeared in court on 30 August 2001, the Trial Chamber held that he was entitled to defend himself, as he had requested, rejecting the prosecution's suggestion that defence counsel be assigned to him. In doing so, the presiding judge, Richard May, referred to the ICTY Statute and Rules which, he maintained, reflected customary international law.[26] Several months into the trial, the Trial Chamber still considered it 'not normally appropriate in adversarial proceedings' to impose defence counsel. In response to further applications from the prosecution in November 2002 and April 2003, the Trial Chamber reiterated its position, recalling US law, especially the *Faretta* case, and international jurisprudence.[27] In September 2003, the Trial Chamber again rejected the prosecution request to introduce counsel, instead reducing the trial schedule still further, to only three days a week.[28]

Two years into the trial, with over 60 days lost due to Milosevic's health issues, and the start of the defence case postponed five times, the dignity of the proceedings was becoming seriously compromised.[29] Milosevic refused to answer questions,[30] making lengthy, irrelevant speeches during the cross-examination of witnesses, disparaging comments about the tribunal,[31] and bullying witnesses. While professional defence counsel would have been held in contempt of court, Milosevic had no incentive to heed repeated warnings from the Bench. Self-represented defendants, not bound by lawyers' ethical codes, are free to wreak havoc on the system in numerous ways.

Milosevic's health issues resulted in the trial being adjourned on 13 occasions during the prosecution case,[32] and with the defence case about to open on 22 September 2004, a new Trial Chamber following Judge May's death the previous May decided to reassess his ruling.[33] It found that the minimum guarantees set out in Article 21(4) were mere 'elements in the overarching requirements of a fair trial'[34] and, in the interests of a fair and expeditious trial, Milosevic's medical condition called for defence counsel to be imposed to lead in questioning witnesses and making submissions.[35]

In the circumstances, it would have been legitimate to assign counsel against Milosevic's wishes, in line with the case law of the EctHR, but the reason the Trial

Chamber gave – delays due to his poor health – lacked legal precedent. Obstructive behaviour is the main reason for the ICTY to limit self-representation, but the threshold for such behaviour is at the discretion of the trial chamber. In the US *Faretta* case, the Court recognized the right to self-representation was not 'a license not to comply with the relevant rules of procedural and substantive law' and that a trial judge may terminate self-representation by a defendant who deliberately engages in serious and obstructionist misconduct.[36] In Milosevic's case the Trial Chamber, while noting the Faretta case, chose not to apply that test. Instead, it was Milosevic's bad health which caused the Bench to restrict his right to self-representation. Two doctors independently found that 'the most likely explanation for the resistant nature of his hypertension was his failure to adhere to his prescribed treatment regime' After taking blood samples, it was found that the concentrations of Metoprolol, a prescribed medication, from the samples were clearly lower than should be expected with the daily intake prescribed. There was also the presence of an unknown drug not contained in Milosevic's medication list.[37] Crucially, however, the Trial Chamber stressed that its decision was not based on these findings.[38]

On 1 November 2004, the Appeals Chamber ruled against the Trial Chamber, falling just short of finding that it had abused its discretion. It conceded, with Judge Meron presiding, that the right to self-representation was a qualified and not an absolute right.[39] It disagreed, however, with the Trial Chamber's assessment of the Order of Modalities, which 'relegates Milosevic to a visibly second-tier role in the trial' which, it held, was grounded on a fundamental error of law.[40] The Appeals Chamber referred to the UN Human Rights Committee 'proportionality principle' that any restrictions 'must be the least intrusive instrument amongst those which might achieve the desired result; and they must be proportionate to the interest to be protected'.[41] It ruled that, while defence counsel should be imposed, the Trial Chamber should work to minimize the practical impact of this formal assignment and, when Milosevic was physically capable of doing so, he should take the lead in presenting his case. The Appeals Chamber based Milosevic's ability to do so partly on his 'vigorous' two-day opening statement, made without apparent difficulty, ruling that the Trial Chamber's failure to 'impose a carefully calibrated set of restrictions on Milosevic's trial participation' was 'an improper exercise of the trial court's discretion'.[42]

The Appeals Chamber decision had important implications for later trials. Subsequent defendants took their cue from *Milosevic* and the Trial Chamber's handling of his case. The weakness in the Trial Chamber's order was in basing it on Milosevic's poor health rather than, as the Prosecution proposed, a 'premeditated policy of deliberate obstructionism by engaging in disruptive courtroom behaviour as well as by sabotaging his medication regimen to artificially induce periods of poor health' which, the Appeals Chamber conceded, might in principle have justified the imposition of counsel on an unwilling defendant.[43]

Following the Appeals Chamber ruling, the situation did not improve. There were further delays due to Milosevic's poor health, and a minimal courtroom schedule of four hours daily, three days a week was continued, during which

Milosevic continued to provide irrelevant information, interrupted counsel and witnesses, corrected interpreters, and defied the authority of the Court.[44] The proceedings were further complicated by Milosevic's flouting of procedural rules which would have had ordinary defence counsel expelled from the courtroom. He refused to comply with orders or disclose materials, file witness lists or produce experts, and rejected written submissions, and spent much time in political grandstanding.[45] The judges were reluctant to cut him off because allowance was being made for his insufficient grasp of legal relevancy although, ironically, this could in itself have been a reason to impose counsel in the interests of an expedient and fair trial.[46] More seriously, Milosevic blackmailed the Court by encouraging defence witnesses to refuse to appear if he was not allowed to question them himself.[47] Throughout this, the Trial Chamber bent over backwards to maintain the appearance of fairness and continued to reject the prosecution's call for appointed counsel to take over.[48] According to former ICTY judge, Patricia Wald, 'As long as Milosevic remained at the helm in a seemingly endless trial conducted on a "banker's hours" schedule, the court projected a disheartening sense of powerlessness, a coup which doubled Milosevic's own popularity at home'.[49]

Milosevic had little to lose, but there were other measures, apart from imposing counsel, which might have been effective if introduced early on.[50] Karadzic had three legal advisors, three case managers and two investigators at the pre-trial phase, along with a large number of *pro bono* international lawyers to assist him with his defence case. He was also allowed funding for certain facilities. And at Scheveningen, there were many privileges not normally available to remand prisoners in national states which could have been withdrawn.

Opinion Polls in Serbia and Republika Srpska followed patterns similar to those in Germany after the Second World War.[51] Milosevic's popularity doubled during the trial from reviled leader to the fourth most popular person in Serbia behind a rock star, a basketball star and another politician. He ran for parliament, and won a landslide election from the courtroom, knocking on its head the idea that the tribunal would discredit the 'Greater Serb' ideology.[52]

Michael Scharf, a leading critic of the ICTY practice of permitting indictees to represent themselves, considered that allowing Milosevic to defend himself could be argued to have undermined the UN Security Council goal of re-educating the Serbs about crimes committed under Milosevic's regime. 'The judicial proceedings . . . transformed Milosevic from a disgraced politician who had been ousted by a popular revolt into one of the most esteemed public figures in Serb history'.[53]

The Milosevic case illustrated the pitfalls inherent in permitting high-level politicians to defend themselves.[54] Del Ponte believed that the judges' lack of resolve from the outset, with their concerns for a fair trial, created a situation which was unfair to everyone, and set a precedent for other would-be *pro se* indictees.

Krajisnik: 20 years for crimes against humanity

Momčilo Krajisnik, co-founder and leading member of the Serb Democratic Party (SDS), and president of the Bosnian Serb Assembly from 1991 till November 1995, served as a member of the RS National Security Council and, from June to December 1992, was a member of the expanded RS presidency. He was indicted on 25 February 2000 for genocide, war crimes and crimes against humanity, through his participation in a JCE. As Radovan Karadzic's 'right-hand man' throughout the war, he was considered by some to be more extreme in his policies.[55] He was arrested by IFOR on 3 April 2000 and transferred to The Hague.[56]

In late May 2005, weeks before the closure of the prosecution case, Krajisnik wrote to the Registrar under Rule 45(F) of the Rules of Procedure and Evidence, and addressed the Trial Chamber directly, stating that he had decided to conduct his own defence in future, and requesting to be informed of his rights.[57] On 18 August, the Chamber denied the request on the grounds that Krajisnik had not convinced the Court that he had reached this decision unequivocally. He had also sought additional funding to be paid to Pale-based investigators, who turned out to be family members, friends or associates.[58] A second ground for denying Krajisnik's request was the potential disruption to proceedings due to the long adjournment needed for his new team to be operational.[59] The Trial Chamber considered the case would collapse in the hands of Krajisnik who had demonstrated, in his limited questioning of witnesses between May and July 2005, that he did not know how to run a criminal case; he misunderstood procedure, asked improper questions and revealed details of protected witnesses.[60] Exceptionally, however, Krajisnik was allowed to supplement his counsel's cross-examination with his own questions to witnesses, pending the final decision on his request to represent himself.[61] Krajisnik's request followed just months after the Milosevic Appeals Chamber had ruled that Milosevic could continue to defend himself, and Šešelj's subsequent assertion of his right to self-representation.

On 27 September 2006, Krajisnik was acquitted on both genocide counts, but sentenced to 27 years imprisonment on five counts of crimes against humanity, including persecution, extermination, murder, deportation and forced transfer.

In February 2007, Krajisnik again requested to represent himself, the first defendant to seek self-representation on appeal. On 11 May, the Appeals Chamber, Judge Fausto Pocar presiding, granted Krajisnik his request, with Colin Nicholls assigned as *amicus curiae*.[62] On 28 February 2008, US attorney Alan Dershowitz was granted the right to provide legal assistance to Krajisnik on the issue of JCE.[63] In reaching its decision, the Appeals Chamber leant heavily on the *Milosevic* decision of 1 November 2004.[64] Despite the seriousness of the crimes he had been convicted for, and Krajisnik's brief track record of self-representation at the trial stage, the Chamber nonetheless saw 'no case-specific reasons why any right to self-representation possessed by Mr Krajisnik should be curtailed'.[65] It, therefore, focused on possible distinctions between the trial and appeal stages, on which the Statute offered no guidance.[66]

In a separate opinion, Judge Mohamed Shahabuddeen supported the Appeals Chamber decision, citing *Aleksovski* and *Simic* that a fair trial right is encompassed in Article 3(d) of the Geneva Conventions, and may be construed in international customary law.[67] But what constitutes a fair trial? The issue of self-representation caused one Appeals Chamber judge to resign from the bench. Wolfgang Schomburg, a senior ICTY and International Criminal Tribunal for Rwanda (ICTR) appeals judge, in an excoriating analysis of the majority decision, wrote

> If I were tasked to show that international criminal jurisdiction cannot work I would draft the decision in the same way as was done by the majority in the Appeals Chamber.[68]

In his 30-page-long opinion, Judge Schomburg referred to 'a long line of unfortunate decisions by the appellate chamber, such as the decision in *Prosecutor v Milosevic* of 1 November 2004 and most recently the decision in *Prosecutor v Šešelj* of 8 December 2006'. Schomburg claimed that those decisions completely disregarded the fact that, in the interests of fair proceedings, very many countries assign counsel both at trial and on appeal from the time when a serious sentence was expected.[69]

> The Appeals Chamber's jurisprudence is based on a false dichotomy which assumes that the right to defend oneself negates the right to be assisted by counsel.[70]

Referring to the brevity and lack of serious discussion in the Appeals Chamber decision, Schomburg proceeded with a detailed comparative analysis of transnational and national law and jurisprudence, and that of other international criminal tribunals and courts. He concluded that neither under the ECHR nor in the states of the former Yugoslavia did the defendant have the right to defend himself in serious cases. In the ICTR, the Rules of Procedure and Evidence were amended with Rule 45*quater*, for counsel to be assigned in the interests of justice, in appeal as well as trial proceedings.[71] Even in Anglo-Saxon law, the role of the accused changes dramatically once convicted, as the US Supreme Court in the *Martinez* case found that the defendant no longer enjoyed the presumption of innocence, nor was he entitled to special treatment.[72] Schomburg concluded that

> in appellate proceedings it is not only the behaviour of an accused as such that justified a restriction of the right to self-representation but the nature of those proceedings. The different role of an accused at the appellate level allows for a greater restriction of the right to self-representation than may be justified at trial . . . even trained lawyers cannot effortlessly navigate the proceedings on appeal.[73]

He also pointed out that Krajisnik had indeed been obstructive in not making a bona fide attempt to obtain counsel despite requesting it, stalling for several months after the trial judgement, and subsequently indicating that he wished to represent himself with the assistance of a 'legal team'.[74] In this way, Krajisnik, a convicted war criminal, had the best of both worlds – he was in control of his case, with the opportunity to prolong, procrastinate, confuse and otherwise endanger the integrity of the proceedings and buy time – especially through the necessity of massive translations of documents – which he would spend in the relative comfort of Scheveningen, while having his time there credited against his ultimate term in a national prison where he would receive the same treatment as any other convicted criminal. Krajisnik's delaying tactics and obstructionist attitude continued after Judge Schomburg's resignation from the case, despite the efforts of succeeding judges to assist in moving the proceedings forward.[75] Twelve years later, Karadzic would play a similar game at his appeal, with some success.

Self-representing defendants generally had a large team of lawyers, often financed by the tribunal, or working *pro bono* behind the scenes. In Krajisnik's case, his bid to represent himself on appeal was made in order to gain time and more financial resources to secure the appointment of a high-level defence counsel, notably Alan Dershowitz. Krajisnik himself had neither legal training nor a sound command of one of the tribunal's official languages, as well as a lack of understanding of court procedures.[76]

On appeal, Krajisnik again demonstrated his inability to abide by Court rules and regulations in the examination of witnesses.[77] Yet, on 17 March 2009, Krajisnik's sentence was reduced by seven years, his purpose in large part achieved. He had spent nearly nine years in the detention unit and was to spend less than four years in a British prison, being granted early release in September 2013.

Once back in Bosnia, Krajisnik sought a high media profile to argue against his conviction. In 2016, he was allowed to promote his book, with a revisionist account of the Bosnian war at the Belgrade Youth Centre. In an hour-long interview in November 2018, broadcast on youtube, Krajisnik interestingly commented that Republika Srpska was a 'gift from God'. The interview revealed him as an unreconstructed nationalist, in total denial of his role in the bloodshed of the early 1990s.[78]

Tolimir: life imprisonment for genocide

Zdravko Tolimir, a former Bosnian Serb Army general, was indicted, amongst other things, for genocide and extermination allegedly carried out in July 1995 by Serb forces against Bosnian Muslims in Srebrenica and Žepa. He was transferred to The Hague in June 2007 when he insisted on conducting his own defence. He benefited from both the Milosevic and Krajisnik precedents, refusing to accept Court and prosecution material provided to him on the basis that he could not read Serbian (his native language) in the Latin script. His request was dismissed orally on 11 December 2007, as was his subsequent appeal.[79] On 30 June 2008, Tolimir was given a final warning by Judge Prost that his continuing refusal of documents amounted to persistent and obstructive conduct, impinging directly on a fair trial.[80] Tolimir's advisor did not fulfil the qualification requirements of defence counsel and was denied cross-examination of witnesses, although he was allowed in the courtroom.

Tolimir's obstructive behaviour caused costly delays, but it gained him substantial time. Although sentenced to life imprisonment, Tolimir died after nearly nine years at Scheveningen, having never served time in a national prison.

Praljak: 20 years for persecutions, cruel treatment and wilful killing

Slobodan Praljak was on trial for war crimes against Bosnian Muslims in the Bosnian war. The Trial Chamber, in an attempt to straddle and balance the competing fair trial rights – the right to represent himself and the right to a fair trial – permitted Praljak to question witnesses in court on issues where he had personal expertise, while he was still represented by lawyers. Praljak abused the opportunity in asking personal questions.

There were many reasons why it was inappropriate for Praljak to represent himself. As the prosecution pointed out, the length of the trial judgement (2,500 pages), the 6 accused and 26 counts for crimes in 8 municipalities and detention camps over a year and a half made the case immensely complex.[81] In addition, the six accused in this case maintained conflicting positions on civilian versus military authority and responsibility, involving the potential for conflict.[82]

The handling by the Trial Chamber and Appeals Chamber of Praljak's right to represent himself in part was a clear illustration of the more relaxed approach of the tribunal on self-representation vis-à-vis the EctHR.[83]

*

Both Vojislav Šešelj and Radovan Karadzic were to benefit from the precedents of the Milosevic and Krajisnik cases but handled their own defences in different ways. Šešelj's case was specific, in large part due to the composition of the Trial Chamber, and is considered separately.[84]

Radovan Karadzic: 40 years for genocide

The trial of Radovan Karadzic, following Milosevic's death, was to be the trial of trials for the crime of crimes – genocide – which Karadzic was alleged to have committed, both in the Bosnian municipalities in 1992 and in Srebrenica in 1995. With Karadzic virtually running his own trial, he had considerable scope, as with the earlier *pro se* defendants, to present an alternative version of the Bosnian war.[85]

By the time Karadzic arrived at The Hague in July 2008, the trials of Milosevic, Krajisnik and Šešelj had established a comfortable path through the route of self-representation. He had at his disposal all the tools for a successful *pro se* trial which would not have been available to him had he been arrested in 1995 when first indicted for genocide and crimes against humanity. He also benefited from the revisionism and denial which had permeated Bosnian Serb and Serbian politics in the intervening years, along with the shifting of international attention to other areas. Karadzic's 13 years of freedom had served him well in more ways than one. The tribunal, on the other hand, had for seven years – since Milosevic first stood in the dock in 2001 and declared his intention to represent himself – been battling on the legal, political and financial fronts to address all the issues arising from the imprecise terms addressing the right to self-representation in the ICTY Statute and Rules.

So, had it learned any lessons from the experience? It would appear not many, in spite of the addition of a provision to its procedural rules, authorizing the Trial Chamber to assign counsel to represent the accused where firmer control was required.[86] Despite the lack of any legal qualifications or training, his declared purpose of disrupting the tribunal, and having been indicted on multiple counts for the most egregious crimes against humanity, Karadzic was permitted to represent himself, and to cross-examine the victims of those crimes from the defence counsel's position in court, elevating him to the level of the legal defence team, with his personal dignity enhanced.

The status of counsel carries special responsibilities and privileges, including access to the files, to confidential information, the right to make binding declarations such as filing requests, motions and appeals and, by Rule 97, to guarantee this confidentiality. Karadzic would, therefore, have access to all the details concerning protected witnesses, but without the associated confidentiality obligations which would ensure their protection. The ICTY's entrance requirements are relatively lenient.[87] Defence counsel is not required to pass a bar exam before being permitted to practice before the ICTY, as some have advocated. The Rules of Procedure and Evidence (Rules 44–46) list the seven qualifications required for counsel,

1 Be admitted to the practice of law, or be a university professor of law.
2 Be proficient in one of the working languages of the tribunal.
3 Be a member of good standing of an association of counsel practising at the tribunal recognized by the registrar.
4 Not be found guilty or disciplined concerning profession.
5 No criminal convictions.
6 Not have engaged in conduct . . . which is dishonest or otherwise discreditable to a counsel, prejudicial to the administration of justice, or likely to diminish public confidence in the ICTY or the administration of justice, or otherwise bring the ICTY into disrepute.
7 Not have given misleading information about qualifications to act as counsel.[88]

No accused could satisfy all those requirements, and most, including Karadzic, would meet few, if any.[89]

Karadzic's bid for self-representation was buttressed in part by his engagement of a retinue of international lawyers, some working *pro bono*, to guide him through the pre-trial process, but also by a tribunal which had become somewhat jaded, and increasingly removed from the atrocities which had brought Karadzic to The Hague. One of the thorniest issues in *Šešelj*, the eligibility of his legal team, had been circumvented by Karadzic in engaging an international lawyer, Peter Robinson, to assist him, mostly from behind the scenes. Eight defence team members for Karadzic were funded during the pre-trial phase, in addition to standby counsel, with a support staff of its own, which rather begs the question, to what extent a self-representing accused genuinely conducts his own defence.[90]

Karadzic rejected the five lawyers initially provided for choice and requested one from Serbia or Bosnia, which was declined by the registrar, and Richard Harvey was appointed, suggesting a divergence from *Šešelj* where the Appeals Chamber had indicated that defendants have a right to select their own standby counsel.[91] Šešelj's obstructionist behaviour, it seems, was the main reason for his being granted the right to choose standby.

One particularly contentious issue which arose in the pre-trial phase was the funding of Karadzic's legal associates. Karadzic argued that a self-represented accused should receive the same financial support as an accused represented by counsel, minus remuneration for lead counsel, which was initially rejected by the Registrar.[92] The ICTY president did, however, grant most of Karadzic's demands, including a lump sum of 750 remunerable hours a month for funding his defence team,[93] although this did not prevent Karadzic from repeatedly complaining that he had insufficient resources to analyse material disclosed by the prosecution.[94]

The trial date was set for October 2009, Karadzic's request for ten further months to prepare having been rejected, with the Trial Chamber holding that he had failed to use the time appropriately, devoting most of it to his purported agreement with the US negotiator, Richard Holbrooke. The Appeals Chamber upheld the Trial Chamber decision, assessing that many of Karadzic's limitations were linked to his decision to self-represent.[95] 'Completion Strategy' concerns may also have influenced the judges' decision. Arguing he was unprepared, Karadzic refused to appear in court, upon which the Trial Chamber ordered the registrar to appoint standby counsel to take over if Karadzic proved obstructive, with the trial to resume on 1 March 2010.[96]

Apart from the opportunity, as with other *pro se* defendants, to use his trial as a public platform for promoting a revised version of the war, Karadzic used his skills as a psychiatrist to intimidate and patronize some of his witnesses. The first witness, Ahmed Zilic, a former production manager in a mine, who had testified for the prosecution in previous trials, was asked by Karadzic about his children and grandchildren, irrelevant to the trial, but indicating that Karadzic was monitoring the witness's growing family, which may have felt threatening to a less seasoned witness.[97] Karadzic also patronizingly intimated that the witness was on the defensive: 'I'm not attacking you. There's no need to defend yourself'.[98] He made lengthy comments, rather than ask questions and, while ostensibly summarizing, in fact reinterpreted the witness's remarks, practices which were only occasionally censured by the Bench.[99] Karadzic also frequently introduced documents which were not on the list and proceeded to question witnesses on the contents.[100] Prosecutor Alan Tieger summed up the situation:

> The commentary . . . is not a reflection of Mr Karadzic's experience or lack of experience in the courtroom. He knows very well the prohibition and the nature of the commentary, and wilfully persists on doing so . . . it happens far more frequently than anyone is really in a position to explicitly note in the

record or object to. Otherwise, . . . I'd be on my feet all the time and the Court would be making admonitions much more often than it already is.[101]

Witnesses called by the prosecution were mercilessly cross-examined by Karadzic, albeit in a measured and even at times deferential manner, Karadzic having learned from the Šešelj example that not all judges would tolerate the bullying displayed by Šešelj during his trial. This led the Trial Chamber not only to overlook a considerable number of Karadzic's falsehoods, threats and digressions but also to defer to him before some witnesses.

Prosecution witness, Almir Begic, whose father was killed at the Markale market massacre, was forced repeatedly during Karadzic's cross-examination to watch videotapes of his father's prosthetic leg in his attempt to challenge evidence of VRS responsibility for the massacre.[102] Cross-examining prosecution witness Ramiz Mujkic (KDZ041) who had lost 13 relatives in the bus massacre in June 1992, Karadzic launched into lengthy statements without asking a question and introduced documents not translated into English, a practice he adopted with other prosecution witnesses.[103]

On 21 and 22 April 2010, KDZ064, a protected witness who had survived the Srebrenica genocide, was cross-examined by Karadzic for nearly five hours.[104] Fortunately, in view of the ordeal he underwent, it was his sixth time of testifying. When Karadzic attempted to ethnically categorize him, the witness instead retorted that 'whoever attacks the country should be somebody to defend himself from', Judge Kwon twice asked the witness to calm down, advising him, '[P]lease understand the Defence is entitled to ask you questions'.[105] When quizzed about the 1992 Cutileiro ethnic division map which the witness said he did not wish to see, Kwon again instructed him, 'I would like you . . . to just answer the question. That's the best way for you to assist the Chamber'.[106]

When objecting to repeated questioning on his municipality, Zvornik, the witness was this time lectured by Judge Morrison:

> The question that you must address your mind to, Mr. Witness, is this, that we are the ones, the Judges, who need this information. Whether you are interested or not interested is a matter for you, but you've got to understand that we are interested. We need to know these things in order to make a proper determination of the case. So I understand that this is a difficult exercise for you, but please bear in mind that this is information which we need to conduct this case fairly and properly.[107]

The judge's reprimand of the witness was not only wrong since Karadzic's maps *were* irrelevant to the case but also patronizing. Morrison's response indicated an ignorance of why maps produced by Karadzic, proposing the ethnic division of Bosnia, should be upsetting to the witness, as well as irrelevant. The judges also took no account of the fact that during the whole exchange Karadzic had not asked a clear question.[108] They had reprimanded the wrong person.

The third member of the Trial Chamber, Judge Melville Baird, then entered the fray:

JUDGE BAIRD: We fully appreciate how you feel. We really do. But now what Judge Morrison and Judge Kwon have said, I will also say. Dr Karadzic is entitled to . . . cross-examine you. If when you hear the question you find you don't understand it, then let us know . . .

WITNESS: Judge, sir, I understand you well, but you don't understand me. You're listening to what Karadzic is reading, and that has nothing to do with my statement or testimony. I'm not interested in that. I'm not a politician. I'm not a military analyst. I have my rights too.

JUDGE BAIRD: You do indeed have your rights and we would not allow those rights to be trampled on, but he also has his rights. And we are there now to balance, to ensure that both sets of rights are respected.[109]

But were they? The judges, in cautioning the witness, yet permitting Karadzic lengthy diversions into political propaganda which the witness was not in a position to respond to, in fact indulged the defendant while disrespecting the rights of the witness.

There were also numerous security lapses. The following exchange, when Karadzic asks the witness questions about his brother's children, is illustrative:

KARADZIC: Can you tell us the names of his sons?

WITNESS: No I can't. He has just one son.

KARADZIC: Your Excellencies, might we go into private session for just one second to hear the name of the man's son?

KWON: Very well. [Private session][110]

Here, the Trial Chamber was treating Karadzic as a *bona fide* defence counsel, bound professionally to confidentiality, whereas they were in fact letting the proverbial fox into the henhouse. Protective measures in court were superfluous once the information was in Karadzic's hands. After many such breaches, the prosecutor, Alan Tieger, voiced his concerns about repeated questions from Karadzic revealing protected information:

> I want to underscore again the concern about the need to comply with protective measures and the need for significantly greater rigour in ensuring that the linkage between protected information and information divulged openly in court is not made. I think that would apply as well to any questions that are asked about why protective measures were sought or granted, that should be in private session. And I can't underscore more forcefully the need to be cautious.[111]

Judge Kwon merely responded,

> I hope the accused Mr. Karadzic, understood it as well, and then the Chamber will pay attention more robustly on the matter.[112]

Kwon did not see fit to censure Karadzic, instead again lecturing the witness.

> Sir, the Chamber understands that you have raised some concerns with the Victims and Witnesses Section about the manner in which you were treated during your evidence yesterday. . . . It is the nature of the legal process at this Tribunal that all witnesses are questioned both by the party who has called them and by the opposing party, in your situation being the accused Mr. Karadzic, who is entitled to cross-examine you not in the capacity of an accused person, but in the capacity as Defence counsel for himself. I understand that that might be something that is difficult for you to understand, but that is a Rule of this Tribunal. When a witness enters the witness box to be cross-examined, he or she has to accept that he or she will be challenged, and sometimes with vigour. Therefore, often during such cross-examination, questions are put which are difficult or may be perceived to be impolite or improper by the witness being asked them. It is the Chamber's role and duty to prevent a witness from being harassed, insulted, or verbally abused during cross-examination, as well as to ensure that questions asked are relevant to the case. The Chamber will intervene in these circumstances, as we did yesterday on one occasion. Otherwise, as advised by my colleague Judge Baird yesterday, it is for you, the witness, to answer the questions put to you to the best of your ability and not for you to ask why such questions are being asked or to refuse to respond. We are sorry if you feel that you were unjustly treated yesterday. The Chamber was far from criticising you, but we merely wanted to provide you with guidance that seemed necessary. Please bear in mind that it is the accused, Mr. Karadzic, who is on trial here and who faces serious penalties if he's ultimately convicted of the charges against him. You are giving evidence that will assist the Chamber in making its final determination of those charges, and Mr. Karadzic is entitled to challenge your evidence as well as your own credibility.[113]

The judge here was putting the whole weight of the Court, including that of the defence counsel (Karadzic), behind his lecture. This was a seasoned witness who would have been well aware of court processes. The condescending tone and language were inappropriate, but picked up by Karadzic who added, 'I'm also concerned I didn't upset you'.[114]

Karadzic continued his cross-examination in the same vein for nearly five hours, introduced untranslated documents in cross-examination, and tendered them for admission before translation, as the presiding judge's main concern often appeared to be more about the process of admitting documents into evidence than ensuring the rights of the witness.[115]

On 5 and 6 May, Fatima Zaimovic, head paediatric nurse at Sarajevo's Kosevo hospital during the war, testified for the prosecution on child casualties. Cross-examining, Karadzic asked the witness her maiden name, and irrelevant questions about her husband and son, attacking the witness in relation to her son's position in the Bosnian army. He again produced maps which, despite the witness's protestation, Judge Kwon allowed, advising her, 'He wants the judges to be familiar with the map and we are not'.[116]

On the following day, Karadzic continued with questions about gunfire and tanks around the hospital and her house. The witness protested at the line of questioning, and was reprimanded by Judge Baird for objecting.[117]

Not content with distorting proven facts himself, Karadzic also guided leading prosecution witnesses into altering their evidence on crucial issues. BBC journalist Martin Bell, for instance, was cajoled into agreeing with Karadzic that there was no centralized command and control of the army before 20 May 1992, when the JNA pulled out of Bosnia. Bell partly retracted this and other responses to Karadzic's cross-examination on re-examination by the prosecutor.[118] Karadzic even distorted evidence offered by his defence witnesses, as in the case of UNPROFOR general, Paul Conway, who, according to Karadzic, had marked the position of a Bosnian Army mortar as the direction from which the shells were fired on the Markale market in late August 1995, whereas the witness had merely marked the position of a Bosnian Army mortar position he discovered in December 1995.[119]

In cross-examination, Karadzic was permitted lengthy diversions, mostly irrelevant to his indictment, where he presented a skewed version of central issues in the Bosnian war. In his defence case, he brought in a large number of convicted war criminals, along with many who had thus far escaped indictment, who challenged adjudicated facts, such as the Srebrenica genocide, responsibility for the Markale market massacres, conditions in the camps in 1992, mass expulsions of civilians from Višegrad and elsewhere, as well as Karadzic's personal and command responsibility in all of this. A qualified defence lawyer with the required accreditation, along with a presiding judge who kept close rein on proceedings, would have ensured less squandering of resources, and a more accurate rendering of the facts.

In view of the way Karadzic's conduct during his trial was handled by the Trial Chamber, it may be questioned whether the defendant's right to a fair trial was accorded priority over the victims' right to justice? And, in view of his indictment for genocide, his lack of legal qualifications and his dubious criminal past, was the decision to permit Karadzic to represent himself, with the assistance of a retinue of highly paid lawyers and advisors, justified in the circumstances?

Karadzic had several advantages in coming to trial towards the end of the tribunal's mandate. Apart from enjoying extensive legal assistance from the outset, and being permitted to occupy the defence lawyers' position in court with the right to quiz/pressurize/threaten his victims directly, he benefited from the advantage of a considerable distance in time from the events, during which international attention had moved on.

The question of tribunal resources was crucial. Many high-level politicians, military personnel and other key players in the atrocities of the 1990s had not been indicted, partly due to lack of sufficient resources, especially in the early stages of the tribunal's work, which has, amongst other things, resulted in a less than complete record of the 1990s Balkans wars.

Conclusion

The ICTY's position on the right to self-representation underwent several shifts over the years, from an absolute right facilitated by an *amicus curiae*, to facilitating standby counsel, to counsel imposed in the interests of justice, to pretend to defend oneself, and finally to pretend to defend oneself while assisted both by counsel behind the scenes and in court accompanied by an *amicus curiae*.[120] Equally, legal aid entitlement was inconsistent. Milosevic was granted funding only for certain facilities, while Karadzic was funded for five full-time individuals, while both Krajisnik and Praljak had difficulties in securing funding on the basis that they were not indigent.

Prior to the Milosevic trial, conventional wisdom had it that 'he who represents himself has a fool for a client' a quote originally attributed to Abraham Lincoln, the reasoning being that even someone fully conversant with international criminal law may not have the necessary inner distance to the case. Self-representing defendants at the ICTY, mostly former high-ranking military or political figures not conversant with the substantive and procedural criminal law and tribunal practice, fell into a different category, however. Aware that the overwhelming evidence would have been likely to preclude their acquittal, they used their time in court to advance their personal reputations, primarily for the benefit of the public at home who watched proceedings daily on TV, but also to present a version of the war which challenged previously adjudicated facts.

The question therefore begs – should defendants indicted for heinous crimes, including genocide and crimes against humanity, have been permitted to conduct their own defence? Should they have had access to sensitive material which risked jeopardizing the safety of witnesses and victims? Should they have been granted privileged access without the responsibilities which any accredited lawyer would have? Unlike professional lawyers who stood to be sanctioned, or even disbarred in the case of serious misconduct, the *pro se* indictee had nothing to lose.

If ICTY jurisprudence demonstrates anything on the *pro se* issue, it is that there should not be the option of self-representation for major offenders, as in the civil law system. In the case of the ICTY, it amounted to an abuse of procedure, diminished efficiency, and encouraged unnecessarily lengthy trials favouring indictees, often at a painful cost to survivor witnesses forced to undergo questioning by the very person they perceived as directly responsible for their suffering and loss.

Finally, the ongoing battle in Yugoslavia's successor states in establishing the history of the 1990s wars, where revisionism and denial still prevails, has not been assisted by trial chamber practice, which in some cases has allowed virtual free rein to *pro se* defendants.

The Šešelj case was to become a graphic illustration of the abandonment of the principles of justice, where a self-defending indictee, combined with an overindulgent judge, led to the acquittal of one of the most notorious paramilitary leaders in the Bosnian and Croatian wars.

Notes

1 Judge Richard May, *Prosecutor v Slobodan Milosevic,* 30 August 2001, p. 18.
2 See Stefan Trechsel, 'Rights in Criminal Proceedings Under the ECHR and the ICTY Statute–A Precarious Comparison', in *The Legacy of the International Criminal Tribunal for the Former Yugoslavia,* ed. Bert Swart, Alexander Zahar and Goran Sluiter, Oxford University Press, 2011, p. 185.
3 International Covenant on Civil and Political Rights, Article 14(3).
4 European Convention on Human Rights, Art. 6(3).
5 Patricia Wald, *Tyrants on Trial: Keeping Order in the Courtroom,* Open Society Justice Initiative, September 2009, p. 40.
6 Trechsel, op. cit., p. 188.
7 Ibid. Stefan Trechsel was Professor of Criminal Law and Procedure in the law schools of Fribourg, St. Gallen and Zurich, and from 2006 acted as an *ad litem* Judge at the ICTY, including the third contempt proceedings against Vojislav Šešelj.
8 Criminal Procedure Act of the Federal Republic of Yugoslavia, Article 13.
9 Ibid. Article 17.
10 Ibid. Articles 318 and 331.
11 Criminal Procedure Code for the Federation of Bosnia and Herzegovina, Article 66. www.legislationline.org
12 Section 140 of the German Code of Criminal Procedure.
13 Articles 274 and 317 of the French Code of Criminal Procedure.
14 Article 70 of the Bulgarian Penal Procedure Code.
15 Report of the Human Rights Committee, UN GAOR, 52d Sess., UN Doc. A/52/40 www.unhchr.ch/tbs/doc.nsf>.
16 237-B European Court of Human Rights (ser.A) (1992).
17 1997-IV European Court of Human Rights, 1074.
18 American Convention on Human Rights, Article 8(2)(d). But see Wald, op. cit., p. 41, for dissenting US judges.
19 M. Cherif Bassiouni, Human Rights in the Context of Criminal Justice: Identifying International Procedural Protections and Equivalent Protections in National Constitutions, 3 Duke J. J. Comp.& Int'l L. 235, 284 (1993).
20 In 1975, the US Supreme Court unequivocally recognized a defendant's right to self-represent.
21 *Faretta v California,* op. cit.
22 *McCaskey v Wiggins,* 465 U.S. 168 (1984).
23 In 1970, the US Supreme Court in Illinois ruled that removal of an accused from court was not a violation of the defendant's Sixth Amendment right to confront the witness against him in a public trial if, after being warned that a repetition of his disruptive conduct would mean removal, he insisted on behaving in a disruptive manner, disturbing the court proceedings. *Illinois v. Allen,* 397 U.S. 337 (1970).
24 *Martinez v Court of Appeal of California,* 528 U.S. 152, 162 (2000).
25 See Judith Armatta, 'Justice, Not a Political Platform, for Milosevic', *New York Herald Tribune,* 8 October 2004.
26 *Prosecutor v Milosevic,* 3 July 2001, T.16-18. The right to self-representation as a rule of customary international law was disputed by some scholars, and not claimed in the two subsequent Trial Chamber decisions. See Boas, pp. 208–209 and Michael P. Scharf and Christopher M. Rassi, 'Do Former Rogue Leaders Have an International Right to Act as Their Own Lawyers in War Crimes Trials?' *Ohio State Journal on Dispute Resolution* Vol.20, 2004, pp. 1, 14.
27 *Prosecutor v Milosevic,* 18 December 2002, p. 14574, 4 April 2003.
28 Ibid., 30 September 2003, T.27021-63. In August 2002, the Trial Chamber, on advice from Milosevic's doctor, allowed four consecutive days of rest following every two weeks of trial.

29 See Cerruti (2009) 40 Georgetown J of Intl L 919–984.
30 Ibid., 3 July 2001, p. 2.
31 For instance, 29 October 2001, pp. 66–69; 11 December 2001, pp. 134–140. See also Scharf & Rassi, op. cit.
32 *Prosecutor v Milosevic*, 'Reasons for Decision on Assignment of Defence Counsel', 22 September 2004, para. 54.
33 Patrick Robinson presiding, O-Gon Kwon, and Iain Bonomy.
34 Ibid., para. 32. 'The right to represent oneself must therefore yield when it is necessary to ensure that the trial is fair', para. 34.
35 *Prosecutor v Milosevic*, 'Reasons for Decision on Assignment of Defence Counsel', 22 September 2004. See Gideon Boas, *The Milosevic Trial: Lessons for the Conduct of Complex International Criminal Proceedings*, Cambridge University Press, Cambridge, 2007, pp. 213–218.
36 *Prosecutor v Milosevic*, ibid., para. 45, citing *Faretta v California*, 422 U.S. 806 (1975) and *Illinois v. Allen*, 397 U.S. 337 (1970).
37 *Prosecutor v Milosevic*, 'Reasons for Decision on Assignment of Defence Counsel', 22 September 2004, para. 61.
38 Ibid., para. 67.
39 Decision on Interlocutory Appeal of the Trial Chamber's Decision on the Assignment of Defense Counsel', 1 November 2004, para. 12.
40 Ibid., paras. 26–17.
41 Compilation of General Comments and General Recommendations Adopted by Human Rights Treaty Bodies, HRI/GEN/1/Rev.6, 12 May 2003, p. 176, cited in Decision on Interlocutory Appeal of the Trial Chamber's Decision on the Assignment of Defense Counsel, 1 November 2004, 17.
42 Ibid., para. 18. The Appeals Chamber ruling was faulted by Stefan Treschel, as not referring to any *travaux preparatoires*. Treschel op. cit.
43 Ibid., para. 18, n.55.
44 See Boas, op. cit. on this.
45 *Prosecutor v Milosevic,* 15 December 2004, pp. 34520–34533, 34555–34563. See also, 'A Role for Assigned Counsel', 15 December 2004, Judith Armatta, globalpolicy.org, and Alison Freebairn, Institute of War and Peace Reporting, 17 November 2005.
46 Directive on the Assignment of Defense Counsel, pursuant to Rules 44 and 45 of the Rules of Procedure and Evidence, www.icty.org/en/sid/304. See also Damaska, (2005) 3 J Int. Criminal Justice 3, 4.
47 Gideon Boas, *The Milosevic Trial: Lessons for the Conduct of Complex International Criminal Proceedings*, Cambridge University Press, 2007, pp. 154, 158–159.
48 *Prosecutor v Milosevic,* T.16 and 20 January 2006.
49 Wald, op. cit., p. 32.
50 See Michael Scharf, 'Maintaining Control of War Crimes Trials', UN Audiovisual Library of International Law, http://legal.un.org/avl/ls/Scharf_CLP.html
51 Ibid. on German public opinion of Nuremberg trials after WWII.
52 Ibid.
53 Michael A. Newton and Michael P. Scharf, *Enemy of the State: The Trial and Execution of Sammam Hussein*, St. Martin's Press, 2008, p. 160. According to Gideon Boas, senior adviser to the *Milosevic* trial chamber, '[t]he Milosevic trial serves as a chilling warning to the failure to manage the issue of self-representation, while appellate rulings in the Šešelj case have turned those proceedings into a circus'. Gideon Boas, 'Self-Representation Before the ICTY: A Case for Reform', *Journal of International Criminal Justice*, Vol.9, 1 March 2011.
54 See also Human Rights Watch Report. Conduct of Proceedings, on the Milosevic trial. www.hrw.org/report/2006/12/13/weighing-evidence/lessons-slobodan-milosevic-trial

55 Biljana Plavsic, Interview, 24 March 2016. www.youtube.com/watch?v=WYCYbZPu0YU
56 See Chapter 8 for a more detailed discussion of Krajisnik's indictment.
57 *Prosecutor v Krajisnik*, T.13399, 25 May 2005 and T.13415-7 and 13439-40, 26 May 2005.
58 Ibid. Reasons for Oral Decision Denying Mr Krajisnik's request to proceed unrepresented by Counsel. 18 August 2005, paras. 7 and 18. The Registry found that Krajisnik had sufficient financial means to contribute US$9,589 per month to his defence costs, which he was not paying to his Hague-based defence team. A compromise was proposed, whereby the Registry would grant up to US$1,000 per month towards the costs of the Pale-based investigators.
59 Ibid., para. 33. The Trial Chamber found that the defence team was far from dysfunctional, as Krajisnik had intimated.
60 Ibid., para. 34. See, for instance, Krajisnik's questioning of Biljana Plavsic. *Prosecutor v Krajisnik*, 7 July 2006, T.26966.
61 Reasons for Oral Decision Denying Mr Krajisnik's request to proceed unrepresented by Counsel. 18 August 2005, and Trial Judgement, para. 1245.
62 Since the job of *amicus curiae*, as the name suggests, is traditionally to assist the court, the appointment of Colin Nicholls in the Krajisnik case was unusual in that he was appointed by the Appeals Chamber to argue in favour of Krajisnik's interests. Decision on Self-Representation, para. 19.
63 Krajisnik had wanted Dershowitz to represent him as counsel, but the issue of Dershowitz's fees could not be resolved, hence his considerably more limited role in Krajisnik's defence. *Prosecutor v Krajisnik*, 26 March 2007, p. 27.
64 *Prosecutor v Krajisnik*, Decision on Momcilo Krajisnik's request to self-represent, on counsel's motions in relation to appointment of *amicus curiae*, and on the prosecution motion of 16 February 2007, 11 May 2007, para. 9.
65 Ibid., para. 10. This was based on Krajisnik having no health problems, his early right to self-representation on appeal and no opportunity for obstruction stemming from self-representation since he had had assigned counsel.
66 Apart from Krajisnik's 27-year prison sentence, 27,000 pages of trial transcript and sophisticated case law complicated appellate procedures. See Wald, op. cit., p. 41.
67 Ibid. Separate Opinion of Judge Shahabuddeen, paras. 2 and 3.
68 *Prosecutor v Krajisnik*, Fundamentally Dissenting Opinion of Judge Schomburg on the Right to Self-Representation, para. 1. Judge Schomburg was formerly a Senior Public Prosecutor and Judge in Berlin, a Judge of the German Federal Supreme Court (Bundesgerichtshof), and Under-Secretary of State (Staatssekretär) in the Berlin Department of Justice.
69 Ibid., para. 4.
70 Ibid., para. 2.
71 Ibid., para. 58.
72 Ibid., para. 30, citing *Martinez v Court of Appeal of California*, 528 U.S. 152, 162 (2000). See also Wolfgang Schomburg, 'The Role of International Criminal Tribunals in Promoting Respect for Fair Trial Rights', *Northwestern Journal of International Human Rights*, Vol.8, Issue 1, 2009.
73 Ibid., paras. 63 and 71.
74 Ibid., para. 65, citing Request to Extend the Deadline for Filing an Appeal Against the Judgement, 17 October 2006, 12 February 2007.
75 See, for instance, Judge Meron's efforts to accommodate Krajisnik at later status conferences, 5 July 2007, 2 November 2007.
76 Prosecuting counsel, Alan Tieger, claimed Krajisnik was not effective in his own defence, citing the judgement where he was considered 'a witness of very low credibility' SENSE, 19 November 2013. See also Wald, op. cit., p. 45 on Appeal Court decision.

77 See, for instance, Krajisnik's examination of witnesses George Mano, 3 November 2008, pp. 370–373, 374, 378–379, 428, Stefan Karganovic, p. 472, and Nicholas Stewart, 11 November 2008, pp. 647–648.
78 Momcilo Krajisnik, Interview, Ugao TV, 26 November 2018.
79 *Prosecutor v Zdravko Tolimir*, Appeals Chamber Decisions of 28 March 2008 and 18 June 2008.
80 'Tolimir Warned that Disruptive Conduct will lead to Imposition of Defence Counsel', ICTY Press Release, 30 June 2008.
81 http://icr.icty.org/LegalRef/CMSDocStore/Public/English/Response/NotIndexable/IT-04-74-A/MRA23704R0000438775.pdf
82 Ibid., para. 5.
83 See *Prosecutor v. Prlić et al.*, Decision on Praljak's Appeal of the Trial Chamber's 10 May 2007 Decision on the Mode of Interrogating Witnesses, 24 August 2007, and Decision on Slobodan Praljak's Appeal of the Trial Chamber's Decision on the Direct Examination of Witnesses Dated 26 June 2008, 11 September 2008, para. 22. See also Sluiter, Rights in Criminal Proceedings under the ECHR and the ICTY Statute, op. cit., p. 175.
84 See Chapter 7.
85 Elberling, commenting on Karadzic representation, argues that counsel representation limits severely the chance for the accused to bring 'their special knowledge of their home country and its conflict into the courtroom'. Tribunal practice, however, indicated that self-representing defendants misused the privilege. www.haguejusticeportal.net/Docs/Commentaries%20PDF/Elberling_Comment%20on%20Karadzic_EN.pdf#page=3&zoom=auto,0,470
86 Rules of Procedure and Evidence, Rule 45ter, adopted 8 November 2008.
87 See Nancy Armoury Combs, *The Legacy of the International Criminal Tribunal for the Former Yugoslavia*, op. cit. [1], pp. 298–301.
88 The Directive on the Assignment of Defence Counsel IT 1/94, 29.6.2006, and 11 July 2006, No. 1/94 & 22 July 2009 (ethical conduct).
89 Along with Momcilo Krajisnik, Karadzic was arrested in Sarajevo in 1984 for fraud and embezzlement. *Economist*, 24 March 2016, and www.globalpolicy.org/component/content/article/165/29638.html
90 The Trial Chamber established the parameters for the functioning of legal associates and case managers in considerable detail at an early stage, with two support members in the courtroom, and one legal associate with the right of audience, limited to addressing the Bench on legal issues. *Prosecutor v Radovan Karadzic*, 8 October 2009. Karadzic had three legal advisers, three case managers and two investigators at pre-trial phase, along with a large number of pro bono international lawyers to assist him. For further discussion by several contributors on self-representation in Rights in Criminal Proceedings under the ECHR and the ICTY Statute, op. cit.
91 See Rules of Procedure and Evidence, Rule 44, 8 December 2006.
92 The European Court of Human Rights would probably also reject this, arguing that the defendant had a choice.
93 Decision on Request for Review of OLAD Decision on Trial Phase Remuneration, *Prosecutor v Radovan Karadzic*, 19 February 2010, para. 45.
94 Karadzic was censured for this, and for searching for information that may be of marginal importance, by the presiding judge. Ibid., 8 February 2011, T.11294.
95 Ibid., 13 October 2009, 24. See also Ivanisevic, Balkan Insight 29 October 2009.
96 Ibid., 5 November 2009.
97 Ibid., 21 & 22 April 2010. See also Chapter 12.
98 Ibid., 13 April 2010, T.1067.
99 Ibid. T.1068. See also Karadzic's cross-examination of General Rupert Smith. Ibid. T.11477-11482.

100 Ibid., 21 June 2011, T.15062. During the testimony of Dragan Kezunovic, the prosecutor pointed to 12–13 pages of cross-examination by Karadzic on document D447 which was not on the list, and of which the prosecution had not been notified.
101 Ibid.
102 Ibid., 16 December 2010.
103 Ibid., 25 February 2011, T.12422-30.
104 Ibid., 21 April 2010, T.1287-1292.
105 Ibid., T.1302 and 1304.
106 Ibid., and T.1305.
107 Ibid. T.1307. Judge Kwon, supporting Morrison told the witness, 'I don't find your non-cooperation very helpful'. Ibid. T.1310.
108 See Prosecutor Julian Nicholls, ibid. T.1308-9. See also T.1355 & 1367.
109 Ibid. T.1369.
110 Ibid. T.1314-1315.
111 Ibid., 22 April 2010, T.1394.
112 Ibid.
113 Judge Kwon, ibid. T.1397-8.
114 Ibid.
115 Ibid. T.1351 & 1377.
116 Ibid.
117 Ibid.
118 14 and 15 December 2010, T.9808-9809, and T.9926-9931.
119 'Karadzic "amends" witness's statements', SENSE, 17 October 2012.
120 Schomburg, op. cit.

7 The Šešelj trial

A miscarriage of justice?

I am in no way hostage to anyone who would be an enemy of the Serb people. I myself [am] totally impartial, unbiased, and am governed by no one.

– Jean-Claude Antonetti[1]

Vojislav Šešelj was initially indicted on 14 February 2003 on 11 counts of crimes against humanity and war crimes. He and Judge Jean-Claude Antonetti, the presiding judge at his trial, both arrived at the ICTY in the same year. The combination of a defiant defendant and a compliant judge took self-representation to a different level. Both appeared to share a messianic view of their own prowess, and contempt for the workings of the ICTY to a point where the trial became dysfunctional, and the tribunal's reputation impaired.

Šešelj surrendered to the tribunal just days before the assassination of the Serbian Prime Minister, Zoran Djindjic, and travelled to The Hague the following day. He had been indicted on 14 counts of crimes against non-Serbs in Bosnia-Herzegovina, Croatia and Serbia, and with participation in a JCE for the forcible permanent removal of non-Serb civilians from a third of Croatia, large areas of Bosnia and Herzegovina and parts of Vojvodina.

Significantly, Šešelj did not seek temporary release.[2] In July 2003, the presiding judge at his trial was requested by the Serbian authorities to approve Šešelj's interrogation at The Hague, in connection with a pending investigation against him and others on suspicion of being associated with the assassination of Djindjic.[3] Twenty-four other suspects were already being held in detention in a Belgrade prison, reason enough for Šešelj's voluntary surrender to the ICTY. On 3 August 2003, he was interrogated at some length by the Serbian judiciary.[4]

The timing of Šešelj's arrival at The Hague was crucial also in relation to the Milosevic trial, where the Trial Chamber, just weeks earlier, had rejected the prosecution's call for the imposition of defence counsel, despite numerous delays and Milosevic's obstructive behaviour, on the basis that it was 'not normally appropriate in adversarial proceedings such as these', so Šešelj felt with reason that he was on firm ground in his insistence on defending himself.[5] There would also presumably have been ample opportunity at the detention centre to confer and mutually confirm their respective positions.

Pre-trial

From the outset, Šešelj made openly clear his intention to damage or destroy the tribunal. At the first hearing three days after his arrival, he invoked his right to self-representation,[6] setting the scene for years of litigation, and challenging not only the prosecution but the judges, the registry and numerous witnesses. The record of Šešelj's self-representation illustrated the many drawbacks in permitting high-ranking defendants to represent themselves, but also threatened to bring the whole tribunal into disrepute.

During the pre-trial phase, Šešelj submitted numerous motions and complaints, handwritten in Serbian Cyrillic, all needing translation, using valuable resources and delaying proceedings. During this time, there were no fewer than four successive presiding judges. Šešelj demanded that 12 judges, assigned co-counsel, and the main prosecution team be removed from his case. Although his demands were not directly met, the people he had targeted did, in fact, mostly leave before the case came to trial, signalling to Šešelj that he could control proceedings simply by pressing his demands.

Šešelj's pre-trial period, lasting from February 2003 to November 2007, a record even for the ICTY, was noted for its lengthy procedures and used subsequently by Šešelj and his team to argue injustice, despite his personal responsibility for most of the delays. But it was not in any way in his interest to return to Serbia at that time, where his name was linked to the Zemun gang deemed responsible for the death of Zoran Djindjic.[7]

At the first hearing on 26 February 2003, with Judge Wolfgang Schomburg presiding, and Daniel Saxon, Hildegard Uertz-Retzlaff and Kimberley Fleming prosecuting, Šešelj deployed an array of obstructionist tactics aimed at unsettling the court and demonstrating his intention to bring down the tribunal. Amongst other things, he claimed he could not understand the interpreters who used Croatian, rather than Serbian.[8] The claim was dismissed at the next hearing, and Standby Counsel assigned, but valuable resources had been used to investigate a flippant complaint.[9] Humour was another device tried by Šešelj to undermine proceedings:

> In my country, it is customary for the Judges, the Prosecutors, and Tribunal employees to wear normal, decent, civil clothing . . . the Judges wearing strange clothing in black, red, and the Prosecutor's in black and white . . . associates me with the inquisition of the Roman Catholic Church, and psychologically I find this unacceptable . . . I have lost 18 kilogrammes because of my psychological frustration due to your robes . . . I expect to be boiled in a cauldron . . . tortured, killed.[10]

On 21 May, Šešelj applied to have three judges disqualified from the hearing on grounds of bias: Judge Schomberg due to his nationality, and Judges Agius and Mumba, both Catholics, due to an alleged long history of conflict between the Serbian Orthodox and Catholic Churches. His request was rejected on 10 June by a full Appeals Chamber, presided by Theodor Meron, as frivolous, and an abuse of process, wasting more valuable resources.[11]

By July 2003, Šešelj was discovering more effective ways of obstructing court proceedings. He refused to use a laptop for his numerous submissions to the court, or to accept court documents in electronic format. The already overstretched translation units on a fixed budget were forced to translate Šešelj's lengthy submissions, handwritten in Cyrillic, into English and French.[12]

A further issue concerned Šešelj's chosen legal assistants, members of the Serbian Radical Party (SRS), for whom he was demanding substantial fees, despite none of them having sufficient knowledge of the Court's official languages to handle legal material, and most of them legally unqualified. The rules for defence counsel insisted that they should be practising lawyers or university professors of law.[13] Šešelj claimed that, although his advisors did not fulfil these conditions, they were efficient in their submissions.[14] This missed the point. Since they were not members of a legal institution, they were unaccountable.

On 21 August, the Trial Chamber found that, despite warnings, Šešelj persisted in trying to turn the tribunal 'into a stage for his private, non-forensic purposes', and saw no alternative but to assign counsel to represent him.[15] The Appeals Chamber reversed the decision, on the basis that Šešelj had not been specifically informed that he would lose his right to self-representation if his obstructive behaviour persisted, but left open the possibility for the reassignment of counsel, should such behaviour persist.[16] Five days later, Standby Counsel was reappointed.

Judge Schomburg was moved to the Appeals Chamber in October 2003, and Carmel Agius took over as presiding judge, evidently under the impression that he would remain for the whole pre-trial stage.[17] It was at this point, however, that Jean-Claude Antonetti, newly arrived at the tribunal and appointed as a permanent judge, joined the pre-trial Bench, where he lost no time in exerting his influence.[18]

At Judge Agius's first Status Conference on 29 October 2003, Šešelj announced that he had prepared some 300 pages of evidence, as well as 80 of his published books, containing his speeches, interviews, and court proceedings largely irrelevant to the indictment. He demanded they be translated. Initially, Agius assumed a tough stance, warning Šešelj against making political speeches, and suggesting he suffered from delusions of grandeur. Agius also advised Šešelj that he needed assistance in finding his way through court procedures,[19] and censured him on several counts, frequently reminding him that he was neither a practising lawyer, nor a professor of law, 'do try to remember that I am the Judge here and you are the accused, and that this is no special case and . . . you will be dealt with like every other accused here'.[20]

During Agius's time as presiding judge, three issues dominated proceedings – the method of disclosure, document translation, and the composition and financing of Šešelj's chosen advisory team.[21] In early 2005, Šešelj stepped up the pressure by demanding a Rwanda judgement of over 500 pages in hard copy, in Serbian.[22] But what was also now emerging as an impasse in progressing the case was the failure of the three pre-trial judges to reach a common position on Šešelj's increasingly outlandish demands. Agius outlined the problem:

> A request made by Mr. Šešelj for the issuance of a subpoena in the hands of the governments of the United States, the United Kingdom, Germany,

> France, Italy, Austria, Hungary, Croatia, and the Federation of Bosnia and Herzegovina, for the production of the Trial Chamber for all documents that are in the possession of their respective intelligence services mentioning the accused or the Serbian Radical Party, especially information relating to the conflict in the former Yugoslavia, including statements, plans, programmes, transcripts, and intercepts from the first appearance of such mentioning until present. As I said, the draft is ready. *There's only one remaining feedback to come from one of the Judges.*[23]
>
> The issuance of a subpoena to His Holiness Pope John Paul II, who is now deceased, all cardinals, archbishops, bishops and dignitaries of the Roman Catholic church for the production to the Trial Chamber of all documents and information in its possession relating to the conflict in the former Yugoslavia, including statements, plans, programmes, and stenographic records from the beginning of the pontificate of the late His Holiness Pope John Paul II until present. As I said, *the draft is ready as soon as I get the feedback from the third Judge, I will proceed with handing down or signing the decision.*[24]
>
> . . . the other two Judges and myself . . . meet regularly to deal with the various motions . . . both from the Prosecution and from you. *Some of course are my exclusive domain as Pre-Trial Judge, others need to be agreed to and decided collegially.*[25]

On 30 May 2005, the Prosecution team announced that they were basically trial ready, and merely awaited decisions from the judges before disclosing materials on hold. They also confirmed that they would be in a position to file their witness and final exhibit list once they had been advised about protective measures and the amendment.[26] Yet, it was to be another two-and-a-half years before the trial began, due largely to the judges' failure to reach a common position on how to address Šešelj's increasingly obstructive tactics.

Nearly a year later, the judges were still unable to reach a decision on disclosure and other issues and, on 4 May 2006, the ICTY president assigned Šešelj's case to a different trial chamber. Judge Agius was replaced by Alphonse Orie, another seasoned judge, who also adopted a tough approach. From what later ensued, however, it was evident that Judge Antonetti had played an active part in the judges' deliberations, frustrating decision making.

Judge Orie was under the impression that he would see the trial to its conclusion.

> As matters stand now, I will preside over the case. On the 12th of May, I . . . designated myself as the Pre-Trial Judge in this case . . . there is a fair chance that the Chamber which will finally hear the case will consist of Judge Robinson, myself, and an Ad Litem Judge still to be appointed.[27]

With Antonetti removed from the Bench, the new panel reestablished the rules, limiting the length of motions, and issuing a decision on the format of disclosure.[28] On 21 August 2006, following further obstructive behaviour on Šešelj's part, counsel was reassigned.[29] On Šešelj's abusive response, Orie pressed the priority button, disallowing the translation. Šešelj responded by demanding to be escorted from the courtroom. Orie clarified the Trial Chamber's position:

> There is an argument regarding the delicate balance that is necessary between the rights of the accused and the interests of the victim and witnesses and the need to create this balance by having proper regard to the particular circumstances of this proceeding . . . in the particular circumstances . . . delayed disclosure is perfectly appropriate. We are dealing here with an accused who has publicly declared his intention to destroy this Tribunal, who has constantly flouted and flaunted the Rules of this Tribunal, and who has already publicly harassed and intimidated Prosecution witnesses.[30]

The threat to prosecution witnesses was already known before the start of the trial, but it would take years to be acted on. A lengthy discussion ensued on witness protection concerning disclosure and the rights of the Defence to a fair trial. Prosecutor Dan Saxon outlined the problem.

> I am not suggesting here that the Defence would disclose information. . . . The Defence, however, has to disclose the names of these particular witnesses to its investigative staff, and they, in turn, will have to start to ask questions about these people in the region, and that's how we fear their identity will get at least known to certain people, including the police, and that means, from then on, the witnesses would be in a risk situation. . . . In addition, certain temporary protective measures that I am not able to address right here now in the presence of the Defence . . . can only be kept in place for a very limited time-period.[31]

His comments were prescient. But arguably the most significant issue at this point was the Trial Chamber's proposal to reduce the scope of the indictment, which the prosecutors vehemently opposed. Judge Orie reminded the prosecutors that under the rules, the Trial Chamber could even direct this. On 30 May 2006, Rule 73 *bis*(D) the phrase that the Trial Chamber '*in the interests of a fair and expeditious trial, may invite the Prosecutor to reduce the number of counts charged in the indictment*' had been added, and Rule 73 *bis*(E) also changed, with the result that the decision on the number of counts and additional time to present evidence was transferred from the prosecutor to the Trial Chamber.[32]

Prosecutor Hilda Uertz-Retzlaff outlined the implications of this:

> For an accused of this level of leadership and responsibility, that is indeed a very expeditious trial . . . we would urge the Trial Chamber not to require the reduction of the scope of the indictment at this point. . . . The accused is not just a member of a JCE that acts in always the same way in [a] huge number of municipalities. The situation in each of the named municipalities that we have addressed in the indictment is quite specific as to the goals of the accused and the . . . means employed . . . we have an accused who physically commits

> or instigates some of the crimes charged . . . then the question is: Which one of the other few municipalities to drop and still have the ability to present the scope and conduct of the criminality of this accused? . . . For instance . . . in relation to the municipality of Brčko, we did not charge the murders and the ethnic cleansing practices applied per se. We only picked one particular camp because we want to show the, in particular, forced labour aspects . . . and the sexual assaults of this case. Or . . . in relation to Bjeljina . . . it is not that we charged for each and every indictment the full scale of the ethnic cleansing means that were applied . . . if we . . . cut certain municipalities, we will lose whole chapters of criminal conduct.[33]

Months later, with Antonetti as pre-trial judge, Šešelj's indictment was reduced by several counts.[34] Antonetti later declared that he himself had been instrumental in changing the rules:

> I was the one who really advocated this – there was a new rule added to the Rules, Rule 73*bis* (D). This has an advantage; it allows the Prosecutor to reduce the number of counts and to also fix a number of crime sites or incidents. Based on that, Trial Chamber III ordered the Prosecution to apply the provisions of Rule 73*bis*. Therefore, the Prosecution removed Counts 2, 3, 5, 6, and 7 from the indictment.[35]

The decision was to have a crucial impact on the presentation of the prosecution case, reducing significantly the magnitude of Šešelj's alleged crimes. Later, it was also to impact on the Karadzic and Mladić cases.[36]

*

The prosecution estimated that the 11 protected witnesses' examination-in-chief would be finished by Christmas. Judge Orie advised Šešelj's imposed defence counsel that if he did not receive instructions or relevant information from Šešelj, he would not be allowed to cross-examine.

> It is on the basis of the behaviour of Mr. Šešelj until now in these proceedings and on the basis of the other reasons given in the decision of this Chamber, that the Chamber does not wish Mr. Šešelj to continue to represent himself.[37]

Orie's ruling was not to prevail. Two days later, Šešelj demanded his removal, along with that of judges Patrick Robinson and Frank Hopfel.[38] Although Šešelj's Motion was rejected, the Appeals Chamber, on 20 October, reversed the Trial Chamber decision, holding that the Trial Chamber should have warned him that counsel would be imposed if the disruptive conduct continued.[39]

Šešelj was presented with two alternatives: either submit to tribunal rules and regulations which would considerably reduce his scope for obstructive behaviour, call the tribunal's bluff, or resort to blackmail through staging a hunger strike.

Šešelj was not new to hunger strikes, having conducted one in the 1980s.[40] The ICTY was presented with the choice of calling Šešelj's bluff in return and risking his dying as a 'hero', casting a shadow over the tribunal's work, or to succumb to his demands. In calling his bluff, the ICTY would have retained its authority and integrity, albeit at the risk of another detainee dying in custody.[41] But the judges opted for what, at the time, may have appeared the safer option. Yet their decision was to lay the grounds for years of abuse of process, protected witnesses' exposure to danger, a massive waste of resources and eventually a judgement contradicting previous tribunal jurisprudence.

Šešelj began his hunger strike on 11 November, allegedly in protest against the tribunal's failure to meet his demands, including the banning of visits by his wife. A more likely motive for the hunger strike was an attempt to boost his party's ratings ahead of Serbia's elections.[42] On 27 November, Šešelj boycotted the first day of his trial and, following a warning that failure to appear at the trial could mean surrendering his right to self-defence, counsel was again reimposed.

On 8 December, the case reappeared before the Appeals Chamber, at which point Šešelj was considerably weaker. Fearing negative publicity, the Appeals Chamber reinstated his right to self-representation and subsequently prohibited the Trial Chamber from imposing standby counsel, unless necessitated by Šešelj's behaviour.[43] This placed Šešelj in a stronger position than before. He promptly ended his 28-day hunger strike, and his trial was suspended till he was fit to resume.

The decision confirmed earlier Appeals Chamber rulings on self-representation, setting the scene for years of mismanagement of Šešelj's trial. He had spent three-and-a-half years engaged in a mission he had declared at the outset – to discredit and destroy the tribunal, a mission already partly accomplished.

*

Following Orie's departure, Jean-Claude Antonetti was appointed as presiding judge for both the pre-trial conferences and the trial itself, a position he retained for over nine years, till the judgement in March 2016. Antonetti was to permit Šešelj's abuse of both prosecutors and expert witnesses, giving Šešelj to understand his sympathetic approach right from the outset. The writing was already on the wall in Antonetti's 2005 dissenting opinion when he argued against his colleagues that Šešelj should have all documents in hard copy and in his own language.[44]

A former *Conseiller Justice* to French president Jacques Chirac, with limited courtroom experience, Antonetti, at his first Status Conference as presiding judge, declared his agreement with Šešelj on most of the contentious issues, while himself displaying some of the illusions of grandeur Agius had attributed to Šešelj.

> We are now at a stage for the first time in the history of international law that we have a case that is starting from zero because certain problems weren't or could not have been resolved. . . . I have hearings every day, but in the

> general interest I accepted to deal with this case because I believed it would be possible for me to re-establish a dialogue and make it possible for this case to re-commence[45]
>
> Mr Šešelj had the right to defend himself. . . . It was a difficult struggle because a number of Judges refused to recognise this right. And then unfortunately, Mr. Šešelj had recourse to hunger strike which caused significant problems. The Appeals Chamber was seized of the matter, and in its wisdom it recognised the fact that Mr. Šešelj had the right to defend himself. As far as I am concerned, we will never be conceiving the idea of imposing amicus curiae or counsel on Mr. Šešelj.[46]
>
> The Pre-Trial Judge needs to prepare the trial as best he can; and as such, I'm concerned by these questions *if other colleagues were not concerned.* I think nowadays everyone has the same view. And to have professional and competent Pre-Trial Judges, this will help us to do our work better.[47]

Apart from the uncollegial comment on the contributions of previous judges, Antonetti came close to sanctioning hunger strikes as an effective means for indictees to prevail. He was equally adamant on disclosure:

> Mr. Šešelj wanted to have documents covered by Rule 65 to 68 in his possession. I was completely in disagreement with my colleagues as far as this issue is concerned, since I believed that the accused must have hard copies of the Prosecution's exhibits in his own language. . . . As far as this issue is concerned, I will not budge.[48]

What Antonetti refused to recognize here was that full disclosure by the prosecution to the defence, as prescribed under Rule 66, meant disclosing details of vulnerable witnesses to Šešelj, who was not under the confidentiality restraints imposed on professional lawyers.

On the question of delays, the prosecution reminded Antonetti that the OTP had been trial ready for a year.[49] Undeterred, the presiding judge demonstrated his empathy with the accused:

> I have the distinct impression, Mr. Šešelj, that you found yourself in front of a wall and that having the impression that no-one was listening to you, the only solution you found was to go on hunger strike. There [are] certain positive factors in your behaviour. You voluntarily surrendered to the Tribunal, you started filing motions that could be justified, whenever you were summoned to a hearing your behaviour was quite normal, you testified in the Milosevic case and there were no incidents in the course of that testimony . . . as an accused were quite ready to cooperate with the needs of international justice. . . . you were involved in a number of demands for dismissal of Judges. I counted 12 and two Presidents of the Tribunal were also concerned, and I said, well, it's very curious that I'm not one of the

> Judges . . . who was singled out by you . . . I'm impartial as far as you're concerned, and I will severely examine each and every element of the case. You may request that I be dismissed, but in such case I would be much surprised.[50]

On the prosecution's alleged shortcomings, Antonetti remarked,

> I was surprised to find out that . . . a trial had not yet started. The preparatory stages hadn't been dealt with. The procedure that we are following means that the Prosecution and the accused must engage in a certain form of dialogue. . . . I also intend to ask the Prosecution to review a certain number of motions that they filed *while you were in your sickbed*, in spite of the fact they continued to inundate the Chamber with motions . . . both parties and in particular Prosecution, have to respect the provisions of the Statute.[51]

Waving aside prosecutor Saxon's reminder that some very substantial motions had been before the Trial Chamber since the previous Autumn, Antonetti intimated that the delays were due to the prosecutor:

> Time must not be wasted, and to avoid wasting time, you should present your case in a logical manner . . . before you think that I'll just allow statements and transcript to be admitted into evidence, let me tell you, that's out of the question.[52]
>
> Leave aside what happened in the other Chambers. I have a different method of work and you have surely understood that. Therefore, on my part you will have very precise directives with which you will conform in such a way that when the trial starts, it will do so under good conditions.[53]

Saxon countered,

> Your Honour referred to the accused's behaviour before this Tribunal during the past four years, and . . . remarked that in his learned opinion the accused's behaviour was quite normal, at least with respect to his behaviour during hearings . . . the Prosecution has a very different perspective on this matter, and . . . believes that the record of hearings and litigation and decisions by Trial Chambers and the Appeal Chamber of this Tribunal describe a very different situation and –

but Antonetti had the last word:

> Mr. Saxon, this is not about lighting the fire again. We're starting off from zero. . . . All he wants is for his rights to be respected, and everyone may take note of that, the Prosecution in particular.[54]

Antonetti was evidently attempting to lay down new ground rules at the pre-trial stage before the full panel of judges had been appointed, but was aware that he would be likely to face opposition:

> I believe that in order to work well one must have . . . hard copy documents, not in electronic form. But . . . my colleagues may not agree with me . . . the accused should have the translation in CD or a hard copy and in his own language. But the other judges may not share my point of view.[55]

Antonetti may not have been fully confident of his position in legal terms, but was determined to have his own interpretation of the rules fully in place by the time the trial began.[56] Other concessions included supporting Šešelj's demand to sit in the defence counsel's position in the first row rather than in the dock, in order to have equal visual standing with the prosecutor.

> I too . . . had considered . . . that the accused should be . . . close . . . to their counsel . . . and the registry at the time in another trial had let me know that for security reasons it was not possible. I did not quite understand the security reasons. I don't think you are going to assault me or assault anybody here, nor any witness, nor Madam Prosecutor or her assistants. So I did not very well understand the position of the registry on this score . . . I will discuss the matter with the Registrar. And I will see to it that you would be as close as possible. I think it is obvious, but perhaps for others it is nonsensical.[57]

Antonetti presumably knew that sitting in the defence counsel position lent Šešelj a certain authority, before both witnesses and his audience at home, which his situation hardly merited. He also agreed to Šešelj's request for an adjoining room to his cell:

> It is simple . . . to make a door in the partitioning wall so that these two cells would be connected . . . so that you can move from one to another to work as you like.[58]

Soon afterwards, a wall was knocked down to accommodate Šešelj's request. Antonetti later suggested Šešelj may even need a third room for his documents.[59]

At the next status conference, familiar contentious issues arose. Christine Dahl, now the senior prosecutor, relying on an Appeal Chamber decision of 17 April 2007 approving electronic disclosure, was promptly overruled by Antonetti who reminded her that the Trial Chamber could exercise its discretionary power to avoid prejudice to the accused. Dahl was to undergo several clashes with Antonetti, as he made a number of unsupported assertions, suggesting she was inefficient, inexperienced and less cooperative than the accused, accusing her of lying, playing on words, playing 'cat and mouse' with him, and using him as 'the prosecution's toy boy', as well as misinterpreting arguments.[60] During the pre-trial conferences, the registry also came in for criticism from Antonetti in the presence of the accused.[61]

With a penchant for citing tribunal rules, Antonetti used Article 21 of the Statute to argue that Šešelj had the right to defend himself, but the Article did not extend to his right to have all documents in his own language, and in hard copy. Nor did it guarantee payment for legal assistance in cases where the defendant was unable to prove indigence. Much of the subsequent pre-trial conference time was taken up with these and similar points, including the crucial issue of witness protection.

At the next status conference, the issue of Šešelj's associates' legal fees arose. A self-representing accused is entitled to the reimbursement of legal counsel costs under certain conditions, but there were two main problems. Firstly, Šešelj had been unable to prove his indigence due, allegedly, to his wife's failure to declare her assets and, secondly, his associates did not fulfil the legal requirements laid down by Rule 44 of the Statute. Compounding this, some of his team, including Aleksandar Vucic (later to become Serbia's prime minister), had taken to the streets supporting Ratko Mladić.[62] Šešelj's three main 'legal' advisors, Vucic, Zoran Krasic and Slavko Jerkovic, were appointed as associates by the registry as Šešelj's condition for ending his hunger strike, but the registry now refused to certify them since they did not meet the legal standards required. They were also active members of the Serbian Radical Party and refused to recognize the legality of the tribunal.[63]

The issue which dominated the status conference, however, was disclosure. The previous year, David Hooper, Šešelj's assigned counsel, had been handed a large number of documents, disclosed electronically in English, which Antonetti now insisted Šešelj should receive in hard copy in his own language, according to Rules 66 and 68. Šešelj claimed that around 207,000 potentially exculpatory documents were involved. According to Antonetti:

> Rule 66 states that the Prosecution is under the obligation to disclose to the accused in his own language all the documents that are going to be adduced or that are likely to be exculpatory material. The accused should have these in his own language and in a hard copy format. This is a legal obligation. . . . As far as I'm concerned, Rule 68(A), Rule 68(i), clearly indicates that the documents must be disclosed in a hard copy format. . . . I understand that you have a technical problem, if you have a great number of documents, and if you felt that the electronic format was a way of finding a solution here, no, this is not the case.[64]

Rule 66(A)(i) in fact states that 'the Prosecutor shall make available to the defence in a language which the accused understands . . . copies of the supporting material which accompanied the indictment' but does not stipulate the format. Rule 68(i) equally does not specify the format, and Rule 68(ii) states that the prosecutor 'shall make available to the defence, in electronic form, collections of relevant material held by the Prosecutor'.[65] But the final decision lay in the hands of the Trial Chamber.[66] Using his authority to manage the trial under new rules, Antonetti overruled a decision made by a previous judge on 4 July 2006, authorizing electronic disclosure,[67] reminding the prosecutor that if she did not meet her obligation, she could be liable for prosecution.[68] He appeared to question the wisdom of that same judge's decision on Rule 67 (Additional Disclosure), not to include hundreds of pages of quotations from Šešelj's books, copies of prior speeches, allegations against popes, and similar.[69] Antonetti also failed to reprimand Šešelj for inappropriate behaviour and sexist remarks directed at the prosecutor: 'Ms Dahl, Ms Dahl, he did not insult anybody. Do not relapse into mistakes in the past'.[70]

Witness protection and contempt

There was evidence of intimidation of prosecution witnesses as early as 2006.[71] Antonetti would have been aware of this, and despite it not being consistent with the rules, refused witnesses' testimony to be supplemented by written statements.[72] Insisting that the prosecutor produce a witness list in advance, he advised Šešelj that 'just a few days from now, you will get the list of protected witnesses. And then all those who are not on the list, you'll be able to mention them'.[73]

It fell to the prosecutor to explain the danger to witness safety of such a procedure:

> I disagree with the interpretation and advice you're giving to Mr. Šešelj of what would be appropriate once he is [given] the list of protected witness . . . many witnesses because of the victimisation that they have suffered are to be referred to solely by their pseudonym and in an abundance of caution given the nature of the allegations against Mr. Šešelj that we tread very carefully and precisely upon what is considered appropriate when identifying people in session. . . . Mr. Šešelj uses this Status Conference to send a message to people who are preparing to come and tell the truth before this Tribunal that they will be branded traitors. . . [and]liars, that frightens people and it is wrong to send that message out of this courtroom in an attempt to dissuade people from coming before this Tribunal under oath to tell the truth. [74]

A further dispute between Judge Antonetti and the prosecutor arose over Šešelj's associates. On 21 December 2006, Vucic, Krasic and Jerkovic had signed a confidentiality agreement with the registry, and became privileged associates of Šešelj, with access to confidential information regarding the case, as well as to the courtrooms, and to have privileged communications with Šešelj and regular visits to the Detention Unit, with the tribunal covering their travel expenses.[75] On 17 August 2007, Antonetti confirmed that Šešelj would be permitted associates who were not fully fledged lawyers, to be paid from tribunal funds, despite not fulfilling most of the main conditions of Rules 44 and 45 of the Rules of Procedure and Evidence.[76] Three contempt cases ensued after Šešelj intentionally disclosed the identities of several protected witnesses. Challenging Antonetti, Šešelj demonstrated his contempt for tribunal Rules:

> My legal assistants do not have oral or written knowledge of either English or French, and they will never learn those languages. My legal assistants will never have proper membership in associations of lawyers capable to appear before foreign courts. First of all because they are not counsel, they're not lawyers, and they do not need to be members. And second, I simply prohibit them from becoming members of such associations.[77]

Antonetti now backtracked, faulting the registry for the apparent confusion.

> I can reassure you that you will be in charge of your own defence. The only minor problem that still needs to be resolved is that you need to inform the Registry. . . . I really don't know why they are demanding this. It's almost as if you're deliberately trying to obstruct this trial. They know that Mr. Jerkovic is a lawyer, but they want you to specify it. I think it's excessive, it's unnecessary . . . you had given three names to the Registry, and those names had been accepted by the Registry So I fail to see why once the Registry has accepted those names, they would no longer do it. . . . There could be some controversy as to paragraph E . . . we just need to interpret this in broad terms. . . . I remind you that this is the first decision in the history of international or national justice. So this is going to be remembered.[78]

The prosecutor strongly objected:

> It is not possible to waive the requirement that accredited Defence associates be licensed and qualified. . . . That role should not be denigrated by accrediting unqualified individuals. It is unwise to allow such an assault on the dignity of this Tribunal. There cannot be the payment of funds from the international taxpayer to unqualified persons who are not licensed to give legal advice and carry with them no ethical obligations to either the accused or this Tribunal. Those ethical obligations are fundamental to safeguard fair play and the pursuit of justice.[79]

Recalling the Appeals Chamber decision of 11 September in *Krajisnik*, which reached a contrary result on payment to Defence associates for individuals who choose to represent themselves, she urged the judges to reconsider.

Antonetti promptly retorted,

> I stop you just now, Mrs. Dahl. The decision of the Appeals Chamber, I know it . . . certainly better than you do. Secondly, I have been extremely clear. Never, ever will I reconsider the decision which I have made. Never. So there's no need even to talk about this. . . . Thirdly, you are . . . stating untruths. You are talking about the integrity of the assistants of Mr. Šešelj, but

> this problem has already been settled . . . Mr. Šešelj had given three names of three individuals to the Registrar, and among these . . . were the three names I mentioned to you. There was never any problem therefore, so don't come back by the back door to question this. For the Registry, there is no problem left. The only residual problem consists of knowing among the three which is the one who would be in charge of the question of the financial assistance. It has to be a barrister. Among the three, Mr. Jerkovic is a barrister. Therefore, on this matter, no problem.[80]

Antonetti again refused to acknowledge the real concerns at issue, namely, the protection of vulnerable witnesses. Consequently, the personal details of several protected witnesses, including their real names, their pseudonyms in the case, and their occupations and addresses, became publicly available in Serbia before the trial began.[81] His ruling, along with his insistence on the order of witness presentation, jeopardized witness security.[82]

In January 2008, the prosecutor launched an investigation into Aleksandar Vucic, a senior member of Šešelj's defence team, for allegedly disclosing the identity of a protected prosecution witness. On 10 June 2008, the Trial Chamber ruled that there was insufficient evidence to prove 'beyond reasonable doubt' that he had violated the court order. After the prosecution appealed, the Appeals Chamber ordered the Trial Chamber to review its decision, and an independent *amicus curiae* was appointed by the Trial Chamber to conduct the investigation, to avoid a conflict of interest. In the decision, which was made public on 2 September 2008, the *amicus curiae* ascertained that the *actus reus* of contempt of court existed – Vucic had disclosed the identity of a protected witness – but a *mens rea*, the intent to violate the court order protecting the witness's identity, could not be established. Although the Appeals Chamber accepted the prosecution argument that it was not necessary to present evidence 'beyond reasonable doubt' for proceedings to be instituted – a *prima facie* case was sufficient – it returned the case to the Trial Chamber.[83]

In 2016, Vucic, now prime minister of Serbia, refused to extradite the Serbian Radical Party members accused of contempt, claiming it might affect Serbian security, fuelling suspicion that earlier allegations against him for witness intimidation could come to light.[84]

On 15 August 2008, in disregard of the track record of Šešelj's team, the Trial Chamber ordered the prosecutor to disclose to Šešelj the list of future prosecution witnesses. Hearings were suspended on 26 August when the prosecutor refused to disclose the witness list to Šešelj, pointing out that it would place them in a 'vulnerable position' and expose them to intimidation and persecution by Šešelj in court, and by his assistants outside. On 17 September 2008, the Appeals Chamber dismissed the prosecution's appeal against the Trial Chamber decision, noting that the prosecution 'does not claim that Šešelj and his legal advisors have intimidated and threatened all prosecution witnesses', which meant that the prosecution could call witnesses who were not exposed to pressure and threats of the accused and his legal advisors, and the trial could continue, pending the decision on the motion to assign counsel.[85]

Due to allegations of witness intimidation, and to protect the integrity of the proceedings, on 11 February 2009, Šešelj's case was adjourned by Majority decision (Judge Antonetti dissenting), since it was not possible to guarantee that the protected witnesses' testimony would be given freely, and to safeguard their security.[86]

Under Rule 77(A)(ii) of the ICTY Rules, Šešelj was held in contempt of court and, on 24 July 2009, sentenced to 15 months' imprisonment.[87] The second and third contempt cases against Šešelj related to the first, namely, that in violation of a court order the books in question publishing the names of protected witnesses had still not been removed from Šešelj's website. Yet where was the incentive? As Šešelj himself pointed out, he had already served the sentence, and more, at Scheveningen.[88] It was even counterproductive, in that the level of interest in Šešelj's writings in Serbia was raised by the publicity from the tribunal. Judge Stefan Treschel's Partly Dissenting Opinion on the length of the sentence was therefore moot.[89] The inadequacy of ICTY provisions for witness protection was exposed by the very person who flagrantly exploited them.

> Not only do I accept the fact that I am the author of the book, I'm very proud of being the author of that book, and it is thanks to these legal proceedings that there is a lot of interest in the book. On my internet site several thousand copies have been photocopied and reproduced, so I'm very satisfied.[90]

Later, in her Partially Dissenting Opinion, Judge Lattanzi was to pay special regard to the 'climate of intimidation, blackmail, threats and fear to which the Prosecution witnesses [were] subjected'.

> The numerous statements 'given' to the defence team by individuals, some of whom were already on the 65 *ter* list of Prosecution witnesses, provide further proof of the climate of intimidation that reigned over the trial. The purpose of these statements was to refute evidence given *viva voce* and they frequently arrived by fax – in Serbian – the day, or several days, after the testimony. The Chamber decided to stop admitting them due to their lack of reliability and *prima facie* probative value. The Accused, however, read them out in the courtroom so they are recorded in the transcripts of the hearings.[91]

Lattanzi observed that this climate of intimidation was completely and erroneously ignored by the majority in the judgement.[92]

Trial

Šešelj's trial began on 7 November 2007, nearly five years after his arrival at The Hague. The vitriol previously reserved for the prosecutors and registry was now extended to prosecution witnesses. The first expert witness called on 11 December, Anthony Oberschall, an eminent sociologist of social movements in Europe, with 40 years' experience, was promptly challenged by Šešelj.[93] This followed a ruling by the Trial Chamber before Oberschall entered the Court, pursuant to Rule 94*bis*, that the witness should be heard *not* as an expert witness, but merely as a prosecution witness, undermining Oberschall's testimony from the outset.[94] When further information provided by the OTP substantiated that the witness had sufficient knowledge to act as an expert witness, Antonetti announced that the Court would decide on the probative value of Oberschall's testimony at the end of the hearing.[95]

> I believe that I am a Judge within the Tribunal who has the most experience in presiding or taking part in hearings, and I have learned from my experience that 80 per cent of the time is taken by the Prosecution.[96]

Yet the first day of the examination-in-chief was mostly taken up with lengthy interventions from Šešelj and Antonetti.

When the prosecutor objected to Šešelj's cross-examination methods, Antonetti, while mildly reproving Šešelj, managed to convey his agreement with him.

> I must say, Ms. Dahl, that I do not agree with your point of view. Mr. Šešelj tackled the issue of credibility. . . . I don't like to have useless objections that are a waste of time. . . . Mr Šešelj . . . you may think that the Prosecution did not do their work properly or not thoroughly enough, but do not attack her personally.[97]

Šešelj, undeterred, continued to humiliate the witness, quizzing him on issues outside the scope of both his indictment and the witness's remit, including his knowledge of physics and mathematics, and his religious affiliation.[98] In support of Šešelj's line of questioning, Antonetti reminded the Court that, since it was an adversarial procedure, the defence had a right to ask questions to check the credibility of a witness using the resume provided by the prosecution, which the prosecutor disputed.

> Mr. Šešelj's examination is not a traditional adversarial common-law cross-examination. . . . This is arguing with the witness. We didn't ask Dr. Oberschall to focus his analysis on the indictment or to cherry-pick the speeches to try to help us prove the case. We gave him 44 volumes of material and he made a search for key words and phrases and analysed those parts of the speech, in terms of propaganda, threat discourse, sending threat messages, and all of the themes that we've talked about for two days.[99]

The following month, the issue of disclosure again arose when Antonetti reminded the prosecutor of the Chamber's ruling on 5 November 2007, dealing with the requirements of the Prosecution under Rule 68, that it should disclose as quickly as possible in hard copy and in a language understood by the witness, namely, 'some 3,000 documents that Prosecution has identified using key words given by the accused',[100] a request that was impossible to fulfil in the two days Antonetti stipulated. Compounding the pressure on the prosecutor, Šešelj demanded that she be investigated under Rule 77 for contempt.[101] When Dahl requested the Chamber's direction on whether she should file a response, Antonetti advised her, 'you are free to . . . respond to the filing by Mr. Šešelj if you wish to, but you have to do so quickly if you want to because we are to issue this decision shortly'.[102] A discouraging start to a contentious session, which Antonetti compounded, commenting, 'we could probably save time if I was asking the questions, but this is not provided for in the Rules'.[103]

The second prosecution witness, Goran Stoparic, gave evidence on Šešelj's hate speech. Stoparic was on the ICTY relocation programme, which Šešelj used as a basis to discredit him as a witness.[104] A former Scorpion, he had received subsistence payments from the ICTY under relocation abroad. Šešelj indicated that he knew in which Western country Stoparic was now living.[105] A discrepancy emerged between the original statement supplied to the tribunal in 2006 and the witness's evidence in January 2008. Antonetti denied the prosecutor's request under Rule 89(F) to admit the earlier statement, recalling Rule 92*ter* of which he claimed to be the 'father', a consequence of which was that the statement could not be compared with conflicting evidence subsequently given in court.[106] Occurring right at the beginning of Stoparic's evidence, this cast doubt on the witness's credibility from the outset. Claiming that the statement had been written by OTP officials, Šešelj's cross-examination was accompanied by frequent tirades of nationalist propaganda for domestic consumption. He produced documents in Serbian, some in virtually unreadable handwritten Cyrillic, which had not previously been declared to the prosecution or the judges.[107] Judge Lattanzi was moved to warn Šešelj more than once on 'self-testifying', but it was mainly left to the prosecutor to remind the presiding judge on procedure, which Antonetti mostly dismissed.[108]

Yves Tomic, the third prosecution witness, who produced an expert report on the Greater Serbia ideology, also came under challenge.[109] The Trial Chamber decided it would assess the relevance and probative value of the expert report, and rule whether it should be admitted into evidence, Antonetti again potentially compromising Tomic's testimony from the start:

> The Rules, which is a binding document, is inspired by the common-law system in which you have expert witnesses who come upon the request of parties without having the Judges saying anything beforehand. It's true that in another civil – law system you would not have this waste of time. In another legal system where Judges appoint independent expert witnesses who come to testify with an adversarial discussion by the parties, after that only, we would save a lot of time, but for reasons that escape me another system was preferred in which the Prosecution has their experts and you, yourself, will have yours.[110]

Antonetti frequently criticized the common law system, while setting aside the fact that under civil law, a system used by both his (the French) and Šešelj's governments, there was little or no right to self-representation.

The prosecutor's examination-in-chief on 29 and 30 January 2008 was interrupted frequently by both Šešelj and Antonetti, including an irrelevant debate on the correctness of the term referring to the people of Slovenia! On 5 February, Šešelj began his cross-examination by declaring his goal to discredit the expert report injecting it, as earlier, with nationalist propaganda, introducing copious material, often in Serbian and not introduced in the examination-in-chief, and repeatedly insulting the witness, without censure from the Bench.[111] Šešelj also disregarded the witness's remit, quizzing Tomic in detail on his knowledge of the Serbian state from the twelfth century.[112] Antonetti encouraged Šešelj with fulsome praise, even suggesting the witness's remit should have included earlier centuries.

> It is very difficult to follow Mr. Šešelj, who has encyclopaedic knowledge and he has so many facts in mind. . . . Mr. Šešelj, I'm aghast at the level of your education. You seem to practically know everything about everything.[113]

Šešelj's unorthodox method of cross-examining throughout the prosecution case met with little censure from the Bench. When it came to the testimony of Reynaud Theunens, an OTP military analyst who had already testified in several ICTY trials, Antonetti evidently felt a prior briefing was required.

> As you know, the cross-examination is made up of leading questions, and it can be quite an ordeal for a witness. Please do not be surprised at the way some questions may be put to you or at the tone that may be used when putting these questions to you, but the Judges will be there to control the proceedings. As you know . . . the cross-examination has for its aim to test the credibility of the witness, and the second purpose of the cross-examination is to check that what the witness has stated in his answers to the Prosecution or in his report is accurate. So as I said, cross-examination can turn into quite an ordeal for an expert witness.[114]

Antonetti's subsequent questioning of witness Theunens, which occupied much of the examination-in-chief, indicated his doubts about the standard of the tribunal's prosecution analysts.[115] Yet, despite his corrective to the witness to be 'extremely specific' and asserting that the three judges on the Bench were 'highly qualified', Antonetti then contradicted himself by asking if the JNA was a member of the Warsaw Pact.[116]

Another expert witness, Andras Riedlmayer, Director of the Documentation Centre for Islamic Architecture at Harvard University, had testified at a number of ICTY trials, as well as in the ICJ case, on the destruction of cultural heritage in the Balkan wars.

The examination-in-chief, during which Riedlmayer gave a Powerpoint presentation, was interrupted on numerous occasions by both Šešelj and Antonetti, on issues which would have been more appropriately raised in cross-examination. The witness was required to explain in some detail what a Powerpoint presentation meant, and to explain why he had not also included the destruction of Serbian artefacts in his report. It was left to the prosecutor to remind the judges that Šešelj had not been indicted for the destruction of Serbian religious and cultural facilities.[117] As the presentation proceeded, more interruptions ensued, Šešelj complaining about a lack of translation, requiring the witness to repeat dates already supplied.[118] The interruptions were indeed so numerous that the following week, Antonetti evidently felt it necessary to refer to them, recalling his earlier warnings to Šešelj, possibly to mitigate his own failure to exercise control.[119] But the presentation was arguably deprived of the powerful impact it might have had without unnecessary interruptions.

In the cross-examination, where there was the opportunity to challenge the witness on his presentation, Šešelj chose to ignore the evidence presented and the accompanying report, and instead focused on discrediting Riedlmayer personally, accusing him of bias, erroneously suggesting that he had misrepresented his academic record, and using ridicule and abuse in an attempt to undermine him.[120] Although Riedlmayer ably defended his position, it was again left to the prosecutor to object, while Šešelj indulged in lengthy detours, requiring Riedlmayer to provide information on political and constitutional issues unrelated to his report or expertise, without being cautioned by the Chamber. Antonetti's rules for Šešelj, however, were somewhat different, as he reassured him that

> if the objections are aimed at destabilising you or, rather, to interrupt the thread of your arguments, then we will intervene. And if we can't take time off, we have other means of coping with the problem. I have said this many a time.[121]

There was a total of 99 witnesses for the prosecution, although many changed their evidence in court, as a result of coercion or intimidation by Šešelj and his associates.[122] Jovan Glamocanin, for instance, after four years' cooperating with the prosecutors, retracted his evidence, and was summoned by the Trial Chamber to testify as a court witness. Glamocanin left the Serbian Radical Party in 1994 and only returned in early 2008 when he was elected a deputy at the local elections. He claimed that, in early 2001, the then Serbian prime minister Zoran Djindjic had convinced him it was necessary to eliminate Šešelj politically from the Serbian scene, and allegedly pressured Glamocanin to cooperate with the ICTY. In May 2003, Glamocanin was approached by OTP investigators and signed a detailed 20-page statement about the role Šešelj played in crimes in Croatia, Bosnia and Vojvodina. He was granted protection measures after claims of fear for his family's safety. In cross-examination, Glamocanin made peace with Šešelj, but also with the Trial Chamber, when warned of the risks of perjury, stating that he was convinced of the integrity of the judges, and intriguingly noted 'the particular sympathy the Serbs have for Judge Antonetti who had restored their faith in the Serb-French friendship'.[123]

Aleksandar Stefanovic, first secretary general of the SRS, also made a *volte-face* with a similar story, claiming that he had been pressured by Djindjic to discredit Šešelj before the ICTY. Prosecutor Dahl in re-examination recalled that Stefanovic had signed his first statement with the OTP on 12 February 2003, and only retracted it on 16 May 2008, when he informed the OTP of his wish to change sides and testify for the defence. Only then did he refer to Djindjic's alleged pressure on him, just one month after Šešelj first produced his theory about a 'pact' between Djindjic and Carla Del Ponte. [124]

Nebojsa Stojanovic, in statements in 2004 and 2006, claimed that Milorad Lancuzanin Kameni 'issued the order to kill all Croats under arms', ordering his group 'to shoot every Croat they came across' and personally saw 'Šešelj's men beat up and cut the throats of five men who had surrendered'. In court in 2008, however, Stojanovic denied '90%' of the contents of his earlier statements.[125] Prosecutor Dan Saxon, present at the interviews, had confirmed their validity before Stojanovic was brought in. Declared a hostile witness, Stojanovic in court denied what he had previously stated in an interview. He was warned of the risks of perjury but was not charged.

These three insider witnesses were amongst the 38 involved in Šešelj's motion of contempt against senior ICTY prosecutors, including Carla Del Ponte, Hildegard Uertz-Retzlaff and Daniel Saxon, for alleged intimidation, blackmail, bribery and abuse of witnesses. Šešelj's motion against the prosecutors was first lodged on 23 March 2007. In response, Presiding Judge Antonetti ordered what the prosecutors called an unwarranted, vague and far-reaching investigation against 'dozens of persons' based on spurious accusations made by people close to the SRS.[126] The prosecutors urged the Appeals Chamber to revoke the Trial Chamber decision and reinstate the previous decision, which ruled that all such issues would be postponed till the end of the trial, or for the ICTY president to appoint an independent chamber to decide whether to institute contempt proceedings. On 22 December 2011, following a report by an independent *amicus curiae*, the Trial Chamber, in an eight-page decision, dismissed Šešelj's motion for contempt. Antonetti's Separate Opinion of 26 pages, essentially agreed with the decision but argued that the *amicus* had 'failed to achieve his objective' and should have interviewed Šešelj and all the witnesses. Judge Lattanzi issued a partially dissenting opinion, calling for more transparency, and claiming that an *inter partes* version with minor redactions would have been useful to the Parties in the preparation of their final briefs or their closing arguments, and it could especially have assisted the Chamber in determining the credibility of witnesses in the ongoing main case against Šešelj.[127]

Earlier that year, Antonetti had dissented from the Majority who ruled against Šešelj's acquittal under Rule 98 *bis* of the Rules of Procedure and Evidence.[128]

Judgement

The 110-page Judgement in *Šešelj* left most observers stunned, not only at Šešelj's acquittal but at the lack of legal reasoning to support the verdict.

This was not the only issue. Initially scheduled for 30 October 2013, the Judgement was delayed till 31 March 2016 due to the dismissal of Judge Harhoff from the case, and his replacement by Mandiaye Niang on 31 October 2013. From Senegal, Niang's previous legal experience had been mainly at the ICTR registry, where he had worked since 1997. He was first appointed as an international judge (at the Rwanda Tribunal) in September 2013, just one month before his assignment to the Šešelj trial.[129] Due to his parallel assignment at the lengthy and complex *Popovic et al.* Appeal case on 31 October 2013, however, Niang was not free to begin familiarizing himself with the Šešelj case until 30 January 2015 when the Popovic trial ended. Yet just five months later, in June 2015, he declared himself ready to pronounce judgement on one of the longest and most complex trials in the tribunal's history, which involved the review of 17,554 pages of transcripts, 1,399 documents, 900 exhibits, and 99 witnesses,[130] without the benefit of having participated in any of the proceedings.[131]

Judge Niang and Presiding Judge Antonetti by majority acquitted Šešelj on all counts.[132] It was left to the third judge, Flavia Lattanzi, to record her dissent, which she did in a blistering 49-page analysis of the Majority verdict.[133] As she noted at the beginning of her 'Partially Dissenting Opinion', the title was a euphemism since she dissented on all but one count.

One of the main arguments threading through the Majority Judgement was harsh criticism of the prosecutor. Lattanzi, while conceding that the prosecution could have done better, argued that it was the Trial Chamber, in its former and current composition, which was mainly at fault, especially regarding Šešelj's behaviour towards witnesses, and his obstruction of the proceedings, which led to the contempt cases.[134] She maintained that the lack of reasoned opinion addressing law and fact made it difficult to exercise in full the right to lodge an appeal of the judgement.[135]

The Majority held that there was insufficient evidence to 'irrefutably establish' the existence of a widespread and systematic attack as an element of crimes against humanity, describing it as an armed conflict between enemy forces. It sought to justify the overwhelming evidence of criminal conduct as merely a lawful contribution to the war effort.[136] Lattanzi, by contrast, pointed to the ample evidence which was cited in what she called 'a disorderly manner in the footnotes', with no real analysis.[137] The same applied to the *actus reus* where elements, such as the means used by Šešelj to influence the perpetrators, were not taken into account by the Majority.[138] Incendiary hate speech was viewed by the Majority as morale boosting for the Serb forces.

In many cases, the Majority did not refer to applicable case law, and not at all in the war crimes section, ignoring previous case law where it was affirmed that a Trial Chamber does not have to discuss at length all ICTY case law, but merely to identify the precedents.[139] Where the Majority did do so, Lattanzi considered that it strayed from the well-established jurisprudence of the ICTY, without offering the slightest justification.[140] Equally, *dolus eventualis* as an alternative form of *mens rea* for instigation and aiding and abetting was not mentioned at all, despite the case law on this being well established.

On the events leading up to the war, the evidence on record, indicating that the difficulties began when Serbia, under the Milosevic regime, tried to impose hegemony on the other republics, was disregarded by the Majority. Judge Lattanzi referred to the Decision of 10 December 2007, established facts, in outlining the events.[141] On the crucial issue of witness's later retraction of written evidence, the intimidating behaviour of Šešelj in court, broadcast in Serbia and on the SRS website, revealing identities of protected witnesses, Lattanzi opined that the proper course of action would have been to lend more weight to the prior written statements than to the *viva voce* evidence in court.[142]

The Majority in *Šešelj* also contradicted the Karadzic Judgement the week previously, where Šešelj was identified as a key member of the JCE.[143] Yet, the Majority argued strenuously that Šešelj was not a member of the JCE, confusing the ultimate political objective of JCE members and the criminal means to achieve it, disregarding Šešelj's contribution to permanently and forcibly removing non-Serbs from large parts of Croatia, Bosnia and Vojvodina through the commission of serious crimes.

Lattanzi concluded that the Majority had lost sight of what characterizes the jurisdiction of a Chamber of the tribunal:

> The majority intended not only to give an 'original' reading of the reasons underlying the armed conflicts which took place . . . but it also wished to reinterpret a large part of international humanitarian law, applicable in times of armed conflict. In so doing, it showed total disregard, if not contempt, for many aspects of the application and the interpretation of the law as set forth in the case-law of the ICTY and ICTR . . . with this Judgement we have been thrown back centuries into the past, to a period in human history where we used to say. . . '*Silent enim leges inter arma*'.[144]

*

Šešelj was provisionally released in October 2014 on health grounds, without conditions, [145] and his judgement took place in his absence since, once back in Serbia, Šešelj declared he would not return to The Hague voluntarily.[146] Following his release, he travelled through Serbia, giving long speeches and interviews, which resulted in a sharp increase in membership of the ultranationalist Serbian Radical Party. He was also free to participate fully and formally on the Serbian political stage. [147] In late 2016, he gained a seat in the Serbian Assembly.

In August 2016, the prosecutor asked the Appeals Chamber to reverse the 'vitiated' judgement and convict Šešelj, or go for a retrial.[148]

Conclusion

The repercussions arising from the Šešelj judgement reach well beyond the ICTY. In the short term, the acquittal of one of the most notorious Serbian paramilitary leaders meant that Šešelj was free to participate in the Serbian political arena at the highest level. In 2016, he led his party back into parliament as the strongest opposition force and was a leading candidate in the 2017 Serbian presidential elections. It also contributed to a significant increase in ultranationalist activity in Serbia, with longer-term consequences for the wider region.

The judgement cast tribunal jurisprudence into confusion on several issues, including JCE and aiding and abetting, leaving an unsettled record to the International Criminal Court, and other *ad hoc* international tribunals. The handling of the trial raised questions about the interpretation of the ICTY Rules of Procedure and Evidence, allowing for the untrammelled abuse of court officials and witnesses, and a failure to provide clear guidelines on disclosure, to determine the parameters of self-representation, the required qualifications and financing of a *pro se* defence team and, not least, to ensure full witness protection where needed. In a change of rules, the ICTY presidency left judges in complete control of the trial, without the cheques and balances previously provided by legal officers and others, which paved the way for the presiding judge to exercise virtually full control over one of the longest, most complex, and certainly most mishandled, trials in the ICTY's history.

It might have been expected, with Šešelj's pre-trial track record culminating in his hunger strike, that the newly appointed Presiding Judge Jean-Claude Antonetti would exercise considerable caution in his approach to the case. Antonetti's numerous concessions to Šešelj at all stages of the trial could have been viewed, albeit at a considerable stretch, as an effort to bring a contentious trial to a conclusion at all costs, avoiding deadlock, another death in custody, or a trial *in absentia*. Yet, as Šešelj insulted and bullied prosecutors and witnesses with impunity, pushing well beyond the boundaries of acceptable conduct, the presiding judge in open court joined him in deriding prosecutors, expert witnesses, the registry, and even his colleagues in the judiciary, often echoing, and at times even surpassing, Šešelj's own litany of grievances against the tribunal.

Antonetti's strategy began soon after he arrived at The Hague, when he set in motion an arrangement which would accord more powers to the presiding judge, virtually driving the legal officers out of the picture. This, broadly reflecting the civil law system, made the presiding judge supreme in court and finally, in the absence of a jury, a powerful player in the judgement, too.

To some extent, the path was paved for Šešelj from the outset in his bid for self-representation. The precedent set in *Milosevic*, where the former Serbian president was at times able to manipulate the court to his advantage, supported by favourable Appeals Chamber decisions, offered Šešelj insight into the possibilities for handling his own trial. His deliberate defiance of the rules dented witnesses' confidence in the effectiveness of protective measures guaranteed by the ICTY and, more importantly, exposed them and their families to reprisals in Serbia. The three contempt cases against Šešelj were arguably a misuse of tribunal resources since, as Šešelj himself pointed out, he had already served the sentences delivered at the contempt trials, so there was little incentive to comply with court orders, and witness intimidation continued.

The judgement took the case to another level. The tribunal's suspension of Judge Harhoff, just a month before judgement, led to the appointment of a new judge who had not participated in any of the proceedings, and who had little trial chamber experience. Just a few months to become familiar with a complex case lasting 13 years was now apparently deemed sufficient time in which to reach a judgement.

There was also a crucial international dimension. The failure by the major world powers and institutions to respond effectively in the early stages of the war, substituting firm action with abortive 'peace' plans and conferences culminating in a peace settlement at Dayton, acceptable to all sides, created the impression that a civil war had taken place, with a consequent symmetry of guilt. This facilitated the Majority in *Šešelj* to conclude that the crimes were in the context of war, and therefore legitimate.

Finally, the lack of accountability at trial chamber level contributed to the misuse of power on the part of the presiding judge over nearly ten years and a subsequent miscarriage of justice, resulting in the acquittal of one of the leading players in the crimes against humanity and war crimes in Croatia, Bosnia and Vojvodina.

Notes

1 Judge Jean-Claude Antonetti, *Prosecutor v Šešelj,* Status Conference, 5 June 2007, T.1215-6.

2 See commentary by Nenad Canak and Dejan Anastijevic on the timely absence of Šešelj at the time of Djindjic's assassination. Vojislav Šešelj: Raspakivanje, 2011. www.youtube.com/watch?v=hMydWzdakQ8

3 *Prosecutor v Šešelj*, Status Conference, 3 July 2003, T.110-112.

4 New evidence indicating Šešelj's possible involvement in the assassination of Zoran Djindjic emerging as late as 2010 and 2011, continued to make The Hague a safer place to stay. Novi dokazi o vezi Šešelja i tomica sa ubistvom Djindjica, *Blic*, 6 July 2010, and Šešelja saslusati zbog ubistva Djindjica, *Vesti*, 4 May 2011. *Vesti* reported that if Djindjic was released from detention at The Hague, he would face interrogation in connection with Djindjic's assassination. Dejan Anastasijevic, a journalist for *Vreme*, claimed that Šešelj was behind an attempt to kill him and his family. Dejan Anastasijevic: Vojislav Šešelj stoji iza atentata na mene i porodicu, *Blic*, 4 July 2010.

5 Judge Richard May, *Prosecutor v Milosevic*, 18 December 2002, T.14524.

6 *Prosecutor v Šešelj,* Initial Appearance, 26 February 2003, T.5-6.

7 In the Djindjic assassination trial, a collaboration witness, Dejan Milenkovic, gave detailed testimony about Šešelj's ties to the late Zemun gang leader, Dusan Spasojevic. Another collaborating witness Zoran Vukojevic, who was later murdered, also linked Šešelj and Spasojevic in his testimony, and claimed the latter funded Šešelj's election campaigns and the construction of his house. *B92*, 18 October 2006.

8 'I don't know what the word "opci" means, "poprilicno", then "tocka", a word I heard several times. I don't know what "zapadni srijem" means. I assume it's a geographic term, but I don't know in which country in the world it is situated. I don't know what "obrana" means or "obrane"'. Šešelj, *Prosecutor v Vojislav Šešelj,* Transcripts, T.29-30, 44.

9 Ibid. Decision on Prosecution's Motion for Order Appointing Counsel to Assist Vojislav Šešelj with his defence, 9 May 2003, para. 22.
10 Status Conferences, 28 October 2003, T.150, and 17 February 2004.
11 Decision on Motion for Disqualification, 10 June 2003.
12 See Zahat, 2008, 256.
13 ICTY Rules of Procedure and Evidence, Art. 44 & 45.
14 Status Conference, 30 May 2005, T.396.
15 *Prosecutor v Vojislav Šešelj*, Decision on Assignment of Counsel, 21 August 2003, paras. 73–80.
16 Ibid. Decision on Appeal Against the Trial Chamber's Decision on Assignment of Counsel, 20 October 2006, paras. 22–26.
17 Ibid., 29 October 2003, 116.
18 ICTY Press Release, 23 September 2003.
19 Status Conference, 14 June 2004, T.228, 243, 257 and 259.
20 Judge Agius, Status Conferences, 17 February 2004, pp. 193, 195, and 14 June 2004, T.228.
21 Apart from the payment of Šešelj's large team of advisers, Šešelj's family were allegedly uncooperative in disclosing their financial status. The registration of his advisers was also problematic since they did not fulfil Rule 44.
22 Status Conference, 31 January 2005, T.308-9.
23 Status Conference, 30 May 2005 T.348. Italics added.
24 Ibid., pp. 348–350. Italics added. Šešelj also requested the Trial Chamber to issue a subpoena to the OTP to produce all documents on the formation of the Serbian Guard and Panthers, paramilitary groups and their participation in the conflict in the former Yugoslavia, and for all documents where his name was mentioned in any case before the tribunal. P. 357.
25 Ibid. T.362. Italics added.
26 Ibid. T.376.
27 Status Conference, 19 May 2006.
28 Status Conference, 4 July 2006.
29 David Hooper was assigned as lead counsel, assisted by Andreas O'Shea. Status Conference, 14 September 2006, T.570.
30 Ibid. T.577-578.
31 Ibid. T.598.
32 Rules of Procedure and Evidence, 17 December 2004 and 22 September 2006.
33 See T.585-590 for the prosecutor's full argument against cutting indictments.
34 Second Amended Indictment, 25 July 2007.
35 Judge Antonetti, Status Conference, 22 May 2007, T.1173.
36 See Chapter 12 for M. Cherif Bassiouni's comments on the ICTY view on this.
37 14 September, T.605-606.
38 Motion to Disqualify Judges Alphonsus Orie, Patrick Robinson and Frank Hopfel from the Trial and Appeals Proceedings, Submission 221. 2 October 2006, The Motion was based on prejudice citing, inter alia, Orie's involvement as amicus curiae in the Tadic case.
39 Decision on Appeal against the Trial Chamber's Decision on Assignment of Counsel, 20 October 2006, Judges Fausto Pocar (presiding), Mohamed Shahabuddeen, Mehmed Guney, Andresia Vaz and Theodor Meron.
40 In May 1984, Šešelj went on a hunger strike when on trial in Sarajevo, which he ended after 48 days.
41 Two previous deaths of senior Serb(ian) politicians in custody earlier that year (Slobodan Milosevic and Milan Babic), may have influenced the tribunal's decision.
42 Šešelj's Serbian Radical Party (SRS) support had slipped from a high point of 36% to around 30% since July. 'Šešelj Hunger Strike a Publicity Stunt', *Balkan Insight*, 23 November 2006.
43 Appeals Chamber Decision, 8 December 2006, para. 20. The alternative would have been a trial *in absentia*, where international lawyers are still sharply divided.

For discussion on this, see www.IBA-ICC-report-trials-in-absentia-in-Int-Criminal-Justice-2016.pdf

44 Decision on the Accused's Motion to Re-examine the Decision to Assign Standby Counsel, Opinion Dissidente du Juge Antonetti, 1 March 2005.

45 Judge Antonetti, Status Conference, 13 March 2007, T.929-931. Also: 'My question was a very important question, like all the questions I put', 16 January 2008, T.2435.

46 Status Conference, ibid. T.928. This reasoning was possibly based partly on Antonetti's apparent ignorance of Šešelj's former career, claiming incorrectly that Šešelj was a professor of law, a position Šešelj had never held. See, for instance, Status Conferences, 13 March 2007, p. 927 and 27 September 2007, T.1520.

47 Ibid., 13 March 2007, T.968. Italics added.

48 Ibid. T.928.

49 Christine Dahl, Status Conference, 5 June 2007, T.1187-1188.

50 Status Conference, 13 March 2007. T.933-935.

51 Ibid. T.932. Italics added.

52 Ibid. T.968-974.

53 Ibid. T.981-982. Antonetti was later on several occasions to indicate to the accused his criticisms of the tribunal. On the issue of Šešelj refusing to stand when the judges enter the Court, Antonetti commented: 'I suppose you are doing this because you said that you contest the existence of the Tribunal, and, therefore, it is your way of showing that you are opposed to the Tribunal. So this, of course, is your choice. And I may understand your position myself, but I'm not alone'. Status Conference 27 September 2007, T.1480.

54 Ibid.

55 Ibid. T.1011 and 1034.

56 See, for instance, Goran Sluiter, 'Compromising the Authority of International Criminal Justice How Vojislav Šešelj Runs His Trial', *Journal of International Criminal Justice Oxford University Press*, 23 March 2007, T.529-536.

57 Status Conference, 2 May 2007 T.1090-1091.

58 Judge Antonetti, Status Conference, 11 March 2007 T.978, and 4 April 2007, T.997 and 1011.

59 'I had the distinct impression that you did not have enough space. That was my impression upon visiting you. You have a lot of documents, and it might be good that the Detention Unit administration give you another room'. Judge Antonetti, Status Conference, 6 November 2007, T.1678.

60 Status Conferences, 2 May 2007, T.10634, 22 May 2007, 1144, 5 June 2007, 1237, 1292-1294, 4 July 2007, 1332, 1379-80, 1387-8, 17 August 2007,1530, 1532, 27 September 2007, 6 November 2007, 1703-4, 1718-9, 1723-4.

61 See, for instance, Status Conferences 2 May 2007, T.1090-1091, 17 August 2007, T.1371.

62 Status Conference, 5 June 2007, T.1212. Vucic worked as a journalist in Pale from 1992–3. He joined the Radical Party in 1993 and became General Secretary of the SRS in 1995. As Minister for Information in 1998, he underwrote a law about public information, resulting in *Nasa Borba* and other journals being banned. Just days after the Srebrenica genocide, on 20 July 1995, Vucic famously declared: 'If one Serb is killed, we will kill 100 Muslims' (ubijte jednog Srbina, mi cemo stotinu Muslimana). www.youtube.com/watch?v=UGqv9CJbd3U www.youtube.com/watch?v=-m0kMkHnpwQ Vucic in Glin 1995.

63 Aleksandar Vucic, accused of leaking witness identities, was later, as Serbian prime minister, to write to the tribunal, protesting strongly about its treatment of Serbia and its legal representative, Sasa Obradovic, particularly concerning three Radical Party officials – Vjerica Radeta, Jovo Ostojic and Petar Jojic – against whom an arrest warrant had been issued, accusing them of threatening two protected witnesses at Šešelj's trial, and offering them bribes of 500 Euros not to testify at the trial. 'Serbia Sends Complaint to Hague Court', Balkan Insight, 12 February 2016.

64 Judge Antonetti, Status Conference, 5 June 2007, T.1237.
65 ICTY Rules of Procedure and Evidence.
66 See www.icty.org/x/cases/Šešelj/acdec/en/070417.pdf Appeals Chamber Decision on form of disclosure, 17 April 2007, paras. 19 and 20. Šešelj's interlocutory appeal was dismissed, but the Appeals Chamber allowed for reconsideration by a new Trial Chamber.
67 Status Conference, 4 July 2006, T.534. Antonetti participated in the vote at a plenary session on 28 July 2004, giving increased authority to Trial Chamber judges, in the interests of a fair and expeditious trial.
68 Status Conference, 5 June 2007. See Status Conference, 4 July 2007, T.1325-1342 for full exchange between Antonetti and the prosecutor on the issue.
69 Status Conference, 5 June 2007, p. 1252. Judge Orie had ruled on 22 November 2006 that Šešelj's bid to have additional material included was not within Rule 67. Status Conference, 22 November 2006, pp. 812–813.
70 Judge Antonetti, T.1292-3.
71 Status Conference, 14 September 2006, T.578.
72 Judge Antonetti, 23 October 2007, T.1601-2.
73 Ibid. T.1672.
74 Christine Dahl, T.1673.
75 Decision on the Accused's Oral Request to Reinstate Messrs Zoran Krasic and Slavko Jerkovic as Privileged Associates, 10 February 2010, 2.
76 Status Conference, 17 August 2007, T.1365.
77 Šešelj, ibid., p. 1368. Later, the head of Šešelj's legal associates Slavko Jerkovic resigned from the SRS and Šešelj's defence after a stormy showdown with Šešelj. www.pressonline.rs/info/politika/100677/srs-napustio-clan-tima-za-odbranu-Šešelja.html
78 Ibid., 27 September 2007, p. 1522. Rule 45 E states that 'Where a person is assigned counsel and is subsequently found not to be lacking the means to remunerate counsel, the Chamber may, on application by the Registrar, make an order of contribution to recover the cost of providing counsel'. Rules of Procedure and Evidence. For further comment by Antonetti on the Registry, see his Concurring Opinion, 31 March 2016, paras. 23–26.
79 Status Conference, 17 August 2007, T.1372. See Rule 44, Rules of Procedure and Evidence.
80 Ibid., 27 September 2007, pp. 1530–1532.
81 www.blic.rs/vesti/hronika/dejan-anastasijevic-vojislav-Šešelj-stoji-iza-atentata-na-mene-i-porodicu/dq48w1k
82 The Prosecution argued for delayed disclosure and protection measures for certain vulnerable witnesses, which Antonetti disputed. For heated exchange between Prosecutor Dahl and Judge Antonetti on this, see Ibid. T.1378-1392.
83 Order issuing a Public Redacted Version of 'Decision of the Prosecution's Appeal against the Trial Chamber's Decision of 10 June 2008', *Prosecutor v Šešelj*, 2 September 2008.
84 'Serbia's Refusal to Extradite Radicals Raises Suspicions' Balkan Insight, 3 November 2016. See also https://justicehub.org/article/un-tribunal-clashes-serbia-over-witness-intimidation
85 SENSE, 17 September 2008.
86 *Prosecutor v Šešelj*, Decision on Prosecution Motion for Adjournment with Dissenting Opinion of Judge Antonetti in Annex, 11 February 2009.
87 This was affirmed on appeal on 19 May 2010.
88 'The sanctions for contempt of court are symbolic. For somebody who has been in prison for seven years, they are even ludicrous' *Prosecutor v Šešelj*, First Contempt Case, 7 May 2009, T.94.
89 Ibid. Third Contempt Case, Partly Dissenting Opinion of Judge Treschel, 28 June 2012, p. 61.

90 Ibid. First Contempt Case, 7 May 2009, pp. 29–30. According to Šešelj, during one promotion approximately 3,000 attended.
91 Ibid. Judgement. Partially Dissenting Opinion of Judge Flavia Lattanzi – Amended Version, Volume 3, 31 March 2016, para. 6.
92 Ibid., para. 7.
93 For discussion of Oberschall's testimony in relation to hate speech, see Richard Ashby Wilson, *Incitement on Trial: Prosecuting International Speech Crimes*, Cambridge University Press, 2017, pp. 199–208.
94 *Prosecutor v Šešelj,* Decision on Anthony Oberschall's Status as an Expert, 30 November 2007.
95 Ibid., 11 December 2007, T.1950-53.
96 Antonetti, Status Conference, 27 September 2007, T.1494.
97 Antonetti, 12 December 2007, T.2144.
98 Ibid. T.2101-210, 2112-3. Šešelj suggested the witness was lacking in intelligence. Ibid., p. 2148. Antonetti's ineffectual response prompted Judge Lattanzi to intervene and reprimand Šešelj. Ibid. T.2150-2151.
99 Ibid. T.2104, 2143.
100 *Prosecutor v Šešelj*, 15 January 2008, T.2294.
101 Ibid. T.2306.
102 Ibid. T.2306-7.
103 Ibid. T.2379.
104 Ibid., 22 January 2008, T.2560-2565.
105 Ibid.
106 Ibid. T.2407.
107 Ibid., 24 January 2008 T.2753.
108 See, for instance, T.2753-4, 2761, 2787, 2790, 2792-3 2807 and 2821.
109 Decision on the Qualifications of Expert Yves Tomic, 15 January 2008.
110 Ibid., 29 January 2008, T.2852-3.
111 Ibid., pp. 3176–3177, 3181, 6 February 2008, T.3203-4 and 3258. Judge Lattanzi reprimanded Šešelj several times for 'self-testifying'.
112 Ibid. T.3203-5.
113 Ibid. T.3212.
114 Ibid., 14 February 2008, T.3630-1.
115 Ibid. T.3564-5.
116 Ibid., 14 February 2008, T.3712-3.
117 Ibid., 22 May 2008. T.7274-7290.
118 Ibid. T.7291-7303, 7306-7307, 7308-7309, 7313-7314, 7316-7317, 7321, 7325-7327, 7328-7340, 7345-7346, 7348-7350, 7351, 7353-7354, 7356-7359, 7361-7362, 7366-7367. *Prosecutor v Šešelj*, 27 May 2008, T.7400-7401, 7404-7405, 7407. The digressions were unnecessary since, as the witness pointed out, they were covered in the accompanying report, and most of Šešelj's interruptions were matters for the cross-examination.
119 Ibid., 27 May 2008, T.7376.
120 'We just see your photographs here, and we see that you're a mediocre photographer who goes on a trip, forgetting his flash, and then cannot take the right kind of pictures because he doesn't have enough light. And you listened to what casual passersby have to say. So you're a mediocre-level photographer and an expert in listening to occasional stories told by passersby; right?' Vojislav Šešelj, ibid., T.7424.
121 Judge Antonetti, ibid., T.7387.
122 See *Prosecutor v Vojislav Šešelj*, Partially Dissenting Opinion of Judge Flavia Lattanzi–Amended Version, Volume 3, 31 March 2016, para. 6, n.4. Witnesses VS-033, VS-1055, VS-2000, VS-067, Asim Alic, Perica Kolbar gave statements to the defence team, having been on the list of prosecution witnesses.
123 'New Elements in Šešelj's Conspiracy Theory', SENSE, 10 December 2008.

124 'Prosecutor Accuses Prosecution Witness of Lying to Court', SENSE, 26 November 2008. Antonetti later rated Glamocanin's and Stefanovic's evidence as 'fair', on a level with that of experts Theunens and Riedlmayer. 'Concurring Opinion of Presiding Judge Jean-Claude Antonetti attached to the Judgement', 31 March 2016, T.461-467.
125 Withdrawal of Signature, Denial of Statement, SENSE, 23 July 2008.
126 SENSE, 15 October 2010.
127 Partially Dissenting Opinion of Judge Lattanzi on the Decision on Vojislav Šešelj's Motion for Contempt against Carla Del Ponte, Hildegard Uertz-Retzlaff and Daniel Saxon, 28 December 2011.
128 Antonetti only upheld Counts 1, 10 and 11 of the indictment, 98 *bis* Hearing, 4 May 2011.
129 See *Rule of Law Through Human Rights and International Criminal Justice, Essay in Honour of Adama Dieng*, Cambridge Scholars Publishing, 2015, Mandiaye Niang, p. 4.
130 See Antonetti, Concurring Opinion, op. cit., p. 16. Antonetti declared that, unlike in the Milosevic case where the new judge relied on a document prepared by the legal team, Judge Niang satisfied himself and Judge Lattanzi that he had done so satisfactorily. However, later (and in reference to the decision on Šešelj's early release) Antonetti contradicts himself, opining that 'familiarisation with the record . . . takes at least a year'. Concurring, ibid., p. 109.
131 For discussion on this, see http://opiniojuris.org/2013/12/16/final-nail-ictys-coffin/
132 Megan Fairlie raises the interesting question of whether the judges would have been on an equal footing, and whether it was feasible to believe that the new judge's views would legitimately test the perspectives of the judges who had been present throughout the trial. If not, and if the two remaining judges disagreed, to which would the new judge be likely to defer. http://opiniojuris.org/2013/12/16/final-nail-ictys-coffin
133 *Prosecutor v Vojislav Šešelj*, Partially Dissenting Opinion of Judge Flavia Lattanzi– Amended Version, Volume 3, 31 March 2016.
134 Ibid., I. The General Climate of Intimidation, paras. 2–3.
135 The Appeals Judgement, in exonerating Šešelj of crimes in Croatia and Bosnia was arguably a reflection of the Prosecution's dilemma in lodging an adequate appeal. See Chapter 12.
136 See also interview with Flavia Lattanzi, 'Perché sono contraria all'assoluzione di Šešelj' [Why I am against Šešelj's acquittal] Radio Popolare, 7 April 2016. www.radiopopolare.it/2016/04/assoluzione-seseli-giudice-italiana-contraria-alla-sentenza/
137 Partially Dissenting Opinion of Judge Flavia Lattanzi, op. cit.
138 Ibid., para. 12.
139 Ibid., para. 14. *Prosecutor v Enver Hadzihasanovic & Amir Kubura,* Appeals Judgement, 22 April 2008, para. 13.
140 Ibid., para. 18.
141 Ibid., paras. 26–31.
142 Ibid., para. 22.
143 *Prosecutor v Radovan Karadzic*. Judgement 24 March 2016, 'Knowledge and acts of named alleged JCE members', T.1254.
144 Lattanzi, op. cit., paras. 143–144 and 150, 'In times of war, the law falls silent' (Cicero's *Pro Milone*, 52 B.C). See also the statement by Chief Prosecutor Serge Brammertz, who viewed the judgement as a 'fundamental failure by the majority to perform its judicial function'. MICT Press Release, 6 April 2016.
145 This was a majority decision, with Judge Niang dissenting on the grounds that there were not sufficient guarantees that Šešelj would return when required.
146 See 'Professor Vojislav Šešelj's Respondent's Brief, Mechanism for International Criminal Tribunals', MICT-16–99-A, 19 December 2016, paras. 410–412. In his response to the Prosecution Appeal Brief, Šešelj informed the MICT that this was

his final communication and he would not participate in any further proceedings, nor return to The Hague, even for an appeal judgement, if any.

147 Šešelj boasted that in 12 years the tribunal had not found him guilty of a single crime. See www.youtube.com/watch?v=tj6YmdPrBrs published 6 January 2017.

Yet, according to Antonetti, reintegrating a politician in social and political life contributed to the restoration and maintenance of peace in the region in taking part in democratic political dialogue. Concurring Opinion, op. cit., p. 100.

148 'Prosecutor: Convict or Retry Šešelj', SENSE, 30 August 2016.

8 The ICJ judgement in *Bosnia and Herzegovina v Serbia and Montenegro*

Introduction

In different ways, the ICJ judgement in February 2007 was a landmark for both Serbia and Bosnia, in contributing to the historical record of the 1990s wars. For Bosnia, winning its case would have secured official endorsement that an international conflict had taken place, rather than a civil war, confirming ICTY findings. Serbia, as a state, would have carried the stigma of responsibility for genocide in its recent past. Reparations, including financial, may have been recommended, with failure to comply impeding Serbia's progress towards EU and NATO membership.

As it was, the ICJ did not find Serbia responsible for the Bosnian genocide, merely for failing to prevent it. The Court also ruled that genocide had occurred in Srebrenica alone over a matter of days. Serbia's ultranationalist president at the time, Vojislav Kostunica, continued to pursue his dubious rapprochement policy with Republika Srpska, integrating further the para-state into Serbian economic structures. RS president, Milorad Dodik, meanwhile, pursued his efforts to divide Bosnia with renewed vigour, and assistance from the international community as divisions in Bosnia became increasingly entrenche.

*

It was almost 14 years after Bosnia and Herzegovina first instituted proceedings against the FRY that a 17-judge panel at the ICJ handed down its judgement in the case brought by Bosnia against Serbia and Montenegro.[1] It was the first state-level lawsuit to be heard at the ICJ in respect of alleged violations of the Genocide Convention. The judgement met with a mixed response from lawyers and other commentators, both within the region and internationally. Antonio Cassese, the first president of the International Criminal Tribunal for the Former Yugoslavia (ICTY), joined a number of international lawyers in opining that the judgement should be greeted with considerable ambivalence. His assertion, that the Court's decision 'attempts to run with the hare and hunt with the hounds',[2] is examined here through some of the main issues raised in the proceedings and judgement.

Legal proceedings on behalf of Bosnia and Herzegovina were first instituted by University of Illinois professor Francis Boyle on 20 March 1993 when the Bosnian war was at its height. In June 1995, the Belgrade team filed a response, arguing that the Court had no jurisdiction, claiming *inter alia* that the FRY had no involvement in Bosnia, and that Bosnia was not party to the Genocide Convention. The Court dismissed these preliminary objections on 11 July 1996, finding that it had jurisdiction under Article IX of the Genocide Convention to hear the case. In 1999, Serbia filed a separate case at the ICJ, alleging genocide on the part of a number of NATO states during the bombing campaign in March of that year, but later damaged its own case by arguing that the ICJ had no jurisdiction over it since the FRY was not a UN member until 1 November 2000. The Court, in light of this and other arguments, revisited its jurisdiction, which it ultimately re-established. It also, after lengthy deliberation in the merits, confirmed that State responsibility can arise under the Convention for genocide.[3]

Two main questions remained to be answered: was genocide committed in Bosnia and Herzegovina? If so, was the State of Serbia responsible?

Was genocide committed in Bosnia and Herzegovina

> *The court fails to explain why the deliberate slaughter of civilians in Brčko in 1992, the torture and execution of Muslims in Foča, were legally different in kind from the Srebrenica murders.*[4]

Genocide law, although relatively simple in theory, is extremely difficult to prove in a court. In determining whether genocide was committed in Bosnia and Herzegovina, the ICJ was bound by the Articles of the Genocide Convention and took the safe route, concluding through close examination of Article II of the Convention as it applied to events in Bosnia and Herzegovina between 1992 and 1995, that genocide *was* committed, but only in Srebrenica in July 1995. This broadly mirrored ICTY judgements where, despite a number of genocide indictments, there have been few convictions, all for Srebrenica. Unlike the ICTY, however, which is limited territorially and temporally in bringing about genocide convictions in the case of individual indictments, the ICJ is in a position to adopt a more holistic approach to the Bosnian war, and the widespread and systematic nature of events, in drawing its conclusions. In confining its findings to genocide in Srebrenica in July 1995, the ICJ declined to make full use of its position as a civil court.

Since the term 'genocide' was coined by Polish lawyer Raphael Lemkin in 1944, its interpretation has often been a matter of some contention in legal circles.[5] This is partly because there has been little case law on the crime[6] and because of the difficulty in proving special intent due to contrasting approaches to the *mens rea* requirement. There have also been problems in determining the protected groups under the Genocide Convention, and in identifying *actus reus* and the application of the term in relation to the number of people killed, relative to the population as a whole. Until the establishment of the ICTY in 1993 and the ICTR in 1994, the only judicial proceedings in which the definition of genocide had been interpreted were at the Eichmann trial in Israel in 1961. While there is some overlap between genocide and crimes against humanity in that both represent the most heinous of crimes forming part of a wider or systematic practice, genocide became a category of its own, in requiring a special intent (*dolus specialis*) to destroy, in whole or in part, a protected group of people. It was *dolus specialis* with which the ICJ Court was most concerned in determining whether genocide had been committed in Bosnia and Herzegovina. Rosalyn Higgins, presiding over the ICJ proceedings, although stressing that the Court should not follow the lines of other courts in terms of burden of proof or how to interpret particular conventions such as the genocide convention, did state that the Court 'should be extremely aware of what our sister courts are doing'.[7]

The standard of proof in determining individual criminal responsibility is 'beyond a reasonable doubt'.[8] For state responsibility, there is no uniform standard but, according to Andre Nollkaemper,

> the standard of proof in interstate proceedings is . . . based on the balance of evidence submitted by both parties rather than on the 'beyond reasonable doubt' threshold and therefore generally will be lower than the standard of proof that applies in matters of individual responsibility.[9]

Nollkaemper stressed, however, that for such serious matters as genocide, 'an international court arguably should translate the seriousness of the allegations into a more stringent standard of proof', citing the Dissenting Opinion of Judge Shahabuddeen where he referred to Corfu,[10] which the Court also recalled in considering burden of proof.[11] Despite extensive reference to ad hoc tribunal jurisprudence, the Court declined to follow the broader approaches to the Genocide Convention adopted in some ICTY judgements where judges, citing geographic and temporal limitations, have often tended to qualify their acquittal on genocide by emphasizing the lack of evidence. In Stakic, the Trial Chamber found against genocide 'only on the basis of the evidence in this concrete case',[12] while the Stakic Appeals Chamber judged that 'the Trial Chamber's compartmentalised mode of analysis obscured the proper inquiry'.[13] Similarly, in dismissing the genocide charge in Jelisic, the Trial Chamber emphasized that it was not stating 'that there was no genocide in Brčko in May 1992 but merely noting that the elements presented do not allow it to conclude that such "all inclusive" genocide was committed'.[14] The Trial Chamber in Brdjanin similarly qualified its dismissal of genocide charges.[15]

In the *Akayesu* case, the ICTR Trial Chamber held acts of rape and sexual violence to form 'an integral part' of the destruction process of the Tutsi as a group 'and could therefore constitute genocide'.[16] Despite the findings of the December 1992 Warburton Report, however, which already noted evidence of some 20,000 cases of rape, and evidence from a number of ICTY cases, *Krnojelac* in particular, suggesting its occurrence was not random or sporadic but a systematic process, with long-term consequences, the Court was not persuaded that rape and other sexual atrocities in Bosnia were part of the larger picture, indicating a slow destruction process.[17]

On the extent of destruction required, the Trial Chamber in *Jelisic* proposed both a quantitative and a qualitative criterion, and adopted an expansive approach to 'in part', stating that 'the intention to destroy must target at least a substantial part of the group'[18] should mean either

> a large majority of the group in question or the most representative members of the targeted community. . . . Genocidal intent may therefore be manifest in two forms. It may consist of desiring the extermination of a very large number of the members of the groups. . . . However, it may also consist of the desired destruction of a more limited number of persons selected for the impact that their disappearance would have upon the survival of the group as such.[19]

As has been observed elsewhere, however, the latter 'involves complex value judgments as to the worth of "ordinary" members of the group [which] often requires arbitrary delimitations'.[20]

ICTR jurisprudence has also included the serious impairment of physical or mental capacities within the context of genocide, where the term was interpreted to include, in addition to 'acts of torture', a wide range of 'inhumane or degrading treatment, and persecution . . . without limiting itself thereto'.[21] The Trial Chamber in *Akayesu* constructed subpaI(c) of the Genocide Convention as 'the methods of destruction by which the perpetrator does not immediately kill the members of the group, but which, ultimately, seek their physical destruction'.[22] The *Krstic* judgement also suggested that cultural genocide may be 'an important indicator of the intent to perpetrate physical genocide',[23] although legal commentators differ on this.[24] The Court adopted a more restricted interpretation. The Trial Chamber in *Blagojevic*, in recalling the opinion of Judge Shahabuddeen in the *Krstic* Appeal Judgement, determined that 'what was originally intended to be excluded from the definition of the crime was cultural genocide [did] not in itself prevent that physical or biological genocide could extend beyond killings of the members of the group'.[25] He found that 'the intent certainly has to be to destroy but, except for the listed act, there is no reason why the destruction must always be physical or biological', arguing that it is the group which is protected, constituted by characteristics binding it together as a social unit.[26] It could, by this token, be argued that the group, also through large-scale expulsions, was destroyed, since it no longer existed as a group within Bosnia and Herzegovina. Indeed, the majority in the *Krstic* Appeals Chamber held that

> forcible transfer could be an additional means by which to ensure the physical destruction of the Bosnian Muslim community in Srebrenica. The transfer completed the removal of all Bosnian Muslims from Srebrenica, thereby *eliminating even the residual possibility that the Muslim community in the area could reconstitute itself*.[27]

In Srebrenica, to date, relatively few Muslims have managed to return, and these have not generally enjoyed equal access to essential services, a situation which prevails in towns throughout Republika Srpska, where there was a Muslim majority before the war.[28] The Court applied that criteria only to Srebrenica, however, resting its rejection of that interpretation on the *travaux preparatoires* of the Convention, and the Sixth Committee approach, as confirmed by the International Law Commission (ILC).[29]

*

The methodology employed by the Court involved an approach which, in general terms, was arguably fragmentary rather than comprehensive. In examining the alleged facts presented by the Bosnian team, the Court examined each crime, or set of crimes, individually, separating municipalities from camps, and Srebrenica from all else, an indication of the judges' tendency to adhere closely to ICTY methodology and jurisprudence which potentially impeded the synergism required in determining civil responsibility.

Considering firstly (a) whether the killings which had taken place in the municipalities (excluding Srebrenica) and camps, and (b) whether 'serious bodily or mental harm' had been caused to the protected group, fell within the scope of Article II of the Convention, the Court held that although the requirements of the material element, as defined by the Convention had been fulfilled, the specific intent (*dolus specialis)* had not been 'conclusively established'. [30] The Court reached the same conclusion for Article II(c) 'encirclement, shelling and starvation',[31] based mainly on the ICTY *Galic* case which had been confined to Sarajevo, however.[32] The Bosnian Serb Army (VRS) military offensive in the UN 'safe area' of Gorazde in April 1994 was referred to by the Court but solely in relation to the targeting of the hospital, cutting off the water supply, and the detention of UN personnel.[33] The judgement omitted the most important consequence of the Gorazde offensive, namely, that over 700 people were killed, and nearly 2,000 wounded, in less than three weeks.[34] Neither did the Court consider the numerous casualties amongst Bosniaks in Srebrenica and elsewhere in the Drina valley in early 1993, resulting from VRS military operations, backed by paramilitary groups. The scale of the 1993 Srebrenica onslaught has led some commentators to conclude that the genocide started at that time, only culminating in July 1995.[35]

The Court, in considering the deportations and expulsions, adhered firmly to the argument that 'an essential motive of much of the Bosnian Serb leadership – to create a larger Serb State, by a war of conquest if necessary – did not necessarily require the destruction of the Bosnian Muslims and other communities, but their expulsion'.[36] On the destruction of Bosnia's cultural heritage, the Court found conclusive evidence of destruction of the historical, cultural and religious heritage in Bosnia and Herzegovina 'albeit in a limited geographical area'.[37] The Court thus apparently accepted the Serbian team's unsubstantiated argument that the municipalities included in the expert report only[*sic*] amounted to 25% of the territory of Bosnia and Herzegovina, concluding that it did not fall within Article II of the Convention.[38]

In confirming genocide in Srebrenica, the Court relied heavily on the *Blagojevic* and *Krstic* judgements,[39] but failed to draw broader conclusions from the landscape of the war as a whole. Citing *Krstic* and *Blagojevic*, the Court dated the genocide from 12/13 July 1995 by VRS forces who, it would appear, suddenly acquired genocidal intent.[40] Yet, according to the Srebrenica Report, the information that the decision to kill the men of Srebrenica 'might have been taken only after the fall of Srebrenica' emanated from Serb sources.[41] It was clearly to Serbia's advantage to argue that the decision was not made *before* the fall of the enclave due to solid information concerning the involvement of VJ forces and military units from Serbia at that time. Yet ICTY jurisprudence is not conclusive enough to support the Court's ruling that the genocide occurred only from 12/13 July 1995. The Court did not satisfactorily address the conundrum of why the VRS forces should have taken the enclave and subsequently slaughtered over 7,000 people, rather than continue the slow process of attrition pursued for more than three years across Bosnia. Also, despite extensive citation of ICTY jurisprudence, the Court did not amplify why the *dolus specialis* which, it held, existed in the case of Srebrenica, could not be inferred from the wide-scale pattern of atrocities committed over many communities, where tens of thousands of Bosnian Muslims had been killed.[42] A further anomaly in the Court's finding that the group had been destroyed in Srebrenica was that the majority of the people in Srebrenica at the time the enclave fell to Serb forces had fled from other areas of Bosnia so it could be argued that, technically, they were not part of that group.[43]

The Court held that the motive to create a Greater Serbia did not require the destruction of the group, but its expulsion,[44] but failed to explain why, if this was the case, so many in the group had been killed or tortured in a consistent pattern of events. Ignoring the *Jelisic* judgement, the Court concluded that *dolus specialis* 'has to be convincingly shown by reference to particular circumstances, unless a general plan to that end can be convincingly demonstrated to exist'.[45] This test is consistent with the ICTY holding in *Brdjanin*.[46] The *Brdjanin* judgement was limited to the indictment, however.[47] And the *ad hoc* tribunals have in some instances applied a lower threshold.[48]

While conceding (citing *Krstic*) that

> where there is physical or biological destruction there are often simultaneous attacks on the cultural and religious property and symbols of the targeted group . . . which may legitimately be considered as evidence of an intent to physically destroy the group,[49]

the Court dismissed *dolus specialis* elsewhere in Bosnia, but failed to offer a more plausible reason for the systematic wide-scale atrocities against the protected group and the destruction of their cultural heritage other than by reference to ICTY genocide indictments, where the lack of a conviction resulted in many cases from either the death of the defendant, dropped charges due to plea bargaining or, as already noted, were limited by the scope of the indictments.[50]

An undoubted influence on the ICJ Court was the ICTY *Krajisnik* judgement (September 2006) which fell between the merits and judgement of the *Genocide* case. This was an immensely important case due to the seniority of the defendant, the territorial breadth of the indictment, and the Trial Chamber's dismissal of both genocide charges, on the grounds that there was insufficient evidence of *dolus specialis*.[51]

Momčilo Krajisnik, from October 1991, was president of the Bosnian Serb Assembly and chaired all but one of the 23 sessions held between that date and December 1992.[52] Additionally, Krajisnik's membership of the five-member presidency which also acted as the commander-in-chief of the Bosnian Serb Republic, served to formalize and consolidate the authority he wielded, together with Karadzic, over all state structures.[53] The *Krajisnik* Trial Chamber concluded that some of the crimes investigated met the requirements of the *actus reus* for genocide, but its legal findings in the genocide section were unusually brief. [54]

> The evidence does not show that the crime of genocide formed part of the common objective of the JCE in which the Accused participated. . . . Statements and speeches of the Accused and others . . . hinged on two main ideas, namely that Serbs had to separate from Muslims and Croats . . . and that there existed historically Serb territories. . . . The discriminatory remarks uttered by the Accused . . . served . . . to retrospectively legitimize the forcible removal. They did not reveal an intent to destroy an ethnic group in whole or in part.[55]

Examining the instances of extermination, the Chamber considered the number of victims relative to the total number of Bosnian Muslims and Croats in the village or detention centre where the crimes occurred, and found the killings themselves to be 'in no instance . . . sufficient to make a conclusive finding on whether the perpetrator had a genocidal intent'.[56] The Trial Chamber was also presented with schedules listing 21 separate multiple killings in detention camps and 59 outside detention facilities in 18 municipalities, and estimated on that basis that at least 3,000 had been exterminated, holding that Krajisnik had command responsibility.[57] In 13 of the 21 camps, however, the numbers killed were unspecified in the schedule, reference merely being to 'hundreds' (the Omarksa detention camp) 'dozens' (the Čajniče camp) or 'a number'. Crucially, the unspecified killings were not reflected in the number quoted in the judgement.[58] Similarly, for unspecified killings in the municipalities.[59] In sentencing, the Trial Chamber acknowledged that the impact of the crimes

> on the entire Muslim and Croat community in Bosnia-Herzegovina [has] been profound. The consequences of the crimes of which Momčilo Krajisnik has been found guilty as a co-perpetrator in a JCE will persist in Bosnia- Herzegovina for decades, affecting hundreds of thousands of people.[60]

The Chamber nonetheless concluded that there was no evidence that genocide was committed in the indictment municipalities, 'which . . . is only to say that the evidence is not conclusive beyond reasonable doubt as to the commission of genocide'.[61]

In the ICTY cases, with the exception of *Krajisnik*, the dimensions of the crimes were not always fully discernible due to the inevitable geographic delimitation involved in trying individual perpetrators. The ICJ on the other hand, was better placed to take a broad overview. The ICJ judgement was undoubtedly aided by *Krajisnik* which was at that point the only case, apart from *Milosevic*, where crimes committed throughout Bosnia were considered by the tribunal.

Yet the role of the ICJ is different from that of the ICTY, since the Court was in a position, unlike Tribunal judges, to examine the entire spectrum of events without the restriction of temporal or geographic limitations. But its findings did not reflect its different role. Moreover, in ICTY (and especially ICTR) cases where a more flexible interpretation of certain aspects of the Genocide Convention was adopted, the Court tended to eschew any broader interpretation of the Convention, provoking a number of commentators to claim that it set its threshold so high as to render a genocide finding virtually impossible.

Was Serbia as a state responsible for genocide?

> *I urge that arbitrators take care not to give the articles undue or unquestioned authority. . . . By too great and casual a deference to the lex generalis of the ILC draft articles, arbitrators may unconsciously undo the lex specialis of the parties.*[62]

The Court's restriction of the genocide to Srebrenica[63] significantly facilitated its dismissal of State responsibility on the part of Serbia. The judgement essentially revolved around the competing tests of *Nicaragua*[64] and *Tadic*,[65] and the differing levels of control required in the respective cases. The Court, referring to customary international law, with special focus on the ILC 2001 Articles, found the *Nicaragua* control test the most appropriate to the case. The *Nicaragua* and *Tadic* judgements are examined as they relate to the findings of the Court in the *Genocide* case, with particular reference to ILC Articles 4 and 8 as they influenced the case, and to ICTY jurisprudence and other relevant literature.

The 13-year delay before the *Genocide* case came to court allowed the Court to benefit from the jurisprudence of the *ad hoc* tribunals the case. Yet close adherence to ICTY jurisprudence in relation to the genocide charges could have been misleading since, apart from the limited scope of the tribunal vis-à-vis the ICJ, as discussed earlier,[66] a number of genocide indictments were withdrawn,[67] some genocide defendants died before or during proceedings,[68] and for others plea agreements were negotiated.[69]

The ICTY Decision of 16 June 2004 on the Acquittal Motion under Rule 98bis of its Statute, filed by the *Amici Curiae* in the Milosevic case, is instructive. The ICTY judges dismissed the *Amici Curiae* motion for acquittal, holding that there was sufficient evidence to indicate that genocide had been committed in Bosnia, and that

> the Accused was a participant in a joint criminal enterprise, which included members of the Bosnian Serb leadership, to commit other crimes than genocide and it was reasonably foreseeable to him that, as a consequence of the commission of those crimes, genocide of a part of the Bosnian Muslims as a group would be committed by other participants in the joint criminal enterprise, and it was committed.[70]

The Trial Chamber considered that there was also evidence that Milosevic aided or abetted, or was complicit, in genocide, and that he had failed to take measures to prevent the genocide, or punish the perpetrators.[71] Seven municipalities were listed in which genocide was allegedly committed, including Srebrenica.[72] While acquittal motions do not constitute legal proof of responsibility – and Milosevic's untimely death precluded a final judgement – it is not clear from the judgement that the Court considered the ICTY Decision on the acquittal motion in the context of State responsibility for genocide.[73]

In applying the high standard of 'beyond reasonable doubt', the Court may have been guided by its judgement in the *Corfu Channel* case, yet such a standard, according to Ruth Wedgwood and others,[74] exceeds the demands of civil liability, and in trying to meet that standard, the court declined to draw any adverse inference against Belgrade, even though the Serbian Defence Council documents the Respondent provided to the court were heavily redacted. As one observer noted, however, 'the court has a consistent policy of citing its own decisions and would only depart from a previous one in very rare circumstances'.[75] The ICJ judgement in the *Genocide* case bore out this observation.

*

The *Genocide* case pivoted around the level of control required to demonstrate the nexus between the Serbian State organs and the Bosnian Serb political and military organs or agents. In seeking to establish the precise nature and degree of control required for the attribution of wrongful acts, *Nicaragua* and *Tadić* came up with different answers.

The case of *Nicaragua* concerned the responsibility of the United States for violations of international humanitarian law by the *contras*, but since the *contras* were not organs of the United States, the Court had to formulate tests for attribution of their acts to the United States. Two alternative control tests were devised, to determine (i) whether or not the relationship of the *contras* was so much one of dependence on the one side and control on the other that it would be right to equate the contras, for legal purposes, with an organ of the US government, or as acting on behalf of that government[76] and, if not, (ii) whether they were under the effective control of the state, that is to say, whether they were financed by the State, whether the State coordinated and supervised their action, or had issued specific instructions for each action.[77] In the judgement, the *Nicaragua* Court found that there was insufficient evidence to demonstrate either level of control.[78] The ICTY Appeals Chamber in the *Tadic* case[79] departed from the *Nicaragua* judgement[80] in holding *inter alia* that, in regard to armed groups, the test for State responsibility was whether those groups were under the *overall* control of the State.[81] This did not necessitate the State issuing instructions for, or exercising control over, each specific operation in breach of international law.[82]

The Court rejected the *Tadić* Appeal test in favour of *Nicaragua*, observing that

> the ICTY was not called upon in *Tadić*, nor is it in general called upon, to rule on questions of State responsibility, since its jurisdiction is criminal and extends over persons only. Thus, in that judgment the Tribunal addressed an issue which was not indispensable for the exercise of its jurisdiction.[83]

On the other hand, the issue in question in the *Genocide* case, as Cassese argued, was 'whether or not the appraisal of customary international law made by the ICTY was more persuasive than that by the ICJ'.[84]

Having thus admonished the ICTY Appeals Chamber, the Court held that 'the situation is not the same for positions adopted by the ICTY on issues of general international law which do not lie within the specific purview of its jurisdiction'.[85] The Court further concluded that the overall control test argument presented by the ICTY in the *Tadić* Appeal was 'unpersuasive',[86] observing that it 'has the major drawback of broadening the scope of State responsibility well beyond the fundamental principle governing the law of international responsibility'.[87]

The *Genocide* case differs from the *Nicaragua* case in several crucial aspects. The *contras* did not seek to incorporate Nicaragua into the United States, whereas the common aim of Serbs from Bosnia, Croatia and Serbia was the creation of a 'Greater Serbia', in which non-Serb elements were to be expelled, eradicated or reduced to minority status. And, while the *contras* were Nicaraguan and claimed neither US nationality nor citizenship, for Bosnian Serbs[88] ethnicity took precedence over nationality since, although Bosnian by nationality, they considered themselves Serb.[89] The historical contexts of the two cases are also entirely different. The United States and the *contras* were not the product of the dismemberment of a single entity. By contrast, the 'organic unity of RS and the FRY simply represents the continuation of a long common history'.[90] Lastly, the United States did not create the *contras*, whereas the VRS was the creation of the FRY[91] and the Yugoslav National Army (JNA).[92]

It was the ILC Articles and commentaries which were to prove the decisive factor, however, in determining the outcome of the case.

The ILC 2001 Articles established a number of paradigms of attribution of individual and group conduct to a state under customary international law. The Articles themselves do not define a standard of control for attribution, but the commentaries implicitly approve the effective control test in the *Nicaragua* judgement for attributing State responsibility,[93] and were regarded as central to the Court's approach in the *Genocide* case.

Chapter II of the Articles, concerning 'attribution of conduct to a State', rests on two main pillars, Article 4 and Article 8.[94] These two Articles were referred to in some detail by the Court in determining whether the Srebrenica genocide was attributable to the State of Serbia on the basis of the conduct of its organs (Article 4), or conduct directed or controlled by the State (Article 8). Article 4, reflecting a rule of customary international law, reads,

1 The conduct of any State organ shall be considered an act of that State under international law, whether the organ exercises legislative, executive, judicial or any other functions, whatever position it holds in the organization of the State, and whatever its character as an organ of the central Government or of a territorial unit of the State.
2 An organ includes any person or entity which has that status in accordance with the internal law of the State.[95]

In considering attribution under Article 4, the Court held that the VRS was not a *de jure* organ of the FRY, since it did not have that status under its internal law.[96] From this, it was concluded that there was no evidence to support a finding that the Srebrenica genocide was perpetrated by an entity having the status of an organ of Serbia, although the Court conceded that there was considerable evidence of 'direct or indirect participation' by the Yugoslav Army (VJ), along with the VRS, in the years prior to the Srebrenica events, and of financial support to the VRS.[97] The Court also acknowledged that the FRY had provided substantial support to the Republika Srpska, including payment of salaries and other benefits to some officers of the VRS, although this did not automatically make them organs of the FRY.

Those officers were appointed to their commands by the President of the Republika Srpska, and were subordinated to the political leadership of the Republika Srpska. In the absence of evidence to the contrary, those officers must be taken to have received their orders from the Republika Srpska or the VRS, not from the FRY. The expression 'State organ', as used in customary international law and in Article 4 of the ILC Articles, applies to one or other of the individual or collective entities, which make up the organization of the state and act on its behalf. . . . The functions of the VRS officers, including General Mladić, were however to act on behalf of the Bosnian Serb authorities, in particular Republika Srpska, not on behalf of the FRY; they exercised elements of the public authority of the Republika Srpska.[98]

This poses a problem, however, in that the Court appears to view 'Republika Srpska' as if it were a legal entity referring to 'the President of the Republika Srpska', and to 'the public authority of the Republika Srpska',[99] notwithstanding the fact that it was an illegal para-state until ratified as an entity (although not a state) within Bosnia and Herzegovina through the Dayton Accords in late 1995.[100] The Court seemingly accorded undue credit to the Serbian team's reiterated argument that there is 'substantial evidence of the status of the Republika Srpska as an independent State'.[101]

In stating that the salaries of only 'some officers of the VRS' were paid by the VJ, the Court inferred a lesser level of support than was formerly conceded.[102] The Court also stated that those 'officers were appointed to their commands by the President of the Republika Srpska', contradicting evidence provided by the Bosnian team.[103] In regard to the status of the VRS, the Court additionally appears to ignore ICTY jurisprudence where it was held that

> throughout 1991 and 1992, the Bosnian Serb leadership communicated with the SFRY leadership on strategic policy in the event that [BiH] would become independent. The Trial Chamber is satisfied that these factors, coupled with the continued payment of the salaries of the VRS officers by Belgrade indicate that, after 19 May 1992, *the VRS and the VJ did not constitute two separate armies* despite the change of name. . . . No consequential material changes actually occurred . . . the military objectives and strategies, the equipment, the officers in command, the infrastructures and the sources of supply also remained the same. In addition, the JNA military operations under the command of Belgrade that had already commenced by 19 May 1992 did not cease immediately and the same elements of the VJ continued to be directly involved in them. Further active elements of what had been the JNA remained in [BiH] after the purported 19 May 1992 withdrawal.[104]

On the basis of this finding, it could be surmised that Serbia, through the VJ and VRS operating as one army, was responsible under Article 4 for *all* the acts of the VRS in Bosnia and Herzegovina, even those not specifically under the control of Belgrade or committed *ultra vires* against its explicit instructions, which includes the Srebrenica genocide. The Serbian team argued that Serbia's control over Bosnia lessened in the course of the war, but the hierarchy of authority at Dayton seems to suggest that this was not the case. In fact, a central argument for Serbia's complete control of the Bosnian Serb organs throughout the war in Bosnia and Herzegovina and afterwards is that, in November 1995, the Serbian president, Slobodan Milosevic, was designated as the chairman of the Serb delegation at the Dayton Peace Conference on behalf of the Bosnian Serbs as well as of Serbia; it was Milosevic who signed the GFA which guaranteed Republika Srpska's fulfilment of the Agreement, with no objection from the Bosnian Serb leaders.[105]

One of the problems in interpreting the ILC Articles is, as de Hoogh points out, that the commentaries do not seem to provide clear criteria for determining whether a person or entity constitutes an organ of the State, notwithstanding the absence or denial of that status under internal law.[106] The ILC, however, did note that the way in which powers were conferred on an entity, the purpose of the powers, and the degree to which the entity can exercise the powers, were important factors.[107] There is also some ambiguity in regard to terminology, in distinguishing 'organs' from 'agents'. Although it was agreed that 'organs' should refer to Article 4, with the term 'agent' being reserved to Article 8, there appears to be some confusion on this within the ILC. De Hoogh concludes that the phrase 'de *facto* organ' should be applicable to Article 4, 'by virtue of the supplementary role of international law under Article 4, paragraph 2'. [108] This is particularly relevant to the *Genocide* case, since it implies more flexibility than the Court exercised when it concluded that 'neither the Republika Srpska, nor the VRS were *de jure* organs of the FRY, since none of them had the status of organ of that State under its internal law'.[109]

Based on the strict control test of *Nicaragua* and the ILC Articles, and evidently persuaded by the arguments of the Serbian team, the Court, adopting a conservative interpretation of the level and nature of control required to demonstrate the required nexus, declared Serbia not to be responsible for the Srebrenica genocide under Article 4.

ILC Article 8 deals with attribution of conduct of a person or group of persons who do not enjoy the status of an organ but are under the instructions of, or directed or controlled by, the state.

> The conduct of a person or group of persons shall be considered an act of a State under international law if the person or group of persons is in fact acting on the instructions of, or under the direction or control of, that State in carrying out the conduct.[110]

Under this formulation, it is difficult to find State responsibility for the Srebrenica genocide since in most cases it will be impossible to prove a direct order by the state to a non-state actor acting as its proxy. States today have learned from the Nazi experience, so there is unlikely to be a smoking gun, or a Wannsee Conference, showing Serbia plotting genocide in Bosnia.[111]

The previous draft Articles did not contain specific requirements on instructions or directions, but used an abstract formulation on attribution of acts of persons or groups of persons in fact acting on behalf of the state.[112] The final Articles do not define a standard of control for attribution, but the ILC commentary cites the second *Nicaragua* test, namely, of effective control,[113] while States in submissions to the ILC made no comments regarding standards of control.[114] The Court clarifies its position on Article 8 at the outset in support of the effective control test of *Nicaragua*, without discussing any of the difficulties in drawing over-close parallels between *Nicaragua* and the *Genocide* case:

> This provision must be understood in the light of the Court's jurisprudence on the subject, particularly that of the 1986 Judgment in the case concerning *Military and Paramilitary Activities in and against Nicaragua*.[115]

The Court was also clearly guided by the commentaries on the ILC Articles:

> It must . . . be shown that this 'effective control' was exercised, or that the State's instructions were given, *in respect of each operation* in which the alleged violations occurred, not generally in respect of the overall actions taken by the persons or groups of persons having committed the violations.[116]

The ILC commentary to Article 8 expanded the definition within the Article itself.

> More complex issues arise in determining whether conduct was carried out 'under the direction or control' of a State. Such conduct will be attributable to the State only if it directed or controlled the *specific operation* and the conduct complained of was an integral part of that operation.[117]

This narrowed the field considerably, making it extremely difficult to link the Srebrenica genocide to Serbia, given the timespan of the occurrence of the genocide as determined by the Court, namely, after 12 July 1995. In other words, the operation over the preceding days to take over the enclave, where there was evidence of VRS involvement, *and* of coordination with Belgrade, was not considered.[118] Additionally, no convincing evidence of VJ participation had been produced by the Bosnian team for the Srebrenica genocide, rendering Article 8 virtually irrelevant to the case.

Special Rapporteur James Crawford had proposed the more stringent form of wording for persons acting on the instructions of a State, or under its direction or control, for specific operations for State attribution.[119] Since this limitation does not appear in Article 8 itself, however, it might be regarded as a guideline, rather than a hard-and-fast rule, and in the commentary, it is also noted that

> [i]n any event it is a matter for appreciation in each case whether particular conduct was or was not carried out under the control of a State, to such an extent that the conduct controlled should be attributed to it.[120]

As De Hoogh points out, 'the text of Article 8 does not exclude application of the standard of overall control, speaking as it does of control, and the revised commentary suggests a case-by-case analysis'.[121]

The Court also reflects the ILC Articles in drawing a firm distinction between the test for determining that a conflict is international in nature (*Tadić*) and the test of involvement required for state responsibility, namely, the 'effective control' test (*Nicaragua*) 'for a particular act committed in the course of the conflict',[122] holding that the 'overall control test' used in *Tadić* 'has the major drawback of broadening the scope of State responsibility well beyond the fundamental principle governing the law of international responsibility'.[123] Application of the 'effective control test' also facilitated the Court's dismissal of the role of the Scorpions, whose members were shown on a graphic video filmed by the executioners themselves, killing six young Bosniacs from Srebrenica.[124] Yet, despite the Scorpions being considered by a number of commentators to be a Serbian police unit, and consequently a *de jure* organ of Serbia,[125] the Court held that there was insufficient evidence to indicate that they were acting in complete dependence on Serbia.

The Court's insistence on strict adherence to the Nicaragua decision, and the corresponding ILC Articles which upheld that decision in respect of State responsibility, beg the question of a possible conflict of interest, since Ian Brownlie, the leading counsel for Serbia in the Genocide case, both in 1996 and 2006, also had a strong voice as a long-standing member of the ILC in the final form of the 2001 ILC Articles.[126]

In contrast, a former long-serving ILC member, Paul Reuter, specializing in the law of State responsibility, stressed the technical complexity of this branch of law, and the 'inherent difficulties' in codification as a pre-legislative function which call for 'more flexibility and less dogmatism'.[127] The ICJ did not appear to have heeded this ad.

*

Legal experts differ on whether *Nicaragua* or *Tadić* was the more applicable case in determining State responsibility, but the Court's choice was consistent with its decision to dismiss the incidence of genocide in Bosnia, other than in Srebrenica in 1995. The Court decided that *Nicaragua* was the preferable jurisdiction, even though *Tadić* shared the same history as the *Genocide* case and was, by a number of commentators, considered the most appropriate precedent.

Through its ruling, the Court set aside ICTY jurisprudence in *Brdjanin*, that the Bosnian Serb Army and the Yugoslav Army did not constitute separate armies, along with a substantial volume of evidence suggesting intent to destroy the group through a systematic pattern of events, and by attrition, in the besieged towns and enclaves across Bosnia, and in the camps. The Court was also unable to explain how the VRS, after over three years resisting genocide, finally – and suddenly – acquired intent within the space of hours, following their capture of the Srebrenica enclave.

The Court's determination, that the genocide in Bosnia was confined to the Srebrenica massacres starting on 12/13 July 1995, was reached through close adherence to the letter of ILC Articles 4 and 8 (2001). Before 19 May 1992, on the other hand, when there *was* conclusive proof of Serbia's complete control over the Bosnian Serb political and military leadership, and of its direct involvement in the systematic mass murder and other crimes under the Genocide Convention, the Court found that there was insufficient proof of genocidal intent. Bosnia's case, therefore, fell between two stools.

The judgement: some legal and political considerations

> *Realpolitik was ever the enemy of justice.*[128]

One of the most controversial of the Court's rulings was that Serbia was not complicit in the Srebrenica genocide, but could have prevented it.[129]

The Court defined the parameters within which the question of complicity in genocide would be examined. Determining that 'complicity' in the sense of Article III(e) of the Convention includes 'the provision of means to enable or facilitate the commission of the crime',[130] the Court focused on that aspect, holding that although the term does not exist in the law of international responsibility, it is similar to the 'aid or assistance' term found in customary international law on State responsibility. The 2001 ILC 2001 Articles were, therefore, considered an appropriate reference point. Article 16 states that

> a State which aids or assists another State in the commission of an internationally wrongful act by the latter is internationally responsible for doing so if: That State does so with knowledge of the circumstances of the internationally wrongful act; and The act would be internationally wrongful if committed by that State.

Article 16 is not directly relevant to the case since it refers to relations between *States*, while the *Genocide* case addresses attributability of a State to an *entity*. The Court, while acknowledging this, saw 'no reason to make any distinction of substance between Article III(e) of the Convention – "complicity in genocide", and Article 16 of the ILC Articles – "aid or assistance" '. On that basis, the Court saw its task as examining

> whether organs of the respondent State, or persons acting on its instructions or under its direction or effective control, furnished 'aid or assistance' in the commission of the genocide in Srebrenica, in a sense not significantly different from that of those concepts in the general law of international responsibility.[131]

On the question of *dolus specialis*, the Court held that

> the conduct of an organ or a person furnishing aid or assistance to a perpetrator of the crime of genocide cannot be treated as complicity in genocide unless at the least that organ or person acted knowingly, that is to say, in particular, was aware of the specific intent (*dolus specialis*) of the principal perpetrator. If that condition is not fulfilled, that is sufficient to exclude categorization as complicity . . . the sole task of the Court is to establish the legal responsibility of the Respondent, a responsibility which is subject to very specific conditions.[132]

The parameters set enabled the Court to conclude that there was insufficient evidence to meet the conditions because it was not established beyond any doubt that the FRY authorities supplied, and continued to supply, the VRS leaders when they were clearly aware that the genocide was about to be carried out, or already under way.[133]

The decisive point in this connection, the Court held, was that the Bosnian team had not conclusively shown that 'the decision to eliminate physically the adult male population of the Muslim community from Srebrenica was brought to the attention of the Belgrade authorities when it was taken'.[134] The Court recalled that since it had been established that the Bosnian Serb authorities made the decision 'shortly before it was actually carried out', it could not be concluded that at the crucial time [between 13 and 16 July 1995] the FRY had supplied aid to the perpetrators of the genocide 'in full awareness that the aid supplied would be used to commit genocide'.[135] From this, the Court held that Serbia was not responsible for complicity in genocide.

The difference between responsibility for preventing and punishing genocide and complicity in genocide, the Court held, was one of conduct, not result.

> There are two main differences; they are so significant as to make it impossible to treat the two types of violation in the same way . . . complicity always requires that some positive action has been taken to furnish aid or assistance to the perpetrators of the genocide, while a violation of the obligation to prevent results from mere failure to adopt and implement suitable measures to prevent genocide from being committed.[136]

The Court set the parameters in assessing a State's discharge of its obligation as, firstly, 'the capacity to influence effectively the action of persons likely to commit, or already committing, genocide', which in turn depends on the distance of the State from the scene of events, and on the strength of the political and other links.[137]

The Court held that a State's obligation to prevent, and its corresponding duty to act, 'arise at the instant that the State learns of, or should normally have learned of, the existence of a serious risk that genocide will be committed'.[138] Complicity then, according to the Court, resulted from commission, and breaching the obligation to prevent from omission. This, according to some commentators, is not an absolute distinction.[139] In drawing this fine line between complicity and breach of the obligation to prevent genocide, the Court found Serbia to be in breach of the latter only.

Four of the judges voted against the majority on the issue of complicity. Judge Bennouna opined that the parameters set by the Court extended well beyond the Genocide Convention, and pointed to the Court's omission to provide a definition of complicity which left unanswered the question of whether the accomplice should share the *dolus specialis* of the main perpetrator.[140] Bennouna considered that the Court should distance itself from that requirement, as advanced by the Serbian team since it 'goes against the generally accepted definition of complicity' and leads to the 'absurd' result of assimilating accomplice and main perpetrator.[141] As evidence that Belgrade knew that genocide was intended, Bennouna recalled the presence of a number of VJ officers at Han Pijesak (the VRS headquarters), considering it inconceivable that they had not informed their superiors.[142] He also referred to the meetings between Mladić and Milosevic, as quoted in the Srebrenica Report, the presence in Srebrenica of the Scorpions, a force under the control of the Serbian interior ministry, and the close military ties between the VRS and VJ, as sufficient evidence to demonstrate Serbia's complicity in the Srebrenica genocide.[143]

Judge Keith, also voting against the majority finding on complicity, pointed out that not only the Belgrade leadership but the wider international community knew of the deteriorating security situation in the Srebrenica area, as demonstrated by Security Council resolution 1004 under Chapter VII of the UN Charter.[144] On 13 July 1995, Judge Keith stressed, UN military observers reported that they had been informed by General Mladić that there were several hundred dead Muslim soldiers in the enclave.[145] He also recalled the meetings between Milosevic and Mladic in Serbia, the first meeting just days before and the second within two days of the commencement of the massacres, and concluded,

> Given President Milosevic's overall role in the Balkan wars . . . his specific relationship with General Mladic, and his involvement in the detail of the negotiations of 14 and 15 July, by that time he must have known of the change in plans made by the VRS command on 12 or 13 July and consequently he must have known that they had formed the intent to destroy in part the protected group.[146]

The Court's finding implies that the Serbian authorities remained in the dark while the killing was in progress and widely reported. Other commentators have also expressed concern at the Court's finding on complicity. Professor Damaska opined that

> if the Serbian government knew about the massacre in Srebrenica, its failure to use its influence on Republika Srpska to avert the tragedy should have been judged by the Court as being accessory to (aiding) the crime. . . . Instead . . . the Court accepted that the government was aware only of the possibility that the massacre might occur. This led the majority of the judges to reach the somewhat hasty conclusion that Serbia was responsible for failing to prevent genocide but not for aiding its execution.[147]

A fundamental problem is the unrealistically high standard of proof for finding Serbia legally complicit in genocide. As Cassese argued, one can be guilty of complicity in a crime 'by not stopping it while having both the duty and power to do so, and when through one's inaction, one decisively contributes to the creation of conditions that enable the crime to take place'.[148] The Court relied on the ILC Articles, which were not altogether applicable to the *Genocide* case, to support what many commentators consider to be the very fine line between complicity in genocide, and violation of the obligation to prevent genocide.

The Court devoted substantial time to considering Serbia's compliance with the obligation to punish the crime of genocide, including lengthy deliberation on whether the ICTY constitutes an 'international penal tribunal' as laid down in the Convention, an issue which had already been examined and resolved elsewhere.[149] The Court's determination that Serbia 'failed in its duty to co-operate fully with the ICTY' (other than the declaration that Serbia was in breach of the Convention), merely echoed numerous statements by the Office of the Prosecutor at the

ICTY, and by other international institutions and leaders. It also had no effect in practical terms, at least in the short run.

*

One of the most controversial aspects of the ICJ judgement was the Court's refusal to require from Serbia the full, unredacted version of the Serbian Supreme Defence Council documents, essential to proving a nexus between the Serbian authorities and the Bosnian Serb Army.

The Serbian Supreme Defence Council (SDC), a senior decision-making body based in Belgrade, decided in 1993 to formalize support for VRS officers in Bosnia by establishing a body within the Yugoslav army called the 30th personnel centre.[150] Portions of the SDC records made public suggest that Belgrade was making payments to VRS officers as late as 2001.[151] The SDC agenda included the military budget, promotions and the retirement of generals. The records consist of over 50 documents of minutes and transcripts of wartime meetings of Yugoslav political and military leaders, including Slobodan Milosevic, and were frequently attended by the Bosnian Serb general, Ratko Mladic.[152] The Council met three times immediately after the Srebrenica massacres, but SDC records for July 1995 are missing even from the secret archives.

Serbia obtained permission from the ICTY to keep the major part of the archives secret. According to one Serbian official, there was major concern that the evidence might influence the ICJ case.[153] It took two years before the Belgrade government handed over the documents to the ICTY prosecutors. Before the handover, however, a legal team from the Serbian foreign ministry insisted, on grounds of 'national security interests' that the documents be edited to keep them from harming their case at the ICJ.[154] Vladimir Djeric at the Serbian foreign ministry was later quoted as commenting to lawyers in Belgrade, 'We could not believe our luck'.[155] The redacted version was used extensively at the Milosevic trial to substantiate allegations that the VRS was supported by Serbia. Lawyers who saw the archives claimed that they addressed Serbian control and direction even more directly, 'revealing in new and vivid detail how Belgrade financed and supplied the war in Bosnia, and how the Bosnian Serb Army, officially separate from 1992, remained virtually an extension of the Yugoslav Army'.[156]

Before the start of the ICJ *Genocide* case, the Bosnian team had requested that the Court require Serbia to release the SDC documents unredacted, or to issue a formal note of refusal, under Article 49 of the ICJ Statute:

> The Court may, even before the hearing begins, call upon the agents to produce any document or to supply any explanations. Formal note shall be taken of any refusal.[157]

The Court rejected the Bosnian team's request with the laconic comment that 'the Applicant has extensive documentation and other evidence available to it, especially from the readily accessible ICTY records',[158] a statement closely replicating the Serbian team's own reasoning.[159] Not having demanded the SDC documents, the Court was not in a position to comply with the requirement under Article 49 of the ICJ Statute to note the Respondent's refusal, or to offer a satisfactory explanation. Instead it merely noted that

> [a]lthough the Court has not agreed to either of the Applicant's requests to be provided with unedited copies of the documents, it has not failed to note the Applicant's suggestion that the Court may be free to draw its own conclusions.[160]

ICJ President Rosalyn Higgins, in a later interview, declined to comment as to why the judges had not subpoenaed the uncensored archives, commenting that it was not the practice of the court to discuss its findings: 'The ruling speaks for itself'.[161] According to some international lawyers, the court might have wished to avoid a diplomatic showdown with Serbia, and the fact that it was a civil, not a criminal, court meant that it was more used to relying on documents before it, than to 'aggressively pursuing evidence'.[162] The decision had serious political implications, however.

Three of the judges criticized the failure. ICJ Vice-President Al-Khasawneh of Jordan noted, 'Regrettably the court failed to act. . . . It is a reasonable expectation that those documents would have shed light on the central questions'. Severely criticizing the Court's refusal to meet the requirement of Article 49, Judge Al-Khasawneh referred to the *Corfu Channel* judgement which ruled that where a State is victim of a breach of international law, it is often not in a position to provide direct proof of facts indicating responsibility.[163]

> Such a State should be allowed a more liberal recourse to inferences of fact and circumstantial evidence. This indirect evidence is admitted in all systems of law, and its use is recognised by international decisions.[164]

Ad hoc judge Ahmed Mahiou of Algeria pointed out that none of the reasons given by the Court were 'sufficiently convincing', including the fear of creating an impression the court was taking sides, that it might intrude on the sovereignty of a state, or that it might be embarrassed if Serbia refused.[165]

The Bosnian team, which had pursued its request at the merits stage and in the second round of the merits, seemed to be slightly at odds as to the importance of the documents.[166] Sakib Softic, the Agent of the Bosnian team, acknowledged that the documents were very important and would be useful to their case, but believed that the material already at the Bosnian team's disposal was sufficient.[167] Phon van den Biesen, the Deputy Agent, felt that the uncensored documents would probably have demonstrated that the Bosnian Serb forces were agents of Serbia, controlled by Belgrade.[168] Joanna Korner, QC, also part of the Bosnian team, surprisingly considered from the outset that the case for State responsibility for genocide was impossible to win.[169] Lawyers interviewed in The Hague and Belgrade thought the outcome might have been different had the ICJ issued a subpoena for the documents directly from Serbia. 'It's a question that nags loudly' according to Diane Orientlicher. 'Why didn't the court request the full documents? The fact that they were blacked out clearly implies these passages would have made a difference'.[170] Natasa Kandic, director of the Humanitarian Law Centre in Belgrade, expressed shock at the Court's inaction. 'It was well known in the Serbian government that the archives spelled out the responsibility of the state'.[171]

ICJ President Rosalyn Higgins stressed before the case opened that solely political concerns could not be allowed to influence the ICJ's legal reasoning.[172] Christian Tomuschat, however, stresses the far-reaching consequences of the judgement in light of Serbia's envisaged entry into the European Union. On the issue of reparations, he points to 'intellectual weaknesses' in the 'summary fashion in which the Court has dealt with the issue of satisfaction':

> Logic would seem to require that the failure of the Serbian Government, specifically acknowledged by the Court, to halt the mass killing in and around Srebrenica, should give rise to an obligation to compensate for the damage suffered by the victimized population and thereby also the State of Bosnia and Herzegovina.[173]

The Court held that although Serbia was in violation of the Convention on the Prevention and Punishment of the Crime of Genocide, it was 'inappropriate to find that the Respondent is under an obligation of *restitutio in integrum*'.[174] Clearly, life could not be restored to the dead, but ILC Article 36 intimates that compensation should be paid. The Court appears to suggest that there was no nexus between Serbia's violation of the obligation to prevent genocide and the resultant massacres.[175] But, as Tomuschat argues, the Court should have shifted the burden of proof to Serbia, 'to show that even if . . . the FRY had taken appropriate measures, the Bosnian Serbs would nonetheless have carried out their criminal plans,'[176] especially in view of the Court's failure to insist that Serbia surrender the full version of the Serbian Defence Council documents.

The Court 'in an extremely short passage of its holdings' concluded that a declaration that the Respondent had failed to comply with its obligation to prevent genocide was sufficient.[177] There are, however, clear precedents in international law for a range of forms of satisfaction, including symbolic monetary compensation.[178] Also, in stating that the Applicant had itself suggested a declaration as the most appropriate form of satisfaction,[179] the Court created the impression that the Applicant did not seek full reparation.[180] Tomuschat concludes that 'the reader must disagree with the Court's observation that the Applicant itself had limited the scope of its demands, thereby implicitly compelling the Court to apply the proposition *ne ultra petita*.'[181] He argues that the Court's response to Bosnia's request for guarantees of non-repetition is also unsatisfactory:

> The ILC has clarified in its Articles on State Responsibility that assurances and guarantees of non-repetition do not specifically pertain to the secondary obligations arising from a breach of a (primary) rule of conduct, but should

> be considered as an articulation of the duty of performance itself in situations where the willingness of the author State to abide by its duties has been put in question through its own conduct.[182]

The close ties between Serbia and RS, and the culture of revisionism and denial which continues to prevail in Serbia 18 years after the deposition of Milosevic, do not augur well for Bosnia's the longer-term stability, or for the security of the non-Serb inhabitants in RS.[183] Significant also is the fact that it took four years following the ICJ judgement for the Serbian authorities to comply with their obligations under Article I of the Genocide Convention, to surrender Ratko Mladic to the ICTY. In Tomuschat's view, Serbia, having continued to shield Mladic, 'makes itself an accomplice *ex post* of genocide'.[184]

*

The Court's finding against Serbia's complicity in genocide was controversial, particularly when interfaced with its holding that Serbia should have acted to prevent the genocide from occurring, and necessitated a degree of semantic acrobatics which still left its ruling unsatisfactorily explained.

The failure on the part of the Court to require Serbia to submit the full unredacted version of the Serbian Supreme Defence Council documents, and its consequent inability to comply with its Statute under Article 49 to note any refusal to do so, left many questions unanswered, and was undoubtedly one of the main barriers to achieving a measure of acceptance of the verdict on the part of Bosnia's Muslims.

On the issue of reparations, the stakes were high. Not only would Serbia have had the stigma of being the first state in history to be pronounced responsible for genocide by an international court, but it would have been rendered in significant debt which it would have been hard-placed to meet. It might also have created a wider precedent, and possibly triggered claims from Croatia, which had a similar suit pending. On the other hand, even symbolic monetary compensation might have been instrumental in assisting Serbia gradually to come to terms with the role of the Milosevic regime in the Bosnian war.

Conclusion

The ICJ judgement was hailed with some relief in Belgrade since, with neither censure nor punishment, the fact that Serbia was merely faulted for not preventing genocide was a moot point. In a compromise decision, the highest legal international body had *de facto* exonerated Serbia from responsibility for the Bosnian genocide. A decision against Serbia would undoubtedly have given rise to a degree of international embarrassment, not least in that highly placed EU representatives and other international players had been working closely, even dining, with the Serbian president in the days leading up to the Srebrenica massacre. The ICJ, in what many regard as one of the least satisfying decisions the Court has ever rendered, unwittingly reflected ongoing trends in international policy in the region. As one commentator noted, 'International institutions represent international policy, which twelve years ago permitted all this to happen. It would have been naïve to think that they would behave differently today'.[185] Western leaders generally view Serbia, the largest of Yugoslavia's successor states, as an important factor for stability in the Balkans and, over time, international institutions have given away much of their leverage in appeasing Serbia through repeated concessions, despite the entrenched culture of denial regarding its role in the 1990s' wars, and the nationalist tendencies still prevailing in much of the state's political, military and religious hierarchy.

In Bosnia, opinion was, predictably, divided. While in RS there was rejoicing, in the Federation, the ICJ judgement was met with dismay and, as relations between the communities deteriorated, an initiative was launched by the Srebrenica municipal assembly to withdraw that municipality from Republika Srpska, which was not surprisingly overruled by the then High representative Christian Schwartz-Schilling as not according with the Dayton Agreement.

Ambivalence in the judgement also gave rise to further disputes as to the character of the war and Serbia's part in it, and led to questioning of RS legitimacy which, in turn, radicalized the behaviour of the entity's leader, Milorad Dodik. The following year, the question of a referendum on RS independence was explicitly mooted in an RS assembly resolution for the first time, marking the beginning of a serious new crisis in the region.

Epilogue

In February 2017, just days before the deadline for review expired, Bakir Izetbegovic, the Bosniak member of the Bosnian presidency, submitted an application for review, which was supported by neither the Croat nor Serb members, Dragan Covic and Mladen Ivanic. Ivanic went so far as to write independently to the ICJ, expressing his opposition to the application. The application was duly rejected by the ICJ registrar within ten days of its submission, on a technical point, namely, that Sakib Softic, the original applicant, no longer had a mandate, although the ICJ Statute contained nothing to indicate that his mandate was no longer valid. It would have been unforeseen that a state accused by another state of genocide would be opposed by government officials within that state.

The whole episode stirred considerable tensions in an already more volatile Bosnia than was the case in 2002, when the earlier application was submitted. The media and outside commentators focused mainly on issues such as the Court's letter in May 2016 to Softic, informing him that he was no longer eligible. Had Softic made this public at the time, there would have been the opportunity to challenge the Court on the legal basis of its decision. It may also have galvanized more support for the Bosnian case. As it was, Softic and his team were open to accusation by both earlier supporters and the opposition of a lack of transparency, and even deceit. There was also criticism of the 'last-minute' rush, after ten years of virtual silence on the issue, with the suggestion that the action was merely a sop to survivor groups who had long campaigned for a revision.

These criticisms have some validity but, in the final count, it is the issue itself which should have merited more focus and debate – the disfunctionality of the Bosnian state due to weak central institutions legitimized at Dayton, the exposure of increasing divisions along ethnic lines within Bosnia, as opposed to 2002, and the irony of an entity (RS), whose political and military leaders had been convicted for genocide and whose successors continue to support those leaders, having a crucial say in the rejection of a review of a genocide case.

According to some analysts, Bosnia and Herzegovina's request was a maladjusted move in timing and legal foundations, motivated more by the political opportunism of the *Stranka Demokratske Akcije* (SDA, Muslim nationalist-conservatives) than by legitimate legal and historical reasons.[186] In any event, it strengthened Belgrade's revisionist position, as well as contributing to increasing regional polarization.

Notes

1 *The Case Concerning the Application of the Convention on the Prevention and Punishment of the Crime of Genocide (Bosnia and Herzegovina v. Serbia and Montenegro),* hereinafter *Bosnia v Serbia,* or the Genocide case.
2 Antonio Cassese, 'A Judicial Massacre', *Guardian,* 27 February 2007.
3 Case Concerning application of the Convention on the Prevention and Punishment of the Crime of Genocide, International Court of Justice, Judgment, 26 February 2007, para. 182.
4 Ruth Wedgwood, 'Milosevic's Last Waltz', *New York Times*, 12 March 2007.
5 Although defined in World War II, neither Article 6(C) of the Charter of the Nuremberg International Military Tribunal nor Article II (1)(C) of Control Council Law No.10 envisaged genocide as a separate category of crimes against humanityAntonio Cassese, *International Law,* Oxford University Press, Oxford, 2005, p. 443.
6 Much of the analysis of the Convention has issued from political and social scientists, historians and journalists.
7 Emir Suljagic. 'ICJ Chief on Bosnia Genocide Case' Interview in *DANI.*
8 Article 66(3) ICC Statute.
9 Andre Nollkaemper, 'Concurrence Between Individual Responsibility and State Responsibility in International Law', The International and Comparative Law Quarterly, Vol.52, Issue 76, July 2003, p. 630. Andre Nollkaemper is Professor of Public International Law and International Relations at the University of Amsterdam.
10 Ibid. 'The standard of proof varies with the character of the particular issue of fact . . . a higher than ordinary standard may . . . be required in the case of a charge of "exceptional gravity against a State"' Judge Shahabuddeen, Dissenting Opinion, *Qatar v Bahrain,* ICJ Reports (1995) 63, referring to *Corfu Channel* 17.
11 Judgment, p. 76, para. 209.
12 *Prosecutor v Stakic,* IT-97-24. Trial Chamber Judgment, para. 46.
13 Summary of Appeals Judgement for Milomir Stakic, 22 March 2006.
14 *Prosecutor v Jelisic*, Trial Chamber Judgment, 14 December 1999. This was a complex case where the Trial Chamber acquitted Jelisic on genocide charges pursuant to Rule 98 bis(B), which the Appeals Chamber considered to have led to an 'incorrect assessment of the evidence'. Appeals Chamber Judgment, 5 July 2001.

15 'On the basis of the evidence presented in this case, the Trial Chamber has not found beyond reasonable doubt that genocide was committed in the relevant ARK municipalities from April to December 1992'. *Prosecutor v Brdjanin,* Trial Chamber Judgment, 1 September 2004.
16 *Prosecutor v Akayesu*., para. 662. The trial chambers in the *Kayishema* and *Ruzindana* cases and in the *Musema* case held the same view
17 ICJ Judgment, p. 127, para. 354, and *Prosecutor v Krnojelac*, IT-97-25-T, Judgment, 15 March 2002, para. 440.
18 *Prosecutor v. Jelisic,* Judgement, para. 82.
19 Ibid. In the *Sikirica* case, on the other hand, the Trial Chamber found the only common denominator to be that the victims were all of military age. *Prosecutor v Sikirica,* IT-95-8-I, Judgment on Defence Motions to Acquit, para. 80.
20 Payam Akhavam, 'Contributions of the International Criminal Tribunals for the Former Yugoslavia and Rwanda to Development of Definitions of Crimes against Humanity and Genocide', *American Society of International Law*, April 2000.
21 *Prosecutor v. Akayesu,* Judgement, para. 504. This may overlap with the broader genus of crimes against humanity, however.
22 Ibid., para. 505. It was determined that This could include 'subjecting a group of people to a subsistence diet, systematic expulsion from homes and the reduction of essential medical services below minimum requirement'. Ibid., para. 506.
23 *Prosecutor v. Karadzic and Mladic* IT-95-5-R61, 11 July 1996, para. 94. Katherine Southwick, 'Srebrenica as Genocide: The Krstic Decision and the Language of the Unspeakable', *Human Rights and Development Law Journal*, Vol.8, Issue 188, 2005.
24 See Southwick, ibid. Also Schabas, who views the organized evacuation of women and children as significant evidence that the intent was not to destroy the group physically. Schabas, ref p. 46. Payam Akhavam, on the other hand, concluded that 'both immediate and slow death clearly fall within the purview of genocide and its conception of physical destruction'. Akhavam [note 20].
25 The *travaux preparatoires* of the Genocide Convention were cited, where a distinction was made between physical and biological genocide, on the one hand, and cultural genocide, on the other [UN General Assembly resolution 96(1), 1946]. *Prosecutor v. Krstic,* Appeal Judgement. Partial Dissenting Opinion of Judge Shahabuddeen.
26 Ibid., para. 50.
27 *Prosecutor v. Blagojevic,* Judgement, [note 39] para. 661, quoting from *Krstic* Judgement, IT-98-33-A, 19 April 2004. Italics in original.
28 Author's discussions with returnees.
29 'As clearly shown by the preparatory work for the Convention . . . the destruction in question is the material destruction of a group either by physical or by biological means, not the destruction of the national, linguistic, religious, cultural or other identity of a particular group'. *Yearbook of the International Law Commission* 1996, Vol. II, Part Two, pp. 45–46, para. 12, quoted in Judgment, p. 124, para. 344.
30 Judgment, paras. 276, 277 and 319. The Court summarily dismissed the occurrence of genocide under Article II(d) and I of the Convention as unproven due to insufficient evidence.
31 Genocide Convention, Article I(c).
32 *Galic*, IT-98-29-T, Trial Chamber Judgment, 5 December 2003, para. 593.
33 Judgment, para. 327.
34 *Annual Report of the International Helsinki Federation*, Vienna, 1995, p. 34.
35 See Matton, and UN Information Notes, April 1993. The Srebrenica Report commented that in April 1993, Serb paramilitaries held Srebrenica for several weeks, when Bosnian Muslims were expelled from their homes in many areas, but also subjected to more serious abuses, a large number being killed. Report of the Secretary General

Pursuant to General Assembly Resolution 53/35 (1998) – *Srebrenica Report,* para. 33. [herinafter *'Srebrenica Report'*].

36 Judgment, p. 120, para. 334, and p. 133, para. 372.

37 Ibid., p. 123, para. 343.

38 Ibid., p. 124, para. 344.

39 The *Blagojevic* Appeals Chamber reversed the genocide charge after the ICJ Judgment. *Prosecutor v. Blagojevic,* IT-02-60-A, Appeals Chamber Judgment, 7 May 2007, p. 48, para. 124.

40 Judgment, p. 108, para. 297. The *Krstic* and *Blagojevic* judgements are not clear as to when the planning of the Srebrenica massacres actually began, although *Blagojevic* concluded that the *dolus specialis* was formed before 12/13 July. In determining individual criminal responsibility in either case, the actual date was of less importance than for the *Genocide* case. See *Prosecutor v Krstic,* IT-98-33-T, Judgment, 2 August 2001, paras. 572–598, and *Prosecutor v Blagojevic*, IT-02-60-T, Judgment, 17 January 2005, para. 674.

41 *Srebrenica Report* [note 36], p. 68, para. 345.

42 As chronicled in the Srebrenica Report, 'most of the territory captured by the Serbs was secured by them within the first 60 days of the war . . . During those 60 days, approximately one million people were displaced from their homes. Tens of thousands of people, most of them Bosnian Muslims, were killed'. *Srebrenica Report* [note 14], p. 6, para. 6.

43 The Court cited *Krstic* where it was held that the destruction of one-fifth of the Srebrenica community 'would inevitably result in the physical disappearance of the Bosnian Muslim population at Srebrenica'. *Krstic* Appeals Chamber Judgment, 19 April 2004, paras. 28–33, cited in Judgment, p. 105, para. 293. Zarko Puhovski has argued that 'to say that there was no genocide in Munich, but that in Buchenwald some kilometres away there was genocide, would be an improper interpretation of reality . . . Many people found in Srebrenica had come from elsewhere, driven there by the military operations in Herzegovina, north-eastern Bosnia, and so on. In other words, the issue was wrongly posed in a factual sense'. Zarko Puhovski, President of the Helsinki Committee for Human Rights in Croatia. Interview in *DANI*, 2 March 2007.

44 Judgment, p. 133, para. 372.

45 Ibid., p. 133, para. 373. The Appeals Chamber in *Jelisic* concluded that while a plan or policy is important in proving special intent, it is not a legal ingredient of genocide. *Prosecutor v Jelisic*, Appeals Chamber Judgment, para. 48. The reference to 'particular circumstances' reflects Article 8 of the International Law Commission, and is discussed further on.

46 *Prosecutor v Brdjanin* Judgment (1 September 2004) para. 970.

47 The Court may also have been guided by its ruling in the *Corfu Channel Case* test, that charges 'must be proved by evidence that is fully conclusive'. *Corfu Channel Case* (1949) ICJ Rep. 4, 18. See, however, Tomuschat who disagreed that the Corfu Channel case was an appropriate parallel due to the 60-year time lapse and the fundamentally different factual background. Christian Tomuschat, 'Reparation in Cases of Genocide', *Journal of International Criminal Justice*, Vol.V, Issue 4, 2007, p. 905–912.

48 *Prosecutor v Jelisic* [note 21], para. 47, *Prosecutor v. Krstic*, Judgment, para. 21, and *Prosecutor V Akayesu*, Judgment, 2 September 1998, para. 523.

49 *Prosecutor v Krstic*, Trial chamber Judgment, 2 August 2001, para. 580.

50 See Sandesh Sivakumaran, 'Decisions of International Tribunals: International Court of Justice, Application of the Convention on the Prevention and Punishment of the Crime of Genocide (*Bosnia and Herzegovina v Serbia and Montenegro*) Judgment of 26 February 2007', *The International and Comparative Law Quarterly,* Vol.56, July 2007, p. 700, for further discussion of this.

51 Ibid., para. 867.

52 *Prosecutor v. Momcilo Krajisnik,* Part 2, Political precursors, para. 69.
53 Ibid., paras. 180, 181 and 187. Radovan Karadzic was president of the Bosnian Serb Republic and of the SDS. His former capacity vested him with the authority to define the Bosnian Serb Army (VRS), establish a system of command, define the demarcation of military territory and issue combat regulations. Ibid., para. 189.
54 Ibid. Part 4, Municipality crimes, para. 292. The Trial Chamber's findings in the Brdjanin case on genocide were considerably more detailed, despite only 13 municipalities being under consideration.
55 Ibid., p. 1092.
56 Ibid., p. 868.
57 *Prosecutor v. Krajisnik.* Part 6, para. 1093.
58 See Ibid., para. 1094.
59 Thirty of the 59 incidences referred to were unspecified numbers. In Visegrad, for instance, 'hundreds' of killings were testified as having occurred. In cases where the numbers killed were unspecified, these were apparently assessed by the Trial Chamber in single figures, arriving at a total figure of just over 3,000.
60 Ibid. Part 7, Sentencing, 1151.
61 Ibid., p. 1095.
62 David D. Caron, 'The ILC Articles on State Responsibility: The Paradoxical Relationship Between Form and Authority', *The American Journal of International Law,* Vol.96, 2002, p. 872.
63 *Prosecutor v Tadic,* Appeals Chamber Judgment (IT-94-1-A), 15 July 1999. There is significant evidence of the involvement of Belgrade, the JNA and, later, the VJ in the Bosnian war, as well as of Serbian paramilitary groups, both before and after 19 May 1992 when the alleged handover to the VRS took place. This was acknowledged by the Court but, in view of the Court's dismissal of genocide outside Srebrenica, that evidence was irrelevant to the ICJ case.
64 *Case Concerning Military and Paramilitary Activities in and against Nicaragua (Nicaragua v United States of America* (1986) ICJ Reports, 14.
65 *Prosecutor v Tadic,* Appeals Chamber Judgment, 15 July 1999.
66 The *Stakic* Appeal Chamber suggested that a different verdict might have been reached had a global overview been adopted. *Prosecutor v Stakic*, Judgment, 22 March 2006, para. 56.
67 *Prosecutor v Erdemovic*, 7 October 1997, and *Prosecutor v Meakic,* Amended Indictment, 18 July 2001.
68 *Prosecutor v Milosevic, Prosecutor v Kovacevic, Drljaca,* First Amended Indictment, 23 June 1998.
69 *Prosecutor v Plavsic*, Plea Agreement, 30 September 2002, and *Prosecutor v Nikolic*, 2 December 2003, para. 63.
70 *Prosecutor v Milosevic,* Decision on Motion for Judgement of Acquittal, 16 June 2004, para. 323(3), Judge Kwon dissenting.
71 Ibid., para. 323(4 and 5).
72 The other municipalities were Brcko, Prijedor, Sanski Most, Bijeljina, Kljuc and Bosanski Novi. Ibid., para. 323(1).
73 The Court considered the Decision on the acquittal motion in the context of Serbia's obligation to prevent genocide. Judgment, p. 157, para. 437.
74 Wedgwood, op. cit. and Cassese. Roger O'Keefe Deputy Director of the Lauterpacht Institute at the University of Cambridge, also opined that 'the ICJ can decide to convict on the balance of probabilities rather than beyond all reasonable doubt'. 'Serbia and Montenegro on Trial for Genocide', *Institute of War and Peace Reporting*, 22 February 2006.
75 Robert Cryer, Nottingham University. Quoted from 'Serbia and Montenegro on Trial for Genocide', *International War and Peace Reporting*. Special Report, 22 February 2006.

Rosalyn Higgins commented for the same report: 'we are extremely aware of our own prior judicial decision making and we certainly try to be consistent'. Ibid.

76 *Nicaragua* [note 65] Judgment, para. 109.

77 Cassese, 2nd edition, pp. 248–249.

78 *Nicaragua* [note 65] Judgment, paras. 109–110.

79 Dusko Tadic was indicted for crimes against humanity, war crimes and grave breaches of the Geneva Convention. *Tadic,* op. cit., Indictment.

80 The *Tadic* Appeals Chamber went even further, declaring that the *Nicaragua* test did not seem to be consonant with the logic of international law on State responsibility. *Tadic,* op. cit., para. 116.

81 Ibid., para. 137.

82 Ibid. See also Cassese, op. cit., p. 249.

83 Ibid., p. 144, para. 403.

84 Cassese, op. cit., p. 249. The *Tadic* test is broadly supported by the jurisprudence of the European Court of Human Rights, which held in the *Loizidou* case that Turkey was responsible for acts by the so-called Turkish Republic of Northern Cyprus which is an integral part of Cyprus. The Strasbourg Court held that 'the obligation to secure, in such an area, the rights and freedoms set out in the Convention derives from the fact that such control whether it be exercised [by the State concerned] directly, through its armed forces, or through a subordinate local administration'. *Loizidou v Turkey (Preliminary Objections)* 23 March 1995, *Reports of Judgments and Decisions 1995, Series A. No.310*, para. 62, p. 24 or (Merits) 18 December 1996, *Reports of Judgements and Decisions, Series A, 1996-VI*, para. 52, pp. 2234–2235, quoted by Pellet, CR.2006/8, para. 59.

85 Judgment, p. 144, para. 403.

86 Ibid., para. 404. The weight attached by the Court to the *Nicaragua* control tests was evident in its extensive citation of *Nicaragua* to substantiate its findings. See Judgment, Section VII (3) and (4), paras. 391, 394, 399, 401 and 402.

87 Ibid., para. 406.

88 Here the reference is to Serbs in Bosnia who supported the Social Democratic Party (SDS) led by Radovan Karadzic, and not those who supported the Bosnian government.

89 In order to avoid a situation where Bosnian Serbs would be deprived of the protection of the Geneva Conventions, the Appeals Chamber in *Tadic* held that it was unimportant whether the victims and perpetrators of grave breaches held the same nationality, which amounted to 'replacing the nationality criterion by an ethnicity criterion'. Andre J. J. de Hoogh, 'Articles 4 and 8 of the 2001 Articles on State Responsibility, the *Tadic* Case and Attribution of Acts of Bosnian Serb Authorities to the Federal Republic of Yugoslavia', *British Yearbook of International Law*, 2001, p. 288. See also ibid., p. 266.

90 Pellet, CR.2006/0, p. 63, para. 57.

91 The Federal Republic of Yugoslavia, as Serbia and Montenegro were then known.

92 See de Hoogh [note 89] on the status of the *contras*., p. 269.

93 The United States was accused of specific individual violations of international law which made it more imperative to establish effective control of the operations. *Nicaragua* [note 65], p. 65, para. 115.

94 The Court specifically stated that none of the other ILC Articles dealing with attribution were applicable. Judgment, p. 149, para. 414.

95 Draft Articles on Responsibility of States for Internationally Wrongful Acts with commentaries, 2001. Text adopted by the International Law Commission at its 53rd session in 2001. United Nations 2005.

96 Judgment, para. 386.

97 Ibid., para. 388.

98 Ibid.

99 Ibid.

100 The term 'Republika Srpska' only came into use outside Serbia and the Serb-controlled territories from late 1994, when the Contact Group began to envisage a two-entity state for BiH. David Owen's contemporaneous account of events, for instance, refers to 'Republika Srpska' very seldom, and then not as a state. David Owen, *Balkan Odyssey*, Gollancz, 1995. Owen's work was copiously cited in evidence by the Respondent.

101 Ian Brownlie, CR.2006/16, p. 39, para. 115. The Respondent moves from this sophistry to argue that 'as of May 1992 General Mladic no longer accepted instructions from Belgrade' (Ibid.), and also uses Republika Srpska's supposed independence to argue against the Applicant's comparison with the *Loizidou* case. For a view supporting the Applicant's position on *Loizidou*, see de Hoogh, op. cit., pp. 271–274.

102 See, for instance, *Prosecutor v Brdjanin* IT-99-36-T. Judgment, 1 September 2004, para. 151.

103 In March 1992, Bogdan Subotic, 'Minister of Defence' in the 'Serbian Republic of BiH' was appointed to the rank of general by the Supreme Defence Council in Belgrade; in May 1995 General Mrksic was appointed by Belgrade to become the 'Commanding Officer' in the army of 'Republika Srpska Krajina'. CR.2006/8, pp. 54–55, paras. 61–63. General Mladic distributed on behalf of the VJ a document called 'Instructions for Command and Co-ordinated Action in Anti-Aircraft Defence and Air Support', instructing recipients to ensure efficient coordination between the VRS and VJ air defences. *Prosecutor v Milosevic,* IT-02-54, Exhibit No. P505, tab.4(a), cited by Pellet CR.2006/8, pp. 50–51, paras. 38–39.

104 *Prosecutor v Brdjanin* [note 52], para. 151. Italics added.

105 Annexes to Dayton Agreements (A/50/790), and *Tadic* Appeals Judgement paras. 157–160. It was actually the Serbian Foreign Minister, Milan Milutinovic, who signed the letter by which Republika Srpska undertook to comply with the Agreement.

106 De Hoogh [note 89], p. 266.

107 ILC Articles 2001, Commentary, Article 5 (now Article 4), para. 6.

108 De Hoogh points out that Special Rapporteur James Crawford uses the word 'agency' in relation to Article 8 in the First Report at 8. De Hoogh [note 89], p. 268, n.70.

109 Judgment, p. 138, para. 386. The Applicant had claimed that all VRS officers were *de jure* organs of the Respondent (Judgment, para. 387) and the Court did not discuss any distinction between *de jure* and *de facto* organs. Other commentators have also opined that a *de facto* organ must act in essentially the same was as a *de jure* state organ. De Hoogh opines, 'It seems right . . . to reserve the phrase "de facto organ" for an organ considered as such by virtue of the supplementary role of international law under Article 4, paragraph 2' [note 89], p. 268.

110 ILC Articles 2001, Article 8.

111 The Wannsee Conference was a meeting of senior Nazi officials on 20 January 1942, to inform senior governmental officials of plans for the 'Final solution to the Jewish question'. Ton Zawaan, of the Amsterdam-based Centre for Holocaust and Genocide Studies, observed, however, that genocidal intent may have been difficult to prove even in the case of Hitler, since 'he never issued an order directing his subordinates to kill Jews'. 'Milosevic and Genocide: Has the Prosecution Made the Case?' *Observer,* 27 February 2004. See also the Declaration of Judge Bennouna, dissenting on Count 4 of the Judgement, who points out that it is rare for a State to announce its intention of destroying a protected group. Dupuy argues, however, that it would be necessary to show the genocidal intent of the government official who orders the commission of genocide to establish state responsibility. Pierre-Marie Dupuy, 'International Criminal Responsibility of the Individual and International Responsibility of a State', in *The Rome Statute of the International Criminal Court: A Commentary*, ed. A. Cassese, P. Gaeta and J. R. W. D. Jones, Oxford University Press, Vol.2, 2002,pp. 1095–1096.

112 First Report on State Responsibility, James Crawford. Addendum 5. UN Doc. A/CN.4/490. Add.5, 22 July 1998 at 16, quoted in Milanovic [note 56].

113 ILC 2001 Articles. Article 8, Commentary (4) and (5).
114 Ibid. Comments and observations received from Governments. A/CN/4/488, 25 March 1998.
115 Judgment, p. 143, para. 399. See also Marko Milanovic on the *Nicaragua* parallel. www.ejiltalk.org/the-icj-and-evolutionary-treaty-interpretation/
116 Ibid., para. 400. Italics added.
117 ILC (2001) Articles, Art.8, Commentary (3). Italics added.
118 The Court recalled the Respondent's submission regarding evidence of military operations in July 1995 being coordinated with Belgrade and the VJ. Judgment, p. 147, para. 411.
119 ILC (2001) Articles, Art.8, Commentary (3) and (4).
120 Ibid. Commentary (5). The previous draft of the Articles did not specify requirements of instructions, direction or control. First Report on State Responsibility by James Crawford, Addendum 5, UN Doc.A/CN/4/490.Add.5, 22 July 1998 at 16 et seq., quoted in Milanovic [note 56], p. 582, n.159.
121 De Hoogh [note 89], p. 290.
122 Judgment, para. 405.
123 Ibid., para. 406.
124 The video, presented at the Milosevic trial, is available at http://jurist.law.pitt.edu/monitor/2005/06/srebrenica-killings-video-icty.php
125 Srdja Popovic, a distinguished Serbian lawyer, commented that 'the Court made an obvious factual mistake in stating that the Scorpions were a paramilitary formation, when in fact they were a Serbian police unit'. Srdja Popovic, *Feral Tribune,* 2 March 2007.
126 Ian Brownlie, in one of his most controversial cases, also represented the FRY against NATO, after the bombing of Kosovo. When he appeared for Serbia at the ICJ, colleagues reportedly attempted to dissuade him, but he cited the 'cab-rank principle', saying he remembered which side the Serbs had fought on during the Second World War. Obituary, *Independent*, 25 February 2010.
127 Referred to by Dupuy in 'Reviewing the Difficulties of Codification: On Ago's Classification of Obligations of Means and Obligations of Result in Relation to State Responsibility', *The European Journal of International Law*, Vol.10, Issue 2, 1999, p. 385. Dupuy, ibid.
128 A. C. Grayling, *The Heart of Things: Applying Philosophy to the 21st Century*, Phoenix, 2005, p. 161.
129 'That Serbia is responsible for not having prevented a genocide in which it was not complicit makes little sense'. Cassese.
130 Ibid., para. 419.
131 Ibid., para. 420.
132 Ibid., paras. 421–422.
133 Ibid., paras. 422–423.
134 Ibid.
135 Ibid.
136 Ibid.
137 The Court referred to the ILC Articles in support of its findings. ILC (2001) Articles. Article 14, para. 3.
138 Judgment, para. 431.
139 See, for instance, Sandesh Sivakumaran, 'Case concerning the application of the convention on the prevention and punishment of the crime of genocide (*Bosnia and Herzegovina v Serbia and Montenegro*), Judgment of 26 February 2007', *The International and Comparative Law Quarterly*, Vol.56, July 2007, p. 704.
140 Judge Bennouna opined that 'the *mens rea* required of the accomplice is not the same as that which lies with the main perpetrator, that is, the specific intent (dolus specialis)

to commit genocide, and it cannot be otherwise, since to require that intent would mean assimilating accomplice and co-perpetrator'. The *Genocide* case, Judgment. Declaration of Judge Bennouna (author's translation from the French).

141 Ibid.

142 Ibid. Judge Bennouna cites the report of the *Netherlands Institute for War Documentation*, 10 April 1992.

143 Ibid.

144 The *Genocide* case, Judgment. Declaration of Judge Keith, para. 11.

145 Ibid., para. 12. This was supported by the Srebrenica Report. *Report of the Secretary-General Pursuant to General Assembly Resolution 53/35 (1998), UN Srebrenica Report*, paras. 353–356, 359 and 371.

146 Ibid.

147 Mirjan Damaska, 'The ICJ Judgment on Genocide in Bosnia-Herzegovina', *Nacional* (Zagreb) 12 March 2007. Mirjan Damaska is Sterling Professor of Law at the Yale Law School. In the jurisprudence of the *ad hoc* tribunals, aiding and abetting has been distinguished from complicity. Schabas considers the distinction unjustified, however, as aiding and abetting is a classic form of complicity. William A. Schabas, *Genocide in International Law: The Crime of Crimes*,Cambridge University Press, 2000, p. 293. For further discussion on this, see Marko Milanovic, 'State Responsibility for Genocide: A Follow-Up', *European Journal of International Law*, Vol.18, Issue 4, 1 September 2007, pp. 669–694.

148 Cassese, op. cit.

149 *Prosecutor v Tadic*, 10 August 1995, and 2 October 1995.

150 *Prosecutor v Milosevic*, 17 June 2003, p. 22619. Testimony by Zoran Lilic, President of the FRY from 1993 to 1997, and member of the Serbian Defence Council. See also 'Lilic Testifies Against Milosevic' Emir Suljagic, *Tribunal Update, Institute for War and Peace Reporting*, 9–13 June 2003.

151 Ibid. and 18 June 2003, p. 22675. The annual allocations for members of the 30th personnel centre (about 4,000 recipients) were approximately 8 million Euros, according to Lilic.

152 *Prosecutor v Milosevic*, p. 22619. Testimony by Zoran Lilic.

153 There was no legal basis for the withholding of the records from the public . . . It served only one purpose: to keep Belgrade's responsibility from public scrutiny and, signifiantly, from the 'International Court of Justice'. Geoffrey Nice, QC, lead prosecutor at the Milosevic trial. Letter to *The International Herald Tribune*, 16 April 2007. *Jutarnji List*, 11 September 2007. See also 'Serbia's darkest pages hidden from genocide court', Marlise Simons, *The International Herald Tribune,* 8 April 2007.

154 See Chapter 9 for a more detailed discussion on this.

155 'Justice at what price?' *Institute of War and Peace Reporting (IWPR)*, Report 407, 19 May 2005.

156 Ibid.

157 Statute of the International Court of Justice, Article 49.

158 Judgment, para. 206. ICJ Vice-President Al-Khasawneh observes that this comment is 'worse than [the Court's] failure to act'. Judgment, Dissenting Opinion of Vice-President Al-Khasawneh, p. 10, para. 35.

159 'The applicant State has deployed enormous numbers of documents in these proceedings and has had access to the archives of the ICTY'. Ian Brownlie, the *Genocide* case, [note 3] Merits, CR.2006/3, p. 25, para. 16, and CR 2006/38, para. 2.

160 Judgment, para. 206.

161 Quoted in 'Serbia's darkest pages hidden from genocide court', Marlise Simons, op-ed, *International Herald Tribune (IHT),* 8 April 2007.

162 William Schabas, Antonio Cassese, quoted in *IHT*, ibid.

163 Dissenting Opinion of Vice-President Al-Khasawneh, p. 216, para. 35.

164 Ibid. Cited from *Corfu Channel (United Kingdom v Albania)* Merits, Judgment, ICJ Reports, 1949, p. 18.
165 Opinion Dissidente de M. Le Juge Mahiou, paras. 57–63.
166 Judgment, p. 76, para. 205.
167 'Could Key Records Have Altered ICJ Ruling?' Merdijana Sadovic, *Tribunal Update, Institute of War and Peace Reporting,* 9 March 2007.
168 'This would have made Serbia liable for the Srebrenica genocide. We believe all this can be found in the documents'. Phon van den Biesen, 'Some observations on the ICJ Judgment', *Bosnia Report,* No.55–56, Spring/Summer 2007.
169 Ms Korner said she had endeavoured at the outset to persuade other members of the Bosnian team that the case was unwinnable. Discussion with the author, Tuzla, Bosnia-Herzegovina, 29 September 2007.
170 Simons, *International Herald Tribune,* 8 April 2007.
171 After the verdict, Kandic met with a member of the Serbian team: 'He was very pleased, but I confronted him . . . you did not tell the truth'. He replied 'It's normal. Every country will do everything possible to protect the state'. *International Herald Tribune,* ibid.
172 'What I think the court must never do is to say we know "x" is the right legal answer, but we mustn't give it because there might be negative political implications if we did'. Rosalyn Higgins, 'Serbia and Montenegro on Trial for Genocide', *IWPR,* 22 February 2006.
173 Tomuschat.
174 An interesting comparison is the ICJ decision in the *Factory at Chorzow* case which stated that reparation 'must, so far as possible, wipe out all the consequences of the illegal act and reestablish the situation which would, in all probability, have existed if that act had not been committed'. PCIJ Series A, No.17, p. 47, quoted in Judgment, p. 164, para. 460.
175 Judgment, paras. 461–462.
176 Tomuschat [note 178]. Tomushat argues that the two orders issued by the Court in 1993 required the FRY 'to take all measures within its power to prevent commission of the crime of genocide'. Order of 8 April 1993, *ICJ Reports* 1993, p. 3, 24.
177 Tomuschat points out that while the ILC Articles do not explicitly mention a financial dimension to satisfaction, 'Article 37(2) is not exhaustive as may be easily gleaned from its wording' Ibid.
178 For instance, the *Rainbow Warrior* Case. Award of 30 April 1990, *Reports of International Arbitral Awards XX,* pp. 217, 272 para. 118, quoted in Tomuschat, ibid.
179 Judgment, p. 165, para. 463.
180 According to Tomaschat, the Court used 'a fairly misleading formulation . . . On this point, one simply has to contradict the Court'. Tomuschat [note 66].
181 Ibid.
182 Ibid. Article 30 deals with cessation and non-repetition, but those remedies are not included in Article 34. The official ILC commentary, therefore, states that such assurances and guarantees should be better treated 'as an aspect of the continuation and repair of the legal relationship affected by the breach'. James Crawford, *The International Law Commission's Articles on State Responsibility,* Cambridge, 2002, p. 232, quoted in Tomuschat, ibid.
183 See Sabrina P. Ramet, 'The Denial Syndrome and Its Consequences: Serbian Political Culture Since 2000', *Communist and Post-Communist Studies,* December 2006. Ramet considers that the 'habits of mind associated with the denial syndrome' are so deeply rooted that they will require a generation before they subside. In the Serbian parliament, the Serbianization of Republika Srpska continues. See 'Omarska – Fifteen Years On', Chris Keulemans, *DANI,* 26 June 2007, and 'Unisteni tragovi nekadasnjeg zivota u Banjoj Luci' (Banished traces of former life in Banja Luka), *Oslobodjenje,* 2 July 2007.

184 Tomuschat, ibid.
185 Mark A. Drumbl, *Professor of Law & Director*, Transnational Law Institute, University of Washington, *Globus* (Zagreb), 2 March 2007, quoted in Bosnia Report, New Series 55–56, January–July 2007.
186 For wide-ranging views on the Application, see interviews with Kasim Trnka, Florence Hartmann and Rasim Muratovic, and articles by Smail Cekic, Enis Omerovic, Sakib Softic and Ahmed Kulanic. *Stav*, No.106, Sarajevo, 16 March 2017.

9 Insider critics

The cases of Florence Hartmann and Frederik Harhoff

To be acceptable to democratic states and publics, an international court should make available the logic and effect of its rulings.[1]

The ICTY's ethics were challenged and brought to public notice in two unrelated cases, when a tribunal official and a judge, in 2007 and 2013 respectively, questioned decisions taken by its judiciary. The first was an established journalist and author, and former *porte-parole* of the ICTY, Florence Hartmann, who faulted two Appeals Chamber decisions relating to document disclosure. The second case arose when a serving *ad litem* judge, Frederik Harhoff, criticized recent tribunal judgements where accused persons, previously holding senior positions in the government or military, had been acquitted. Notwithstanding their hitherto unblemished professional records, both endured harsh consequences as a result of their actions.

Insider critics – or whistleblowers – are legally protected in many countries, at least on paper.[2] Yet the fate of a number of individuals who have sought in recent years to explain or expose the functioning of states and public institutions, and to establish the facts, would appear to suggest otherwise. Punishments have ranged from shunning and isolation to job loss, and even death.[3]

Florence Hartmann and Frederik Harhoff both committed a cardinal error in the eyes of the tribunal, in exposing some of the inner workings of the Court and casting a long shadow over its reputation and public record. Although dissimilar in many respects, contextually and in delivery, the cases merit closer study for the manner in which they were handled by the tribunal, especially in view of the wider political implications of their actions.

The tribunal chose not to address the legitimate issues raised, but rather to 'shoot the messengers', imposing punishment disproportionate to the deed, while diverting attention from vital questions to which the public had, and still has, a right to answers.

Florence Hartmann

On 14 September 2009, French journalist, author and former ICTY official Florence Hartmann was convicted by a Specially Appointed Trial Chamber of the

ICTY of contempt of court for disclosing confidential tribunal information.[4] Hartmann was the first foreign journalist to be convicted on this charge, and the only former ICTY employee to be tried for contempt.

Hartmann's revelations were not earth-shattering, since the practical effect of the decisions had been widely reported in the media well before the publication of her texts. She was nonetheless charged with violating Rule 77(A)(ii) of the Rules of Procedure and Evidence (RPE), which allows the tribunal to bring contempt charges against any individual who knowingly and wilfully interferes with the administration of justice by disclosing information relating to proceedings in violation of an order of the Chamber. Since the rule is not actually mentioned in the Statute, some scholars were led to question the tribunal's power to punish contempt.[5] The ICTY is, arguably, anyway a poor venue for handling contempt proceedings, especially where the Court is one of the injured parties, raising issues of cost, objectivity and legality.[6]

Hartmann's conviction rests on two pieces of work. In August 2007, her book *Paix et Chatiment* was published, which contained information relating to two Appeals Chamber decisions, including the contents and alleged effect of those decisions.[7] The following January, an article by Hartmann was published online by the Bosnian Institute, alleging that in two confidential decisions the Appeals Chamber had declined to release transcripts of meetings of Serbia's Supreme Defence Council (SDC), purportedly containing evidence of Serbia's involvement in the Srebrenica genocide.[8]

Background

The deputy prosecutor in the Milosevic case, Geoffrey Nice, had been battling to acquire the SDC documents for over a year, without which he was not prepared to indict Milosevic for genocide in Sarajevo and Srebrenica.[9] Belgrade firmly resisted releasing the documents, contravening Serbia's obligations to cooperate with the tribunal.[10] To overcome the impasse, Carla Del Ponte wrote to the Yugoslav (FRY) foreign affairs minister, Goran Svilanovic in May 2003, agreeing to withhold from the public certain passages, provided the protection measures demanded by Belgrade were 'reasonable', and in conformation with tribunal Rules of Procedure and Evidence, under Rule 54 *bis* (F).[11] Reassured by Del Ponte's letter, Belgrade agreed at the end of May for an expert from the OTP to consult a selection of the archives over a period of two days under stringent conditions. No copies were to be made, nor notes taken. The expert was able to confirm on examining the documents, however, that they indicated that Milosevic was the architect of the Bosnian war, and the Bosnian and Croatian Serb armies totally under his control.[12] This was subsequently confirmed in other testimony before the ICTY and in various reports.[13]

This revelation ended the deadlock within the OTP and, on 30 July 2003, following an application by the prosecutors, the Trial Chamber (judges Richard May, Patrick Robinson and O-Gon Kwon, Judge May presiding) renewed the injunction to Belgrade to release the documents. Belgrade promptly raised an objection, at which point prosecutor Geoffrey Nice informed the media.[14] The Belgrade authorities declared this a breach of trust and turned to the judges.

At an ex-parte meeting between the judges and Serbian state representatives which followed in October, to which the OTP was not invited, the Trial Chamber acceded to much of Serbia's request, interpreting the rules to permit blackouts to protect Serbia's 'vital national interest'. The prosecutor was denied the right to appeal the ruling. The documents were available in full to the Milosevic Trial Chamber who found sufficient evidence to deny Milosevic's request for acquittal but were denied to the plaintiff and judges at the International Court of Justice (ICJ), with the result that the ICJ did not have the benefit of a full record. It was agreed that the judges could use the documents to determine the culpability of Milosevic, but would not be able to cite confidential extracts in the public record of the judgement. Serbia also convinced the Chamber that the documents, excluding the most compromising extracts, should be used for the Milosevic trial only, and not divulged to any other court.[15] The judges had bought Serbia's argument relating to 'vital national interests'. Nothing in the tribunal rules, however, permits judges to grant protective measures in order to conceal from another court evidence of possible state responsibility for genocide. A third-party government considering cooperation with an international court would wish to know that sensitive information would be protected. Serbia was not a third-party government, however, but the instrument used by Milosevic to advance his war aims.

Del Ponte now felt released from her earlier promise to Svilanovic and asked for a hearing before the Chamber, but without success. The Chamber remained convinced, however, that losing the case of Serbian State responsibility for genocide before the ICJ would result in immeasurable damage to a country whose economy was already in ruins, and could endanger the current tenuous peace.[16] Hartmann claims that, in doing so, the judges were accomplice to a lie in apparently ignoring that 'vital national interests' had already been invoked to justify crimes which they were now charged to judge.[17]

In March 2016, Hartmann repeated the charge that tribunal judges had improperly and unlawfully struck a deal with Serbia, aimed at denying victims of mass atrocities access to information critical to their ability to obtain reparations. This might indicate tribunal thinking in arresting her at The Hague on the day of the Karadzic judgement – where there was a high media presence, and hundreds of Bosnian genocide survivors and others gathered at the ICTY gates – as a pre-emptive move to forestall further public debate. Unfortunately for the tribunal it misfired, as holding Hartmann in captivity along with defendants accused of crimes against humanity merely highlighted its confused sentencing policy.

At the time, Svilanovic himself admitted that the request was to avoid responsibility at the ICJ, where a suit for civil damages brought by Bosnia against Serbia under the Genocide Convention might end in costly reparations. In doing so, he unwittingly acknowledged the veracity of the SDC documents and their potential in proving Serbia's role in the Bosnian war. Hartmann records Svilanovic's comment at a meeting in Del Ponte's office on 3 October 2003: 'If we aid in convicting Milosevic of genocide, our State will be equally condemned for genocide by the ICJ, and we would have to pay billions of dollars in reparations to Bosnia

Herzegovina'.[18] This was backed by a source at the Serbian foreign ministry, who did not wish to be named.

> The SDC was involved in decisions about Serb forces in Bosnia and Herzegovina, and this had our lawyers worried. We gave them a kind of offer. We provided them with what we might have and what the procedure for sharing the documents would be if they were interested in introducing them.[19]

Svilanovic and his colleagues were surprised at their apparent easy victory. Vladimir Djeric, Svilanovic's legal advisor later observed, 'while we didn't have much success negotiating with the prosecution, we had more success with the court'.[20] It was viewed as a major triumph in damage limitation for Serbian diplomacy and legal skills. Serbia also feared that another consequence of the documents coming to light could be the unravelling of the Dayton Agreement, which had established the para-state, Republika Srpska.

Tribunal insiders interviewed by the Institute for War & Peace Reporting (IWPR) pointed out that agreeing to Belgrade's terms was the only way the Trial Chamber at least would gain a clearer picture of Milosevic's role in the Bosnian war.[21] Indeed, on 16 June 2004, it held that there was sufficient evidence to sustain a *prima facie* criminal finding of genocide against Milosevic.[22] Months later, additional Serbian military files came to light that reportedly revealed Ratko Mladic to be a serving officer in the Yugoslav Army (VJ), placing Serbia directly in the chain of causation of the Srebrenica genocide.

A HRW report later summed it up:

> The Milosevic trial opened the door on these state secrets. Evidence introduced at trial showed how those in Belgrade and the Federal Republic of Yugoslavia financed the war; how they provided weapons and material support to Croatian and Bosnian Serbs; and the administrative and personnel structures set up to support the Croatian Serb and Bosnian Serb armies. In short, the trial showed how Belgrade enabled the war to happen. As a former United Nations (UN) official testified, 'The [Serbs] relied almost entirely on the support they got from Serbia, from the officer corps, from the intelligence, from the pay, from the heavy weapons, from the anti-aircraft arrangements. Had Belgrade chosen even to significantly limit that support, I think that the siege of Sarajevo probably would have ended and a peace would have been arrived at somewhat earlier rather than having to force them militarily into that weaker position'.[23]

It later emerged in testimony that Ratko Mladic had been promoted on 16 June 1994 by Zoran Lilic, then president of the FRY (not by Karadzic, the Bosnian Serb president).[24] According to Hartmann, the five Appeal Court judges considered that the plea of 'national state interests' was not admissible and that the *Milosevic* Trial Chamber was wrong in 2003 to use the argument of national security to justify protection measures. Hartmann records that, rather than correct the error and lift those measures, the Appeals Chamber concluded that Serbia had a legitimate expectation that guarantees given two years earlier still applied. On 21 September 2005, the OTP again attempted to have the measures lifted. In response, on 6 December 2005, the new judge, Iain Bonomy, replacing Judge May, along with Judge Robinson, decided (with Judge Kwon dissenting) to annul the protective measures in place since 2003. Belgrade applied and obtained a provisional suspension of the Decision. On 6 April 2006, the Appeals Chamber, in a Decision marked 'confidential', Judge Pocar again presiding, annulled the Trial Chamber decision of 6 December, with the result that the documents remained inaccessible to the ICJ.[25] The ICJ judges, extraordinarily, did not even attempt to acquire them, and they were denied to the Bosnian team.

'In the Case of Florence Hartmann'

On 27 August 2008, Florence Hartmann was indicted 'In a Specially Appointed Trial Chamber', with Judge Carmel Agius presiding, on two charges of contempt of the ICTY,

> punishable under this Tribunal's inherent power and Rule 77(A)(ii) of the Rules, for knowingly and wilfully interfering with the administration of justice by disclosing information in violation of an order of the Appeals Chamber dated 20 September 2005 and an order of the Appeals Chamber dated 6 April 2006 through means of authoring for publication a book entitled *Paix et Chatiment*, published by *Flammarion* on 10 September 2007. . . [and for] authoring for publication an article entitled 'Vital Genocide Documents Concealed', published by the *Bosnian Institute* on 21 January 2008.[26]

Following her indictment, numerous non-governmental organizations (NGOs) and human rights groups in the region signed a press release condemning the tribunal's action and pointing out that the information disclosed by Hartmann was already in the public domain.[27] The NGOs also criticized the tribunal decision to accept Serbia's request to keep the SDC documents under wraps, a position held *inter alia* by Geoffrey Nice, who wrote to the ICTY chief prosecutor before she made the Agreement, stating that there was no reason in law for any part of the transcripts to be protected.[28]

The case revolved partly around the issue of freedom of expression, revealing a marked difference in emphasis between the ICTY Special Chamber and the Amicus Curiae Brief, exposing the substantial tension between the principles of freedom of expression and the fair administration of justice. The Amicus Brief, on Behalf of Article 19, focused on freedom of expression principles developed in international law.[29] Recalling the Universal Declaration of Human Rights 1948, the European Convention of Human Rights 1950, the International Covenant on Civil and Political Rights 1966, the American Convention of Human Rights 1969 and the African Charter on Human and Peoples' Rights 1981, along with several case studies, the Brief quoted the case of the *Observer and Guardian v UK (1992)*, in which the European Court summarized key principles substantially adopted in subsequent ECtHR judgements:

(a) Freedom of expression constitutes one of the essential foundations of a democratic society; subject to paragraph 2 of Article 10, it is applicable not only to 'information' or 'ideas' that are favourable received or regarded as inoffensive or as a matter of indifference, but also to those that offend, shock or disturb. Freedom of expression, as enshrined in Article 10 is subject to a number of exceptions which, however, must be narrowly interpreted and the necessity for any restrictions must be convincingly established.
(b) These principles are of particular importance as far as the press is concerned. While it must not overstep the bounds set, inter alia, in the 'interests of national security' or for 'maintaining the authority of the judiciary', it is nevertheless incumbent on it to impart information and ideas on matters of public interest. Not only does the press have the task of imparting such information and ideas: the public also has a right to receive them. Were it otherwise, the press would be unable to play its vital role of 'public watchdog'.

The Brief went on to analyse case law pertaining to the administration of justice and contempt, citing *Sunday Times v UK*, where the European Court observed that '(t)here is a general recognition of the fact that the courts cannot operate in a vacuum', and that 'whilst the mass media must not overstep the bounds imposed in the interests of the proper administration of justice, it is incumbent on them to impart information and ideas concerning matters that come before the courts.' . . . [30] In *Dupuis v France*, the European Court, citing the Council of Europe's Committee of Ministers' Recommendation that the public had a right to receive information, stressed 'the importance of media reporting on criminal proceedings to inform the public and ensure public scrutiny of the functioning of the criminal justice system'.[31] This case was of central relevance to *Hartmann* in that it demonstrated that the fact that confidential information had been disclosed did not determine whether the person disclosing the information should be convicted of contempt of court. In *Weber v Switzerland*, a journalist was convicted for having disclosed the existence of a confidential judicial investigation but, since the essence of the information was already in the public domain and the investigation near completion, the European Court found that the disclosures were unlikely to prejudice the investigation.[32] In *Guja v Moldova*, the European Court found a violation of Article 10 but considered that the public interest may have been strong enough to override even a legally imposed duty of confidence.[33] A further important consideration, according to the European Court, was the 'chilling effect' of a journalist's conviction, even if the fine imposed was moderate.

> The reasoning is well-established in the Article 10 jurisprudence; the fact of a person receiving a criminal conviction is <u>in itself</u> capable of discouraging

> open discussion of matters of public concern, so the imposition of even a moderate fine does not negate the chilling effect.[34]

Article 19 found the ICTY's attempts to suppress its legal reasoning and punish Hartmann for exposing the truth were 'depressingly inconsonant' with its stated mission to bring 'transparent international justice' to the area.[35]

> [O]ther than damaging the moral authority of the ICTY there is little to counterweigh the palpable public interests served by Hartmann's report on the controversy. That one of the primary purposes of the ICTY (the pursuit of truth) was compromised in order to pursue another fundamental purpose (bringing Slobodan Milosevic to justice) may be justifiable to some, but its moral value is ambiguous and clearly merits proper investigation and debate.[36]

The arguments of the ICTY Special Chamber, on the other hand, focused on the boundaries of exercising freedom of expression as found in Article 10(2) of the ECHR, which may be subject to such 'formalities, conditions, restrictions or penalties as are prescribed by law and are necessary in a democratic society for preventing the disclosure of information received in confidence, or maintaining the authority and impartiality of the judiciary'.[37] The Chamber's focus on the provisions of the ECHR pertaining to penalties may have been intended to address suggestions that in punishing those found guilty of contempt of court, it may be violating the principle of *nulla poena sine lege*.

In asserting its inherent power to deal with allegations of contempt, the Special Chamber studiously followed the precedent established in *Tadić*.[38] The Trial Chamber's main argument focused on the protection of confidential information relating to court proceedings, against the right to freedom of expression. Relying on *Jovic* and *Margetic*, the Chamber dismissed Hartmann's claims that 'criminalisation of her conduct would, in the circumstances, constitute a violation of her fundamental rights and, thus, be *ultra vires* of the statutory powers and jurisdiction of the Tribunal'. In the *Jovic* and *Margetic* cases, two Trial Chambers at the ICTY had confronted the need to weigh the right to freedom of expression and freedom of the press against the equally critical need to protect confidential information related to court proceedings.[39] The *actus reus* and *mens rea* of contempt were examined, the Chamber ruling that Hartmann acted with knowledge that her disclosure violated the Appeals Chamber order in publishing her book and article.[40] The Chamber dismissed the Defence argument, considering it 'wholly lacking in merit', including the selective prosecution claim that Hartmann was targeted while 'others very publicly discussed the reasoning and purported effect of the impugned decisions without exposing themselves to contempt proceedings'.[41]

> In making its findings, the Chamber has relied upon those arguments by the parties that it considers relevant to the issues which are the subject of the specific charges against the Accused. It has not discussed a number of arguments that it considers to be wholly lacking in merit. It is the discretion of the Trial

> Chamber as to which legal arguments to address, and, [w]ith regard to the factual findings, the Trial Chamber is required only to make findings of those facts which are essential to the determination of guilt on a particular count. It is not necessary to refer to the testimony of every witness or every piece of evidence on the trial record.[42]
>
> The Defence argument of selective prosecution, for example, finds no basis in either fact or law. . . . In this respect, the Chamber finds that evidence that other persons may have committed similar acts to those alleged in the Indictment is irrelevant to the case at hand, as it does not prove or disprove any of the charges against the Accused.[43]

The Trial Chamber's dismissal of the Defence's selective prosecution arguments, that the Defence has 'no basis in either fact or law', is interesting in light of the Appeals Court decision in *Celebici*, where that Chamber held a contrasting position:

> The breadth of the discretion of the Prosecutor, and the fact of her statutory independence, imply a presumption that the prosecutorial functions under the Statute are exercised regularly. This presumption may be rebutted by an appellant who can bring evidence to establish that the discretion has in fact not been exercised in accordance with the Statute; here, for example, in contravention of the principle of equality before the law in Article 21. This would require evidence from which a clear inference can be drawn that the Prosecutor was motivated in that case by a factor inconsistent with that principle. *Because the principle is one of equality of persons before the law, it involves a comparison with the legal treatment of other persons who must be similarly situated for such a comparison to be a meaningful one.* This essentially reflects the two-pronged test advocated by Landžo and by the Prosecution of (i) establishing an unlawful or improper (including discriminatory) motive for the prosecution and (ii) establishing that other similarly situated persons were not prosecuted.[44]

The Chamber also recalled that Florence Hartmann had signed a confidentiality agreement on joining the ICTY so, in legal terms, she broke this in violating a Chamber order and disclosing information not in the public domain. But did she wilfully interfere with the administration of justice, as alleged in the Judgement?[45] There is a subtle difference between 'disclosing information in violation of an order of an Appeals Chamber' and knowingly and wilfully interfering with the administration of justice. It can equally be argued that justice was better administered by the publication of the documents than by withholding their publication.

In determining the appropriate penalty, the Chamber pointed to 'the need to deter future wrongful disclosure of confidential information by the Accused or any other person'.[46] But, again, the question begs: why should that information be confidential? Whose interests did it serve? Third-party sovereign states, perhaps, who are not directly implicated in the issue. But in this case, it was Serbia, not a third-party state, which was directly implicated, and which continued to violate tribunal laws.

Ruth Wedgwood summed it up.

> The public study of procedural rulings and potential misfires of international war crimes tribunals remains important in figuring out how to assure fair procedures in future international trials. . . . But we should avoid such misfires in the future. It does not advance the cause of international criminal justice to threaten a person who described the boggled procedure with criminal contempt.[47]

The international dimension

It may be wondered why the tribunal judges succumbed so easily to Serbia's arguments, even when they did not stand up to scrutiny, and at a time when Serbia was blatantly violating its obligations before the ICTY in refusing to surrender major war crimes indictees.

The tribunal was already under fire for indicting a far greater number of Serbs than any other ethnic group. In the environment of the early 2000s, after Milosevic's transfer to The Hague, followed by several other indictees from Serbia, the perceived need to play into Serbia's hands on the issue of the SDC documents in order to obtain further cooperation in arresting major war crimes indictees, seemed to be paramount in ICTY thinking. There was also the implied threat of potential major civil unrest in Serbia, consequent to the publication of the documents.

Hartmann's allegations against Western leaders may also have played a part. The book's sub-title: 'The Secret Wars of Politics and International Justice' may have rung alarm bells, as British, French, American and other diplomats and politicians were named.[48] Hartmann later claimed that British diplomats threatened her with court action, but didn't follow through.[49] As Ruth Wedgwood commented, 'The explosive nature of this contempt case . . . turns on the aching quality of the international community's underlying failure in Bosnia'.[50]

The reasons behind major world power appeasement of the Milosevic regime throughout the war, and into the post-Milosevic era, have been analysed by a number of scholars.[51] A variety of reasons have been offered, including the perception of Serbia as a factor for stability in the region.[52] Forcing Serbia into a position where it would be liable for significant reparations would scupper that position. It may also not be irrelevant that the ICTY, an *ad hoc* tribunal founded by the UN Security Council, was dependent on funding from the UN.

The decision by two Appeals Chambers at the ICTY held in secret, to withhold the documents from other courts and from the public, resulted in the ICJ being deprived of essential material in adjudicating the Serbian State's responsibility for genocide in Bosnia and Herzegovina, making it difficult not to conclude that, in this case, misplaced political considerations trumped the law.

Conclusion

The court's confidentiality rules surrounding key papers from the Serbian government archives, apart from compromising proceedings in another court, means that Serbian people will be denied information concerning their leaders' role in the Bosnian war for years to come. Ignorance of the true role of the Milosevic regime in the 90s wars has reinforced a culture of denial and blame, preventing a genuine understanding of the wars. The lack of transparency means that others wishing to use the archives as evidence will be unable to access them, contrary to the stated aims of the tribunal.

The ICTY has never denied any of Florence Hartmann's revelations, merely castigated her for publishing them. Tribunal judges have in effect ruled that someone who reveals facts which may have direct relevance to the administration of justice in another court should, in violating the tribunal Rules, receive a criminal conviction, while the State itself (Serbia) should be exonerated both from full disclosure of documents and from the consequences of disclosure, including possible State reparations for genocide in Bosnia. It could be argued that, in this instance, the ICTY was trebly wrong – firstly, for concealment of documents under a false interpretation of the rules, secondly for convicting the whistleblower, and thirdly for not offering an adequately reasoned explanation for her conviction.

Ruth Wedgwood and others have argued for the transparency of international criminal courts (ICCs), even when dealing with sovereign states, and that there can be no secret jurisprudence, unavailable to debate and critique by an audience of lawyers, political leaders, and citizens. In the case of Florence Hartmann, no witness was endangered, no sealed arrest warrant thwarted, and the Milosevic case to which the decisions pertained ended with his death in 2006.

The tribunal has, over the years, been beset by time, logistical and financial constraints and, not least, by political pressure, both from within the former Yugoslav states and internationally. By placing its judicial ruling on public record, it may have provoked controversy, but in keeping its ruling secret, it opened itself to suspicion and mistrust.

In sentencing Florence Hartmann to incarceration in the same building as major war crimes indictees, subjected to similar conditions and given a criminal record, not to mention the 'chilling factor', and the resultant loss of work, with potential psychological and financial consequences, the tribunal has not lived up to the ideals of its early days. Nor has it provided other international courts with the kind of example necessary for establishing a healthy working environment.

Frederik Harhoff

For the first time since its establishment, the International Criminal Tribunal for the former Yugoslavia (ICTY) disqualified one of its judges, *ad litem* judge, Frederik Harhoff, following his letter criticizing a number of acquittals which he felt indicated a change of direction in the tribunal's jurisprudence in key areas.

Harhoff was by no means alone in his view of the acquittals which had sparked off widespread reaction from lawyers and other observers even before Harhoff's letter. The acquittals of Gotovina and Markac, as well as that of the Serbian general, Momčilo Perišić, and Serbian secret service chiefs Jovica Stanisic and Franko Simatovic had provoked a storm of protest amongst international lawyers, human rights groups and other judges, who claimed privately that legal jurisprudence applied in earlier cases had been rewritten, especially on aiding and abetting. It was just days after the acquittal of Stanisic and Simatovic that Harhoff wrote his letter. Jovica Stanisic was head of the Serbian State Security Service of the Ministry of Internal Affairs (MUP) during the Bosnian war, where Simatovic was also employed. They were indicted for four counts of crimes against humanity and one count of the violations of the laws or customs of war. The *Economist* summed up the general view:

> The credibility of the International Criminal Tribunal for the Former Yugoslavia in The Hague is in shreds and few understand the reasoning behind recent judgments. This seems to be the consensus of comments made in the wake of two landmark judgements last week. In one the Croatian state was implicated in war crimes in Bosnia during the 1992–1995 war. And in another, Serbian officials were acquitted.[53]

Harhoff framed his criticism in the form of an email to 56 lawyers, friends and associates on 6 June 2013, in which he raised serious concerns about the acquittals, accusing the tribunal's president, Theodor Meron, of pressurizing his colleagues, and even alluding to US/Israeli military intelligence influence. The email was soon leaked to the Danish media.[54]

On 9 July 2013, Vojislav Šešelj filed a motion to recuse Judge Harhoff from his case on the basis of the letter which he alleged indicated, *inter alia*, an anti-Serb bias.[55] In response, ICTY President Theodor Meron who had been cited in the Motion assigned it to Vice-President Carmel Agius for consideration. The case was heard on 28 August before Judges Bakone Justice Moloto, Liu Daqun and Burton Hall, Judge Moloto presiding. The Trial Chamber was divided in its Decision on the interpretation of the letter and the fate of Judge Harhoff, as were outside lawyers and other observers. The Majority found that

> By referring to a 'set practice' of convicting accused persons without reference to an evaluation of the evidence in each individual case, the Majority, Judge Liu dissenting, considers that there are grounds for concluding that a reasonable observer, properly informed, would reasonably apprehend bias on the part of Judge Harhoff in favour of conviction. This includes for the purposes of the present case. The appearance of bias is further compounded by Judge Harhoff's statement that he is confronted by a professional and moral dilemma, which in the view of the Majority, is a clear reference to his difficulty in applying the current jurisprudence of the Tribunal. In the

> circumstances, the Majority considers that the Letter, when read as a whole, rebuts the presumption of impartiality.[56]

Šešelj claimed that Harhoff was 'overwhelmed with prejudice' against the Serbs, and implied he should be tried for contempt. It was his 508th motion, vastly in excess of the limit imposed by the rules, poorly organized and unconvincingly argued. It was also one of many aimed at removing judges, prosecutors and others from his case.[57]

Judge Liu, in a vigorous Dissenting Opinion, stressed that, while he did not support the manner chosen by Judge Harhoff to express his views, he considered Šešelj's allegation of bias against Harhoff to be unfounded, including Šešelj's reference to previous judgements in which Harhoff had deliberated.[58] Liu pointed to the high threshold necessary to disqualify a judge and that, 'while bias on the part of a judge undermines confidence in the administration of justice, so too would disqualifying judges on the basis of unfounded allegations of bias'.[59] He expressed concern with

> the cursory approach taken by the Majority in assessing whether the email would lead an informed person, with knowledge of all the relevant circumstances, to reasonably apprehend bias on the part of Judge Harhoff in favour of conviction of accused before the Tribunal.[60]

He also opined that the Majority had failed to properly contextualize Harhoff's statements and to address the surrounding circumstances, including Harhoff's experience as a judge and professor of law.[61]

Šešelj's reference to 'previous judgements' mainly concerned Rasim Delic's case, analysis of which occupied nearly a third of Šešelj's lengthy motion.[62] His long-winded analysis of *Delic* attempted to prove that Harhoff, in acquitting Delic on several counts, was prejudiced in favour of Bosnian Muslims. Previously commander of the main staff of ABiH, General Delic received a three-year sentence for failing to take the necessary measures to prevent or punish crimes committed by subordinates at two camps in July and August 1995.[63] According to Šešelj, Harhoff 'practically acquitted' Delic. It was a shaky argument, not least in that Delic *was* convicted, and sentenced. So, arguably, far from demonstrating a perception of bias, the Decision indicated a lack of bias on Harhoff's part, since it was the presiding judge, Justice Moloto who dissented, holding that Delic should be acquitted on all counts. Nonetheless, as on numerous previous occasions, Šešelj won the day, while Harhoff was disqualified from his case, just weeks before judgement day.

Following the Majority decision, Harhoff wrote an Internal Memorandum, where he rejected the allegation of bias and explained the circumstances under which he had expressed his concern over the tribunal's change of course, which raised the bar for prosecuting high-ranking commanders who knew about crimes perpetrated by their subordinates. In attempting to understand the rationale behind the judgements, Harhoff explained that countries engaged in armed conflict, such as the United States and Israel, could have an interest in ensuring that international criminal law did not develop standards which could lead to the conviction of generals as members of a Joint Criminal Enterprise, or for aiding and abetting crimes in which they were not direct participants. Crucially, as Harhoff noted, his letter did not mention Šešelj, who was not a military commander. He confirmed that he held no prejudice towards Serbs, Muslims or Croats, or 'even against generals as such'.[64] Harhoff's Internal Memorandum was not taken into consideration, however, on the dubious grounds that he was not a party to the trial.

The publication of Harhoff's letter heralded fierce debate amongst international lawyers, human rights representatives and the media, and exposed deep divisions amongst the permanent judges at the tribunal.[65] While most lawyers appeared to agree that Harhoff's action was unethical in view of his position as a sitting judge, opinion was divided as to whether he should be disqualified from Šešelj's case or, indeed, removed from the tribunal since, unlike at the ICC, neither the Statute nor the rules specifically addressed the issue. On the other hand, there seemed to be general agreement that Harhoff should have been heard in the process of disqualification.[66] Also, while judges are bound not to disclose their deliberations or to discuss cases on which they were sitting, there is no rule which forbids discussion on other matters relating to the tribunal. It was unfortunate that Harhoff named the tribunal's president, Theodor Meron, who was, arguably, in a position to influence not only the outcome of major trials, as Harhoff alleged, but the Trial Chamber which was to deliberate on the Harhoff case. The assignment of Justice Moloto as presiding judge arguably sealed Harhoff's fate, in view of Moloto's strong Dissenting Opinion in *Perišić*.[67]

More unfortunate was Harhoff's US/Israel innuendo, leading some commentators to become embroiled in a debate which at times lost sight of the real issue, namely, the change of tribunal jurisprudence on 'specific direction', which could impact not only on future judgements at the ICTY but also further afield. Predictably, Serbian Radical Party official Zoran Krasic, who had assisted Šešelj during his trial, expressed satisfaction at the allegation of bias and looked to Šešelj's prompt release as, presumably, did Šešelj himself.[68]

On the 'specific direction' saga, lawyers were equally divided.[69] In the Perišić Appeals Judgement, a 'specific direction' requirement was purportedly added to the *actus reus* of aiding and abetting, introducing a new standard to tribunal jurisprudence, rendering it virtually impossible to convict senior military commanders where there was no direct evidence of crimes committed.[70]

As Kevin Jon Keller saw it,

> As the AC explains in *Perisic*, there is no 'old' law of aiding and abetting. The specific-direction requirement was articulated in *Tadić*, the first AC judgment, and has been reaffirmed in every AC judgment but one since. The requirement developed bite for the first time in *Perišić* because, as Judge Moloto explained in his dissent at trial. . . *Perišić* was the first case in which there was significant question whether it was satisfied.[71]

This argument, which traces specific direction back to *Tadić*, was quashed by James G Stewart who, on the basis of two empirical studies found that the stricter standards of proof were only used previously in extremely rare cases, and never to acquit anyone.

> Of the 362 incidents we have coded, 33% mention 'specific direction' or 'specifically directed' in passing by citing the language in Tadić. . . . To the best of our knowledge there is only one reference to 'specific direction' prior to the Tadic Judgment. . . 'specific direction' is only applied as a substantive test to the facts of a case in 2% of incidents. . . [i]n over 98% of aiding and abetting incidents in international criminal law, 'specific direction' is either not mentioned at all in relevant decisions, or it is mentioned in only a single sentence without later application. . . . To the best of our knowledge, there are no acquittals . . . based on 'specific direction' prior to Perišić before any court, national or international.[72]

General Perišić was the first military commander to be acquitted according to the 'specific direction' principle which, contrary to the Appeals Chamber finding, was not settled law.[73] Interestingly, the Special Court for Sierra Leone in *Taylor* rejected the Perišić Appeals Chamber's judgement that the *actus reus* of aiding and abetting liability requires 'specific direction'.[74]

But perhaps more pertinent to the disqualification of Judge Harhoff were the deep divisions within the tribunal and the general working environment.[75] Judges and court officials at the ICTY, speaking on condition of anonymity, confirmed that a mini-rebellion had been brewing against Judge Theodor Meron, the ICTY president, with some of the 18 permanent judges grouping around another candidate for the scheduled election of tribunal president, which Judge Meron was expected to win. One senior court official estimated that around half the judges were uncomfortable with Meron due to his pressure for raising the bar for convictions, setting legal precedents which would protect military commanders in the future.[76] As William Schabas saw it,

> A decade ago, there was a very strong humanitarian message coming out of the tribunal, very concerned with the protection of civilians. It was not concerned with the prerogatives of the military and the police. This message has now been weakened, there is less protection for civilians and human rights.[77]

According to Richard Dicker. International Justice Programme Director at Human Rights Watch, Harhoff raised a legitimate question, especially in the case of General Perišić's acquittal which he called a 'step in the wrong direction', and created 'a very dangerous and undermining precedent' of 'immunising senior officials' on the issue of aiding and abetting liability that had already been applied with the acquittals of Stanisic and Simatovic.[78] This series of decisions set a very high standard for conviction on aiding and abetting, requiring a senior accused to have specifically known that a crime would be committed, and 'practically rules out conviction of senior accused not present', which could potentially have wider consequences. For example, if an international court looked into crimes committed in Syria, aiding and abetting liability would likely be needed to link senior officials to the crimes committed by the Shabiha militias, loyal to Syrian President Bashar Al-Assad.[79]

Professor Jens David Ohlin of Cornell University believed the outcome of the Harhoff case should be seen against the backdrop of 'a culture of silence' that for many years has surrounded the ICTY. 'Criticism from the outside is okay but. . . [Harhoff] went afoul of a culture of not criticizing the court from the inside. That alone explains the negative reaction from inside the court and the drastic remedy'. According to Ohlin, a fairer approach would have been to let all judges determine Judge Harhoff's fate by taking a vote in a plenary session, which he stated was the rule followed by the ICC. [80] Professor Dov Jacobs, critical of Harhoff's letter, nonetheless opined that to justify his dismissal by his 'unprofessional' behaviour suggested that it was a weak institution, incapable of dealing with the issue head on.[81] Hanne Petersen, professor of law at the University of Copenhagen, hoped that the Harhoff case would lead to 'some deep soul-searching within the ICTY', and prompt the UN courts to be more transparent.[82]

The credibility of Theodor Meron was also questioned at the International Criminal Tribunal for Rwanda. IBUKA, a high-profile organization based in Kigali to represent the rights and interests of genocide victims, had repeatedly expressed dissatisfaction with Meron's acquittal decisions and took Harhoff's letter very seriously. Justin Mugenzi and Prosper Mugiraneza, both Rwandan government ministers at the time, were found guilty of conspiracy to commit genocide, and sentenced to 30 years' imprisonment on 30 September 2011, and both were acquitted on appeal on 4 February 2013, with Judge Meron presiding, on the basis that the prosecution had violated its disclosure obligations under Rule 68. The Appeals Chamber conceded that the material not disclosed did not materially impact the cases.[83] It concluded, however, that Mugenzi and Mugiraneza did not necessarily possess the requisite *mens rea* for a conviction for conspiracy to commit genocide, Judge Liu dissenting, or for direct and public incitement to commit genocide.[84] The IBUKA president, Pierre Dusingizemungu, commented that 'it would be a mistake to simply dismiss these cases offhandedly as conspiracy theories, as some less informed people might be inclined to do'.[85]

Conclusion

Of the three appeal judgements which Judge Harhoff criticized, debate continues on the Gotovina/Markac and Perisic acquittals, but the Stanisic and Simatovic case, which had taken its cue from the Perisic appeal judgement, was declared a mistrial, and a new trial under the UN Mechanism for International Criminal Tribunals is currently under way. The cost to taxpayers of UN member states is likely to be extortionate, but the longer-term damage to the tribunal in legal terms could be greater still.

The channel Harhoff chose for his exposure has been strongly condemned by many. On the other hand, had the ICTY been more transparent and permitted open debate on controversial issues, the disagreement could probably have been sorted less contentiously. Of more concern was Harhoff's allegation of a US/Israeli conspiracy, and in attributing a motive to specific foreign intelligence and military quarters, without the requisite proof. As some scholars have pointed out, it would be naïve to discount the likelihood of political interference in the court, given the evidence of its formative years, but specifying countries and naming individuals was perhaps a bridge too far in this instance. What lay at the root of the tribunal judges' recent change of direction is still unclear, although it is not inconceivable that international military considerations played a part.

The focus on legal niceties, both within the tribunal and from some commentators, at times contributed to obscuring the wider picture. Vojislav Šešelj, who brought the Motion, was an ultra-right leader of a wartime paramilitary group which had perpetrated numerous crimes. And, while his 508th motion before the tribunal was taken seriously, Frederik Harhoff, a judge of some considerable professional standing and experience, who merely raised a number of points crucial to the development of international criminal jurisprudence (which were already being discussed privately within the tribunal, and publicly) was disqualified without adequate reason, and removed from the tribunal in disgrace, while the issues he raised continue to be shrouded in secrecy. Šešelj, on the contrary, was vindicated and initially acquitted. The recent acquittals also meant that no Serbian officials were convicted for war crimes in Bosnia and Herzegovina, despite overwhelming evidence that those crimes were mostly orchestrated by the Milosevic regime in Belgrade.

Other important issues included the cult of secrecy, the lack of transparency at the ICTY, and the absence of rules for judges, resulting in a situation where international jurisprudence on aiding and abetting and specific direction is in disarray, and the ICC is still, at the time of writing, unclear on the parameters of JCE liability.[86]

The ICTY decision may be interpreted as being merely extra-cautious, but it could also be seen as hitting back at a judge who had publicly accused its president of poor judgement, or worse. Judge Harhoff was disgraced for blowing the whistle, which undoubtedly sent a signal to the judges remaining, with consequences yet to be fully assessed.

Conclusion

The two cases suggest misjudgement by judges. But where does this leave the reputation of the ICTY? The lack of transparency and confused jurisprudence is not the legacy it might have hoped for and casts a shadow on its overall record. They cost the ICTY more financially, and in reputation, than either issue warranted. Both Florence Hartmann and Frederik Harhoff raised legitimate concerns and were punished for their actions. They were judged by the judges they had exposed or their associates.

It may be hoped that these episodes will in the longer-term trigger a reflection on the system, so as to make international judges independent but accountable in ways similar to most advanced domestic legal systems.

Notes

1 Ruth Wedgwood, Professor of Law and Diplomacy, and Director of the International Law and Organizations Program at the Paul H. Nitze School of Advanced International Studies, John Hopkins University, Washington, DC. 'The Strange Case of Florence Hartmann', *The American Interest*, Vol.4, Issue 6, 1 July 2009.

2 Hartmann herself maintains that she was not a whistleblower, but rather a scout (une eclaireuse) – one who examines or observes in order to obtain information. Florence Hartmann, *Lanceurs d'Alerte: Les mauvaises consciences de nos democraties*, Don Quichotte editions, 2014, pp. 330–331.

3 David Kelly, British scientist and senior weapons inspector, disclosed to a BBC journalist in May 2003, just weeks into the coalition invasion of Iraq, his concerns regarding a government dossier on weapons of mass destruction (WMD). The journalist, Andrew Gilligan, subsequently on BBC Radio 4, without naming Kelly, alleged the government had used false arguments to engage Britain in war. At this point, although the absence of WMD soon became clear, as the initial 'victory' culminating in the ousting of Saddam Hussein was coming under media scrutiny, and the invasion viewed less favourably, the British government could not afford this view to gain momentum and, through its spin doctors and others including sections of the media, outed Kelly and hounded him to the point where he lost his life in a manner still not unequivocally established. The information Kelly had imparted became subjugated to the hunt to identify the whistleblower and, thereafter, record his fate. The BBC also came under fire, resulting in the resignations of its president, Gavyn Davies and director-general, Greg Dyke, with no casualties on the British government side.

4 Under Rule 77 of the Rules of Procedure and Evidence, the tribunal can conduct proceedings for contempt of court.

5 See, for instance, comments by William A. Schabas and Alexander Zahar. http://humanrightsdoctorate.blogspot.co.uk/2008/09/florence-hartmann-prosecuted-for.html, and Kevin Jon Heller 'An Unfortunate Trial Begins at the ICTY' http://opiniojuis.org

6 See also Sluiter, who suggests that jurisprudence and rules offer a confusing picture with respect to the question of whether a person accused of contempt is entitled to the same degree of protection as a person accused of one or more of the 'core crimes'. Goran Sluiter, 'The ICTY and Offenses Against the Administration of Justice', *International Criminal Justice*, Vol.2, Issue 2, 2004, pp. 631, 635.

7 Florence Hartmann, (IT-02-54-R77.5) Appeals Chamber Decisions dated 20 September 2005 and 6 April 2006. *Paix et Chatiment: Les Guerres Secretes de la Politique et de la Justice Internationales,* Flammarion, 2007.

8 The Serbian Supreme Defence Council was allowed to mobilize the army in time of war, to promote and retire generals, to make decisions over financing and logistics, and to approve defence plans put forward by the army chief of staff. The documents go to the heart of how the Yugoslav military was managed at the highest level.

9 Proving the guilt of a head of state nowhere near the multiple crime scenes, and establishing a chain of command where no lawful authority existed, is difficult and time consuming. For the internal struggle within the OTP on this issue, see Hartmann, pp. 112–114. See also comments by the senior prosecutor in *Milosevic,* Nice, op. cit., pp. 56–60.

10 In hearings in March and June 2003, the prosecutors said they had been denied access to 100 priority documents from Belgrade, including the SDC documents. The Trial

Chamber eventually ordered Serbia to produce the SDC documents but refused many prosecution motions for documents from the archives. Djeric commented that had the prosecutors applied more political pressure rather than turning to the court they may have had more success.

11 Rule 54 bis, one of the more complicated, allows governments to request protective measures for documents submitted to the Court, provided the state can prove that making the documents publicly accessible would 'prejudice its national security interests'. Belgrade applied for protection on that basis. ICTY Prosecutor Geoffrey Nice told the Institute of War and Peace Reporting (IWPR) that he had already written to Del Ponte before she made the agreement, explaining that there was no legal reason for any parts of the transcripts to be protected in that way. 'Secrecy and Justice at the ICTY', IWPR, 15 February 2010.

12 Hartmann, pp. 114–115.

13 See, for instance, *Weighing the Evidence: Lessons from the Slobodan Milosevic Trial*, Executive Summary, Human Rights Watch, 13 December 2006. www.hrw.org/report/2006/12/13/weighing-evidence/lessons-slobodan-milosevic-trial

14 'Special Investigation: Justice at What Price?' *Institute for War & Peace Reporting*, 17 November 2005.

15 Hartmann, op. cit., p. 116.

16 This argument was also used by Serbian officials in an attempt to prevent Croatia's entry to the EU. Author's discussion with EU officials, February 2002.

17 Hartmann, op. cit., p. 120.

18 Ibid., p. 118. This author's translation.

19 See 'Special Investigation'.

20 Ibid.

21 Ibid.

22 *Prosecutor v Milosevic,* Decision on Motion for Judgement of Acquittal, 16 June 2004, para. 323. On 26 February 2007, the ICJ found that, while genocide had occurred at Srebrenica in July 1995, and that Serbia-Montenegro had provided the Bosnian Serbs with considerable military and financial support throughout the war, including at Srebrenica, Serbia was not responsible for the actions of the VRS and paramilitaries who carried out the genocide. See Chapter 8.

23 *Weighing the Evidence*, op. cit. See also the testimony of David Harland, 5 November 2003, p. 28706.

24 Former Yugoslav president Zoran Lilic had previously testified to a November 1993 SDC decision formalizing arrangements to fund and support offices of the Bosnian Serb army, and Serb forces in Croatia, through the 30th and 40th personnel centres of the Yugoslav army, to the tune of approximately 800,000 euro, with Bosnian Serb officers being paid not by the RS administration but by Serbia. Professor Radovan Stojanovic, the FRY foreign ministry's legal council chairman, revealed to IWPR in August 2004 the existence of a secret Yugoslav army order from 1993 awarding Mladic a promotion, an order leaked to the Sarajevo media. 'Special Investigation'.

25 Hartmann, op. cit., pp. 121–122.

26 In the Case Against Florence Hartmann, Amended Order in Lieu of an Indictment on Contempt, 27 October 2008. http://www.icty.org/x/cases/contempt_hartmann/ind/en/081027.pdf

27 The Belgrade-based Humanitarian Law Centre issued a press release on 3 November 2007, signed by 34 NGOs, pointing out that the content of the confidential decisions was the subject of numerous press reports and debates following the ICJ Judgement in February 2007, and that it was unclear why Hartmann had been singled out.

28 See 'Secrecy and Justice at the ICTY', Simon Jennings, IWPR, 14 May 2008 and 'How Belgrade Escaped Genocide Charge' by Slobodan Kostic, IWPR, 25 February 2008, for discussion of this. Serbia applied for protective measures under article 54 bis of the RPE, on the basis of 'national security interests', which Del Ponte agreed to

in October 2003. It was arguably unwise of Del Ponte to promise support 'in general terms' for the blackout and exclusions from the documents since she was not in a position to deliver.

29 Amicus Curiae Brief on Behalf of Article 19. 18 February 2010, hereinafter 'Amicus Curiae Brief'. Article 19 is a British-based organization established to defend the right to freedom of expression.

30 *Sunday Times v UK* (1979) 2EHRR 245, para. 65, cited in Amicus Curiae Brief, para. 14.

31 Amicus Curiae Brief, para. 15. In *Dupuis v France,* where there was an ongoing judicial investigation, the European Court accepted that the criminal conviction had a legitimate aim – to protect the secrecy of a judicial investigation – but that the interference was not justified in that case since the information was already partly available to the public. Ibid., para. 18.

32 *Weber v Switzerland* (1990) 12 EHRR 508, cited in Amicus Curiae Brief, paras. 20–21.

33 *Guja v Moldova,* Application no. 14277/04, Judgement, 12 February 2008.

34 Amicus Curiae Brief, para. 23, citing *Campos Damaso v Portugal*, Application No. 17107/05, 24 April 2008. Emphasis in original.

35 'ICTY: Hartmann case troubling', 10 October 2011. www.article19.org/resources.php/resource/2770/en/icty:-hartmann-case-troubling

36 Ibid.

37 Judgment, note 2, 70. See discussion of this in ICTY Special Chamber Decision in Benjamin E. Brockman-Hawe, 'The Case Against Florence Hartmann', *American Society of International Law*, Vol.13, Issue 17, 9 October 2009.

38 *Prosecutor v Tadic,* 31 January 2000, pp. 2545–2554.

39 *In the Case of Florence Hartmann*, Final Trial Brief of Florence Hartmann, 124, 2 July 2009. *Prosecutor v Jovic*, Judgment, 30 August 2006, note 20, 23 and *Prosecutor v Margetic*, Judgement 7 February 2007. Neither the Jovic nor Margetic chambers examined contemporary ECtHR case law on the issue, the Trial Chamber employed balancing competing public interests for the first time. See also Special Chamber Decision in Brockman-Hawe.

40 In a Specially Appointed Chamber, *In the Case of Florence Hartmann*, Judgement on Allegations of Contempt, p. 62. With regard to *actus reus*, the Defence argued that the Appeals Chamber (AC) decisions granting confidential status to the documents protected the documents themselves, not the legal reasoning of the AC decisions. Defence Final Brief, 2 July 2009, 6, and Judgment, 40, 41 and 46.

41 Defence Final Brief, July 2, 2009, 14.

42 *In the case against Florence Hartmann*, Judgement, 14 September 2009, Evaluation of Evidence, 23.

43 Ibid., p. 23, n.53.

44 *Prosecutor v Zejnil Delalic, Zdravko Mucic, Hazim Delic, and Esad Landzo*, Appeals Chamber Judgement, 20 February 2001, 611. Italics added.

45 'The Chamber is satisfied that the Prosecution proved beyond a reasonable doubt that the Accused knowingly and willfully interfered with the administration of justice'. Judgement Summary, 14 September 2009.

46 *Hartmann*, p. 88.

47 Wedgwood.

48 Hartmann recalled that Carl Bildt, on the eve of the Srebrenica genocide, tried to convince the United States to have confidence in Milosevic, who he considered a peacemaker. Other revelations include the fact that, according to Hartmann, none of the main figures present at a White House meeting in early August 1995 were prepared to testify at the ICTY, including Richard Holbrooke and Christopher Hill, despite Wesley Clark not meeting any challenge from Milosevic in two days of cross-examination. Hartmann, op. cit., p. 147. See also Ruth Wedgwood, ibid., and Hodge, op. cit.

49 Hartmann refers to the role of Paddy Ashdown in some detail, including his sacking of Munir Alibabic, pp. 209–212, See also Hodge, op. cit., pp. 180–184 on this.
50 Wedgwood, op. cit., 1 July 2009.
51 For a broad view of the Western response, see *This Time We Knew: Western Responses to Genocide in Bosnia*, New York University Press, 1996, in particular chapters by Brad Blitz, Daniele Conversi and Daniel Kofman.
52 For an analysis of the British role in the region from 1991 until 2006, see Hodge, and for Britain's role in the Bosnian war, see *Unfinest Hour, Britain and the Destruction of Bosnia*, Penguin Press, 2001, and Jane M. O. Sharp, *Honest Broker or Perfidious Albion: British Policy in the Former Yugoslavia–Defence and Security*, Institute for Public Policy Research, 1997.
53 'Two Puzzling Judgments at the Hague', *Economist*, 1 June 2013. Eric Gordy, senior lecturer at UCL School of Slavonic and East European Studies, commented that the record of the recent acquittals now meant that the 'judicial record does not match the historical record', while Chuck Sudetic, author and former ICTY analyst, commented that the new rule 'turns back precedents set at Nuremberg after World War II and does so 20 years after the establishment of the ICTY and might eventually emasculate the capacity of the institutions of international justice to bring to justice the highest-ranking persons responsible for heinous war crimes. Only the actual killers will be punished, not the mass murderers'.
54 Frederik Harhoff email, 6 June 2013, first published in the Danish tabloid newspaper, *BT* on 13 June 2013. www.bt.dk/udland/english-version-murderers-are-being-allowed-to-go-free
55 'Professor Šešelj's Motion for Disqualification of Judge Frederik Harhoff', 1 July 2013, Submission 508 [72 pages in Serbian and English].
56 *Prosecutor v Vojislav Šešelj*. Decision on Defence Motion for Disqualification of Judge Frederik Harhoff and Report to the Vice-President, 28 August 2013, para. 13.
57 Šešelj's Motion, Submission 508, op. cit.
58 *Prosecutor v Vojislav Šešelj*. Decision on Defence Motion for Disqualification of Judge Frederik Harhoff, 28 August 2013. Dissenting Opinion of Judge Liu.
59 Ibid., para. 4.
60 Ibid., para. 6. Rule 15(B)2.
61 Ibid., paras. 8–9.
62 Šešelj's Motion, Submission 508, op. cit., paras. 29–43.
63 *Prosecutor v Rasim Delic*, Trial Chamber Judgement, 15 September 2008.
64 Judge Harhoff's 'Internal Memorandum' made Public, SENSE Tribunal, 5 September 2013. Following the Decision, the Prosecution, two other judges of the Chamber, and Judge Harhoff himself requested clarification on the judge's decision.
65 'Fellow Judges Support Ousted Colleague's Criticism of Hague Tribunal', *Information,* 6 December 2013.
66 But see, 'Brief Thoughts on Judge Harhoff's Disqualification', Kevin Jon Heller, 29 August 2013. http://opiniojuris.org/2013/08/29/brief-thoughts-judge-harhoffs-disqualification/
67 Judge Moloto had allegedly also been very vocal in condemning Harhoff's email in the corridors of the tribunal. *Information*, 6 December 2013. www.information.dk/udland/2013/12/fellow-judges-support-ousted-colleagues-criticism-of-hague-tribunal.
68 Hague Disqualifies 'Biased' Judge from Šešelj Trial, Balkan Insight, 29 August 2013.
69 See, for instance, the discussion at http://opiniojuris.org/2013/08/12/welcome-to-beyond-the-hague-and-a-great-catch-on-judge-harhoff/
70 For further discussion of aiding and abetting and 'specific direction', see Milestones in International Criminal Justice: Recent Legal Controversies at the UN Yugoslav Tribunal, The Royal Institute of International Affairs, held at Doughty Street Chambers, 16 October 2013.

71 http://opiniojuris.org/2013/12/06/judge-harhoff-digs-deeper See also Alex Fielding on alleged hypocrisy of Harhoff, 'Judge Harhoff, Specific Direction and the Perisic Acquittal', Alex Harding, Beyond the Hague, 12 August 2013, and its rebuttal by Marko Milanovic, http://opiniojuris.org/2013/08/12/welcome-to-beyond-the-hague-and-a-great-catch-on-judge-harhoff/ Alex Fielding is a Canadian lawyer currently based in Tel Aviv, and was part of the Perišić Defence Team at the ICTY in 2009.

72 James G Stewart, Assistant Professor at the University of British Columbia Law School. www.ejiltalk.org/specific-direction-is-unprecedented-results-from-two-empirical-studies/. Dr Stewart had also worked at both the ICTY and ICTR. For a wider discussion of liability, see 'The End of "Modes of Liability" for International Crimes', James G Stewart, Leiden Journal of International Law, 2012, 2 November 2011.

73 See Chapter 11.

74 *The Prosecutor v Charles Ghankay Taylor*, Judgement, 26 April 2012. Taylor was found guilty on all 11 counts for both planning and for aiding and abetting, upheld on Appeal, 26 September 2013 in the Special Court for Sierra Leone. The judge concluded that the persons directed by Taylor could only be the perpetrators on the battlefield, but that it would be impossible to establish any direct link between Taylor and the actual perpetrators because he would rarely know who or where they were.

75 These divisions came across in various off-the-record discussions this author has held over the years with ICTY officials past and present.

76 Marlise Simons, 'Hague Judge Faults Acquittals of Serb and Croat Commanders', *The New York Times,* 14 June 2013. ICTY sources also allegedly revealed that a clear majority of the 23 members of the panel of judges (18 permanent judges plus five *ad litem*) concurred in the criticism in Harhoff's letter. According to *Information*, a Danish national newspaper, one judge, who preferred to remain anonymous, commented that Meron was good at seeking out every judge in advance and making deals with them, and managed to get re-elected in October 2013 for a further 2-year term, with 12 votes to 6 against. Meron also decided on the assignation of cases at the MICT, which took over pending cases. Criticism of Judge Meron was also expressed to this author by tribunal officials, on condition of anonymity. www.information.dk/udland/2013/12/fellow-judges-support-ousted-colleagues-criticism-of-hague-tribunal.

77 William Schabas, professor of international law, Middlesex University, London. Ibid.

78 Ibid.

79 Richard Dicker, 'Judge Thrown Off Yugoslav War Crimes Tribunal for Criticising "Change of Direction" in Verdicts', *Independent*, 24 September 2013.

80 'Fellow Judges Support Ousted Colleague's Criticism of Hague Tribunal. https://www.information.dk/udland/2013/12/fellow-judges-support-ousted-colleagues-criticism-of-hague-tribunal?vwo_exp_badges=|32|

81 Ibid.

82 Ibid.

83 *Justin Mugenzi and Prosper Muginareza v Prosecutor*, Appeals Chamber Judgement, ICTR, 4 February 2013, p. 63.

84 Ibid., pp. 91, 140.

85 'Concern over validity of International Criminal Tribunal judgments', IBUKA, Kigali, 20 June 2013.

86 Milestones in International Criminal Justice, 26 October 2013.

10 The Ganic case and Serbia's law courts

Even in overwhelmingly unfair requests, the principal of comity – reciprocal respect for other states' judicial and executive integrity – is often an insurmountable hurdle for transparent justice.[1]

Introduction

On 1 March 2010, a former vice-president of Bosnia and Herzegovina, Ejup Ganic, was arrested by the Scotland Yard Extradition Unit at Heathrow Airport, acting on an extradition warrant issued by the Serbian judicial authorities, Interpol having refused to issue a diffusion notice.[2] The Serbian request held that Dr Ganic was involved in alleged war crimes committed in Bosnia 18 years earlier.[3] He was taken into custody in Wandsworth prison and held there for several days without being informed of his rights, and without contact with his lawyers or the Bosnian embassy in London.[4] He was later released on stringent bail conditions. The extradition hearing began four months later, on 5 July.

The procedural history of the investigation is long and complex. A file prepared by Serbia was handed to *Republika Srpska* which, in turn, passed the case to the ICTY. In 2002–2003, the tribunal reviewed the evidence pursuant to the Rome Agreement of 1996 and found no case to answer against Ganic.[5] The decision was binding on Serbia at the time, but once the arrangements under the Rome Agreement lapsed, the Serbian government argued that the case remained open, and could be investigated by their War Crimes Prosecution Office (WCPO).[6]

Ejup Ganic's arrest coincided with the first day of the trial at The Hague of Bosnian Serb leader Radovan Karadzic, indicted for genocide and crimes against humanity. Since Dr Ganic was a regular visitor to the UK on business, the coincidence was curious. It made the headlines on the BBC and other British media outlets that evening, Ganic's photo juxtaposed with Karadzic's implying, to the casual observer, a moral equivalence between the two former Bosnian leaders and their respective roles in the Bosnian war, lending credence to the 'civil war' theory, 'ancient ethnic hatreds' and similar misnomers applied to the cataclysm endured by Bosnia's people in the early 1990s.

The case raised many issues, including the integrity of the Serbian law courts, the role of the arresting state authorities in the extradition process, the extradition act itself, and the proceedings within the UK which preceded Ganic's arrest, suggesting a political dimension to the case.

The extradition request

The main questions before the Westminster Magistrates' Court, where the hearing was held, were the validity of the Extradition Request itself, and whether Ejup Ganic would receive a fair trial if extradited to Serbia.

The Request was submitted by the Serbian War Crimes Chamber (WCPO) to the Crown Prosecution Service (CPS) in London following proceedings against Ejup Ganic and others initiated in late 2007.[7] It claimed that when Ganic took over the presidency in the absence of the Bosnian president, Alija Izetbegovic, he personally commanded an attack on the military hospital, the JNA Officers' Club and a column of medical vehicles in breach of the Geneva Conventions, as well as issuing the command to attack a JNA column passing through Sarajevo's Dobrovoljacka Street, where a number of soldiers were killed.

The Dobrovoljacka Street attack, also known as the Sarajevo column case, refers to the events of 3 May 1992 when a convoy of JNA troops withdrawing from Sarajevo was attacked, and a number killed. Ganic was released on 11 March 2010 on £250,000 bail, on the strict condition that he remained at a specified address in London. The Bosnian authorities expressed outrage over the arrest and filed their own extradition request for Ganic, arguing that they had first right to try one of their own citizens.[8]

*

On 18 February 1996, Serbia, Bosnia and Herzegovina and Croatia had entered into the Rome Agreement, known as the Rules of the Road (RoR) which, amongst other things, provided that serious violations of international humanitarian law would be considered by the ICTY only if the evidence had been reviewed and deemed consistent with International Legal Standards by the ICTY. The ICTY investigation subsequently carried out concluded on 17 June 2003 that there was no case against Ganic. The ICTY, while not the only court with jurisdiction to try alleged perpetrators of violations of international humanitarian law committed in the former Yugoslavia, takes precedence which can be asserted when a national court is considered unreliable, or when a case may be relevant to other cases being tried at the ICTY.

On closure of the RoR in May 2004, the Bosnian war crimes chamber came into being. Philip Alcock, appointed as international prosecutor for war crimes, conducted an investigation into whether Ganic was responsible for war crimes arising out of the events of 2–3 May 1992, and concluded, as had the ICTY, that there was no evidence whatsoever to connect Ganic with any war crime on 2 May since he only became acting president that evening.[9]

Under the Extradition Act 2003, Serbia falls into category 2 territories which are not required to provide *prima facie* evidence in support of their request for extradition. The Extradition Act states that the Secretary of State must issue a certificate if he receives a valid request for the extradition. The request would be refused, however, if the purpose was deemed to be 'to prosecute or punish the person on account of race, religion, nationality, gender, sexual orientation or political opinions, or if extradited the person might be prejudiced at his trial or punished unfairly for any of these reasons'.[10] Conduct amounting to one or more of the grave breaches of the Geneva Conventions 1949 would also constitute an extraditable offence. 'Grave Breaches' only apply to international armed conflicts which arise between two or more of the High Contracting Parties to the conventions.

Human Rights organizations have questioned the systems of justice in a number of countries considered under the Extradition Act to be safe for extradition, including some EU member states.[11]

*

The standard of the Request indicated that it had been hastily drawn up. There were a number of false and misleading statements which pointed to a clear bias, suggesting that the motives behind it were not purely judicial. It was also negligent and tendentious regarding basic facts claiming, for instance, that, at the time of Bosnia's declaration of independence on 3 March 1992, an 'international armed combat commenced between the Army of Bosnia and Herzegovina and the members of the Yugoslav People's Army – JNA'. This misleadingly gave the impression of a symmetrical armed conflict, whereas Bosnia's defence consisted at that time of several disparate groupings, including the Territorial Defence, a number of paramilitary groups, the Patriotic League, the Green Berets and civil defence groups. On 15 April, the Bosnian presidency ordered the unification of the available forces into a single army, but it was months before that army began to function in any meaningful sense.[12] During the interim, with very few tanks and Armoured Personnel Carriers, and no military aircraft, the hybrid force was pitted against the JNA, the fourth largest army in Europe, which was by then no longer the 'Yugoslav People's Army', but under the total control of the Milosevic regime in Belgrade.

Also misleading was the inference that an international war had erupted following Bosnia's declaration of independence. In putting the Bosnian 'army' first, the extradition request created the impression that the JNA was merely acting *in response to* attacks initiated by the Bosnian 'army', contradicting documented evidence at the ICTY and other courts which clearly revealed a build-up of Serbian aggression over considerable time.

Then there was the blatant omission of the kidnapping of the Bosnian president, Alija Izetbegovic, on the afternoon of 2 May. The Request stated that Ganic

> in the absence of the President of the Presidency Alija Izetbegovic who was that day on the business trip in Lisbon, in capacity of the Acting President of

> the Presidency of Bosnia and Herzegovina personally commanded attack to the Military hospital, JNA Officer's Club and the column of medical vehicles in Sarajevo.[13]

No evidence was produced to support this claim. Ejup Ganic was appointed acting president by Izetbegovic, *after* the latter was detained against his will by the JNA, along with his daughter.[14] The events described took place before Ganic was appointed acting president.[15]

The Request also presented the attacks as occurring out of the blue. Omitted was the fact that, in the early morning of 2 May, JNA armoured cars, personnel carriers and tanks entered the city in a radical escalation of the war in Sarajevo, aiming to divide it in half by taking over the presidency and destroying the main telephone exchange, thereby breaking communication between the various Bosnian forces. Local Bosnian defenders, acting largely on their own initiative, attacked JNA installations where JNA soldiers were present. The concealment of these facts distorted the picture of the events of that day.[16]

Referring to the Dobrovoljacka episode, the Request alleged that Ejup Ganic and JNA General Milutin Kukanjac had agreed on 3 May for 'the unhindered and peaceful dislocation of the Command of the 2nd Military Area from Sarajevo to Lukavica', via a route passing through Dobrovoljacka Street, with the approval of UN General Lewis MacKenzie and EU [*sic*] representative Colm Doyle.[17] This was purely speculative since there was no evidence offered to contradict Ganic's account that he had only agreed to a swap between President Izetbegovic with his daughter and General Kukanjac who, together with 400 JNA officers and men, were trapped at Bistrik headquarters, behind Bosnian government lines.[18] On the morning of 3 May, Ganic went to the UN headquarters, pleading with the UN commander to intervene, as Izetbegovic was the only leader with the moral authority to control the militias in the city who had surrounded the JNA barracks. General MacKenzie, along with Colm Doyle, went to Lukavica where Izetbegovic, held captive, agreed initially to the one-for-one swap with General Kukanjac, then soon afterwards under considerable pressure agreed to pass the order down to his militia to allow safe passage out of Sarajevo for the entire barracks.[19] This was not the deal understood by Ganic and the Bosnian presidency members, nor by the disparate Bosnian forces on the ground who, unlike Izetbegovic who had been away in Portugal, were well aware of the escalating situation on the ground, and of the significance for the Bosnian defence of Sarajevo of the withdrawal of the entire JNA arsenal from the city.

The Request then alleged that Ejup Ganic ordered the attack on the JNA column through 'mutual telephone and radio connection as well as radio connections with unit commanders, and thus they directly managed the attack, coordinating the individual armed actions with the unit commanders who were already in the area'. This claim seems highly implausible, given the chaotic situation on the ground and the breakdown in telephone links across the city, following the JNA sabotage of Sarajevo's central telephone exchange. Neither was any evidence offered in support of the claim.[20]

Interestingly, it was the first time that Serbia had, in writing, declared the war to have an international character. Serbia's consistent defence before the ICJ and the ICTY cases against its military and political leaders was based on the assertion that a *civil*, not international, war had taken place in Bosnia. Yet the case against Ejup Ganic rested on the premise that the war was an 'international armed combat', and that Ganic and others had violated several articles of the Geneva Conventions, a claim argued over 12 pages of the Request.[21] Due to its dependence on the Geneva Conventions, Serbia had to convince the court that the war was international to have any chance of success. Yet if that was so, it meant that Serbia had been responsible for aggression in Bosnia, which it consistently denies.[22]

Abuse of process?

Ejup Ganic's defence team, headed by Edward Fitzgerald, QC, contested the arrest warrant, filing a complaint on 24 June 2010 pertaining to the British Court's competence and the alleged misuse of legal proceedings for political purposes. A hearing consequently held at the Westminster Magistrates' Court in London ruled, however, that there was enough evidence to proceed. The Serbian authorities then swamped the Court with numerous documents several weeks after the deadline for disclosure, many of them irrelevant to the case.[23] This followed the practice of several Serbian defence teams before the ICTY and was possibly aimed at befuddling the defence team late on in the proceedings.[24]

Just three days before the start of the hearing, in a 22-page 'Narrative of the Evidential Materials', The CPS in London, acting on behalf of the Serbian Government, responded that the 'evidential issue' was not relevant, since a *prima facie* case was not required in support of the request.[25] The evidence submitted by Serbia was merely to demonstrate that the WCPO had conducted its own independent *bona fide* investigation, and submitted material from which a reasonable prosecutor could conclude that there was a case to answer.[26] This, the CPS claimed, included new evidence not previously taken into consideration by the ICTY, or by the Bosnian court also investigating the case, in the form of two videotapes and two new witnesses.

The Narrative relied heavily on a contemporaneous report of General Nambiar, then head of UNPROFOR in Sarajevo, referring to the events of 2–3 May 1992, which suggested that 'Moslem Territorial Defence Units', controlled by the Bosnian presidency, initiated the violence in blockading the JNA headquarters on the orders of the Bosnian presidency. General Nambiar, however, had not been personally present. His report rested on information provided by EC monitors.[27] In support of Nambiar's report, the CPS cited the views of General Aksentijevic. Yet, as a senior JNA officer, Aksentijevic was hardly a neutral party.[28]

The CPS claimed that the most straightforward introduction to the events of 3 May 1992 was the contemporaneous video evidence, which included footage not before the RoR. But this was not quite the case. The quality of the tapes was poor in places, and the narrative of the events the tapes allegedly portrayed unclear due to what appeared a cut-n-paste attempt designed to support the Serbian government's version of what happened that day. That this evidence was relied on to such a degree, occupying a considerable section of the Narrative, spoke for the weakness of the overall case against Ganic. As his defence lawyer later observed,

> It is arguable that in extradition cases the CPS has misunderstood its role. It derives its power to conduct proceedings from statute, not a purported solicitor/client relationship. It ought, therefore, to take an independent view of the merits of extradition cases. When a solicitor/client relationship becomes one of agency, independence is a casualty.[29]

*

On 5 July, as the hearing began, the defence team refuted in considerable detail all the arguments set out in the Narrative. On the allegation of grave breaches of the Geneva Conventions, Ganic's defence maintained that the pursuit of these was abusive, and the evidence contained serious and significant omissions, while issues already dealt with by earlier prosecuting authorities had been unjustifiably reopened.[30] The alleged order to attack the JNA officers' club housing enemy officers during an international armed conflict could not be unlawful, given that the events of 2 May 2010, commencing with a massive onslaught by Serb artillery on Sarajevo, had been edited out, and Ganic anyway had no power to give orders at that time. On the alleged attacks on military vehicles and the military hospital, the defence argued that the allegations had been rejected by the Rules of the Road and the evidence offered by the prosecution, both in terms of the 'new' witnesses and the video footage, was unreliable and constituted an abuse. Similarly with the alleged attack on the medical hospital. On the alleged attack on the withdrawing JNA column, the defence pointed out that it constituted armed soldiers, taking with them the kidnapped president Izetbegovic and his daughter as hostages. The event was also investigated by the RoR who found there was no *prima facie* case. The only new witness of any significance was Kovačević but he entered the fray very late in the day, and his credibility was negligible, considering his close association with Ratko Mladic.[31] Ganic's defence team concluded,

> The way the case has been presented is so deeply misleading as to render it an abuse. But it is also an abuse to reopen this matter, and prosecute, after it has been fully investigated by two independent international investigations, and found to be without sufficient foundation to make out a prima facie case.[32]

Extradition hearing

The hearing on Serbia's extradition request began on 5 July 2010 at the Westminster Magistrates' Court, presided over by Judge Timothy Workman. Seven witnesses gave testimony in court for the defence, Philip Alcock, Damir Arnaut,

Christian Schwartz-Schilling, Carole Hodge, Noel Malcolm, Sonja Biserko and Gordana Knezevic. Written testimony was submitted by Paddy Ashdown and Marko Hoare. CPS Prosecutor Ben Watson had informed the court on 24 June that there would be three prosecution witnesses, who remained unnamed due to the huge publicity surrounding the case.[33] Judge Workman gave the prosecution until 4.00 pm on June 25 to disclose the name of witnesses with statements. In the event, the only witness for the prosecution was Milan Petrovic from the Serbian WCPO.

The first defence witness, Philip Alcock, was a former British international prosecutor in the war crimes chamber of Bosnia-Herzegovina's state court, who had spent two years investigating the case.[34] Alcock testified that he had never seen any evidence linking Ganic to the bloodshed of 2 and 3 May, and viewed the trial against him as politically motivated and that there would be a huge risk of prejudice if he went on trial in Serbia.

The second witness, Damir Arnaut, legal and constitutional advisor to the Bosnian presidency, told the court that secret diplomatic efforts were ongoing during the extradition process, including Serbia's promise to withdraw the Request if Bosnia were to accept publicly the Srebrenica declaration adopted by the Serbian parliament on 10 March 2010, which excluded the word 'genocide'. This was a highly controversial issue. In 2009, the European Parliament had adopted a declaration terming the Srebrenica massacre a genocide and requested all countries in the region to adopt similar declarations, condemning the genocide. According to the Serbian foreign ministry, the Request came when the political climate in Serbia was at 'a very sensitive phase', as the declaration on Srebrenica was expected to be adopted in parliament. If Bosniaks criticized the declaration it would be less effective. The Turkish Ambassador had received an assurance from Serbia that they would not send the Request in time for the certification deadline, thus ending extradition proceedings. The UK ambassador in Belgrade, however, confirmed the Request had been received. Arnaut's evidence on this was largely unchallenged.[35]

As for Serbia's witness 'A', Arnaut testified that the witness had approached him unsolicited on 16 March 2010, stating that the investigating magistrate had switched off the tape recording from time to time and that two police officers had approached him, offering employment with the RS police. The Serbian government retorted that Arnaut had attempted to bribe the witness.[36] Yet Arnaut's evidence was to prove crucial. The judge found it to be 'truthful and compelling both in relation to the creditability of witness 'A' and in relation to the political and diplomatic pressures that were being exerted.'[37]

Dr Christian Schwarz-Schilling, High Representative of Bosnia and Herzegovina from 2005 to 2007, opined that the WCPO in Serbia was under political influence and that Ejup Ganic would not receive a fair trial in Serbia due to the importance to demonstrate that Bosnian people were being tried before the WCPO. Dr Carole Hodge pointed to the unreliability both of the evidence of General Lewis MacKenzie due to his association with an American Serbian lobbying group, and to discrepancies in the translation of parts of the videotapes. She also considered the request to be politically motivated and that Dr Ganic, if extradited to Serbia, would be unlikely to receive a fair trial due to the enormous pressure to convict.[38] Dr Marko Hoare also concluded that the prosecution was brought for political reasons, and with the desire to rewrite the history of the Bosnian war, to 'equalise the guilt of the parties'.[39]

Dr Noel Malcolm, who had provided a detailed analysis of the Request, observed that

> In the errors of misrepresentations that I have found it seemed to me there was a pattern. This was not just random incompetence and getting things wrong. All the significant misrepresentations pointed in the same direction [and that there was a culture within Serbia which amounted to] a very powerful current opinion which involves a fundamental denial of the origins, nature and scale of what was done in Bosnia by Serb Forces.[40]

Malcolm concluded that Ejup Ganic, as a very prominent Bosnian Muslim politician, and a Bosnian leader during the war, would suffer prejudice at his trial on grounds of politics and ethnicity.[41] Paddy Ashdown also opined that the request was about politics rather than justice and that Ganic's arrest on the day Karadzic gave his opening statement to the ICTY was no coincidence, but a contrived situation by the Serbian government.[42]

The hearing spilled into a second week during which Sonja Biserko, director of Helsinki Human Rights in Serbia, testified to the political situation in Serbia and the state of the Serbian courts. Gordana Knezevic, former deputy editor of Oslobodjenje, a leading Bosnian daily, gave an account of her personal experience of the widespread attacks by Serb forces across Sarajevo on 2 May.[43]

The only witness called by the Serbian Government was Milan Petrovic, the deputy prosecutor of the WCPO in Belgrade, who would have had the responsibility of prosecuting, were Ganic to be extradited. Petrovic had been a prosecutor in the Jurisic case in which the defendant was convicted and sentenced to 12 years' imprisonment, based upon an alleged agreement made on 27 April 1992 which Petrovic was forced to acknowledge in cross-examination had not in fact been reached, rendering his evidence unreliable.[44]

*

Just days before the verdict was announced, WCPO Chief Prosecutor Vladimir Vukcevic, in an interview with a leading Bosnian Serb daily, recalling that the British Home Secretary had certified the Request, expressed his conviction that Ganic would be extradited to Serbia and travelled to London for the verdict.[45]

He was disappointed. On 27 July 2010, the Westminster Magistrates Court ruled against the Ganic's extradition to Serbia, and he was released. In reaching his verdict, Judge Workman concluded that the proceedings had been brought, and were being used, for political purposes and amounted to an abuse of process.[46]

> Two careful and thorough investigations have concluded that there is no evidence on which charges could be brought against Dr Ganic. The District Court in Serbia issued proceedings at the request of the War Crimes Prosecutor without any further evidence having been obtained. The evidence which has been subsequently obtained is not significant and does not justify any change in the initial decision. In the absence of any significant additional evidence, there would appear to be only two possible explanations, that of incompetence by the Serbian Prosecutors or a motive for prosecuting which is based upon politics, race or religion.[47]

*

Bruno Vekaric from the Serbian prosecution team, announced an appeal, while Snezana Malovic, Serbia's justice minister, denied the allegations, and maintained that previous proceedings in the Serbian war crimes court proved the country addressed war crimes issues professionally. Natasa Kandic, the director of the Humanitarian Law Centre (HLC) in Belgrade, commented that, on the contrary, the judge's words would act as a warning to the Serbian courts to cease politically motivated requests.[48] It seems Kandic was over-optimistic as, the following year, Serbia issued an extradition request to Austria for Jovan Divjak relating to the same event.

Following the verdict, the Serbian president, Boris Tadić, declared he was insulted by the decision of the British court to reject Serbia's extradition request, dismissing the evidence of possible political motivation,[49] while Vukcevic, in an interview with B92, argued that the allegation of abuse of process could not be sustained, given that the British Home Office had certified the Request. After consulting with the CPS in London, on 4 August, however, Vukcevic dropped his bid to appeal.[50]

The Serbian law courts

WCPO was established on 1 July 2003 in Serbia, as a specialized component of the Belgrade District Court, to prosecute perpetrators of crimes against humanity and war crimes, and offences recognized by the ICTY Statute, in former Yugoslavia after 1 January 1991.[51] Under Rule 11*bis* of the ICTY's Rules of Procedure and Evidence, the tribunal could transfer lower-level suspects whose indictments had been confirmed. Yet, by 2007, just one case had been transferred to Serbia.[52]

Serbia's relationship with the ICTY improved after the demise of Milosevic but two patterns remained constant: firstly, that Serbia's cooperation with the ICTY came about only following intense pressure from Western governments and, secondly, the lack of political leadership in addressing the consequences of its past.[53] Although the ICTY contributed to the WCPO through the transfer of expertise and the model of fair process, including training programmes for prosecutors and judges in substantive areas of international criminal law, in the two written opinions the WCPO had issued by August 2007, it had 'made no use of ICTY jurisprudence concerning issues of substantive law'.[54] WCPO Chief Prosecutor Vukcevic was quoted as referring to the training programmes and other encounters with ICTY prosecutors with disdain.[55]

The WCPO record preceding the arrest of Ejup Ganic was mixed, the cases till then considered indicating a continued lack of political will to prosecute those bearing superior responsibility for war crimes.[56] This was partly attributed to the limited political space, although Vukcevic also obscured links between defendants and policies instituted by state institutions in drawing up indictments and presenting evidence.[57] In November 2006, pressure from the Serbian Radical Party in particular, coinciding with Šešelj's hunger strike at the Hague, exerted the strongest pressure resulting, according to Bruno Vekaric, in politicians avoiding public support of the war crimes prosecutor.[58] In April 2008, a plan to assassinate Vukcevic and two others was uncovered.[59] In a survey conducted in Serbia the following month, only a quarter of those polled believed the WCPO would act independently of political pressures.[60] Vukcevic commented that there was 'a kind of obstacle we would meet if we made cases against the most senior officials – we would be exposed to great pressures by the public'.[61]

Various reports had been published on the work of the Belgrade War Crimes Chamber preceding the Ganic case, including by the US State Department, Human Rights Watch, the HLC in Belgrade, and by human rights lawyer, Diane Orentlicher for the Open Society Justice Initiative. Orentlicher concluded that the WCPO record was mixed. A modest number of Serbs had been convicted by the court for war crimes against non-Serbs, but these were mostly small fry – low-ranking perpetrators, and even in the Scorpion case, were no more than middle-ranking members of the Serbian gendarmerie.[62] This indicated the continuing limits in Serbia's political will to prosecute those with superior responsibility. By the end of April 2008, the total number of first-instance trials completed by the WCPO was six, four of which were reviewed by the Supreme Court, which ordered retrials. Part of the problem was attributed to a 'dearth of resources'. The Belgrade War Crimes Chamber had limited funding and inadequate political support for the WCPO, which may have indicated a more systemic problem. There was little public awareness of its work, and reticence from police investigators, two of whom were themselves implicated in, or linked to individuals responsible for war crimes.[63]

Even when a war crimes conviction was secured by the WCPO, the Supreme Court would quash the majority of convictions.[64] Biljana Kovačević-Vuco, director of the Lawyers Committee for Human Rights in Belgrade called the reasoning of the Supreme Court in those decisions 'poorly reasoned and ill-founded', partly due to the fact that many of its members were Milosevic-era appointees.[65]

Belgrade lawyer Dragoljub Todorovic, who represented victims and their families in 11 cases before the Serbian courts, including Muslims, Albanians and Croats, until February 2009, commented,

> The war crime trials in Belgrade represent a specific form of confrontation with the past of the state, its institutions, media, public and Serbian society as a whole. The print and electronic media did not cover these trials sufficiently and adequately. . . . For these reasons, the Serbian public is far from being adequately informed about the evidence derived from the main hearings.[66]

In 2008, the HLC in Belgrade monitored all trials held in Serbia for crimes committed in the context of armed conflicts, as part of regional cooperation on monitoring war crimes trials before national courts.[67] It concluded that the verdict reached by the WCPO in the Scorpions case was led by political rather than legal reasoning, 'in an effort to adjust its stances to the ones of the Serbian authorities regarding the responsibility for genocide committed in Srebenica in the context of the International Court of Justice verdict'.[68]

A US State Department Human Rights Report, published in 2009, noted corruption in the Serbian police and judiciary, harassment of journalists, human rights' advocates and discrimination against ethnic and religious minorities. The State Department also reported death threats against war crimes prosecutor Vladimir Vukcevic and the justice minister, Snezana Malovic. Vukcevic was later to state that his main motive in accepting the post was that Serbian war crimes prosecuted before an international court placed Serbia on the level of less developed countries.[69] Serbia's readiness to address its role in the Bosnian war, it seems, played little part in the establishment of the WCPO.

*

One of the most graphic illustrations of the workings of the Serbian courts, which had undoubtedly influenced the Ganic verdict, was the related case of Ilija Jurisic.

A Bosnian Croat, Jurisic was duty officer in the Tuzla Public Security Centre Operational Headquarters. He was convicted because, on 15 May 1992, he had allegedly relayed an order from the Operational HQ over the radio to all units of the Bosnian Croat forces to attack a convoy of JNA soldiers withdrawing under a ceasefire agreement between Bosnia and the FRY on the JNA's peaceful withdrawal from Bosnia to the FRY.

In the attack, 50 JNA members were killed and another 44 wounded. Jurisic was sentenced by the Belgrade War Crimes Chamber to 12 years imprisonment for use of impermissible means of combat pursuant to Article 148 para 2 in relation to para 1 of the SFRY Criminal Code.

The indictment was filed in Belgrade on 9 November 2007, the Serbian judicial authorities persistently refusing requests by the Bosnian Prosecutor's Office to hand over the case where the latter was already conducting an investigation into the same event, regardless of the fact that the Belgrade court would be unable to conduct hearings on a number of witnesses in Bosnia, pointing to a political motivation on the part of the Serbian judicial authorities to prosecute the case in Belgrade. It was the first case since the establishment of the Belgrade War Crimes Chamber where an indictment was raised before the investigation was completed. No family members of the killed policemen were amongst the witnesses, nor were any other citizens from Tuzla.

According to the Humanitarian Law Centre, the court failed to establish Jurisic's guilt beyond a reasonable doubt and did not check some of the relevant charges, such as whether or not Jurisic had actual authority to give orders to all of the Bosnian Croat armed forces. The defence's proposal to examine witnesses, including Budimir Nikolic, who had knowledge of the activities and authority of Jurisic on that critical day, was rejected by the court. Police officers in the field that day were also not examined. Neither was Mate Zrinic, wounded in the convoy, examined despite the court's obligation to examine all victim-witnesses, possibly because he left the JNA and joined the Tuzla police after that event.[70] The trial started on 22 February 2008, lasting 32 days, with seven expert witnesses and 78 others, including 48 victim-witnesses.

Jurisic was later acquitted, but again retried *in absentia* with the 12 years' imprisonment confirmed.[71] The Jurisic case was just one of many which challenged the integrity of the Serbian courts.

*

Since the Ganic case, there has been little reason for optimism in the Serbian courts. Almost exactly a year later, Jovan Divjak, a 73-year-old retired general with the Bosnian Army, was arrested in Vienna on 3 March 2011 on an extradition warrant issued by Serbia.

Divjak is an ethnic Serb who defected from the former JNA after it bombed Sarajevo in April 1992, and one of the 19 Bosnian officials charged by Serbia over the attack on a JNA convoy in Dobrovoljacka Street, Sarajevo, on 3 May 1992, as it was withdrawing from the city. On 29 July 2011, an Austrian court rejected Serbia's request for Divjak's extradition, and released him, based on lack of evidence, and because there was no guarantee he would receive a fair trial in Serbia.[72] 'The massive restriction of defence rights makes his delivery to the Serbian authorities impermissible', according to the court of Korneuburg, near Vienna.[73]

In March 2015, the situation in the Serbian courts seemed to improve, with many observers seeing a historic step towards justice and reconciliation within the region, with the arrest in Serbia of eight men accused of organizing and executing the massacre of 1,300 Muslims in Kravica, a village near Srebrenica, in July 1995.[74] Yet the start of the trial was postponed from September to December 2016, then to February 2017, till finally on July 13, the Belgrade Court of Appeal ordered the invalidation of the trial on procedural grounds – that the indictments were not authorized by a chief prosecutor, since the position had remained vacant for a year and a half since Vukcevic's departure.[75] The prosecutor was ordered to reformulate the charges and reschedule the trial, which entailed starting from scratch.[76] The HLC responded with a press release raising radical criticisms of Serbia's legislative, executive and judiciary powers, which it alleged were jointly responsible 'for the prolonged void at the head of the prosecution', and the 'systematic obstruction of war crimes proceedings by state authorities', which failed to meet the legal requirements of European integration.[77]

The Bytyqi Brothers' case, where three Bytyqi brothers were killed in Serbia in 1999, still remained unresolved in 2017. The Bytyqi family believe that Goran Radosavljevic, former commander of a special police unit and of the Petrovo Selo training centre, where the three brothers were detained before being killed, is the main suspect in the case. Since retirement, Radosavljevic has remained active in politics as a member of the executive board of Vucic's ruling Progressive Party.[78]

In January 2017, Ramush Haradinaj was arrested at a French airport by police acting on an international arrest warrant from Serbia, which is pursuing separate charges of torture and murder of civilians in Kosovo in 1999. Haradinaj had twice been tried at the ICTY for war crimes against Serbs and acquitted. France held him for several months before rejecting Serbia's demand in June. The Serbian president, Alexander Vucic condemned the French ruling, calling it 'disgraceful, scandalous, unlawful, and above all else, political'.[79] Serbian charges against Haradinaj persisted when he was arrested on a Serbian arrest warrant for crimes against civilians in January 2017 by French border police. In April 2017, the French court rejected the Serbian request and released him.

The British role

The British government's prompt acceptance of Serbia's extradition request was perhaps surprising, given Interpol's refusal to issue an arrest warrant, the inaccuracies and distortions evident even on cursory reading and that two formal investigations into Ganic's role had been carried out and found there was no case to answer. More surprising still were the events leading up to Ganic's arrest.

According to British parliamentary records, Metropolitan police met at New Scotland Yard with officials from the Foreign Office and Home Office on 1 March 2010 to discuss Serbia's Request before Ganic was arrested.[80] Not on official record, however, was what proceeded the meeting.

In an interview after Ganic's acquittal, Damir Arnaut stated that, when Ganic arrived in Britain on 26 February 2010, the British authorities, on their own initiative, got in touch with Serbia, informing the authorities that Ganic was in London, and inviting them to apply for his arrest directly, bypassing Interpol. This Serbia did the following day, through its London embassy. After a meeting attended by ministers from several government departments, the Request was passed to the local court. This would seem to contradict the statement by the British ambassador to Sarajevo, on the day after Ganic's arrest, that the matter was purely judicial, and his government had played no part in it.[81] After Ganic was arrested, Haris Silajdzic, then chair of the Bosnian presidency, asked to see the Home Office minister but was refused, although the minister reportedly received the interior minister of Serbia.[82]

Arnaut's account of the events leading to Ganic's arrest may appear puzzling on the surface but is less so when considered in the context of British policy in wartime Bosnia. Given this, the Serbian authorities might well have expected that the British political and legal institutions worked hand-in-hand, as may be the case in Serbia, and that the Westminster Magistrates Court would do its political masters' bidding, notwithstanding the irregularities in the Request, and the clear abuse of process. Hence the confident presence of Vladimir Vukcevic himself at the judgement. The judgement and the arguments on which it was based demonstrated the independence of the judge, although the Conservative party victory in Britain in May 2010 may also (ironically considering its previous track record in the region) have played a part. A temporary shift of climate within the Foreign Office led by the then foreign secretary, William Hague, included an active interest in Bosnia, and particularly Srebrenica.[83]

British politicians and diplomats since the Bosnian war ended have often sought the moral high ground, distancing themselves from the Foreign Office–led policies of the early 1990s. Labour politicians and supporters have asserted that the British SFOR troops action in Prijedor in July 1997 led to a sea-change in NATO policy in Bosnia. The initiative led by William Hague in Srebrenica could be seen in a similar light – as a concerted move away from the Conservative policies of the 1990s. Bosnia's post-war political decline was arguably sealed at Dayton, however, when ethnic divisions became cemented and nationalists confirmed in power through an internationally brokered agreement.[84]

Why Britain under Gordon Brown's leadership decided actively to assist the Serbian authorities bid to have Ganic extradited to Serbia can be attributed partly to the stringent terms of the 2003 Extradition Act, but it was also a reflection of British policy, which continues to prioritize relations with Serbia, viewed as the most powerful state in the Balkans, a policy which in the 1990s facilitated genocide.

Conclusion

The Ganic case is significant historically and for international law. Ejup Ganic's arrest deflected from the Karadzic trial and attracted global media attention. The conviction for war crimes of a former high-ranking official of Muslim ethnicity, one of the wartime leaders of an enemy country, would undoubtedly alleviate political pressure on the Belgrade prosecutor and be applauded by the vast majority of the Serbian people. It would also suggest a symmetry of guilt, and contribute to the myth that Bosnia's Muslims started the war. The British law courts were used to equalize responsibility for the war, to rehabilitate perpetrators and confuse issues, and to rewrite history.

It was predictable, given the track record of the Serbian law courts on war crimes prosecutions, that the Serbian government should wish to have a senior Bosnian official such as Ejup Ganic extradited to Serbia for war crimes. Given the limitations of the 2003 Extradition Act where no *prima facie* case was required, and traditional British-Serbian relations, the Serbian authorities would have been confident that their request would succeed.

But why did they wait 15 years after the end of the war to attempt to extradite Ejup Ganic? The request coincided with a shift in international interest away from the Balkans, as the situation in the Middle East grew more serious by the day, and as Milorad Dodik, the Republika Srpska leader, became increasingly consolidated in power, against a High Representative who wielded little influence either in Bosnia or internationally. These realities, combined with the acquittal in 2006 of Radovan Karadzic's leading associate, Momčilo Krajisnik, of genocide in Bosnia, and the ICJ judgement in 2007, exonerating Serbia from responsibility for genocide in Bosnia and Herzegovina would have led Belgrade to believe that the rewriting of the Bosnian war record was feasible. The legal risk of acknowledging that an international conflict had taken place – as opposed to a civil war which Serbia had hitherto always maintained – was essential to determining Ganic's violation of the Geneva Conventions. Serbian leaders evidently thought it worth the gamble.

Questions over the fairness and objectivity of the Serbian courts continue at the time of writing. According to the HLC, legal reforms in Serbia are 'purely cosmetic' or nonexistent, words echoed by ICTY Chief Prosecutor Serge Brammertz in his report to the UN Security Council in December 2016, where he observed that none of the commitments by Belgrade on Chapter 23 had been honoured.

Notes

1 Stephen Gentle, partner, Kingsley Napley, 'The High Cost of Politically Motivated Extradition Cases', *The Lawyer*, 16 August 2010.

2 *The Government of the Republic of Serbia v Ejup Ganic,* Second Bundle of Material Submitted on Behalf of the Government of the Republic of Serbia, Ministry of Justice Communication, 17 June 2010, p. 18, para. 47. The Serbian government alleged that 'Interpol did not refuse to issue diffusion notice because it was filed by Serbia but because of the temporary decision applicable to all the countries in Interpol system'. Ibid. See also Roy Gutman, 'Serbia Pursues Ejup Ganic for War Crimes. Or Is It a Vendetta?' *Christian Science Monitor*, 12 April 2010.

3 Ejup Ganic was also president of the Federation of Bosnia and Herzegovina from 1997 to 1999 and again from 2000 to 2001. He holds an ScD (doctor of science) from Massachusetts Institute of Technology, and was the founder, and is currently the chancellor, of the Sarajevo School of Science and Technology.

4 Ed Vulliamy, 'Psihoticna Srbofilia', *Dani*, 5 March 20.

5 Operation Joint Endeavour (IFOR), The Rome Statement, 18 February 1996. https://www.nato.int/ifor/general/d960218a.htm

6 The request for the extension of the investigation of the war crimes prosecutor in Belgrade against Ejup Ganic and others was issued on 29 December 2007, pursuant to Art.243, para. 2 of the Criminal Proceedings Law. Apostille, Belgrade, 5 March 2010.

7 'The District Court in Belgrade, War Crimes Chamber, investigative judge Milan Dilparic, in the investigation against Ejup Ganic et al., on the account of the perpetration of the crime WAR CRIME AGAINST THE WOUNDED AND SICK referred to in Art.143 para. 1 of the Criminal Code of the SFRY etc., upon the request for the extension of the investigation of the War Crimes Prosecutor in Belgrade Ktrz. 6/05 of 28th

November 2008, issued on 29th December 2007, pursuant to Art.243, para. 2 of the Criminal Proceedings Law, the following Ruling against Ejup Ganic' and 17 others: Stjepan Kljujic, Hasan Efendic, Fikret Muslimovic, Zaim Backovic, Jovan Divjak, Emin Svrakic, Jusuf Pusina, Dragan Vikic, Jusuf Prazina-Djapic, Ismet Bajramovic, Nusret Sisic, Musan Kovac, Jovica Berovic, Ibrahim Hodzic, Avdo Panjeta, Jusuf Kecman, Damir Dolan and Samir Cengic. The indictees were either BiH presidency members or members of the BiH Territorial Defence.

8 The Section for War Crimes was set up in the Criminal and Appellate Divisions of the Court of Bosnia and Herzegovina, in March 2005, with jurisdiction to prosecute the most serious alleged war crimes committed in Bosnia.

9 Philip Alcock, Evidence, cited by Judge Timothy Workman, *The Republic of Serbia v Ejup Ganic*, Verdict, para. 30.

10 Extradition Act 2003, Section 81 (a) and (b).

11 Liberty noted that the European convention on extradition has been signed by countries with 'appalling human rights records whose judiciaries in many cases are neither independent nor impartial'. *Guardian*, 19 January 2009.

12 On this, see Mirko Pejanovic, *Through Bosnian Eyes: Political Memoir of a Bosnian Serb*, Purdue University Press, 2004.

13 Extradition Request, p. 3, section 2 ('Alleged conduct').

14 On 2 May 1992, President Izetbegovic was kidnapped on his return from a meeting with European diplomats in Portugal (then holding the EC presidency). Ganic, as his second in command, was appointed by Izetbegovic to take over the leadership of the country during this time.

15 The appointment of Ejup Ganic took place on live TV, being the only institution with functioning telephone lines. Allan Little and Laura Silber, *The Death of Yugoslavia*, London: Penguin Press, 1995, pp. 261–262.

16 Ibid., pp. 255–268.

17 Extradition Request, p. 5 (g). The EU was not formed until 1994.

18 In his memoir published in 1993, General MacKenzie recorded that when he and Doyle went to the JNA Lukavica camp, they entered into negotiations for the one-for-one exchange with General Kukanjac and afterwards for an exchange with Kukanjac together with the 400 soldiers. It was on this basis that the JNA withdrawal took place. *'The Road to Sarajevo' Lewis MacKenzie*, Vancouver: Douglas & McIntyre, 1993, p. 164.

19 *Death of Yugoslavia*, op. cit., p. 264.

20 Although General MacKenzie in his memoirs speculates that Ganic might have issued the command, he also conceded that it could have been a local commander's initiative. 'The TDF (Territorial Defence Force) was very undisciplined at that early stage of its development, and many things didn't go the way they were planned. This might have been one of those times. I suppose we will never know'. 'The Road to Sarajevo', op. cit., p. 171. For MacKenzie's connections to the Serb lobby, see Dele Olojede and Roy Gutman, 'Former UN Leader MacKenzie Speaks on Behalf of Serb Forces', *The Tech*, Vol.113, Issue 29, 23 June 1993.

21 Ejup Ganic and others were indicted for '(a) Attack against the Military Hospital . . . thus violating the rules of international law under Art.19 of I Geneva Convention and the rules under Article 12, para. 1 and Art. 21 and 37, para. 1 and Protocol 1, (b) Attack against the JNA Centre, thus violating the rules of international law under Art.37, para. 1 of Protocol I, (c) Attack against the medical corps vehicles . . . thus violating the rules of international law under Art.19 of I Geneva Convention and the rules under Art.12, para. 1 and Art.21 and 37, para. 1 of Protocol I and (d) Attack against the JNA column in Dobrovoljacka Street . . . thus violating the rules of international law under Art.3, para. 1, Items a) and c) and Art. 19 of I Geneva Convention, the rules under Art.12, para. 1, Art.13, para. 1 and 2 of III Geneva Convention and the rules under Art.21,

para. 1 and Art.37, para. 1 of Protocol I'. *The Government of the Republic of Serbia v Ejup Ganic*, Index to Bundle of WCPO Materials (English translation) 11 March 2010, signed by Investigative Judge, Milan Dilparic.

22 Milos Vasic, *Sudske Neprilike Ejupa Ganica*, Pescanik, 12 March 2010.

23 *The Government of the Republic of Serbia v Ejup Ganic,* Second Bundle of Material Submitted on Behalf of the Government of the Republic of Serbia, Ministry of Justice Communication, 17 June 2010. Judge Workman later referred to 'a substantial amount of evidential material amounting to some 20 lever arch files'. Verdict, para. 1.

24 In the Šešelj case, for example, the defendant produced thousands of documents, including his own books, which he demanded be translated. These were mostly totally irrelevant to his case, but clogged up the system, and delayed proceedings. The most recent example of this practice was the Mladic Defence 'Notice of Filing: Book of Authorities as to Reply to Prosecution's Response Brief on Behalf of Ratko Mladic,' *Prosecutor v Ratko Mladic*, MICT, 29 November 2018. The material, totalling 181 pages, required translation into French. While it was irrelevant to Mladic's case, it would delay and obstruct proceedings.

25 See Gentle, op. cit. for discussion of the relationship between the CPS and the requesting state in extradition cases.

26 In the City of Westminster Magistrates' Court between *The Government of the Republic of Serbia v Ejup Ganic*. Narrative of the Evidential Materials, pp. 1–2, para. 3, 2 July 2010.

27 Narrative, ibid., p. 3, para. 9.

28 Ibid., pp. 4, 11. The Narrative notes, however, that these accounts were at odds with the assessment of Silber and Little in the BBC documentary, *The Death of Yugoslavia,* who viewed the events as part of a broader picture of ongoing attacks by the JNA. Ibid., p. 12.

29 Gentle, op. cit.

30 In the Westminster Magistrates Court. *Serbia v Ganic*. Summary of Submissions of defendant on alleged grave breaches and extradition offence, Ed Fitzgerald, QC and John Jones, 5 July 2010, Note 1.

31 Ibid. Note 3, p. 9, 6.7. As Stephen Gentle later noted 'the client (Serbia) sought to rely on the evidence of a close associate of the indicted (fugitive) war criminal, Ratko Mladic. It is inconceivable that this would happen in a domestic prosecution, with the duties that the CPS has as an independent prosecutor to adduce reliable evidence'. Gentle, op. cit.

32 Ibid. Note 1, p. 11, 5.9.

33 Westminster Magistrates Court, Hearing, 24 June 2010, *Serbia v Ejup Ganic.*

34 Philip Alcock was the international prosecutor in Bosnia until the end of the 2009 and led the investigation until his departure. After Ganic was arrested, he wrote to the Magistrates Court, saying that he had not found enough evidence about Ganic's role.

35 Judge Workman, Verdict, 19, 21 and 22.

36 Ibid., p. 22.

37 Ibid.

38 *Serbia v Ejup Ganic*, Westminster Magistrates Court, 9 July 2010, and Verdict, 27 July 2010, para. 39.

39 Verdict, ibid., para. 25.

40 Ibid., para. 37.

41 Ibid.

42 Verdict, ibid., para. 25. Judge Workman did not take this view into account in considering the evidence, however, holding that it was coincidence rather than design.

43 *Serbia v Ejup Ganic*, 12 July 2010. Gordana Knezevic, a Serbian-born journalist, currently works for Radio Free Europe in Prague.

44 Verdict, op. cit., para. 36.

45 'Vladimir Vukcevic: Za Mladicem Tragamo 24 sata Dnevno', *Nezavisne Novine,* 24 July 2010.
46 Verdict, 27 July 2010, para. 35.
47 Ibid., para. 40.
48 'Srpsko tuzilastvo ne treba da se bavi politikom', *Radio Slobodna Evropa,* 28 July 2010.
49 *Serbian International Radio*, 30 July 2010.
50 See 'Vukcevic: Tvrdnje Ganica besmislene', *B92*, 30 July 2010, for the Serbian chief prosecutor's comment on the verdict and on abuse of process.
51 For internal opposition to the WCC, see 'On Trial: A Lively Start for a New Organized-Crime Court', *The Economist*, 21 May 2005, and Orentlicher, p. 65.
52 According to Diane Orentlicher, 'The Tribunal's failure to transfer other 11bis cases to Serbia reflects, among other considerations, the ICTY's general preference for transferring cases to the state in whose territory the crimes charged by the Hague Prosecutor were committed . . . to Bosnia and Herzegovina in particular and, in one instance, to Croatia'. Orentlicher, op. cit., p. 68.
53 Ibid., p. 50.
54 Bogdan Ivanisevic, *Against the Current–War Crimes Prosecutions in Serbia*, International Centre for Transitional Justice, 2007, p. 25, cited in Orentlicher, p. 71.
55 Orentlicher, ibid.
56 See Humanitarian Law Centre, *Transitional Justice Report: Serbia, Montenegro and Kosovo, 1999–2005*, Belgrade, 2006.
57 Orentlicher, op. cit., p. 75. For the Scorpions' case verdict, see 'Four "Scorpions" Found Guilty', Human Rights House Foundation, 12 April 2007.
58 See Chapter 7.
59 Reuters, 9 April 2008.
60 This survey, carried out by the OSCE, represented a decrease from the two previous years. Orentlicher, op. cit., p. 75.
61 Ibid., p. 76. Interview with Vladimir Vukcevic, 21 November 2006.
62 'As the verdict in the Scorpions case suggests, there are limits to how far the WCC is able or willing to go even when the perpetrators are lower-level perpetrators'. Orentlicher, ibid., p. 83.
63 Ibid., pp. 76–78.
64 The Supreme Court quashed four out of the six convictions up to 2008, and reduced other sentences, or went for retrial. Only one conviction was left intact, i.e. of an ethnic Albanian Anton Lekaj, convicted for the rape of Roma women in Kosovo.
65 Orentlicher, p. 79, and Human Rights Watch, *Unfinished Business: Serbia's War Crimes Chamber*, p. 31, June 2007.
66 www.helsinki.org.rs/doc/dragoljub todorovic.doc. Todorovic represented victims in the following cases: Ovcara, the Scorpions, Zvornik I & II, Sjeverin, Suva Reka, Bytyqi Brothers, Lovas, Podujevo I & II and Strpci.
67 'War Crimes Trials in Serbia', Humanitarian Law Centre (HLC), December 2007, and 'Trials for war crimes and ethnically and politically motivated crimes in post-Yugoslav countries', HLC, 2008.
68 Transitional Justice Bulletin, Fond za Humanitarno Pravo, Belgrade, 13 April 2007.
69 Orentlicher interview with Vukcevic, Orentlicher, op. cit., p. 67.
70 Humanitarian Law Centre, *Belgrade District Court fails to Establish Ilija Jurisic's Responsibility in the Tuzla Convoy Case Beyond Reasonable Doubt*, Press Release, 30 September 2009.
71 For an apposite comment on the Jurisic case, see 'Koga je branio Ilija Jurisic', Miljenko Jergovic, 1 December 2011. www.jergovic.com/sumnjivo-lice/koga-je-branio-ilija-jurisic/

72 For Divjak's eyewitness account of the events of that day, see Jovan Divjak, *Sarajevo, Mon Amour*, Buchet/Chastel, 2004, pp. 71–81.
73 In 2017, the police in Trebinje, Republika Srpska, issued a report to the BiH prosecutor against Divjak, for war crimes and crimes against humanity against civilians. 'Jovan Divjak o prijavi: "Ne znam o čemu se radi" ', *Blic*, 24 May 2017.
74 The arrests in Serbia in March 2015 took place following a cooperation protocol on war crimes, signed in 2013 by the special attorneys of Bosnia-Herzegovina and Serbia, when the authorities finally agreed to share information and evidence to allow the extradition of fugitives, and to give jurisdiction to their foreign counterparts.
75 Serbia's parliament in May 2017 elected Snezana Stanojkovic, the former deputy to the prosecutor, as the country's chief war crimes prosecutor, a position that had been left vacant for a year and a half. *Serbia Selects New Chief War Crimes Prosecutor*, Balkan Insight, 15 May 2017.
76 Osservatorio Balcani e Caucaso, 31 July 2017. www.balcanicaucaso.org/eng/Areas/Bosnia-Herzegovina/The-Kravica-case-and-judicial-cooperation-in-the-former-Yugoslavia-181659.
77 DOCUMENTA: Center for dealing with the past, www.documenta.hr/en/crime-in-srebrenica-kravice.html
78 Dusan Janjic from the Forum for Ethnic Relations commented that the issue of solving the Bytyqi murders was a test of Serbia's readiness to accept what it did in Kosovo. US Urged to Pressure Vucic over Bytyqi Murders, Balkan Insight, 12 July 2017. See also www.balkaninsight.com/en/article/aleksandar-vucic-s-broken-promises-to-america-06-16-2017, and https://bytyqibrothers.org/goran-guri-radosavljevic/
79 *Prospect of Haradinaj Running Kosovo Divides Serbia*, Balkan Insight, 8 September 2017.
80 Response to question by John Whittingdale, *Hansard*, 11 October 2010. The Labour Party was in power till the 11 May 2010. Gordon Brown was prime minister, Alan Johnson home secretary, and David Milliband foreign secretary.
81 Interview with Damir Arnaut, *BiH Dani*, 6 August 2010, *Telegraph*, 27 July 2010.
82 Haris Silajdzic, Interview, www.youtube.com/watch?v=mhNssoeMHIE
83 In 2009, William Hague visited Bosnia on a two-day trip to raise the profile of Project Maja–a Conservative Social Action project, along with six others, including Arminka Helic who had fled from Bosnia in the 1990s. In 2004, she was appointed special adviser to William Hague. *Daily Telegraph*, 13 September 2010, and 'William Hague Fears for Future of Bosnia', *Daily Telegraph*, 12 August 2009.
84 The one ray of hope occurred after the election in 2000, when non-nationalists took over in the Federation, during Wolfgang Petritsch's term as High Representative.

11 Crimes and punishment

Indictments and sentencing at the ICTY

If we cannot find that the Accused aided and abetted those crimes, I would say we have come to a dark place in international law indeed.[1]

Introduction

In timing, scope and content, indictments and sentencing at the ICTY have often reflected the chequered development of the tribunal itself, which in turn was subject to the political exigencies of the major powers at the UN Security Council.

The tribunal has been criticized for its timing and choice of indictments – and for their absence – often depending on the political viewpoint of the critic. The fact that 80% were for Serbs led its detractors on the Serb(ian) side to dub the tribunal a kangaroo court, while the failure to indict certain major players across the ethnic spectrum has at times exposed the tribunal to criticism from all sides.

Sentencing patterns have similarly come under fire, often with good reason, and not least for their inconsistency. While some defendants have been sentenced for life others, perceived to have played equally heinous roles in the conflict, have been handed down minimal sentences, and on occasion been acquitted.

Indictments

In 1993, the war in former Yugoslavia was into its third year with no real prospect of peace. Nor was there any mechanism in place to bring perpetrators to justice. It was not until July 1995, after four years of war, and the fall of Srebrenica, that Karadzic and Mladic were indicted for genocide in Bosnia while Milosevic, generally viewed as having led the war from Belgrade, continued to be central to international peace talks, and had a leading role in shaping the Dayton Agreement. The Croatian president, Franjo Tudjman, also involved in peace negotiations throughout the war, was not indicted, and neither were other Croat(ian) politicians, clearly implicated in the war against Bosniaks in Bosnia and Herzegovina. JNA Generals Kadijevic and Adzic, JNA commanders in the Croatian war in 1991 in which thousands of civilians were killed, escaped indictment.[2] So, too, did Borisav Jovic, SFRJ president, a close ally of Milosevic and an *eminence grise* in Serbian policy in the early days of the war.

The time-frame of some indictments was also questionable. Vojislav Šešelj was only indicted from August 1991 to September 1993, after which it was assumed that he was in conflict with Milosevic. Šešelj's association with Milosevic, despite differences in late 1993, was renewed when Šešelj was appointed deputy prime minister in 1998, a position he held till 2000, yet he eluded indictment for war crimes in Kosovo. Zeljko Raznatovic, aka Arkan, one of the most notorious paramilitary leaders, was indicted in 1997 on 24 counts, but only for crimes committed in September 1995, despite his well-documented role behind assaults in Croatia in 1991, and throughout Bosnia from 1992 to 1995.[3] He was never arrested, and proceedings against him were concluded on his death in 2000. Momčilo Krajisnik, president of the Bosnian Serb assembly till late 1995, and Karadzic's closest associate in decision making in the Bosnian war, was not indicted till 2000, and only then till December 1993. Had the indictment been extended, his involvement in the Srebrenica genocide could have been examined.[4]

The effectiveness of the ICTY indictments was illustrated not least in the official exclusion of Karadzic from the Dayton Peace Conference after being indicted, and from holding office after the war, albeit that he remained RS president well into 1996 and was not arrested despite the many opportunities for NATO troops to do so. Mladic, after his indictment, also disappeared from the military scene although, like Karadzic, his influence in RS continued. Krajisnik, however, participated in the Dayton negotiations and became the Serb member of the Bosnia and Herzegovina presidency in 1996, where he remained for two years. During this crucial post-war period, as one of the key players behind the Bosnian bloodshed, he was in a position to influence events leading to the consolidation of an ethnically 'pure' Serb para-state, Republika Srpska. Biljana Plavsic was also not indicted until 2000. During her time as president of Republika Srpska from 1996–1998, non-Serbs continued to be harassed and expelled from that entity.[5]

The first chief prosecutor, Richard Goldstone, came under heavy criticism for indicting too many 'small fry' with insufficient evidence, while Carla Del Ponte was accused of using indictments as bargaining chips, when former KLA members Ramush Haradinaj and Fatmir Limaj were indicted in exchange for the surrender to The Hague of senior Serbian indictees in the Kosovo war.[6] Louise Arbour, Goldstone's successor, was not in a position to indict Slobodan Milosevic until May 1999 and then only for crimes relating to Kosovo.

The prosecutors were all restricted by external factors. Neither Goldstone nor Arbour were provided with the evidence necessary to indict by outside states who held significant contemporaneous witness/victim testimony acquired from refugees and asylum seekers, and other evidence which could have pointed to Milosevic's role in orchestrating the Bosnian war. While the tribunal's hands were tied by *realpolitik*, international diplomats and politicians continued to negotiate with war criminals and even incorporate them into the post-war settlement at Dayton. It was only, weeks into the NATO action in Kosovo, when Milosevic still bluntly refused to cooperate and his support within Serbia, and from Russia, was rapidly dwindling, that his indictment became a more realistic objective.

Sentencing

With little precedential guidance, ICTY judges were vested with considerable discretion in sentencing, which at times led to inconsistency in both approach and outcome.[7] Sentencing patterns tended to fluctuate according to the time of sentencing, negotiated plea agreements, the composition of judges in both trial and appeal chambers, and other factors.

Plea bargaining

Plea bargaining at the ICTY, a contentious issue, was introduced in the early 2000s at a time when many cases remained to be heard, and the tribunal was under increasing pressure to complete its work. In a number of cases, important concessions were accorded to defendants, including the withdrawal of several counts of their indictments, often resulting in relatively short sentences in relation to crimes committed.

The ICTY did not explicitly address the issue of guilty pleas in its Statute but, in late 1997, adopted Rule 62 *bis*:

> If an accused pleads guilty in accordance with Rule 62 (vi) or requests to change his or her plea to guilty and the Trial Chamber is satisfied that (i) the guilty plea has been made voluntarily, (ii) the guilty plea is informed, (iii) the guilty plea is not equivocal and (iv) there is a sufficient factual basis for the crime and for the accused's participation in it, either on the basis of independent indicia or in lack of any material disagreement between the parties about the facts of the case, the Trial Chamber may enter a finding of guilt and instruct the Registrar to set a date for the sentencing hearing.[8]

The Rule governing the plea agreement procedure (Rule 62 ter) states,

> (A) The Prosecutor and the defence may agree that, upon the accused entering a plea of guilty to the indictment or to one or more counts of the indictment, the Prosecutor shall do one or more of the following before the Trial Chamber: (i) apply to amend the indictment accordingly; (ii) submit that a specific sentence or sentencing range is appropriate; (iii) not oppose a request by the accused for a particular sentence or sentencing range. (B) The Trial Chamber shall not be bound by any agreement specified in paragraph (A). (C) If a plea agreement has been reached by the parties, the Trial Chamber shall require the disclosure of the agreement in open session or, on a showing of good cause, in closed session, at the time the accused pleads guilty in accordance with Rule 62 (vi), or requests to change his or her plea to guilty.[9]

Important concessions were accorded to defendants in the expectation that their pleas would facilitate reconciliation. In sentencing, judges came to recognize a number of factors, including voluntary surrender, prior good character, expressions of remorse and age.

In adversarial legal systems, plea bargaining is widespread. The Sentencing Council in the UK, for instance, determined that

> whereas a court should consider the fact that an offender has pleaded guilty to murder when deciding whether it is appropriate to order a whole life term, where a court determines that there should be a whole life minimum term, there will be no reduction for a guilty plea. In other circumstances: the court will weigh carefully the overall length of the minimum term taking into account other reductions for which the offender may be eligible so as to avoid a combination leading to an inappropriately short sentence; where it is appropriate to reduce the minimum term having regard to a plea of guilty, the reduction will not exceed one-sixth and will never exceed five years.[10]

Yet at the ICTY, where alleged crimes were generally much graver, plea bargaining at times resulted in reduced sentences wholly disproportionate to the gravity of the crimes. Judges justified the use of plea bargains on two main grounds – they saved the tribunal time and resources, and they facilitated reconciliation. Guilty pleas render a trial unnecessary and lead directly to sentencing.

Twenty ICTY defendants pleaded guilty.[11] Their pleas were mostly induced through plea bargaining which the Trial Chamber opined would foster reconciliation and bring a degree of closure to the victims. The judges found Dragan Obrenovic's guilty plea helpful in this respect.[12] Yet other judgements following plea agreements were vigorously opposed by survivors.[13]

The pressure on the tribunal to complete its work by 2009 undoubtedly played a major part in its readiness to accept plea bargains, even for defendants charged with genocide.[14] Some of those, including Biljana Plavsic and Momir Nikolic, managed to have the genocide charges dropped as part of a plea-bargaining arrangement.[15] The lesser crimes that were eventually agreed on meant that the element of intent, crucial to demonstrate genocide, was not examined. It also meant that genocide in Bosnia in 1992, when some of the most egregious crimes were committed, became less easy to prove overall, particularly as Plavsic was a leading member of the joint criminal enterprise, with the result that the tribunal's record of the Bosnian war was compromised.[16]

Similarly with rape and sexual assault crimes in Bosnia, where the plea agreement reached between the OTP and Dragan Zelenovic resulted in seven counts of torture and rape being dropped from the indictment, with the effect of 'editing out the full factual basis upon which a conviction rests'.[17] As a consequence, the overall ICTY record on rape failed to represent a full picture of its systemic and widespread occurrence across Bosnia and Herzegovina.

Expressions of remorse, present in virtually all the plea-bargaining statements, were regarded by the ICTY as mitigating factors. Yet, bearing in mind that most of that remorse came only after several years of evading justice, its sincerity might be doubted. The claim by judges that guilty pleas aided reconciliation, furthering one of the tribunal's three official goals, namely the restoration and maintenance of peace in the former Yugoslavia, was questioned by several international lawyers. In an in-depth survey on the role of ICTY plea bargaining in reconciliation in the region, Janine Natalya Clark found an overwhelming consensus that defendants who expressed remorse for their crimes were being disingenuous, and simply sought to reduce their sentences,[18] while Mirjan Damaska opined that the special features of international crimes and their context reinforce the view that plea bargaining can only be justified on grounds of practical utility.[19]

Plavsic

The case of Biljana Plavsic is a graphic example of the negative consequences of plea bargaining.

As the Serb representative to the Bosnian presidency and co-president of the Bosnian Serb presidency, Plavsic was one of the main political leaders during the Bosnian war, with *de facto* control over the Bosnian Serb army, and full authority to punish or initiate proceedings against soldiers under her command.

Plavsic was indicted in April 2000 and surrendered the following January. She was charged based on individual and superior criminal responsibility on eight counts, including genocide and/or complicity to commit genocide, extermination, murder, persecutions on political, racial and religious grounds, deportation, crimes against humanity and war crimes. Initially, Plavsic pleaded not guilty to all charges and was remanded in the UN Detention Unit till September 2001, when she was provisionally released to Serbia. In December 2002, the Prosecution motion to dismiss seven counts of the indictment, including the two genocide counts, was granted by the Trial Chamber, and Plavsic pleaded guilty to just one count – persecution.[20] This was a controversial decision given the crimes she was charged with and her senior position in orchestrating a genocidal war. The indictment included crimes in 37 municipalities in Bosnia and Herzegovina: Banja Luka, Bijeljina, Bileća, Bosanska Krupa, Bosanski Novi, Bosanski Petrovac, Bratunac, Brčko, Čajniče, Čelinac, Doboj, Donji Vakuf, Foča, Gacko, Hadžići, Ilidža, Ilijaš, Ključ, Kalinovik, Kotor Varoš, Nevesinje, Novi Grad, Novo Sarajevo, Pale, Prijedor, Prnjavor, Rogatica, Rudo, Sanski Most, Šipovo, Sokolac, Teslić, Trnovo, Višegrad, Vlasenica, Vogošća and Zvornik.[21] Senior Prosecutor Alan Tieger described the scale of killings as

> unfathomable, even when we focus on individual municipalities. . . . And although the events took place in 1992, their destructive impact continues to this day. It is reflected . . . not only in the debilitated and shortened lives of camp survivors but in the blighted lives of widows and orphans or of stigmatised rape victims or of depressed and withdrawn children.[22]

Carla Del Ponte added that

> if the accused is on the right path, she still has not gone the full length of her journey . . . she is not willing to provide substantial cooperation with the Prosecutor. Indeed, so far I have not been able to convince her of the need to

> undertake the last step of her journey, of her admitting responsibility . . . that she would be willing to appear as a witness on essential and relevant facts in other trial proceedings.[23]

The prosecution asked for a 15–25-year sentence, while Plavsic's defence argued that a lengthy sentence (more than 8 years) would in effect constitute a lifetime sentence and discourage others from coming forward and contributing to reconciliation.[24] Plavsic's Statement of Guilt, extending to over a thousand words was read to the Court in Serbian. While expressing remorse, Plavsic professed ignorance of the magnitude of the crimes committed by Serb forces, claiming her role in the war was mainly humanitarian.

> I have now come to the belief and accept the fact that many thousands of innocent people were the victims of an organised, systematic effort to remove Muslims and Croats from the territory claimed by Serbs. At the time, I easily convinced myself that this was a matter of survival and self-defence. In fact, it was more. Our leadership, of which I was a necessary part, led an effort which victimised countless innocent people . . . how could our leaders and those who followed have committed such acts? The answer to both questions is, I believe, fear, a blinding fear that led to an obsession, especially for those of us for whom the Second World War was a living memory . . . Although I was repeatedly informed of allegations of cruel and inhuman conduct against non-Serbs, I refused to accept them or even to investigate. In fact, I immersed myself in addressing the suffering of the war's innocent Serb victims.[25]

Yet Plavsic was far from being an underling in the Bosnian Serb leadership. Renowned throughout the 1990s as an uncompromising apologist of 'ethnic cleansing', the self-styled 'Serbian Iron Lady' once defended the purge of Bosnian non-Serbs as 'a natural phenomenon', not a war crime.[26] In Bijeljina in April 1992, with Arkan, stepping over a dead body, she infamously declared that 'six million Serbs can die so that the remaining six million can live in freedom'.[27] In 1994, she equated a specific ethnic group with a disease or illness, declaring that she and other Serbian nationalists were unable to negotiate with the Bosnian Muslims due to genetics. She is quoted as opining that:

> It was genetically deformed material that embraced Islam. And now, of course, with each successive generation it simply becomes concentrated. It gets worse and worse. it simply expresses itself and dictates their style of thinking, which is rooted in their genes. And through the centuries, the genes degraded further.[28]

In its Sentencing Judgement, the Trial Chamber, while acknowledging the gravity, 'massive scope and extent' of the persecutions, found there was 'substantial mitigation', in that Plavsic had surrendered voluntarily, pleaded guilty and expressed remorse in her statement of guilt, and that 'full disclosure' and 'acceptance of responsibility' would promote reconciliation in Bosnia and in the region as a whole.[29] Plavsic's post-conflict conduct was also a factor influencing the judges, as perhaps were her background and education, where her defence team stressed her father's distinguished record, her marriage to a prominent Sarajevo lawyer, and her 'international distinction', including a Fulbright Scholarship.[30]

Several international witnesses who testified at the sentencing hearing may also have unwittingly contributed to the lesser sentence. Former US Secretary of State Madeleine Albright described the accused as the vehicle in Republika Srpska for making sure that the Dayton Agreement was carried out. Robert Frowick said that he viewed Plavsic as attacking corruption and injustice, while former High Representative Carl Bildt described her as courageous in supporting the peace implementation, a firm supporter of constitutional rule, who 'took great personal risk with that'.[31]

The Trial Chamber inclined towards the defence, sentencing Plavsic to 11 years imprisonment, which she served in Sweden. Del Ponte only later recorded that Plavsic's statement was 'full of generalistic *mea culpas*, but lacking compelling detail'.[32] She admitted her 'fundamental error' in not obliging Plavsic to testify against other accused: 'I accepted verbal assurances and was deceived'.[33]

Plavsic's apparent change of heart did not deceive everyone, however. Nobel Peace prize winner and Auschwitz survivor Elie Wiesel addressed the court via a video link from Paris as a prosecution witness, notably urging the judges to consider 'the pain and suffering of all the victims' of Bosnia's war when they considered Plavsic's sentence.[34]

Less than two years into her sentence, Plavsic gave an interview on Banja Luka *Alternativna Televizija*, in which she declared that she had confessed merely to shorten her sentence.[35] In the same year, she produced a book, written in Hinseberg where she was serving her sentence, in which she claimed she was not part of the decision-making process led by Karadzic and Krajisnik, and portrayed her role in the war as mainly humanitarian.[36] In 2006, Plavsic was summoned by the Trial Chamber to testify at Krajisnik's trial, where she complained with no hint of irony that she had been put together with prostitutes, drug addicts and women convicted of murder, whereas she should have been imprisoned with others accused of war crimes. Her comments testified both to her apparent belief that she, as a genocide indictee, was somehow less culpable than her prison inmates, and to her unyielding elitism which reached beyond ethnic prejudices.[37]

On 14 September 2009, ICTY President Patrick Robinson granted Plavsic early release, declaring that she appeared to have demonstrated substantial evidence of rehabilitation and remorse and had accepted responsibility for her crimes. Yet the evidence indicated that Plavsic was far from remorseful and certainly did little to contribute to reconciliation and peace in the region, either before her imprisonment or after her release.

Many share responsibility for mishandling the case – the prosecutors, in withdrawing all but one of the counts, including two for genocide, the judges in imposing a sentence which in no way reflected Plavsic's crimes and, finally, international leaders who supported her unquestioningly in the aftermath of the Bosnian war.

In 1996, when Plavsic was elected president of the Bosnian Serb republic, she became feted in the West as a relative moderate. Despite opposing the extradition of indicted war criminals, and her appeasement of the continued expulsion of non-Serbs from Banja Luka, she was applauded by Carl Bildt and world leaders including Madeleine Albright, British foreign secretary Robin Cook and international development secretary, Clare Short.[38] In the post-war international climate, corruption took shape as a more heinous crime than genocide, and Plavsic, in standing against wartime corruption, was rewarded with international aid and investment.[39] Her role in the war, influential enough to prevail over Milosevic in opposing the Vance Owen Peace Plan in April 1993, was set aside in the interests of *real politik*.

Once granted early release in October 2009, having served just over six years, Plavsic went to live in Belgrade.[40] In 2016, she asserted that Clinton was behind the Srebrenica genocide and, on hearing of Karadzic's sentencing, denied it had taken place.[41] She has since given lengthy interviews on Serbian television, where she is warmly applauded for her heroism and for having secured Dayton for Republika Srpska, as she recognized (which many international observers still appear not to) that the Dayton Agreement which cemented ethnic apartheid, has for many years benefited RS to the detriment of the Federation.[42]

Bosnian Croat cases

Partly in an attempt to counteract claims of ethnic bias, the tribunal issued indictments for a number of Bosnian Croats, including minor players, often on insubstantial evidence. This resulted in early acquittals in several cases and uneven sentencing in others.

The first such case to come to trial was that of Bosnian Croat Tihomir Blaskic, commander of the HVO Armed forces in Central Bosnia from 1992 to 1994. The case was marked by a massive discrepancy between the Trial and Appeals Chamber Judgements. Initially indicted in November 1995, Blaskic surrendered voluntarily on 1 April 1996. On 3 March 2000, he was convicted on 19 counts and sentenced to 45 years' imprisonment, reduced to 9 years on appeal 4 years later, when he was acquitted on 16 of the 19 counts. By this time, Blaskic had already served over 8 years at Scheveningen. The reduction in sentence was due to significant additional evidence presented, following the death of Tudjman in December 1999, and the subsequent opening of Croatia's archives on the order of the new president, Stipe Mesic, in order to dissociate the new government from Croatia's role in the Bosnian war under Tudjman's leadership. Had Tudjman been indicted, and the archives opened sooner, Blaskic would undoubtedly have received a fairer trial.

The case generated considerable publicity, partly due to the length of sentence, but also because of Blaskic's alleged responsibility for the well-documented

Ahmići massacre on 16 April 1993, where more than 100 Bosnian Muslim civilians were slaughtered overnight.[43] The Croatian archives confirmed, however, that the assault on Ahmići was carried out by the special purposes police unit called the Jokers (Dzokeri), commanded by Dario Kordic, president of the Croatian Democratic Union of Bosnia and Herzegovina from 1992 until 1995 and later vice-president of 'Herceg-Bosna'. Kordic was convicted in 2001 for the Ahmići massacre, along with other war crimes and crimes against humanity, and granted early release after serving two-thirds of a 25-year sentence. Mario Cerkez, indicted with Kordic, was sentenced to 15 years but on appeal most of his convictions were overturned and his sentence reduced to 6 years.

In view of the crimes committed in Central Bosnia in 1993, the Kordic and Cerkez sentences were disproportionately short. Blaskic's sentence was three years longer than that of Cerkez which included persecutions and other more heinous crimes. Several other Croat defendants were acquitted on appeal, including Zoran, Vlatko and Mirjan Kupreskic, who had been sentenced in the first instance to terms ranging from six to ten years.[44] Ivan Santic and Pero Skopljak were freed without trial due to lack of evidence. Drago Josipovic and Vladimir Santic received heavy sentences at first instance, but these were reduced on appeal. All those convicted were released early and freed to return to their villages, often to a hero's welcome.

Bosnian military indictments

Between 2001 and 2005, Chief Prosecutor Carla Del Ponte issued indictments for six military commanders from the Bosnian Army (ABiH), generally related to war crimes committed by soldiers under their command.

Enver Hadžihasanović, Amir Kubura and Mehmed Alagic, all senior ABiH officers were charged under the same indictment on 13 July 2001. Hadzihasanovic and Kubura were sentenced to three-and-a-half years and two years' imprisonment, respectively, for failing to take the necessary measures to prevent or punish crimes committed under their command in central Bosnia and Herzegovina in 1993 and early 1994.[45] Proceedings were dropped against Alagic following his death. It was the first tribunal judgement to deal with the presence of foreign Mujahedin combatants in central Bosnia. The crimes, often brutal in nature, were committed by Mujahedin troops, allegedly under the command of Hadžihasanović. The Appeals Chamber concluded, however, that

> the relationship between the El Mujahedin detachment and the 3rd Corps was not one of subordination. It was quite close to overt hostility since the only way to control the El Mujahedin detachment was to attack them as if they were a distinct enemy force. This scenario is at odds with the premise of the Trial Chamber that the El Mujahedin detachment was subordinated to the 3rd Corps. This conclusion further confirms that Hadžihasanović did not have effective control over the El Mujahedin detachment.[46]

Most of the 19 counts in the original indictment were not proven, and the final sentences received were small relative to most ICTY cases, which prompts the question – why were they tried by the tribunal and not in the Bosnian Court?

In this regard, it may be recalled that in May 1998, ICTY Chief Prosecutor Louise Arbour decided to withdraw several cases, for transferral to the Bosnian Court, including that of Zeljko Meakic, the commander of the Keraterm camp who was indicted in February 1995 for genocide and crimes against humanity. Also indicted in 1995 were Momčilo Gruban, Dusan Fustar and Dusan Knezevic, guards at the Keraterm and Omarska camps.[47] The indictment included 'murder, beatings and sexual assault of Bosnian Muslims, Bosnian Croats and other non-Serbs detained in the camps, confinement in inhumane conditions, harassment, humiliation and psychological abuse of Bosnian Muslims, Bosnian Croats and other non-Serbs in the camps'.[48] At that time, they were all still at large. Between 2002 and 2003, they surrendered individually and were subsequently transferred to the Bosnian Court where, in May 2008, they received sentences ranging between seven and 31 years. Arbour explained why she had made the referrals:

> I have re-evaluated all outstanding indictments *vis-à-vis* the overall investigative and prosecutorial strategies of my Office. Consistent with those *strategies, which involve maintaining an investigative focus on persons holding higher levels of responsibility, or on those who have been personally responsible for the exceptionally brutal or otherwise extremely serious offences*, I decided that it was appropriate to withdraw the charges against a number of accused in what have become known as the Omarska and Keraterm indictments, which were confirmed in February 1995 and July 1995 respectively.[49]

Yet Arbour's successor, Carla Del Ponte, abandoned that strategy. In the early 2000s, when the tribunal was still overburdened with cases, she would have been well within her right to transfer the more minor cases. So what was her reason for trying the Bosnian army officers at The Hague, if not political?

Del Ponte at that time was under considerable pressure from all sides. She had frequently clashed with NATO leaders who had failed signally to arrest Karadzic and Mladic, while the Serbian authorities were accusing the tribunal of bias against Serbs in its indictments, while refusing to hand over senior figures indicted for crimes in Kosovo and living openly in Serbia. But her indictments of non-Serbs for lesser offences often failed to stand up to scrutiny at trial.

Sefer Halilovic, former deputy commander in the ABiH, was indicted in 2001. The Trial Chamber found that the Prosecution had failed to prove beyond reasonable doubt that he had either *de jure* nor *de facto* command of the alleged 'Operation Neretva', or that he had effective control over the troops who committed crimes in Grabovica in early September 1993. Halilovic was accordingly acquitted in November 2005, confirmed on appeal.

Rasim Delic, former commander of the Main Staff of the ABiH, was initially indicted in March 2005 for command responsibility, in failing to prevent or punish crimes committed by his alleged subordinates, Mujahedin troops, in July and August 1995. Delic was sentenced by Majority to three years' imprisonment for cruel treatment on the grounds of superior criminal responsibility on 15 September 2008. Presiding Judge Moloto, in a nine-page Dissenting Opinion, disagreed that Delic in 1995 was in a position to enforce his decisions upon his subordinates, including the '*El Mujahed*' Detachment (EMD), and would have acquitted Delic on all counts.

> It is clear that if a decision had been made to confront the EMD by force, the ABiH would have encountered resistance comparable to an enemy force, rather than a force which is under its control. Such a scenario can hardly be reconciled with the theory of 'effective control' as set forth in the Tribunal's jurisprudence . . .[50]
>
> The links of the EMD with the foreign authorities show another area in which the EMD acted independently from the ABiH . . . the EMD's failure to report to its immediately superior unit coupled with the EMD's erratic behaviour towards the orders of the ABiH seriously undermined the command and control of Rasim Delic.[51]

The case went into appeal, but Delic died before the appeals judgement could be announced.[52]

The case of Naser Oric was the most controversial and highly publicized of the Bosnian army officers' judgements. Oric, former commander of the Srebrenica Armed Forces, was first indicted in March 2003 for individual and superior criminal responsibility in the 'wanton destruction of cities, towns or villages, not justified by military necessity', and of superior criminal responsibility with 'murder and cruel treatment' between 10 June 1992 and 20 March 1993. The Trial Chamber found him guilty for failing to take necessary measures to prevent the murder of Serbs detained at the Srebrenica Police Station and Municipal Centre, and for failing to prevent cruel treatment. In June 2006, he was sentenced to two years' imprisonment and immediately released.[53] Two years later, he was acquitted of all charges.[54]

Oric's indictment for crimes in Srebrenica sent shock waves through Bosnia, especially since the tribunal had failed to bring to trial the main indictees for the Srebrenica genocide. The trial of seven other Bosnian Serb military figures indicted for genocide and crimes against humanity in Srebrenica (*Popovic et al.*) began two months after Oric's conviction.[55] The dichotomy between Oric's alleged crimes and those charged in *Popovic et al.* was stark, and indicting Oric at the ICTY was comprehensible only in the context of the political pressure on the OTP at the time. Normally, such a case would have been transferred to the Bosnian Court, and it may be wondered whether Del Ponte fully comprehended the situation in Bosnia in Srebrenica before 1995.[56] As commander of the Srebrenica forces, Oric was regarded as a hero, having led the defence of the area in conditions of extreme deprivation since 1992. His indictment, in the circumstances, was an unfortunate move.

A shift in ICTY jurisprudence

The period from November 2012 was particularly controversial, with surprising acquittals in four major cases at the ICTY in just over six months, all defendants having occupied senior military or political positions during the wars of the 1990s. Although they differed ethnically, geographically and factually, most of the cases challenged previous ICTY jurisprudence.

On 15 April 2011, Ante Gotovina, Mladen Markac, former Croatian generals, charged with crimes against humanity and war crimes, were sentenced to 24 and 18 years respectively, by a unanimous Trial Chamber. On appeal, on 16 November 2012, both were acquitted by Majority. Two weeks later, Kosovar general and former president, Ramush Haradinaj and his subordinate Idriz Balaj were acquitted for the second time on retrial.[57] On 28 February 2013, former Yugoslav Army (VJ) commander Momčilo Perišić was acquitted by a Majority Appeals Chamber, with Perišić having been sentenced in the first instance to 27 years' imprisonment. The final shock acquittal occurred when Jovica Stanisic, head of Serbian State Security Service (SDB) and Franko Simatovic, commander of Serbian Police Operations (JSO) were acquitted by Majority of all charges on 30 May 2013.

*

Gotovina, Markac and Cermak

The first to be acquitted on appeal were Ante Gotovina and Mladen Markac, charged with crimes against humanity and war crimes for their role in Operation Storm (*Oluja*) in August 1995. During the period relevant to the indictment, Gotovina held the post of Lieutenant General in the Croatian Army (HV) and was commander of the Split Military District. Markac was commander of the Croatian Special Police.

The case is of interest not least in that it exposes the opposing international positions in the Croatian and Bosnian wars. While Britain argued that Gotovina was equal in culpability to Mladic and Karadzic and merited a commensurate sentence,[58] the United States considered that Croatia had also been a victim of aggression in 1991 and, since the war was unlikely to end without firm military action, the first step was to break the siege of the Krajina region of Croatia.

The acquittal of the two accused on appeal was controversial for a number of reasons. Besides the huge disparity between the verdicts of the two Chambers, there was considerable disagreement about the facts of the case. Both sides claimed 'ethnic cleansing' had taken place in the Krajina region of Croatia but, whereas the prosecutors alleged they occurred during Operation Storm in August 1995, the defence team argued that they had taken place in 1991 when Serbian forces originally seized the territory.[59] The judges were sharply divided, as were outside commentators.

In the first-instance judgement, the Trial Chamber found that the Four Towns artillery attacks were unlawful based on a so-called Site Impact Analysis, which in turn was based on a 200-metre range of error, the so-called 200-metre Standard, and that all impact sites over 200 metres from their legitimate target were evidence of an unlawful attack. The Appeals Chamber found unanimously that the Trial Chamber had erred in devising the 200-metre standard, without adequate reasoning as to how that margin of error was arrived at, and also that the Trial Chamber had applied its Impact Analysis to all four towns, without sufficient evidence.

The Appeals Chamber held, by majority, that the artillery attacks on the Four Towns were not unlawful and that there was therefore no JCE. Judges Carmel Agius and Fausto Pocar strongly dissented, describing the findings on 'alternate modes of liability' as confirmation of 'the legal confusion' in the reasoning of the Majority. Judge Agius, then vice-president of the tribunal, argued that the issue of 'alternate modes of liability' should not have been raised and that sufficient evidence existed to convict Gotovina on grounds of command responsibility.[60] Agius also opined that the Trial Chamber had clearly established Markac's effective and *de jure* control over the police forces, as well as his 'substantial contribution' to the commission of the crimes.[61] Judge Pocar, a former tribunal president dissented in even stronger tones, calling the reasoning of the Majority in Gotovina 'wrong, incorrect and misleading', and even 'grotesque', claiming that the Majority mischaracterized the Trial Chamber's findings in stating that the trial judgement held that the artillery attack was the 'core indicator' and 'primary means' of the deportation of the Serbs, and thus of the JCE. He concluded with the implicit suggestion that the Majority might have been guided by other than purely legal motives.[62]

Operation Storm (*Oluja*) was a military campaign to take back control. In 1991, approximately 10,000 had been killed and 80,000 Croatians fled, or were expelled, from Serb-occupied areas of Croatia, while in the Krajina, a virtual apartheid was imposed by *Republika Srpska Krajina* (RSK) forces, supported by Milosevic in Belgrade and underpinned by UN troops on the ground, despatched to 'protect' the so-called United Nations Protected Areas (UNPA).[63] On 23 July, the UN 'safe area' of Bihac in Bosnia, under siege for three years, came under heavy assault from Serbian, Bosnian Serb and Krajina Serb forces.[64] Since this occurred just after the fall of Srebrenica and Žepa, also UN 'safe areas', the Bosnian and Croatian authorities had little confidence that the UN would act to save Bihac from a similar fate. Apart from the potential humanitarian consequences, Croatia would have been more exposed to attack. Zagreb had already come under shellfire from RSK forces in May 1995, with seven deaths and over 200 wounded.

It is doubtful whether the Croatian army would have been successful without US support on several levels. The outcome of the 'rehearsal' Operation Flash (*Blijesak*) in May 1995 encouraged the United States to proceed further.[65] US military advisors from Military Professional Resources Incorporated (MPRI) became involved and diplomatic channels were bypassed, with preparation reportedly carried out from the Pentagon via Col. Richard Herrick.[66] The United States supplied the Croatian Army with intelligence on Serb movements in Krajina and the Yugoslav Army on Croatia's eastern borders, in anticipation of a possible counter-attack in eastern Slavonia. In the small hours of 4 August 1995, the United States electronically intercepted and destroyed the Serbian telecommunications devices.[67]

The Balkans had become an important issue for the US president, especially after the fall of Srebrenica. Clinton needed to demonstrate his leadership qualities as he prepared for re-election against US Senator Bob Dole who had repeatedly requested Congress to remove the arms embargo from the Bosnian government forces. It was now increasingly urgent to resolve the impasse and bring the war to an end. The US-brokered Split Declaration, signed by Izetbegovic and Tudjman, permitted HV forces to enter Bosnia to cooperate with the Bosnian army. Operation Storm was a strategic victory in the Bosnian war, especially in ending the siege of Bihac.

In contrast to US reports, the reaction in the UK to *Oluja* was swift and condemnatory, with sections of the British media peddling the notion that hundreds of thousands of Serbs had been 'ethnically cleansed' from Croatia. Comparisons were made with Srebrenica, with some international diplomats, including EU envoy Carl Bildt, suggesting that the Krajina situation was a worse humanitarian disaster.[68]

It has been argued by Serbia that Operation Storm constituted 'ethnic cleansing', and even genocide.[69] This was also a contentious issue amongst Serbian leaders, the RSK commander, Mile Mrksic, arguing that his evacuation order had only been for the Serb civilians to seek temporary shelter in Lika or the woods.[70] An estimated 200,000 Serbs left Croatia but, although many fled the Krajina as a direct consequence of HV military action, there was also an order to evacuate taken by the RSK 'Supreme Defence Council', as acknowledged by Mrksic in testimony at the ICTY.[71]

There were civilian casualties in *Oluja*, as in any war. What was not addressed by the Appeals Chamber Majority was the aftermath, when HV forces and others assaulted or drove out Serbs who remained, looted houses and set villages on fire. An estimated 600 civilians were killed during this time, mostly elderly Serbs.[72] Gotovina and Markac had command responsibility but failed to punish or attempt to recompense the losses sustained. Their acquittals were therefore unsustainable, and left lingering resentment within Serb communities, making it more difficult for refugees to return later to Croatia. The hero's welcome Gotovina received on return from The Hague, as well as reinforcing his alleged innocence, fuelled the ongoing crusade of Croatian nationalists.[73]

Perišić

Momčilo Perišić, a former Serbian general, served as Chief of the General Staff of the Yugoslav Army (VJ) between 1993 and 1998. In 2011, he was sentenced to 27 years' imprisonment for war crimes and crimes against humanity and acquitted on all counts by Majority on appeal 18 months later. When the war broke out, Perišić was commander of the JNA Artillery School Centre in Zadar, and in January 1992, he was appointed commander of the 13th Corps of the JNA in Mostar. In June, he became chief of general staff and deputy commander of the 3rd Army based in Nis and in April 1993 its commander. Under Yugoslav (FRY) law, he was subordinate only to the Yugoslav president and the Supreme Defence Council (SDC). In November 1993, Perišić created the units known as the 30th Personnel Centre for members of the VJ serving in the ranks of the Army of the Republika Srpska (VRS), and the 40th Personnel Centre for members of the VJ serving in the Army of the Serbian Krajina (SVK) These centres provided supplies to senior officers of the different armies in order to cover up involvement of the VJ and Serbia in the Bosnian war.

Perišić was first indicted on 5 February 2005 for aiding and abetting a military campaign in civilian areas of Sarajevo, which killed and wounded thousands between August 1993 and November 1995, and for aiding and abetting in crimes in Srebrenica planned by members of the VJ 30th Personnel Centre. The prosecution alleged that Perišić had reason to know of his subordinates' participation in the crimes but had failed to initiate an enquiry. It was further alleged that on 2 and 3 May 1995, by order of Milan Martic, General Celeketic of the SVK, Perišić's subordinate, ordered a rocket attack with cluster bombs in the centre of Zagreb and Pleso airport, resulting in seven civilians killed and at least 194 wounded.

On 6 September 2011, the Trial Chamber, Judge Justice Moloto dissenting, found Perišić guilty of war crimes and crimes against humanity, and sentenced him to 27 years' imprisonment, holding that Perišić 'knew that it was highly probable that the VRS would forcibly transfer Bosnian Muslims and commit killings and other abuses with discriminatory intent once Srebrenica had fallen under VRS control'. It also found that Perišić had repeatedly used his authority to provide the VRS with logistical and personnel assistance while he knew of their systematic and grave crimes committed against Muslim civilians. Moreover, Perišić continued to offer assistance to the VRS for months, even after being informed of the massacres in Srebrenica.[74]

Judge Moloto, dissenting, viewed the VRS as a legitimate army fighting a legitimate war. Conceding that Perišić 'supported the conflict as a whole' he argued that there was no evidence of 'specific direction' that the logistical assistance provided was for committing crimes, and that Perišić was not at or near the scene of the crimes committed.

> There is no evidence to suggest that such assistance supported the commission of the crimes which occurred in Sarajevo and Srebrenica . . . assisting the VRS wage war per se is not a crime under the Statute. . . . The dependence of . . . a foreign army as a whole, alone does not automatically lead to the only reasonable conclusion that such assistance provided to that dependent army and distributed by that army to its subordinate units was specifically directed as providing those officers . . . with practical support which had a substantial effect on the perpetration of the crimes.[75]

Significantly, a central thrust of Moloto's dissent was the wider implications of convicting a military leader for providing military aid 'aimed at supporting mutual interests such as the deterrence of war, the promotion of regional and global peace, stability and prosperity and other objectives'.[76] During an exchange with Senior Prosecutor Mark Harmon in the closing arguments, Moloto suggested that a ruling against Perišić could have implications for international leaders, political and military, and enquired of Harmon whether the NATO Commanders in Afghanistan would be guilty of aiding and abetting the alleged crimes committed there.[77]

On 28 February 2013, the ICTY Appeals Chamber, Judge Liu largely dissenting, overturned the Trial Chamber's judgement and acquitted Perišić on the grounds that 'specific direction', as an element of the actus reus of aiding and abetting liability, was not proved beyond reasonable doubt and that, while Perišić implemented the Yugoslav Supreme Defence Council's policy of providing support to the VRS through the Yugoslav Army, this policy was not directed at criminal activities as opposed to legitimate war efforts. Without a finding of specific direction, the Appeals Chamber found Perišić not guilty of aiding and abetting VRS crimes in Bosnia. It also found unanimously that there was no evidence beyond reasonable doubt that Perišić possessed effective control over the Serbian Army of the Krajina (SVK) soldiers, who committed crimes during Zagreb's shelling, and that without effective control, Perišić could not be held liable as a superior. On that basis, his convictions relating to SVK crimes in Croatia were reversed.

In dissenting, Judge Liu stated he was not convinced, even assuming specific direction were a required element of aiding and abetting liability that, given the magnitude, importance and sustained nature of the assistance provided to the VRS, an acquittal would be justified.[78] Referring in detail to the Trial Chamber Majority, Judge Liu noted that the specific direction requirement was not applied consistently nor with any rigour in the relevant jurisprudence, and to rely on it was to raise the threshold for aiding and abetting liability to the point of undermining its very purpose.[79] He further observed that, as the highest-ranking officer in the VJ, Perišić oversaw a system which provided considerable practical assistance and institutionalized the provision of logistical assistance to the VRS,[80] and had the power to approve or deny requests. He even encouraged the SDC to maintain the assistance, including considerable quantities of weaponry, and to increase the budget, as well as transferring VJ officers and key personnel to the VRS. Both Karadzic and Mladic, moreover, admitted that the comprehensive assistance of Serbia was essential to the continued existence of the VRS. Liu further noted that in the early stages of the war Perišić received information from several sources of the VRS's criminal behaviour and discriminatory intent relating to violence against Bosnian Muslims, and had contemporaneous knowledge of allegations of VRS crimes in Srebrenica.[81]

Perišić's surprise acquittal led to wide debate in international legal circles which reflected the deeply divided chambers at both trial and appeals level.

Legally, the issue was complex. 'Specific direction' had no solid grounding in customary international law, and the Appeals Chamber placed considerable weight on the Tadić Appeals Chamber Judgement in 1999, which had characterized aiding and abetting as assistance directed to a specific crime with knowledge of that crime, as opposed to JCE liability, which was not codified in the ICTY Statute.[82] Yet, while a number of international decisions referred to the *Tadić* Appeal Judgement, none offered a detailed analysis of the meaning of 'specific direction', and the ICTY had limited and inconsistent jurisprudence on the matter. Over time, the notion of 'specific' became diluted, as aiding and abetting came to cover not a specific crime but a programme of systemic violence or a specific unlawful policy.[83]

There was also the question of the characterization of the VRS – was it a legitimate organization, or a criminal one? If legitimate, the aid and assistance Perišić, as commander of the VJ, provided was also used for legitimate purposes, even though crimes had been committed, and he was not necessarily aware of the uses to which his assistance was being put. Yet is it possible for a military force to act *purely* criminally? Some of its activities must perforce be non-criminal. As VJ Chief of Staff, who regularly sat in on the Serbian Defence Council meetings where these issues were discussed, Perišić should have been aware of crimes committed. Also, many of the VRS members assisted by Perišić were technically members of the VJ, albeit fighting in Bosnia. And the argument that 'geographic distance' is an appropriate measure of remoteness from the scene of the crimes, argued by the Appeals Chamber, and by Judge Moloto, dissenting, is also difficult to sustain in an age of advanced technology where geographic distance is often immaterial.[84]

The time-frame of the indictment itself is equally questionable. Perišić's indictment began in August 1993, a year after the greatest number of atrocities were committed by JNA and VRS forces. Had the indictment been from 1991, a case might have been made for Perišić's role in the Croatian war, when he was commander of the JNA Artillery School Centre in Zadar and, later, of the JNA 13th Corps in Bileća.

The OTP appealed the acquittal but, on 20 March 2014, it was rejected by the Court which declared that the prosecution had failed to establish cogent reasons in the interests of justice for departing from settled tribunal jurisprudence.

The Perišić case sparked vigorous debate amongst scholars of international criminal law on the elements of aiding and abetting liability, and on whether the judgement would impact on the Taylor case in Sierra Leone. Charles Taylor, former president of Liberia, was charged on 11 counts and convicted by the Special Court of Sierra Leone (SCSL) Trial Chamber for aiding and abetting the crimes of the Revolutionary United Front/Armed Forces Revolutionary Council (RUF/AFRC) in Sierra Leone, in providing them with financial support, military training, personnel, arms and ammunition. The facts of the two cases were similar in two important aspects. Firstly, neither Perišić nor Taylor was part of, nor found to have had command responsibility over, the army/group that carried out the crimes in question. Secondly, neither of the accused was in geographical proximity to the location of the crimes. In regard to the specific direction of aiding and abetting, however, the Appeals Chamber of the SCSL, confirming the Trial Chamber judgement, explicitly rejected that 'specific direction' is a distinct element of the actus reus of aiding and abetting.[85]

Stanisic and Simatovic

The Stanisic and Simatovic case was similar to that of Perišić in that all indictees were Serbian nationals, and both cases also revolved primarily around 'specific direction' in aiding and abetting. Jovica Stanisic was head of the Serbian State Security Service (*Drzavna bezbednost*) of the Internal Affairs Ministry, where Franko Simatovic was also employed. They were acquitted by Majority on all counts, but due to Trial Chamber legal errors, the case was remitted for retrial.

Both defendants were accused as JCE members of having directed, organized, equipped, trained, armed and financed secret units of the Serbian State Security which murdered, persecuted and expelled non-Serb civilians from Croatia and Bosnia and Herzegovina between April 1991 and 31 December 1995. They were indicted for four counts of crimes against humanity, and one war crimes count. Both were arrested on 13 March 2003.

After many delays, the trial began in June 2009. On 30 May 2013, both indictees were acquitted, by majority. The judges, Judge Picard dissenting, found that the crimes charged in the indictment were committed by the *Drzavna bezbednost* but held that Stanisic and Simatovic could not be held criminally responsible, and were unable to conclude that the Accused shared the intent to further the common criminal purpose of the JCE. The Chamber also found that the prosecutor had failed to prove beyond reasonable doubt that Stanisic or Simatovic had planned or ordered the crimes. On aiding and abetting, the majority determined that although they rendered assistance to the special units, it was not specifically directed towards committing crimes.

In a hard-hitting 15-page Dissenting Opinion, Judge Picard argued that the *sole* reasonable interpretation of the vast amount of evidence received was that the Accused shared with the other members of the JCE the intent to establish their control by deporting the non-Serb population by criminal means.[86]

> My colleagues have reviewed the evidence in an isolated fashion . . . whereas it is my profound conviction that it is when one surveys the entire picture that one is able to view the situation as it really was. It is likewise necessary, in my view, to assess these events by taking into account the broader military and political context at that time.[87]

She considered that, even applying the current threshold for aiding and abetting to the specific facts of this case, the 'specific direction' requirement could be inferred from the Accused's actions.[88]

> The Accused in this case knowingly funded and armed criminals, and even trained them in illegal warfare (human shields) so that they could commit the crimes which the Accused knew (majority: *must have known*) these men would ultimately commit. If we cannot find that the Accused aided and abetted those crimes, I would say we have come to a dark place in international law indeed. It is a place, in the words spoken by the Honorable Judge Robert

> H. Jackson in 1949, where 'law has terrors only for little men and takes note only of little wrongs'.[89]

Presiding Judge Orie wrote a six-page Separate Opinion in response, largely reiterating the legal arguments set out in the Judgement.[90] In the later *Mladic* Judgement where Orie was also presiding judge, this was extended to all indictees from Serbia previously charged with involvement in a JCE in Bosnia and Herzegovina.[91]

The prosecution appealed, and the Appeals Chamber, on 15 December 2015, found that on the basis of errors in the Trial Chamber Judgement, the case should be retried on all counts of the indictment under Rule 117(C) of the rules, Judge Afande dissenting, and Judge Agius dissenting on aiding and abetting liability. On JCE liability, the Appeals Chamber observed that in deciding on the *mens rea* of Stanisic and Simatovic, the Trial Chamber did not firstly adjudicate whether the elements of *actus reus* of JCE liability were fulfilled. On the issue of 'specific direction' as an element of aiding and abetting liability, the Appeals Chamber cited the Appeals Judgement in *Šainović et al.* which, after reviewing ICTY and ICTR jurisprudence and customary international law, rejected the position adopted by the Perišić Appeals Chamber, declaring it to be 'in direct and material conflict with the prevailing jurisprudence on the *actus reus* of aiding and abetting liability and with customary international law', and held that specific direction is not an element of aiding and abetting liability.[92] Subsequently, the *Popovic et al.* Appeals Judgement also reaffirmed that 'specific direction' is not an element of aiding and abetting.[93]

The decision to remit the case for retrial was based on the fact that it was considered inappropriate for the Appeals Chamber to analyse the entire trial record without having directly heard the witnesses, a decision lamentably not replicated by the Appeals Chamber in *Šešelj*.

Conclusion

The failure to indict timeously (or at all) a number of senior military and political figures involved in the wars in former Yugoslavia, and the limited scope of some other indictments, had several consequences, not least in contributing to the consolidation of an ethnically 'pure' para-state in the middle of Europe which stunted the economic development of Bosnia and Herzegovina, and destabilized it politically. Yet the tribunal's hands were tied by international priorities, including the pursuit of a political settlement without due regard for justice or the realities on the ground, which involved engaging closely with the perpetrators.

Inconsistent sentencing at The Hague has been widely criticized on several levels and reflected different legal systems and individual standards. Plea bargaining, frequently used in national courts in common law countries, may have saved time but proved to be a dubious practice in the context of an international conflict where heinous crimes on a massive scale had been committed. The case of Biljana Plavsic, who was indicted for genocide yet escaped with a lenient sentence, was illustrative, as her opportunism was mistaken for remorse, and her brief presidency of Republika Srpska, and promise to root out corruption, blinded some international observers to her less savoury characteristics.

The ethnic balancing policy espoused by Carla Del Ponte in the early 2000s was a desperate measure to counter claims of partisanship, and encourage the surrender of major indictees from Serbia to The Hague. Although to some extent it was effective, it inevitably involved an imbalance in indictments which fostered resentment amongst communities on the ground and resulted in acquittals of persons who should not have ended up in The Hague in the first place. It was also a waste of time and precious resources.

The surprising acquittals of several senior political and military figures from Serbia, Croatia and Kosovo in 2012 and 2013 divided both judges and international lawyers. Senior tribunal judges were seen to have diametrically opposed views on the evidence, including aiding and abetting, and special direction, which challenged previous ICTY jurisprudence. They also raised the question of external political influence, as some dissenting judges obliquely suggested. The acquittals of Perišić, Stanisic and Simatovic meant that out of over 100 ICTY convictions none were from Serbia proper. This may have stifled Serbia's argument that the ICTY was a kangaroo court, but is likely to have political implications for the region, which are yet to be fully assessed.

Notes

1 Judge Michele Picard, Dissenting Opinion, *Prosecutor v Jovica Stanisic and Franko Simatovic,* Trial Chamber Judgement, 30 May 2013, para. 2406.
2 See interview with Marko Hoare, 'Carla Del Ponte Stopped the Indictment Against Top Serbian Military and Political Officials', *Hrvatski List*, 16 April 2007.
3 *Prosecutor v Zeljko Raznatovic*, Indictment, www.icty.org/x/cases/zeljko_raznjatovic/ind/en/ark-ii970930e.pdf
4 There was no official explanation for the time-frame of the indictment. Author's discussion with Prosecutor Alan Tieger, The Hague, October 1996.
5 See Chapter 4.
6 See Chapter 5, and Hodge, op. cit., pp. 184–190 for competing international agendas in Kosovo.
7 For discussion on this, see 'Sentencing of International Crimes at the ICTY and ICTR: Consistency of Sentencing Case Law, Barbara Hola, Amsterdam Law Forum, Fall issue, 2012.
8 ICTY, Rules of Procedure & Evidence.
9 Ibid.
10 Sentencing Council. Reduction in Sentence for a Guilty Plea. Definitive Guideline.www.sentencingcouncil.org.uk/wp-content/uploads/Reduction-in-Sentence-for-Guilty-plea-Definitive-Guide_FINAL_WEB.pdf
11 Milan Babić, Predrag Banović, Miroslav Bralo, Ranko Češić, Miroslav Deronjić, Damir Došen, Dražen Erdemovič, Miodrag Jokić, Goran Jelisić, Dragan Kolundžija, Darko Mrđa, Dragan Nikolić, Momir Nikolić, Dragan Obrenović, Biljana Plavšić, Ivica Rajić, Duško Sikirica, Milan Simić, Stevan Todorović and Dragan Zelenović
12 Dragan Obrenovic, Guilty Plea Statement, 30 October 2003.
13 See, for instance, Darko Mrdja, https://iwpr.net/global-voices/mrdja-guilty-plea-sparks-anger

14 Theodor Meron, then president of the ICTY, indicated in his report to the UN Security Council in October 2003 that the completion of trials would depend on several factors, including the number of guilty pleas entered, without which the tribunal would be unable to meet its completion strategy.

15 Momir Nikolic, assistant commander for security and intelligence of the VRS at Bratunac, was arrested in 2002 for genocide and crimes against humanity, and initially pleaded not guilty. He changed his plea to guilty the following year and was convicted in 2006 for participating in the murder of thousands of Bosniak civilians. Nikolic agreed to testify in other trials against his former war commanders. He was sentenced to 26 years' imprisonment, reduced on appeal to 20, and spent just 7 years in a Finnish state prison. He was granted early release in 2014.

16 On this, see Michael P. Scharf, 'Trading Justice for Efficiency: Plea-Bargaining and International Tribunals', *Journal of International Criminal Justice*, Vol.2, Issue 4, 1 December 2004, pp. 1070–1081.

17 Ibid. Dragan Nikolic, commander of the 'Susica' detention camp in Brcko, was the first to be indicted by the ICTY in 1994 for subjecting Muslim and other non-Serb detainees to murder, rape and torture and participated in creating an atmosphere of terror in the camp. It was not until 2000 that he was arrested by SFOR. He pleaded not guilty, and it was only in 2003 that he entered a guilty plea. He was sentenced to 20 years on appeal, but served just seven in an Italian state prison and was granted early release in 2013.

18 Janine Natalya Clark, 'Plea Bargaining at the ICTY: Guilty Pleas and Reconciliation', *European Journal of International Law*, Vol.20, Issue 2, 2009, p. 432.

19 Mirjan Damaska, 'Negotiated Justice in International Criminal Courts', *Journal of International Criminal Justice*, Vol.2, Issue 4, 1 December 2004, pp. 1018–1039.

20 See Carla Del Ponte's later account of being deceived by Plavsic. *Madame Prosecutor*, op. cit., p. 161.

21 *Prosecutor v Momcilo Krajisnik and Biljana Plavsic,* Amended Consolidated Indictment, Count 3, Persecutions.

22 *Prosecutor v Biljana Plavsic,* Alan Tieger, 18 December 2002, pp. 626–627.

23 Ibid. Carla Del Ponte, pp. 637–638.

24 Ibid., p. 651.

25 Statement of Guilt by Biljana Plavsic, 17 December 2002, pp. 609–612.

26 BBC, 27 February 2003.

27 Mann, p. 389.

28 Shatzmiller, p. 58.

29 *Prosecutor v Plavsic,* Trial Chamber Judgement, 27 February 2003.

30 Ibid. Factual Basis for Plea of Guilt, 30 September 2002.

31 Ibid. Sentencing Hearing Press Release, 27 February 2003.

32 Del Ponte, op. cit., p. 161, originally in La Caccia: Io e i criminali di guerra', Feltrinelli, 2008, p. 175.

33 Del Ponte, op. cit., p. 161, and La Caccia, p. 175. *Prosecutor v Plavsic,* 17 December 2002, pp. 514–517.

34 *BBC News*, 17 December 2002.

35 Interview with Biljana Plavsic, reported in 'Zatvorski dani B. Plavsic', *B92,* 12 March 2005, and *Glas javnosti,* 13 March 2005, and 'Plavsic retracts war crimes confession', *Daniel Uggelberg Goldberg,* The Local *(Stockholm), 26 January 2009. [Swedish original:* www.vi-tidningen.se/templates/Arti

36 Plavsic reiterated her position to ICTY Prosecutor Dermot Groome, who travelled to Sweden in an attempt to compel her to testify against Milosevic. Del Ponte, op. cit., pp. 161–162, La Caccia, pp. 175–176. Del Ponte claimed in her memoirs that she tried to put Plavsic on trial for violating her plea agreement, but that her endeavour failed.

37 'Zatvorski dani. . . ', op. cit., and *Prosecutor v Krajisnik* 6 and 7 July 2006. Plavsic also refused to testify for the prosecution in the Stakic case.

38 See Hodge, op. cit., pp. 140, 144., and Bildt, pp. 73–80. RS premier, Milorad Dodik later remarked that the aid pledged to RS was beyond all their expectations. *Vecernje novosti,* 11 May 1998.
39 Ibid.
40 RS premier Milorad Dodik provided a government jet to pick up Plavšić and welcomed her to Belgrade, citing 'purely moral reasons' for doing so. He later revealed that he had considered giving Plavšić an office in the Senate.
41 'Biljana Plavsic: Clinton je kriv za zlocin u Srebrenici', *Blic,* 25 March 2016. www.blic.rs/vesti/politika/biljana-plavsic-klinton-je-kriv-za-zlocin-u-srebrenici/k4jxnjc, and *Vecernje Novosti,* 24 March 2016.
42 'Goli Zivot', 9 & 14 August 2014 www.youtube.com/watch?v=UBQe43axhyA; www.youtube.com/watch?v=WYCYbZPu0YU, 24 March 2016.
43 See Hodge, op. cit., pp. 61–68, for analysis of evidence relating to the Ahmici massacre.
44 This may have been partly due to threats and other harassment of witnesses testifying at the tribunal. The witness protection service at The Hague did not cover witnesses once they returned to their villages. See Eric Stover, *The Witnesses, War Crimes and the Promise of Justice in The Hague*, University of Pennsylvania Press, 2007, for discussion of witness testimony in the Lasva Valley Trials.
45 Hadzihasanovic's sentence was originally for five years, reduced on appeal.
46 *Prosecutor v Enver Hadzihasanovic and Amir Kubura*, Appeals Chamber Judgement, 22 April 2008, para. 230.
47 Dusan Knezevic was not a guard at the camps but had sufficient authority to be able to enter and leave the camps at will. *Prosecutor v Mejakic et al*., ICTY Information Sheet.
48 Ibid.
49 Statement by Chief Prosecutor Louise Arbour following the withdrawal of the charges against 14 accused. The Hague, 8 May 1998. Italics added.
50 *Prosecutor v Rasim Delic*, Trial Chamber Judgement, 15 September 2008, Judge Moloto Dissenting, para. 10.
51 Ibid., paras. 18 and 15.
52 This author was informed privately that Delic would have been acquitted on appeal. The tribunal rejected requests from Delic's family for publication of the Appeals Judgement.
53 Oric had already spent over three years in detention at Scheveningen.
54 Judges Liu Daqun and Wolfgang Schomburg appended partly dissenting opinions.
55 *Prosecutor v. Vujadin Popovic, Ljubiša Beara, Drago Nikolic, Radivoje Miletic, Vinko Pandurevic, Ljubomir Borovčanin & Milan Gvero*, indicted between 2002 and 2005. Three were convicted on genocide counts, and all for crimes against humanity.
56 Marko Hoare faults Del Ponte as having a 'muddled' understanding of the chronology and organization of aggression against Bosnia, claiming she did not have a global systemic analysis of the aggression but only the crimes she was familiar with: siege of Sarajevo and Srebrenica massacre.
57 See Chapter 5.
58 On this, see Hodge, op. cit., pp. 193–195.
59 For the 1991 war in Croatia, see Hodge, op. cit. Chapter 1. Between April 1991 and April 1992, between 80,000 and 100,000 Croats and other non-Serb civilians were deported from the SAO Krajina. *Prosecutor v Stanisic & Simatovic*, Judgement, 30 May 2013, Dissenting Opinion of Judge Michele Picard, para. 2373.
60 See also *Serbia v Croatia,* International Court of Justice, 3 February 2015, paras. 467–468.
61 *Prosecutor v Ante Gotovina & Mladen Markac,* Appeals Judgement, 16 November 2012. Dissenting Opinion of Judge Carmel Agius.
62 Ibid. Dissenting Opinion of Judge Fausto Pocar.

63 See 'Impunity for Abuses Committed during "Operation Storm"', *Human Rights Watch Report*, Vo.8, Issue 13, August 1996. On UNPROFOR in Croatia, see Hodge, op. cit., pp. 27–28.

64 'Bosnia Enclave of Bihac Faces 3-Way Siege', *Los Angeles Times*, 25 July 1995.

65 Operation Flash was a strategic victory for Croatia resulting in the capture of territory held by RSK forces around Okučani. The occupied area, situated astride the Zagreb–Belgrade motorway and railroad, had presented Croatia with significant transport problems between Zagreb and eastern Slavonia.

66 Molly Dunigan, *Victory for Hire: Private Security Companies' Impact on Military Effectiveness*, Palo Alto, CA: Stanford University Press, 2011, and for a Croatian account, *Marijan, Davor, Oluja, Zagreb, Croatia: Croatian Memorial Documentation Centre, 2007. See also* Ivo Pukanic, 'US Role in Storm', *Nacional*, 24 May 2005.

67 Former RSK Army commander, Mile Mrksic, a witness in the trial, remarked on the incredible accuracy of the Croatian artillery as it targeted military facilities in Knin and other towns. SENSE, 'Accurate Fire on Military Targets, Random Targeting of Civilians', 19 June 2009.

68 See Bildt, op. cit. Chapter 6, where he refers to Operation Storm (but not Srebrenica) as 'ethnic cleansing'.

69 Application of the Convention on the Prevention and Punishment of the Crime of Genocide (*Croatia v. Serbia*), International Court of Justice, 26 May 2008.

70 UN documents cited by Gotovina's defence team, however, indicated that the plan was to move civilians into Bosnia. The Serb authorities had evidently asked the UN for enough fuel to transport 32,000 refugees to Petrovac and Banja Luka.

71 See also 'Odluku o Povlacenju su Doneli Martic i Mrksic', *Nasa Borba*, August 23, 1995.

72 In Grabovi, for instance, on 25 August 1995, 6 elderly Serb civilians were killed. See also *Croatia v. Serbia,* op. cit. International Court of Justice, 3 February 2015, para. 484, and report by Elisabeth Rehn, Special Rapporteur of the Commission on Human Rights, UN doc. S/1995/933, p. 7, para. 18, cited by ICJ.

73 In 2010, Serbia sued Croatia before the International Court of Justice (ICJ), claiming that the *Oluja* operation constituted genocide. In its Judgement in 2015, the ICJ affirmed that, while the Serbs fled as a direct result of the offensive, it did not constitute a genocide and that there was no 'ethnic cleansing' of civilians. It did, however, confirm that crimes against Serb civilians had been committed by Croatian forces. *Croatia v. Serbia,* ibid., paras. 484–487.

74 See also a report from the Bosnian Ministry of Foreign Affairs, which describes attacks on Srebrenica and Zepa controlled from the VJ command post on Mt. Tara by Perisic. According to the report, units were brought up via the Ljubovija crossing in early July to Srebrenica and the Zepa surroundings. The organized transfer of ammunition and fuel from Serbia allegedly continued during the months when the border between Serbia and Bosnia was supposedly monitored internationally. The monitoring mission, however, never had the technical conditions for effective control. Most crossings were uncontrolled (only 18% controlled), with the numbers of observers constantly on the decline, while the delivery of military aid doubled after January 1995. Military Help from the so-called FRY (S&M) to the so-called RS, August 1994–July 1995. The Republic of Bosnia and Herzegovina, Ministry of Foreign Affairs, August 1995. ICTY doc.03069024-37. See also 'Milosevic Fuels Secret War Across the Drina', *Independent*, 26 July 1995, and *Wall Street Journal*, 1 August 1995.

75 *Prosecutor v Momcilo Perisic*, Trial Chamber Judgement, 6 October 2011, Dissenting Opinion of Judge Moloto on Counts 1–4 and 9–12, paras. 27 and 30.

76 Ibid., para. 32.

77 *Prosecutor v Momcilo Perisic,* pp. 14655–14661, 28 March 2011.

78 Ibid. Appeals Court Judgement, Partially Dissenting Opinion of Judge Liu, 27 February 2013, para. 9. See also Judge Ramaroson's Opinion on 'specific direction'. Opinion Separee du Juge Ramaroson sur la question de la visee specifique dans la complicite par aide et encouragement.

79 Ibid., para. 3.

80 Ibid., para. 5, and Trial Chamber Judgement, para. 1594. Nedo Krayishnik, who had donated large sums of money to Republika Srpska and the military hospital in Belgrade, unwittingly gave evidence that on 18 July 1995, he spent two hours in the company of Perisic and Mladic where there was jovial discussion of the 'liberation' of Srebrenica, and no disagreement between the two. Ibid. transcripts, 3–4 November 2009.

81 Appeals Court Judgement, Partially Dissenting Opinion of Judge Liu, 27 February 2013.

82 Differentiating the two standards enabled the Court to convict Tadic of crimes he had been acquitted of under aiding and abetting since no direct link was established between Tadic and the crimes. See Elies Van Sliedregt, Milestones in International Criminal Justice: Recent Legal Controversies at the UN Yugoslav Tribunal, Chatham House, 16 October 2013.

83 For discussion of this, see Marko Milanovic, 'The Limits of Aiding and Abetting Liability: The ICTY Appeals Chamber Acquits Momcilo Perisic', ejiltalk.org

84 As Milanovic noted, 'it will be practically impossible to convict under aiding and abetting any political or military leader external to a conflict who is assisting one of the parties even while knowing that they are engaging in mass atrocities, so long as the leader is remote from the actual operations . . . and does not leave a smoking gun'. Ibid.

85 *Prosecutor v Charles Ghankay Taylor,* Appeals Chamber Judgement, 26 September 2013, paras. 471–479. The Chamber also noted that the ICTY Appeals Chamber lacked a clear detailed analysis of the authorities supporting the conclusion that specific direction is an element of the actus reus of aiding and abetting liability under customary international law.

86 *Prosecutor v Jovica Stanisic and Franko Simatovic,* Trial Chamber Judgement, Judge Picard Dissenting Opinion, 30 May 2013, para. 2365.

87 Ibid., para. 2367–2368.

88 Ibid., para. 2405.

89 Ibid., para. 2406. Robert H. Jackson, *Nuremberg in Retrospect: Legal Answers to International Lawlessness*, Excerpted from Canadian Bar Association Address, Banff, Alberta, 1 September 1949.

90 *Prosecutor v Jovica Stanisic and Franko Simatovic,* Trial Chamber Judgement. Separate Opinion of Judge Alphons Orie, pp. 868–873, para. 2413.

91 *Prosecutor v Ratko Mladic* Judgement. 'The evidence received by the Trial Chamber did not show that Slobodan Milošević, Jovica Stanišić, Franko Simatović, Željko Ražnatović, or Vojislav Šešelj participated in the realization of the common criminal objective'. Vol.IV, p. 2090, n.15357.

92 In *Sainovic et al.*, the Appeals Chamber rejected the Perisic position. 'The Appeals Chamber disagrees with the holding in the Perisic Appeal Judgement that the Mrksic and Sljivancanin and the Lukić and Lukić Appeal Judgements support that specific direction is an element of the *actus reus* of aiding and abetting . . . the Appeals Chamber has carefully examined the jurisprudence of the Tribunal and the ICTR as well as customary international law, and concludes . . . that "specific direction" is not an element of aiding and abetting liability. . . [and] rejects the approach adopted in the Perišić Appeal Judgement as it is in direct and material conflict with the prevailing jurisprudence on the actus reus of aiding and abetting liability and with customary

international law in this regard'. *Sainovic et al.*, Appeals Judgement Summary, 23 January 2014.

93 'The Appeals Chamber, Judge Niang dissenting in part, finds that Mr. Pandurević has failed to establish any factual or legal error, recalling in particular that "specific direction" is not an element of aiding and abetting liability under customary international law'. *Popovic et al.*, Appeals Judgement Summary, 30 January 2015.

12 The top of the pyramid

Karadzic, Mladic, genocide and the western role

I knew that for the West 10,000 troops would be enough, 5,000 in Zvornik and 5,000 in the Posavina corridor, and the Serbs would be finished.[1]

Introduction

With the death of Slobodan Milosevic, the Karadzic and Mladic trials became the most important in the tribunal's history. Yet, over 20 years after indictment for genocide, their cases were still under appeal. During most of that time both lived freely in Serbia and, since their arrest, have resided at Scheveningen, enjoying privileges unknown in most other European prisons. In the meantime, the tribunal grew ever more distant from the 1990s war crimes it was pledged to address.

On arrival at The Hague, Karadzic argued that US negotiator Richard Holbrooke had promised him amnesty if he retired from active politics. The truth of this may never be known, yet neither Karadzic nor Mladic were arrested following their indictments in 1995, despite international arrest warrants issued by the tribunal, and NATO knowledge of their whereabouts on the ground. Instead, both were secretly included in pre-Dayton talks with Holbrooke, strengthening their defence in court where Karadzic insisted that, while admittedly crimes had been committed, he personally was not responsible. Both he and Mladic brought to their defence convicted war criminals and genocide deniers in an endeavour to promote an alternative version of the Bosnian war, while the discovery in 2013 of Tomasica, the largest mass grave in Bosnia, was excluded from Karadzic's trial, and marginalized in the Mladic judgement.

Meanwhile, at the International Residual Mechanism for Criminal Tribunals (MICT or the Mechanism) which took over from the ICTY in 2018, the Appeals Chamber, while finding Vojislav Šešelj guilty for hate speech in Vojvodina, confirmed his acquittal for war crimes in Bosnia and Croatia, a verdict which did little towards establishing an accurate record of the many atrocities committed under his command.

On trial

Adjudicated facts

The Karadzic case has previously been discussed in relation to self-representation. Karadzic had several other options he would put into play, however, when it came to defending himself in court. One was to challenge the established practice of agreement between prosecution and defence counsel on adjudicated facts.

According to Rule 94 (B) of the Rules of Procedure and Evidence, at the request of a party or *proprio motu*, a Trial Chamber, after hearing the parties, may decide to take judicial notice of adjudicated facts or of the authenticity of documentary evidence from other trials relating to current proceedings. Its use reduces the repetition of testimony and exhibits in successive cases, with the aim of expediting and streamlining proceedings, and narrowing the scope of the litigation to issues particularly in dispute. Approximately 2,300 prior adjudicated facts were entered into the trial record before Karadzic's case began. Sophie Rigney, legal assistant to the Standby Council, argued, however, that the cases revealed a significant shifting in the evidential burden to the accused, which she claimed fundamentally affected the fairness of proceedings. She pointed to the inconsistent record of trial chambers in determining what constituted adjudicated facts. Karadzic, meantime, argued that it would require mounting 'a massive case to rebut the adjudicated facts and assertions of facts in prior statements and testimony', to avoid violating his rights to a fair trial and shifting the burden of proof, and filed for an additional 300 hours.

The inconsistent application of facts between the Trial Chambers alleged by the Karadzic defence was perhaps inevitable given the increasing complexity of some trials and the different judicial systems. Yet, had Karadzic been arrested in 1995 when he was first indicted, the issue of adjudicated facts would not have arisen. Their accumulation was the price (a small one) for 13 years of freedom.

The defence case

Evidence for the defence was heard over 18 months, as Karadzic's witnesses, and others subpoenaed by the Trial Chamber, disputed the Srebrenica genocide, the Sarajevo siege, and responsibility for the 1994 Markale market massacre, painting a totally different picture of the events of 1992–1995, and Karadzic's role therein. Some changed their statements submitted to the OTP once they were in court.[2] Others appeared in court only after guarantees that they would not be arrested for war crimes en route to The Hague.[3] One witness testified on the same day for the Prosecution in *Mladic* and the Defence in *Karadzic*.[4]

Karadzic's defence witnesses included a number convicted by the ICTY or local courts for genocide and crimes against humanity, as well as others who had leading roles in the war under Karadzic's command but had escaped indictment. Amongst them were Momčilo Krajisnik, Stanislav Galic, John/Jovan Zametica, Vujadin Popovic, Milenko Zivanovic, Radoslav Brdjanin, Zeljko Mejakic,

Zdravko Tolimir, Ljubisa Beara, Mico Stanisic, Momčilo Gruban, Milan Martic, Milomir Stakic, Milenko Zivanovic, Vidoje Blagojevic, Miroslav Kvocka, Bosko Mandic, Zdravko Torbica, Gojko Klickovic, Ratko Mladic (who refused to testify), and Vojislav Šešelj.

Military, political and diplomatic figures from the international community were cited by some defence witnesses in support of their arguments, including Lord Carrington, Cyrus Vance, David Owen, Jose Cutileiro, Phillip Corwin, Cedric Thornberry, General Philippe Morillon and General Michael Rose. The testimony of Jovan Zametica, subpoenaed by Karadzic, was of particular note. Zametica had been appointed advisor to Karadzic in February 1994, with responsibility for communications with international institutions. He testified that Karadzic's power did not extend far, that he had agreed to all peace plans, and was not in control of the army.[5] Zametica had been a one-time employee of the International Institute of Strategic Studies (IISS) which, along with other brief academic posts in the UK, might have assisted his credibility in court, albeit that the IISS later disowned him.[6] The Court permitted a lengthy discussion between Karadzic and Zametica about the Srebrenica events, with Karadzic feeding the witness the responses he desired, suggesting a degree of rehearsal.[7] Caroline Egerton cross-examining, discredited Zametica on several issues, including his role in hostage taking, when he threatened that all UN hostages would be killed if NATO attacked. She also reminded Zametica of his BBC Radio interview on 13 July 1995, when he stated that he was informed that the Bosnian Serbs were arresting all Muslim men in Srebrenica in a search for war criminals: 'We are separating the men from women, children and the elderly'.[8] Egerton further referred to a front-page article in *The Independent* on 17 July 1995, entitled 'Bodies Pile Up in Horror in Srebrenica', based on over five hours' footage, showing piles of bodies against a wall riddled with bullet holes. The scene had been filmed in the Srebrenica area on 13 and 14 July by Serbian journalist Zoran Petrovic-Pirocanac and featured in a documentary broadcast by Studio B on 15 July. While this exposed Zametica's lie in denying knowledge of any killings, it also shed light on the degree of international knowledge of the massacres at the time, when negotiations for aid access to Srebrenica was being conducted with Mladic.

Prosecution issues

Due to the tribunal's completion strategy and financial constraints, the prosecutors were restricted in the scope of the indictment, and under heavy pressure to exclude many areas where some of the most heinous crimes against non-Serbs had occurred, amongst them Zvornik, Bratunac, Visegrad, Bijeljina, Doboj, Novo Sarajevo, Bosanska Krupa and Brcko,[9] resulting in the Karadzic indictment for Genocide Count 1 being whittled down to just seven municipalities, and in *Mladic* to six.

In this regard, it has been cogently argued elsewhere that a more systemic problem lay at the heart of the Office of the Prosecution. In his last work, M. Cherif

Bassiouni, often referred to as the 'godfather of international criminal law', examined the consequences of some of the tribunal's rules of procedure and evidence which had been drafted in 1993, in the middle of the Bosnian war.[10]

In Bassiouni's view, the drafters, most of whom were young and had no knowledge of international criminal law, ignored the International Military Tribunals at Nuremberg and Tokyo, and failed to consider that the nature of the Bosnian conflict was more akin to policies and practices that took place in World War II. According to Bassiouni, 'it never made sense to the prosecutors at Nuremberg and Tokyo to look at individual instances of conduct because they were all connected by the same policy and, to a large extent, carried out in the same manner'.[11] Instead of building on the precedents of Nuremberg and Tokyo, the ICTY Rules of Procedure and Evidence were written in such a way as to prevent a holistic approach, whereby the prosecutor could present evidence of a common policy and similar practices. Bassiouni argued that the rules

> left the prosecutor in these individual trials unable to present evidence of the overall context in which alleged crimes were perpetrated. . . [but] instead . . . narrowed the admissibility of evidence to that which directly pertained to the conduct of the accused, without regard to its overall contextual relationship with other similar acts.[12]

This resulted in evidence of the systematic policies employed during the conflict being lost. In the case of mass rape in Foča, for instance, the number prosecuted did not reflect the true nature and overall systemic and largely institutionalized policy of rape and sexual assault in the region throughout the chain of command. Had a holistic approach been adopted, indictments could have expanded the number of those prosecuted, and presented a more accurate picture at the outset of the processes at work across Bosnia and Herzegovina.

As discussed earlier, the ICTY prosecution faced a number of hurdles from the start. With no clearly detailed mandate, as well as logistical and financing issues, a decision had to be made as to the primary criterion for initiating investigations. Two of the lawyers working in the Prosecutor's Office in 1994, Morten Bergasmo and Michael J Keegan, outlined the choices the tribunal faced in light of the staggering number of crimes committed and the potential number of victims and perpetrators.[13] Was it more important to opt for a limited prosecution with a greater likelihood of conviction, or to address more directly the interests of the victims and prove the full nature and extent of the crimes committed, and victimization caused?

In state criminal investigations, investigators are despatched to the crime scene over which, given their authority in the system, they have full access and control; scale is not usually an issue and, where it is, the prosecutor will normally limit the number of charges that present the best chance of conviction. For genocide and crimes against humanity investigated by an international war crimes tribunal, on the other hand, it is the *context* in which the crimes were committed that is more significant. The identity of the actual perpetrator is initially of less concern than the context and establishing who was in charge and responsible for the broader onslaught.

Over 20 years on, the magnitude of the crimes and the linkage between them became increasingly obscured, as prosecutors continued with a 'bottom-up' pyramid approach, positing that it was necessary to begin with evidence against the actual perpetrators in order to establish linkage to the top of the command chain.[14] Yet, how was this so when ICTY Chief Prosecutor Richard Goldstone had considered that there was already sufficient evidence in 1995 to indict both Karadzic and Mladic on two separate genocide counts?

Admittedly, the tribunal was in an invidious position, operating in an environment of war, or early post-war adjustment, where it lacked the authority to make arrests and bring the main perpetrators to trial in the early stages. But its main problem was the lack of cooperation, not merely from the states involved but internationally, at both civilian and military level. An added difficulty was that, unlike in Srebrenica in July 1995, many parts of Bosnia, where equally heinous crimes had been committed, were inaccessible to independent investigators and journalists at the time, and prosecutors were often forced to rely on witnesses who had managed to survive and possessed enough courage to testify before an international court. As time went on, this issue became more acute.

The pyramid approach had an increasing impact on judgements as the years passed, and memories dimmed, and was particularly evident in *Karadzic* and *Mladic*, as demonstrated in their first-instance acquittals for genocide in the Bosnian municipalities in 1992.

Tomasica

At the end of October 2013, a mass grave containing the remains of 370 people killed during the Bosnian war was uncovered at Tomasica, an abandoned iron mine near Prijedor, in an area covering more than 5,000 square metres, and 10 metres deep. Preliminary findings indicated that the mine was used to store bodies of victims killed in the summer of 1992. The bodies were unloaded from trucks, and many of them were later moved to secondary locations. Mladic was aware, as he noted in his war journal on 27 May 1993 referring to the Tomasica site, of Prijedor police force chief Simo Drljaća's request for assistance to remove around 5,000 bodies previously buried in the mine.[15]

In November 2013, ICTY President Meron visited Tomasica, and the following March, the prosecutors in *Karadzic* argued that although the trial was nearly over, the evidence was 'highly probative and directly relevant to the charged JCE . . . in the context of the permanent removal of non-Serbs from Bosnian Serb claimed territory', and that its value outweighed any prejudice that its admission might cause the accused.[16] It would have taken just a day to present, the prosecutors argued, with three expert witnesses ready to testify within weeks. The Trial Chamber, however, denied their request on grounds of expediency, Judge Kwon ruling that the value of the evidence was 'speculative' as the forensic work had not been completed, and that reopening the case would prompt a request from Karadzic to present evidence in rejoinder, resulting in more than 'a minimal amount of additional time to the trial'.[17]

In other circumstances, grounds of expediency might be considered reasonable, given the tribunal's completion schedule. But the judges in *Karadzic* had sat through hundreds of hours of testimony from convicted criminals, genocide deniers, and others ready to commit perjury, who had been accorded virtual free rein to express, and have recorded in the ICTY annals, testimony which was mostly mendacious, and at odds with proven facts. The judges' decision to accept Karadzic's request to reject the prosecution's application considerably advantaged Karadzic over his victims, especially given the Trial Chamber's focus on numbers killed in their ruling on genocide. Their response illustrated graphically the triumph of bureaucracy over justice, particularly in view of the time and expenditure involved in numerous court hearings necessitated by the hundreds of motions submitted by Karadzic since arriving at The Hague.[18]

Just months later, on 26 August 2014, the Mladic trial chamber granted the prosecution's motion to reopen the case-in-chief on Tomasica, ruling that the fresh evidence was relevant and had probative value, also that the delay would not be undue.[19]

Accordingly, several senior expert witnesses gave evidence at the Mladic trial on Tomasica. Thomas Parsons, Director of Forensic Science at the International Commission on Missing Persons, examined on 29 June 2015, testified that

> [the] total from Tomasica was 385 distinct DNA profiles indicating different individuals . . . some of those individuals also had portions of bodies discovered at Jakarina Kosa. But for individuals found only in Jakarina Kosa, there is an additional 211 individuals. In addition we've recently provided information to the Office of the Prosecutor on eight DNA profiles from Jakarina Kosa that have not had matches. So if we add all those – figures together, the number of individuals detected by DNA in both of those graves is 604.[20]

Forensic archaeologist Ian Hanson, who had attended the exhumations of bodies from the Tomasica mass grave on behalf of the International Commission of Missing Persons, testified that 401 'groups' of victim remains in civilian clothing were recovered at that location in 2013. Twelve years earlier, at least 298 bodies had been exhumed in nearby Jakarina Kosa, where they had been transferred from Tomasica. The ground had been probed in 2002 but the probes did not go deep enough and therefore yielded no results.[21]

Demographic expert Ewa Tabeau testified that out of 385 bodies exhumed from the Tomasica grave, a total of 123 were identified as people killed in attacks by

Bosnian Serb forces in Bosniak villages, and the Keraterm camp. She confirmed Thomas Parsons' testimony that 604 people had been exhumed from the Tomasica and Jakarina Kosa mass graves.[22]

None of this evidence was included in the Karadzic trial and, while the *Mladic* Trial Chamber admitted the Tomasica evidence, it was omitted from the judges' analysis of genocide in the municipalities.

The Karadzic judgement

Following a trial record of over 48,000 transcript pages, 95,000 pages of filings and over 190 pages of admitted exhibits, totalling over 330,000 pages of trial record, the judgement came in four ostensibly impressive volumes. Yet the structure of the indictment and the approach adopted by the Trial Chamber illustrate some of the concerns raised by Bassiouni.

The following comments are limited mainly to issues related to the Trial Chamber's findings on Genocide Count 1. The methodology, including the separation of the components and the municipalities, and the focus on individual *proven* numbers killed in relation to the total population in each municipality in determining genocide, was misleading when related to Bosnian war crimes. This approach led the judges to conclude that the sharp discrepancy in the non-Serb population in many municipalities between 1991 and 1995 was mainly the result of removal.[23] The fact that the removal was forcible and frequently resulted in loss of life was not reflected in the Trial Chamber conclusions. The refusal to reopen the case to include evidence on Tomasica further indicates the priority accorded to protocol, as opposed to aiming to produce a more accurate record of the extent of crimes committed in the municipalities.

In considering Count 1, the judges conceded that Serb forces took control of municipalities in Bosnian Serb-claimed territory, during which there was a widespread and systematic pattern of crimes committed against Bosnian Muslim and Croat civilians, and that a vast number were forcibly displaced, resulting in drastic changes to the ethnic composition in the municipalities. They recognized that Karadzic was at the forefront of the Bosnian Serb political and governmental organs and the VRS in promoting the ideology and policies, including the establishment and perpetuation of inhumane living conditions in around 50 detention facilities, where detainees were subjected to torture, beatings, physical and psychological abuse, rape and sexual assault by Serb forces, resulting in serious mental or physical suffering or injury to the victims.[24] The Trial Chamber also found that Bosnian Muslims and Croats were removed from positions of authority and dismissed from their employment in multiple municipalities,[25] that some were killed in mass executions, or following attacks on non-Serb villages,[26] and that the perpetrators chose their victims in the municipalities on the basis of their identity as Bosnian Muslims or Bosnian Croats. The crimes were committed, therefore, with discriminatory intent, facts already confirmed in previous judgements.

Yet these findings were not reflected in the judges' ruling on Count 1, genocide in the municipalities. In referring to Article 4(2) of the ICTY Statute,

> Genocide means any of the following acts committed with intent to destroy, in whole or in part, a national, ethnical, racial or religious group, as such,
>
> (a) killing members of the group;
> (b) causing serious bodily or mental harm to members of the group;
> (c) deliberately inflicting on the group conditions of life calculated to bring about its physical destruction in whole or in part; and
> (d) imposing measures intended to prevent births within the group;

the Trial Chamber was satisfied for the purpose of Article 4(2)(a) of the Statute that members of the Bosnian Muslim and Bosnian Croat groups were killed, and for the purpose of Article 4(2)(b) that 'members of the Bosnian Muslim and Bosnian Croat groups were subjected to serious bodily or mental harm in the Count 1 Municipalities', the acts being 'of such a serious nature as to contribute or tend to contribute to the destruction of the Bosnian Muslims and Bosnian Croats in the Count 1 Municipalities'.[27] Yet when it came to Article 4(2)(c), the Trial Chamber concluded that the genocidal intent, or *mens rea*, was missing:

> While the conditions in the detention facilities in the Count 1 Municipalities were dreadful and had serious effects on the detainees, the Chamber is not convinced that the evidence before it demonstrates that they ultimately sought the physical destruction of the Bosnian Muslims and Bosnian Croats. The Chamber is therefore not satisfied for the purpose of Article 4(2)(c) of the Statute that conditions of life calculated to bring about the physical destruction of the Bosnian Muslims and Bosnian Croats were deliberately inflicted on these groups in the Count 1 Municipalities.[28]
>
> Given that the intent of the named alleged JCE members, including the Accused, is intrinsically connected to all of the evidence on the record pertaining to the existence and the scope of the Overarching JCE, the Chamber conducted a holistic and contextualised assessment of this evidence and will indicate below, where relevant, the appropriate cross-references to these sections.[29]

In doing so, however, the Chamber focused on the ideology and objectives of Karadzic and the Bosnian Serb leadership, and concluded that although speeches and statements made by Karadzic threatened the 'disappearance', 'annihilation', 'vanish[ing]', 'elimination' and 'extinction' of the Bosnian Muslims, the evidence also showed an intent to create an ethnically homogeneous Serb state in Bosnia and Herzegovina, and to separate and remove non-Serbs from Bosnian Serb-controlled territory. The judges stressed the need to consider the statements in the full context in which they were delivered, and not in isolation.[30] They concluded from reported or intercepted phone conversations Karadzic had conducted with various people from 1990, that from 1990 and into mid-1991, the political objective of Karadzic and the Bosnian Serb leadership was to preserve Yugoslavia and to prevent the separation or independence of Bosnia and Herzegovina, which would result in a separation of Bosnian Serbs from Serbia:

> The Accused was passionate about a common Serb identity and working towards creating a unified Serbian nation, which was viewed as an age-old aspiration of all Serbs living in one state. The Accused continued to adhere to this ideology of Serb unity and the importance of creating a Serb state into 1992.[31]

Yet the judges did not appear to take sufficient account of the mendacity and duplicity displayed by Karadzic on numerous occasions, nor of his endeavours to conceal Bosnian Serb leaders' objectives from the international community.[32] In places, the Trial Chamber's analysis displayed an incomplete grasp of the situation on the ground in 1992 and a less than clear understanding of the precise chronology of events. On 18 October 1991, Lord Carrington had presented a plan to all six republics for a loose Yugoslav confederation, which was accepted by five of them, including Bosnia, but rejected by Milosevic on behalf of Serbia. It was only then that the Bosnian leadership under Izetbegovic began its bid for independence. Yet the Trial Chamber alluded to the Carrington Plan merely in passing (citing witness Okun in *Krajisnik*), missing its significance.[33] Serbian Autonomous Areas (SAOs) had been well established across Croatia and Bosnia by that time, ready for the violent takeover of municipalities which they by then controlled.[34]

The credulity displayed towards Karadzic's public statements was further reflected in the judges' consideration of mitigating circumstances, including Karadzic's expression of sympathy to the victims.[35] Hardly the holistic approach the Trial Chamber claimed to have adopted! What the analysis of Bosnian Serb leaders' comments did unwittingly reveal, however, was the steady expansion of their objectives between 1990 and 1995, as they noted little serious international opposition to their war strategy, or indeed to the crimes themselves, as reflected in the 'even-handed' peace plans.

Another issue was the separation of the indictment into four components: the Municipalities in 1992, Sarajevo from 1992–1995, Srebrenica 1995 and hostage taking. This meant that the siege of – and crimes committed in – Sarajevo over three-and-a-half years were not included in the genocide count. It also meant that the significance of the continuum of killings, aggression, rape and sexual assault, and other crimes from early 1992 to 1995 was lost. Undue importance was attached to the 'lull' in 1993–1994, which was simply the result of Serb(ian) territorial objectives having already been largely achieved. The ongoing VRS offensives in the Drina valley, including Srebrenica in early 1993, Goradze in April 1994, and in Bihac, another UN 'safe area' under siege and subjected to frequent attack culminating in Autumn 1994, areas still targeted by the Karadzic leadership, were also omitted from the genocide indictment, not to mention the continuing persecution of non-Serbs in Banja Luka and other Serb-controlled areas.

An additional discrepancy was in the judges' findings relating to Karadzic's overall control, where they concluded that he had *de jure* control over the Sarajevo-Romanija Corps (SRK) and VRS, which he was able to exercise throughout the conflict. Yet, if this was so, how was Karadzic responsible for genocide in Srebrenica *only* from 13 July 1995, when men and women were separated? The practice was hardly new in the Bosnian war, occurring as early as 1992 under Karadzic's leadership.

With regard to the detention/concentration camps, the judges, while acknowledging that 'the conditions in the detention facilities in the Count 1 Municipalities were dreadful and had serious effects on the detainees', were not convinced that the evidence demonstrated that the perpetrators ultimately sought the physical destruction of the Bosnian Muslims and Bosnian Croats. What was not considered here was the 'premature' closure in August 1992 of the most notorious camps, due *solely* to global exposure by US and British journalists which saved countless lives and led to the closure of many of the camps, as inmates were moved to relatively safer environments.

Then there was the fixation on numbers killed. The Chamber held that

> It is well established that where a conviction for genocide relies on the intent to destroy a group 'in part' *such part must be a substantial part of the whole protected group*. The targeted portion must be a 'significant enough [portion] to have an impact on the group as a whole'.[36]

The judges cited earlier ICTY judgements on genocide, including the Krstic Appeal Judgement, in determining substantiality.

> The numeric size of the targeted part of the group is the ***necessary*** and important starting point. . . . The number of individuals targeted should be evaluated not only in absolute terms, but also in relation to the overall size of the entire group. In addition to the numeric size of the targeted portion, its prominence within the group can be a useful consideration. If a specific part of the group is emblematic of the overall group, or is essential to its survival, that may support a finding that the part qualifies as substantial within the meaning of Article 4.[37]

But proportionality does not form part of the Genocide Convention. Had a holistic approach been taken, it would have been possible to conclude that, cumulatively, across many more municipalities than cited in the Count 1 indictment, the Karadzic regime actions were directed towards the removal of non-Serbs from large swathes of Bosnia and Herzegovina by whatever means required, including the killing of tens of thousands of civilians.[38]

The Tolimir Appeals Judgement is of more relevance in this respect. Recalling the *Croatia v Serbia* case concerning *actus reus*, which in turn cites earlier ICTY judgements, the Appeals Chamber found that

> the deliberate infliction on the protected group of conditions of life calculated to bring about its physical destruction in whole or in part covers methods of

> physical destruction, other than killing, whereby the perpetrator ultimately seeks the death of the members of the group. Such methods of destruction include deprivation of food, medical care, shelter or clothing, as well as lack of hygiene, systematic expulsion from homes, or exhaustion as a result of excessive work or physical exertion.[39]

This conclusion, quoting Article 4(2)(c) of the ICTY Statute, could equally have been applied to the detention camps and other killings in 1992, and areas under siege between 1992 and 1995. The Trial Chamber in *Karadzic* opted for a narrower interpretation, indicating inconsistency in ICTY jurisprudence on this important issue.

*

It may be recalled that on 28 June 2012, after the prosecution in *Karadzic* had rested its case, the Trial Chamber, Judge Kwon presiding, found there was insufficient evidence that could lead to a conviction on genocide in the municipalities.[40] This was reversed on 11 July 2013, in a Rule 98 *bis* Appeals Judgement, and the charges reinstated. However, Judge Kwon in the *Milosevic* case had dissented from the Majority, who concluded that there was sufficient evidence that genocide was committed in the municipalities. It was predictable, therefore, that he would maintain that view in *Karadzic*, where he was the presiding judge.[41] This is of particular relevance in light of a later MICT holding, where three judges were removed from the Mladic appeals panel due to alleged possible bias in some of their earlier judgements.

It has been argued by some lawyers that 'the crimes in the municipalities are no less bad simply because they do not satisfy the legal criteria for genocide; their victims are no less dead, and their perpetrators no less culpable'.[42] Agreed on one level, since there is arguably little moral difference between genocide and crimes against humanity. The difference is more practical. Had genocide been determined by the ICTY in the Municipalities in 1992, there would have been an international obligation to act to prevent or halt it, with probable reparations for victims.

The final ICTY judgements

The last days of the ICTY may be more remembered for the dramatic and public suicide of Slobodan Praljak, the former Bosnian Croat general, than for the judgement of Ratko Mladic, the former Bosnian Serb commander whose case was amongst the most important of the 161 cases before the tribunal.

Both judgements were generally expected to be non-controversial. Undoubtedly, that is what the tribunal itself would have wished. But issues which had lain partly dormant in recent years flared up once more, with the ethnic divide deepening, as the Trial Chamber's decision to acquit Mladic for genocide in the Bosnian municipalities exacerbated the injustice already felt by many of Bosnia's non-Serb survivors, while nationalist sentiment within Croat(ian) communities was revived. Bosnian Croat Jadranko Prlic and five others, including Praljak, were convicted in 2013 for war crimes and crimes against humanity in Bosnia and Herzegovina. The case itself had been relatively low key, despite its complexity and length, but Praljak's self-inflicted death overshadowed his crimes, and nationalism in Croatia, and especially in Croat-dominated parts of Bosnia, came instantly to the fore, rendering some of the survivors of their crimes more vulnerable than at any time since the war ended.

Yet, while the Praljak drama may be most widely remembered, and confirmed that leading politicians in Croatia were key figures in a JCE aimed at creating a Croatian entity in Bosnia and Herzegovina through 'ethnic cleansing' of the Muslim population, some of the more recent cases produced verdicts which fell short of justice and risked presenting a skewed record of the Bosnian war, as exemplified in the Mladic judgement.

The genocide in Srebrenica had already been confirmed in a number of ICTY judgements, and at the ICJ, suggesting that the *Mladic* Trial Chamber would follow suit. And, while it was also hoped by many that the Court would rule for genocide in the municipalities (Count 1), it was more realistically expected that it would echo the Karadzic judgement in limiting the Bosnian genocide to Srebrenica. Earlier defendants indicted for genocide in the municipalities from 1992 had all been acquitted on that charge, often based on scant reasoning.[43] But Mladic's acquittal was particularly disquieting, in light of the Trial Chamber's handling of the evidence.

Due to the tribunal's completion strategy and financial constraints, the prosecutors in *Mladic* (as earlier in *Karadzic*) were restricted in the scope of the indictment, and under heavy pressure to exclude many areas where some of the most heinous crimes against humanity had occurred, not least Višegrad, Bijeljina, Doboj and Brčko. The indictment was instead whittled down to just six municipalities. Also, as in *Karadzic*, the judges noted crimes against humanity committed by Serb forces under Mladic's command, including in Bosanski Novi, Novi Grad, Banja Luka, Bjeljina, Ilidja, Kalinovnik, Novo Sarajevo, Pale, Rogatica, Vogošća, Zvornik, Bosanska Krupa, Bosanski Novi, Brčko, Hadžići, Sokolac and Sanski Most, and conceded that brutal mass executions had occurred, with a large number of Bosnian Muslims and Bosnian Croats in some of the municipalities subjected to killings and/or serious bodily or mental harm.

Yet the judges failed to acknowledge the continuum of events from 1992 leading up to the Srebrenica genocide and, in adopting a piecemeal approach to the crimes, essentially accepted the argument put by Mladic's defence team in assessing the percentage of non-Serbs killed in the six municipalities in relation to the total non-Serb population of Bosnia and Herzegovina. Addressing each in turn, in what appeared to be a cut-n-paste exercise, the judges arrived at the conclusion that the proven number killed formed a very small percentage of the whole, not sufficiently 'substantial' to constitute genocide. The majority (Presiding Judge Orie dissenting) went on to hold that the *physical perpetrators* in some municipalities intended to destroy the Bosnian Muslims there as a part of the protected group, but that they formed a relatively small part of that group. Following from this, the judges unanimously held that genocide had not been committed, discounting the distinct pattern of attacks across Bosnia which made it reasonable to assume that those 'physical perpetrators' were under central command and that they felt they could act with impunity. This approach, besides departing from the Genocide Convention, was an exercise in progressive reductionism which failed to embody the essence of the Bosnian war, where nearly a hundred thousand died in 1992, most of them civilians.

A further controversial aspect of the judgement was the declaration that no evidence had been produced by the prosecution to demonstrate that Milosevic, Stanisic, Simatovic, Šešelj and Arkan (Zeljko Raznatovic), all Serbian citizens, were members of the Joint Criminal Enterprise, despite the evidence of the Mladic diaries not available in earlier judgements.[44] This not only challenged previous tribunal jurisprudence but also inferred that Serbia had no part in the Bosnian war, inaccurately rendering, in terms of these last two judgements, Croatia as the only outside state with responsibility.

As in previous indictments, the siege of Sarajevo and its ten municipalities where at least 10,000 civilians had been killed, including 1,500 children, and where up to 3,700 shells a day fell on the city, was considered separately, and not within Genocide Count 1. Although the Chamber found that members of the VRS intended to spread terror amongst the population of Sarajevo and that the infliction of terror was the primary purpose of the sniping and shelling, it did not pay sufficient regard to the linkage with other crimes across Bosnia, and the knock-on effect of the siege, and its profound effect on the psyche and future of the population.[45]

Finally, the Tomasica mass grave finding in 2013, although included in some detail in the evidence, was not reflected in the judgement, relating to genocide in Prijedor. Its significance in respect of the total numbers killed in that municipality was therefore lost.

The Mladic appeal was transferred to the Mechanism where new challenges awaited, as three judges were removed from the appellate procedure on grounds of alleged bias.

From ICTY to MICT

The MICT took over from the ICTY in 2018 with a mandate to perform essential functions previously carried out by the ICTY. On its establishment in 2012, President Theodor Meron declared that the Security Council in establishing the Mechanism 'had helped to guarantee that the closure of the two pioneering *ad hoc* tribunals does not open the way for impunity to reign once more'.[46] Regrettably, its first year's performance did little to merit Meron's optimism, as challenges from defence lawyers in late 2018 revealed chinks in the very fabric of the institution.

Šešelj appeals judgement

On 18 April 2018, the Mechanism issued its final judgement in the Šešelj case. Two years earlier, Vojislav Šešelj had been acquitted on all nine counts of war crimes and crimes against humanity between August 1991 and September 1993.

The Prosecution appealed the judgement, and Šešelj, now residing in Serbia, failed to respond. In his absence, the Appeals Chamber, with Judge Meron presiding, reversed the Trial Chamber's holding that there was no widespread or systematic attack on non-Serbs in Croatia and Bosnia,[47] and found that it had erred in acquitting Šešelj of crimes committed in Hrtkovci (Vojvodina, Serbia). But the judges rejected the prosecution case for Šešelj's involvement in a JCE and held that his other speeches in Croatia and Bosnia, although clearly inflammatory, could not be linked to the crimes committed.

Much of the Appeals judgement focused on Šešelj's hate speech and its alleged incitement linking it to crimes committed, a generally unsettled area of international criminal law. Yet Šešelj's command over the so-called Šešeljevci, and his incitement to them to commit crimes against non-Serbs, was clear from ample contemporaneous video footage. Šešelj himself confirmed the support he received from the Milosevic regime in a later interview:

> The regime in Serbia saw how useful we were. They provided a whole barracks for my volunteers. Serbia did everything for us. The volunteers got uniforms, weapons, and transport to the front, and so on.[48]

Šešelj's involvement in the Vukovar war crimes and his close ties to the Milosevic regime were also recorded in the testimony of Serbian journalist Jovan Dulovic. Then working for *Politika Ekspres*, a pro-regime paper, and with close connections to the Serbian police and JNA, Dulovic overheard Šešelj declare,

> We are all one army. This war is a great test for Serbs. Those who pass the test will become winners. Not a single Ustasha must leave Vukovar alive. . . . The army has shown it was able to cleanse its ranks. We have a unified command consisting of military experts who know what they're doing.[49]

Regarding Šešelj's involvement in war crimes in Bosnia, the Vienna-based Ludwig Boltzmann Institute for Human Rights wrote a detailed report on 'ethnic cleansing' operations in Zvornik from April to June 1992, involving Šešeljevci and other paramilitary groups, which it presented to the UN Commission of Experts.[50] There was also the evidence of protected witness VS-1064, a survivor of the massacre in the Drinjaca Culture Hall in the Zvornik municipality, where *Cetniks* were alleged to have killed 88 Muslims on 30 May 1992.[51] More explicit still was Šešelj's own description of his involvement in Zvornik in early 1992:

> Milosevic was in absolute control. And the operation was planned here in Belgrade. The Bosnian Serbs did take part. But the best combat units came

> from Serbia. These were the special police commandos, called the Red Berets. They are from the secret service of Serbia. My forces took part, as did others. We had prepared this operation carefully. Everything went exactly to plan.[52]

Published in 'The Death of Yugoslavia' in 1995, this interview with Šešelj took place at a time when the international community was negotiating a peace deal with Milosevic, and Šešelj would have spoken with the confidence of impunity.

The Appeals Chamber's conclusion, that Šešelj was not involved in a JCE, contradicted most established tribunal jurisprudence (*Mladic* being an exception), although, according to international defence lawyer Michael Karnavas, 'very rare is the day when the Appeals Chamber will take the time to look at the relevant trial record and other documentary evidence when assessing errors of facts'.[53] The Statute of the Mechanism, whereby judges are to work remotely insofar as possible in order to minimize expenses, may further impact on judicial proceedings, where judges no longer have an office space, staff support, or easy access to trial records. Nor do they have the opportunity, unlike at the ICTY, to discuss factual and legal issues in person, particularly important in the process of finalizing a judgement.[54]

Bearing in mind the mishandling of the Šešelj case by the presiding judge, the intimidation and bullying of witnesses, and the last-minute import of a third judge who had not participated in any of the proceedings, a retrial would have been the most obvious channel for the Appeals Chamber to pursue. Instead, the judges accepted most of the Trial Chamber findings, and sentenced Šešelj to just ten years' imprisonment, which he had already served at the UN Detention Centre, obviating his return to The Hague. Future clashes with Serbia were thus adroitly avoided since, judging by its track record, the Vucic government would have been highly unlikely to extradite Šešelj to The Hague.[55]

At the time of writing, Šešelj remains a member of the Serbian Assembly, and appears frequently on Serbian chat shows, attracting wide audiences, where he freely airs his nationalist views and boasts of his win over the tribunal. He has also recently peddled the long-term Serbian aim of extending its territory to Northern Albania, to gain access to the sea,[56] He also had a stand at the Belgrade Book Fair in October 2018, where school children lined up for autographs and pictures of him.[57]

The presiding judge in the Šešelj first-instance judgement, Jean-Claude Antonetti, meanwhile, remained in service as one of 23 judges on the roster of independent judges at the Mechanism where, as the most long-standing judge after Meron (and Agius), he was to play a crucial role in influencing the Mladic and Karadzic appeal proceedings.

Karadzic appeal hearing

Karadzic's Appeal Hearing on 23 and 24 April 2018 at the Mechanism opened late with Karadzic sitting in the second row, next to his defence team, where he continued to be addressed as 'President Karadzic'. As a war crimes convict, there was no logical reason why he should not be sitting in the dock, especially since attorney Peter Robinson had taken over his defence.[58]

Karadzic appealed on 50 grounds, demanding an acquittal, a new trial or a reduction of sentence. His main points concerned the volume of evidence he was required to rebut, including adjudicated facts which, the Defence claimed, raised fair trial issues since, as a *pro se* defendant, Karadzic was not permitted to testify, and also that the indictment was too broad, inefficient, and could not be adequately defended.

The first issue, the volume of evidence, related directly to the cumulative evidence from many trials, gathered over the 13 years that Karadzic remained at large. The size and complexity of the case were due in large part to the failure to bring him to justice promptly after his indictment, which Karadzic further complicated with numerous motions.

The second point raised by the defence was even more ironic, since a central reason Karadzic would have chosen to represent himself was the freedom it afforded him to self-testify, both through cross-examination of prosecution witnesses and in examining his defence witnesses, which he used to the full, only very occasionally being called to account by the Trial Chamber, mostly on the prompting of the prosecutor. As for the scale of the indictment, it simply reflected Karadzic's involvement either directly, or by command responsibility, in the crimes. More pertinently, as discussed earlier, the indictment had been drastically curtailed on the Trial Chamber's request and represented a truncated picture of Karadzic's role in the war.

Karadzic opened his rebuttal commenting disingenuously, 'I do not want to offend the Trial Chamber who might have been helped by young people with prejudices and lacking local understanding'. Interestingly, he cited major international players Lord Owen, Michael Rose and Lord Carrington in support of his case, adding that Martin Bell, David Harland, and Patrick Treanor (prosecution witnesses) learned things they did not know before.[59]

One of the most telling moments in the Appeals Hearing, however, came when the prosecutor, summing up, focused on the Prijedor case, to argue that genocide had occurred in the municipalities, explaining that to include the many other municipalities would have been too onerous within the scope of the appeals case. Asked by the presiding judge, Theodor Meron, how many people had been killed in Prijedor, she replied that there were 1,200 established victims.[60] This exchange illustrates the problems faced by the prosecution in trying to make the case for Genocide Count 1. In separating the municipalities, the magnitude of the crimes overall in Bosnia became obscured, suggesting that the numbers of proven killed in each municipality were too small to constitute genocide. The Prijedor estimate was further distorted in that it excluded the recent Tomasica findings.

Disqualification of judges

In June 2018, a serious development at the Mechanism threatened the integrity of proceedings in both the Mladic and Karadzic cases. It began with the request by the Mladic defence team that judges Meron, Agius and Daqun be disqualified from the Appeals panel due to potential bias, based on some previous convictions of Bosnian Serbs linked to Mladic. Jean-Claude Antonetti, as the most long-standing judge at the Mechanism after Meron and Agius, assumed the role of acting president (Senior Judge) and accepted the request under Rule 18(A) and (B)(iv).[61] All three judges strongly opposed the decision, declaring in writing that it clearly contradicted established jurisprudence, and harmed the interests of the Mechanism. Nonetheless, they all reluctantly agreed to step down.

The decision had a number of consequences. Firstly, there was the election of Prisca Matimba Nyambe as the new presiding judge. Nyambe, however, could also have been accused of possible bias due to her vigorous 38-page dissenting opinion in the Tolimir judgement, where she questioned established tribunal jurisprudence on a number of issues, and would have acquitted the Bosnian Serb general of all eight charges, including genocide. Referring to the Bosnian 'civil war' and 'decades long hatred between Bosnian Muslims and Bosnian Serbs', Nyambe considered that some of the Bosnian Muslim witnesses 'were inclined to overstate the hardships inflicted on them in Potocari', and challenged the finding that there was a forcible transfer, alleging that civilians had a free choice whether to stay or go.[62] She also suggested, contrary to other reports, that food supplies were sufficient.[63]

More pertinent still were Judge Nyambe's observations about Mladic. She disagreed that Mladic had conducted meetings at the Hotel Fontana in Bratunac in 'an intimidating and dominant' manner, seeing him as 'a well-known general with a commanding presence in a situation of great uncertainty', who was 'welcoming, offering comforts to the attendees such as cigarettes, beer, and sandwiches for lunch,' Nyambe listed Mladic's acts of 'kindness', concluding that he 'clearly left a choice for the population to make their own decisions'.[64] She interpreted the separation of men from the women and children as legitimately screening for war criminals,[65] and challenged the Majority's finding on the scope of the JCE and Tolomir's participation in it, opining that 'small groups of VRS soldiers committed the killings',[66] to 'pay off old scores',[67] and that at least 3,000 men may have been killed in combat.[68]

Following the withdrawals, the Mladic Appeals Chamber in November 2018 consisted, apart from Presiding Judge Nyambe, of Judges N'Gum, Kam, Panton and Ibanda-Nahamya, listed 15th, 18th, 22nd and 23rd in order of precedence, respectively, out of a total of 23 judges on the Mechanism list. This meant that less established, and in some cases less experienced, judges were on the appeals panel of, arguably, one of the most important cases in the tribunal's history.

Removing decision-making from Meron's hands was a development that some may have welcomed, having long felt that Meron's power should be curbed, especially after the controversial acquittals of 2012–2013. Yet was Antonetti really the best person to assume that role, in light of his handling of the Šešelj case, and the Mechanism Statute Code of Conduct?

The Mladic defence team were evidently satisfied with the new Bench line-up. On 6 November 2018, at the first Status Conference since the controversy began,

Mladic's defence counsel, and Mladic himself, made a special point of warmly welcoming Judge Nyambe as the new presiding judge. The Conference lasted ten minutes, during which Mladic read out a statement of health issues which the tribunal medical unit had allegedly failed to address, possibly a prelude to a request (and not the first) for temporary release to be treated in Serbia, which the new Bench, mostly lacking background knowledge, might be more disposed to grant.[69]

Given Judge Antonetti's role in Nyambe's promotion to presiding judge at the Mladic appeal, his 147-page partially dissenting opinion at the Tolimir Appeals Judgement might also be noted, where he expressed Judge Nyambe's dissenting opinion as 'an example to follow'.[70] He agreed with Nyambe that the evidence did not prove beyond reasonable doubt that the transfer of civilians was forcible or unlawful, and opined that Tolimir had not had a fair trial due to the reversal of the burden of proof. Recalling the UN Report (1999) referring to the events in Srebrenica in 1992/3, Antonetti attempted to argue that on 6 May 1992 'the Muslims had started fighting to seize control of Srebrenica from the Serbs'.[71] In doing so, however, he omitted a crucial section of the report (para 33) detailing the takeover of the enclave by Serb forces at the beginning of the conflict, and the expulsions and killings of several hundred Bosniaks.

On Mladic's role in Srebrenica, Antonetti maintained that

> General Mladić took it upon himself to organise new talks at the Hotel Fontana, attended by representatives of the Bosnian Muslim civilians. In the course of these meetings, contrary to what is stated in the Judgement, none of the recordings show any intimidation or authoritarian behaviour on the part of General Mladić towards the participants; on the contrary, he is hospitable and courteous. The video footage that I have seen is particularly edifying as regards the atmosphere and the substance of the discussions.[72]

On the Srebrenica genocide, Antonetti stated,

> I am inclined to accept that there was a 'genocide', but not the kind portrayed by the vague claims of the Prosecution which fails to take into account the actual status of the persons belonging to the protected group of Muslims gathered in Srebrenica.[73]

The judges' dispute then moved on to the Karadzic case. On 25 September 2018, US attorney Peter Robinson, representing Karadzic, requested the removal of President Meron as presiding judge in the Karadzic appeal, citing the Mladic precedent, and previous judgements in which Meron had presided. This was again handled by Antonetti. On 27 September, Meron reluctantly withdrew and appointed William Sekule as presiding judge, which Robinson again opposed for the same reason, upon which Meron appointed judge Ivo Nelson de Caires Batista Rosa. Karadzic's defence then argued before Judge Antonetti that Meron no longer had the competence to appoint judges to the case. As the two senior judges locked horns, there followed a series of motions on all sides, including the prosecution, involving several hearings with different judges, The dispute hinged on the interpretation of Rule 18(A) and (B)(iv) of the Mechanism's Rules of Procedure and Evidence, the prosecutors supporting Meron's position that competence lay with him as president of the Mechanism.

On the face of it, the Defence case was weak. The allegation of possible bias could be attached to many judges who had worked at the ICTY due to the number of previous judgements linked to Karadzic and/or Mladic, and had been deployed previously, mostly without success. It was also questionable why the Karadzic defence team did not act earlier, given that the appeal came 18 months after the trial chamber judgement and five months after Karadzic's appeals hearing.

Then there was the question of jurisdiction, the rules being less than clear on the issue. Equally, if not more, important was judges' accountability. On 9 April 2018, a revised code of professional conduct for judges of the Mechanism was adopted, setting out core judicial principles related to independence, integrity, confidentiality, and outside activities as well as a complaints procedure. The statute states that

> Judges shall be persons of high moral character, impartiality and integrity who possess the qualifications required in their respective countries for appointment to the highest judicial offices. Particular account is taken of candidates' experience as Judges of the ICTR or the ICTY. Not more than two of the Judges on the roster may be nationals of the same State.[74]

There was no explanation of how two judges from Tanzania, Sekule and Masanche, came to be elected to the Mechanism.

*

There were several immediate consequences arising from the debacle. Karadzic's final judgement (originally due in December 2018) was postponed while the new judges familiarized themselves with the case, and his despatch to a national jail consequently delayed, while Mladic rested content that his appeal was in 'good' hands, opening the prospect of 'temporary' release on grounds of health, where the Šešelj precedent could be cited. The longer-term implications of these recent developments are yet to be assessed.

Conclusion

The reluctance of international institutions to locate and arrest those at the 'top' of the pyramid, Radovan Karadzic and Ratko Mladic, immediately following their indictment for genocide in July 1995 or soon thereafter, meant that they had the benefit of freedom for 13 and 16 years, respectively, after the war ended and, when their trials finally began, some witnesses at earlier trials testifying for the same or similar crimes had died or moved on; memories had faded, and others may have simply been reluctant to testify again before a panel of judges distanced from the war, temporally, geographically and linguistically. The trials also came too late to bring about a genuine reckoning with the consequences of crimes committed.

The linkage of crimes across many Bosnian municipalities was made by ICTY prosecutors in several trials but was often lost in the subsequent judgements, with the implication that the most egregious crimes were not committed till July 1995 in Srebrenica. Yet, the Srebrenica genocide was merely the culmination of a process which had begun years earlier. While the Prosecutor's Office recognized – as did the UN Commission of Experts – [75]the genocidal nature of the war from 1992, and issued timely indictments against Mladic and Karadzic for genocide in the municipalities as early as July 1995, the judges 20 years on failed to follow through.

In failing to recognize the wider context of the crimes, and the linkage of events from the outset, some ICTY judges unwittingly reflected the path taken by the UN and major world powers who, setting aside the nature of the war, soft-pedalled their way through years of fruitless, even-handed negotiations with war criminals, and with peace plans based on ethnic division, only acting effectively after the worldwide media exposure of Srebrenica in 1995. The acceptance of the term 'ethnic cleansing' also confused the issue, allowing UN Security Council members to avoid calling the crimes committed in 1992 'genocide', which would have required action under international law on the part of signatories of the Genocide Convention. In confining the genocide to Srebrenica in 1995, signatories of the Convention appeared exonerated, since NATO intervened the following month, followed by a peace settlement at Dayton, achieving a cessation of hostilities.

Karadzic, in his capacity as 'defence counsel', enjoyed privileges unavailable to defendants with *bona fide* counsel representing them, including subtle intimidation which only someone with influence on the ground could effectively exercise. It took a very hardy survivor/witness to withstand the double injustice often meted out in court by defendant and judges alike. Yet Karadzic was simply employing tactics he had used, with some success, with international players in wartime Bosnia, including misinformation and digressions into history, to confuse judges temporally, geographically and culturally remote from the events of the 1990s.

One of the many ironies was that valuable resources saved in cutting out major crime areas in some of the most important trials were subsequently squandered in unnecessarily lengthy proceedings, with months of court time consumed in largely irrelevant argumentation, including propagandist (cross)examination and self-testifying, especially in the Karadzic case, with only occasional censure by the judges, a practice favouring defendants over victim-witnesses.

The crisis at the MICT which flared up in late 2018 raised questions as to the solidity of some of the rules, including judges' accountability and, finally, whether the Mechanism, as it is currently configured, is best placed for addressing some of the most serious cases faced by the ICTY in its existence.

Notes

1 Radovan Karadzic, Interview, *The Death of Yugoslavia*, BBC Documentary, 5/6, 'A Safe Area'. www.youtube.com/watch?v=URZA6r5LLtk. Author's translation.
2 Simo Miskovic, for instance, when interviewed by the OTP, said that he heard about the massacre in 'Room No. 3' in the Keraterm prison camp immediately after the incident, where approximately 150 prisoners were killed in the massacre in late July 1992. In court, the witness claimed that 'this is the first time I hear about the murder of so many people'. See 'Profiteering before Murder', SENSE, 19 December 2013.
3 The Karadzic defence applied for a safe passage guarantee for Dragan Kijac, who headed the State Security Department in the Republika Srpska interior ministry during the war. SENSE, 19 October 2015.
4 Petar Salapura, former chief of the intelligence service of the VRS Main Staff. See 'A Witness for all Seasons', SENSE, 23 June 2013.
5 *Prosecutor v Radovan Karadzic,* Transcripts, p. 42457.
6 The IISS later disowned him, however, removing his monograph on Yugoslavia from its website. For more on Zametica, see Carole Hodge, *The Serb Lobby in the UK*, Donald Treadgold Paper, University of Washington, 1999, and 'Britain and the Balkans', pp. 38, 98.
7 *Prosecutor v Radovan Karadzic,* Transcripts, pp. 42470–42472.
8 Ibid., pp. 42538–42548. BBC Radio 4, 13 July 1995, Exhibit. P6475.
9 Bratunac and Zvornik were included in the Karadzic judgement, but excluded in *Mladic*.
10 Investigating War Crimes in the Former Yugoslav War 1992–1994, M. Cherif Bassiouni, Intersentia, 2017.
11 Ibid., p. 398. See Robert H. Jackson's opening statement before the Nuremberg tribunal. 'My emphasis will not be on individual barbarities and perversions which may have occurred independently of any central plan. One of the dangers ever present is that this Trial may be protracted by details of particular wrongs and that we will become lost in a "wilderness of single instances". Nor will I now dwell on the activity of individual defendants except as it may contribute to exposition of the common plan. The case as presented by the United States will be concerned with the brains and authority [at the] back of all the crimes. These defendants were men of a station and rank which does not soil its own hands with blood. They were men who knew how to use lesser folk as tools. We want to reach the planners and designers, the inciters and leaders', www.roberthjackson.org/speech-and-writing/opening-statement-before-the-international-military-tribunal/.
12 Bassiouni, op. cit., pp. 398–399.
13 Case Preparation for the International Criminal Tribunal for the Former Yugoslavia, Morten Bergsmo and Michael J. Keegan, *Manual on Human Rights Monitoring*, Norwegian Institute of Human Rights, www.jus.uio.no/smr/english/about/programmes/nordem/publications/manual/previous/chapter10.pdf
14 Bob Reid, Chief of Operations, ICTY Office of the Prosecutor, ICTY Final Legacy Lecture Series, 2 November 2017.
15 *Pescanik*, 20 November 2013.
16 *Prosecutor v Radovan Karadzic,* 14 March 2014, and *Institute of War & Peace Reporting,* 21 March 2014.
17 'Tribunal Rejects Tomasica Evidence Against Karadzic', *Balkan Insight*, 21 March 2014. See also 'Prosecutor could have foreseen Karadzic's argument', SENSE, 26 March 2014.
18 Between 2008 and 2018, Karadzic submitted over a thousand motions to the Court, in a bid to frustrate the smooth running of his trial, each involving hearings before a full trial chamber. That this practice was permitted to continue unchecked reflects the tribunal's increasing adherence to UN bureaucracy and legalism over the years.

19 *Prosecutor v Ratko Mladic,* 23 June 2015, T.36184.
20 Ibid., 29 June 2015, T.36416-8.
21 Ibid., 24 June 2015. See also 'Hundreds of "Groups" in Tomasica Mass Graves', SENSE, 24 June 2015.
22 *Prosecutor v Ratko Mladic,* Transcripts, 7 July 2015. See also, www.justice-report.com/en/articles/tomasica-mass-grave-victims-died-in-ethnic-cleansing#sthash.hm7XlGCY.dpuf
23 *Prosecutor v Radovan Karadzic,* Judgement, 24 March 2016, T.1014. For example, in the Foca municipality, the Chamber took judicial notice of the exhumation of 62 male bodies from a mass grave at Jama Piljak on Maluša Mountain but, with the exception of one body which had a name card, Chamber ruled there was insufficient evidence to link those bodies with the scheduled incident. Judgement, p. 359.
24 Ibid. T.250–254, 294–298, 347–354, 395–398, 470–471, 535–536, 540–550, 564, 624–631, 695–755, 785–796, 827–832, 847–854, 870–876, 922–926, 939–944.
25 Ibid. T.240–241, 259, 282, 335–227, 340, 369, 418, 431, 453–456, 807–812.
26 Ibid., pp. 233–242, 272–291, 308, 326–335, 384–390, 418–424, 431–440, 451–467, 508–532, 587–599, 611–621, 642–694, 765–782, 822–824, 835, 861–876, 892–898, 916–917, 930–938.
27 Ibid., pp. 998–999.
28 Ibid., p. 1000.
29 Ibid., p. 1002.
30 Ibid., pp. 1003–1004.
31 Ibid., p. 1023.
32 See, for instance, Judgement, pp. 1121, 1151–1152.
33 Ibid., p. 118.
34 Serbian Autonomous Areas (SAOs) had been created in several areas of Bosnia and Herzegovina before the Carrington Plan was proposed, including Bosanska Krajina in September 1991, an area with 16 municipalities, SAO North-Eastern Bosnia in October 1991, with 3 municipalities, and SAO Herzegovina in May 1991. See also Judgement, pp. 1123–1124.
35 'President Karadžić expresses his deep regret and sympathy to the victims of the crimes charged in his indictment and to their families'. Defence Final Brief, para. 3438. The Trial Chamber also considered Karadzic's age (70) and his conduct at the Detention Unit as mitigating circumstances. *Prosecutor v Radovan Karadzic,* Judgement, pp. 2532–2534.
36 Ibid. Judgement, p. 210, quoted from *Prosecutor v Radislav Krstic,* Appeals Judgement, 19 April 2004, p. 4, para. 12. Italics added.
37 *Krstic*, ibid.
38 Over 100,000 people were estimated to have died in the Bosnian war by 2010, the majority being non-Serbs. The figure remains highly controversial, reflected in these and other reports, and has risen as more mass graves have been discovered, and remains identified, since that time. 'Bosnian war dead figure announced', BBC, 21 June 2007 www.icty.org/x/file/About/OTP/War_Demographics/en/bih_casualty_undercount_conf_paper_100201.pdf https://mihalisk.blogspot.com/2007/10/how-many-and-who-died-in-bosnia.html
39 *Prosecution v Zdravko Tolimir*, Appeal Judgement, 8 April 2015, citing ICJ Croatia v. Serbia Judgment, para. 161, and Brdjanin Trial Judgement, para. 691, Stakic Trial Judgement, paras. 517–518.
40 Ibid., 28 June 2012, T.28762-28770.
41 *Milosevic*, Judge Robinson presiding, concluded that there was 'sufficient evidence the genocide had been committed in Brcko, Prijedor, Sanski Most, Srebrenica, Bijeljina, Kljuc and Bosanski Novi . . . and that the Accused was a participant in a joint criminal enterprise, which included the Bosnian Serb leadership, the aim and intention of which

was to destroy a part of the Bosnian Muslims as a group'. *Prosecutor v Slobodan Milosevic*, Decision on Motion for Judgement of Acquittal, 16 June 2004, paras. 289–291, and Ibid., p. VII, Dissenting Opinion of Judge O-Gon Kwon. On intent, see also 'Namjera za genocid u Bosni i Hercegovini', Enis Omerovic, *Korak*, br. 17, Sarajevo, 2009.

42 Milanovic, www.ejiltalk.org/icty-convicts-radovan-karadzic/

43 Brdjanin, Jelisic, Stakic and Krajisnik were all indicted for genocide in the municipalities in 1992, and acquitted on that count.

44 *Prosecutor v Ratko Mladic,* Trial Chamber Judgement, 22 November 2017, p. 2090, n.15357.

45 See the UN Commission of Experts Report on this.

46 President Theodor Meron, UN Security Council, 7 June 2012.

47 *Prosecutor v Vojislav Šešelj*, Appeals Chamber Judgement, 11 April 2018, para. 70.

48 Šešelj Interview, 'Šešelj u Vukovaru 1991', www.youtube.com/watch?v=kWxGtTykLSY. See also 'Vojislav Šešelj i dobrovolci srpske radikalne stranke u Vukovaru (1991)' where Šešelj states: 'Vukovar is that key point which is necessary to . . . capture'. www.youtube.com/watch?v=kScR8XMTeDs. Author's translation.

49 Armatta, op. cit., pp. 191–192. See also www.youtube.com/watch?v=kWxGtTykLSY where Šešelj comments on the assistance from the Milosevic regime for his group's activities in Vukovar.

50 'Report on ethnic cleansing operations in the northeast-Bosnian city of Zvornik from April through June 1992'. https://web.archive.org/web/20000818030124/www.haverford.edu/relg/sells/zvornik/zvornikrep2b.html

51 Ibid. Prosecution Final Brief, Transcripts, 5 March 2012, p. 17116. See also 'Massacre in Drinjaca', SENSE, 26 June 2008.

52 Interview with Vojislav Šešelj, posted on youtube on 8 April 2011. Kako je Zvornik oslobođen od Zvorničana.mkv. A slightly longer version of the interview is published in *The Death of Yugoslavia*, op. cit., p. 247.

53 Michael Karnavas, http://michaelgkarnavas.net/blog/2018/05/03/Šešelj-appeal-judgement/

54 For a more detailed analysis, see Andrea Carcano, 'Of Efficiency and Fairness in the Administration of International Justice: Can the Residual Mechanism Provide Adequately Reasoned Judgments?' *Questions of International Law*, 30 June 2017.

55 Two contempt indictees in the Šešelj case remain in Serbia, despite numerous attempts by the ICTY to have them transferred to The Hague.

56 Šešelj: Let's exchange the population of the two municipalities – Albanians from Presevo to Strpce, and Strpce to Presevo, Kosovo Sever portal, 28 August 2018. https://kossev.info/Šešelj-lets-exchange-the-population-of-the-two-municipalities-albanians-from-presevo-to-strpce-and-strpce-to-presevo/

57 Navala na Šešelja: deca cekaju u redu, Mondo, 24 October 2018. http://mondo.rs/a1140767/Info/Drustvo/Vojislav-Šešelj-na-sajmu-knjiga-deca-cekaju-u-redu.html

58 The Mechanism proved to be more flexible on Karadzic's funding than the ICTY, which had determined on the basis of two properties owned by Karadzic's wife that he had sufficient resources to fund his own defence. The MICT Registrar initially followed this decision, but 10 days later the Court held that it had erred, and granted Karadzic legal aid. *Prosecutor v Karadzic,* Decision on a Motion for Review of the Registrar's Decision on Indigence, 24 June 2016.

59 In court, Karadzic managed to have Bell confused over a number of facts. *Prosecutor v Karadzic*, Transcripts, 14–15 December 2010. See also Martin Bell's view, where he admits that memory fades over time, and opines that 'an acquittal for lack of sufficient evidence would be more to the tribunal's credit than a conviction unsafely arrived at'. 'Karadzic isn't the only one on trial', *Guardian*, Opinion, 26 October 2009.

60 Karadzic Appeal Hearing, 24 April 2018, www.youtube.com/watch?v=7ZFR6uI8E6w&t=3655s, 59.42 minutes into video.

61 Meron, as president of the MICT, exempted himself since the motion applied to him. 'Biased' Hague judges in Ratko Mladić trial replaced, *Emerging Europe*, 6 September 2018.
62 *Prosecutor v Zdravko Tolimir,* Trial Chamber Judgement, 12 December 2012, Dissenting Opinion of Judge Prisca Matimba Nyambe, paras. 14, 28–32 and 82.
63 Ibid., paras. 29–32. This contradicted copious evidence to the contrary. See, for example, UN Information Notes, June–July 1995, which recorded that supplies Srebrenica plummeting from late May 1995 to a quarter of previous levels.
64 Ibid., paras. 37–38 and 45.
65 Ibid., para. 40.
66 Ibid., paras. 63–65.
67 Ibid., para. 82.
68 Ibid., para. 84.
69 In early December, Mladic requested four days' leave to visit the grave of a recently deceased cousin in Serbia. www.balkaninsight.com/en/article/defense-files-leave-request-for-ratko-mladic-12-10-2018
70 *Prosecutor v Zdravko Tolimir,* Appeals Chamber Judgement, Separate and Partly Dissenting Opinion of Judge Antonetti, p. 9.
71 Ibid., p. 11.
72 Ibid., p. 60.
73 Ibid., p. 73.
74 The Code of Professional Conduct for the Judges of the Mechanism (MICT/14/Rev.1) was originally adopted on 11 May 2015.
75 Bassiouni, pp. 206, 306, and UN Commission of Experts Report, Annex 5 162.

Conclusion

When the International Criminal Tribunal for the Former Yugoslavia (ICTY) was established in 1993, international criminal law was in embryonic form, with no precedent beyond the Nuremberg and Tokyo trials to refer to in addressing some of the most egregious war crimes in Europe since World War II. Since then, the tribunal has overcome numerous obstacles to convict 90 individuals for genocide, war crimes and crimes against humanity, including senior political and military figures. It has also established rape as a crime against humanity and provided an extensive archive for other *ad hoc* tribunals and the ICC.

Yet, at the time of its closure in December 2017, several of the tribunal's stated objectives remained unachieved. In the early days, its main focus was survival, often against almost insuperable odds. Many of the early indictments were for relatively minor offenders, and not always sufficiently supported by evidence. And, while the indictments for Karadzic and Mladic in July 1995 were a major breakthrough, Slobodan Milosevic was not indicted for another four years, and neither Karadzic nor Mladic were arrested at the time despite being easily accessible, casting a shadow over the tribunal's work for well over a decade.

The difficulties began when the Commission of Experts, the precursor to the ICTY, was denied adequate support at Security Council level and wound down prematurely. That unhelpful stance was carried into the early years of the ICTY's existence which received only lukewarm support from most Security Council members, and virtually none at all from Britain. The ICTY's exclusion from the Dayton Peace Conference, where it could have emphasized the importance of challenging impunity, was a further illustration of the international mindset in minimizing the tribunal's role in restoring peace and securing justice.

Instead, the international failure to make arrests following ICTY indictments left the main actors free to wield influence over a civilian population already damaged by years of war. The opportunity to put Mladic and Karadzic on trial at a time when there was a readiness on the part of some Serb political leaders to acknowledge what had taken place and when graphic video coverage of the Srebrenica genocide was still in the public mind worldwide was lost. The trials also came too late to bring about a genuine reckoning with the consequences of crimes committed. Furthermore, over time, outside perception as to the nature of the Bosnian war has become muddied, and the frequent practice of referring to the conflict simply as a 'civil' war misleadingly suggests a symmetry of guilt which has consequences, both in terms of reparations and in the international approach to addressing the current mounting tensions in the region.

The potential power of the ICTY, had it been free to exercise it fully, was illustrated in the indictments of Karadzic and Mladic in July 1995, resulting in their official exclusion from the peace talks, and later from holding public office. Milosevic, however, remained unindicted until May 1999, and played a key role at Dayton and beyond, while the Croatian president, Franjo Tudjman, a co-signatory of the Dayton Agreement, was never indicted, and is posthumously regarded as a hero by many in Croatia. Indicting Milosevic would have been expressly contrary to international policy makers who, although cognizant of his pivotal role in the Croatian and Bosnian aggression, had mostly viewed him from the outset as an essential element in the peace process. The exclusion from Dayton of Kosovo, where there was ongoing human rights' abuse and rising tensions, together with the concomitant failure to indict Milosevic timeously, contributed to the full-blown conflict there three years later.

In attempting to work around the external obstacles to the tribunal's development, ICTY officials made compromises which did less than justice to the victims and tarnished the tribunal's reputation, including the failure to indict leading offenders, uneven sentencing patterns, unwarranted capitulation to Serbian leaders' demands and lenience on self-representation issues. The acquittal or provisional release on sketchy grounds of senior military and political figures was, on occasion, compounded by engagement in trial chamber practice which would not pass muster in most national courts in the European Union or North America.

The ICTY belatedly introduced a code of conduct for judges in 2015. However, Judge Jean-Claude Antonetti, who had acquitted Vojislav Šešelj based on reasoning which dismissed established tribunal jurisprudence, was elected to the panel of 23 judges at the Mechanism, where he played a crucial role as Senior Judge in reconfiguring, at a late stage in the proceedings, the appeals chamber panels in both *Mladic* and *Karadzic*. Antonetti's handling of the Šešelj trial was also, arguably, not in accordance with stated ICTY standards.

The wisdom in disqualifying Judge Frederik Harhoff just weeks before the Šešelj judgement might also be questioned. Was it prudent, based on one lengthy email expressing concerns felt by many at the ICTY and elsewhere, to replace Harhoff with Mandiaye Niang, a recently appointed judge, new to the ICTY and with little trial chamber experience, and expect him in a matter of months to pass judgement on a highly complex case extending over 11 years, without having participated in any of the proceedings? Equally, was Harhoff's dismissal by fellow judges democratically conducted? Who benefited, moreover, by putting Florence Hartmann on trial for contempt of court for revealing information in the public interest which was already mostly in the public domain? Was this in the tribunal's interests or, indeed, a good use of limited resources?

The issue of resources has often been raised as an explanation for less than perfect outcomes. Yet some ICTY defendants, through their legal teams, were awarded massive sums, in comparison with survivors who had travelled to The

Hague and testified, often at considerable risk, only to return home to face their erstwhile aggressors, released after completing just two-thirds of their relatively short sentences.

Then there was the genocide issue. Successive trial chambers have ruled against the case for genocide in the municipalities, based on insufficient numbers killed. Apart from being a questionable interpretation of the Genocide Convention, logic suggests that, if using the numbers criterion, judges should rightly have found for genocide in the municipalities, where there was overwhelming evidence that the number of (mainly Muslim) civilians killed between April and August 1992 across multiple Bosnian towns and villages, was far greater than in Srebrenica in July 1995, a death toll which would have been higher still had it not been for the exposure of the camps by courageous journalists from the United States and Britain. Had genocide been established in 1992, there would have been an obligation for all signatories of the Genocide Convention to act to prevent or halt the carnage.

The ICTY was in some degree both hostage to and a casualty of international wartime policy. Unlike the ICC, the tribunal, established under Chapter VII of the UN Charter, and UN funded, was essentially a political institution (although not in the sense often characterized by Belgrade), and subject to the dictates of the P5 members at the Security Council. From the outset, it found itself at odds with many international diplomats and politicians engaged in securing a peace settlement, who viewed indicting wartime leaders as detrimental to re-establishing peace. While there is no dichotomy *per se* between the pursuit of a political settlement and the pursuit of justice, conflict arises when those whose work it is to bring about a cessation of hostilities are in negotiations with political and military leaders alleged to be responsible for those hostilities, and on whom they depend in their efforts to secure peace.

M. Cherif Bassiouni in his final work describes in some detail how major world powers and institutions frustrated the work of the Commission of Experts and obstructed the establishment of the ICTY. He pulls no punches in identifying some of the main players on the international stage, citing the responsibility of international officials on several levels. Yet the ICTY, despite paying tribute to Bassiouni at the opening of its final legacy conference, devoted just a fringe meeting to discuss his work and the issues raised in his book including, most pertinently, the tribunal's overall approach to the conflict, and the linkage of crimes across Bosnia and Croatia. This linkage was made by ICTY prosecutors in several trials, but often lost in subsequent judgements, where it was not recognized that the Srebrenica genocide was merely the culmination of a process which had begun years earlier, involving the forcible takeover of large swathes of former Yugoslavia – from the destruction of the multi-cultural town of Vukovar in November 1991 and the massacre at Ovcara, to the siege of Sarajevo and the Visegrad and Koricani massacres, from the Foca mass rapes to the mass graves at Ljubija, from the forcible takeover of Prijedor to the fall of Srebrenica in 1995 and the Racak massacre in January 1999. While the Prosecutor's Office recognized, as did the UN Commission of Experts and the European Court of Human Rights, the genocidal nature of the war from 1992, ICTY judges adopted an atomized approach and failed to reflect those findings.

In not recognizing the wider context of the crimes, and the linkage of events from the outset, successive trial and appeals chambers unwittingly echoed the path taken by the UN and major world powers who, setting aside the nature of the war, soft-pedalled their way through years of fruitless, even-handed negotiations with war criminals and peace proposals based on ethic division, acting effectively only after the worldwide media exposure of Srebrenica in 1995. The acceptance of the term 'ethnic cleansing' also confused the issue as it allowed the UN Security Council, and later ICTY judges, to avoid calling the crimes committed in 1992 'genocide', a denotation requiring intervention under international law. Confining the genocide to Srebrenica, on the other hand, exonerated outside powers, since NATO intervened the following month, followed by a peace settlement at Dayton which achieved a cessation of hostilities, albeit also rewarding the perpetrators of genocide with their own ethnically 'cleansed' republic.

*

The ICTY on its website claims that 'by removing some of the most senior and notorious criminals and holding them accountable the Tribunal has been able to lift the taint of violence, contribute to ending impunity and help pave the way for reconciliation'. Yet the relatively short sentences given to a number of defendants, including perpetrators of genocide, enabled them to return home to a hero's welcome, with associated privileges, often at the expense of their victims, some of whom are destined to live as second class citizens in a hostile environment, exposed to the taunts of their former oppressors. This suggests that the ICTY's extensive outreach programme, despite its efforts through numerous films, conferences and other promotional activities, failed signally to reach many of the people in Yugoslavia's successor states. The fact that some of their citizens were responsible for unspeakable war crimes did not penetrate through to Serbia, Republika Srpska, Croat-dominated areas of the Federation or, to an extent, Croatia itself, where a culture of denial prevails. Nationalist or war-corrupted leaders remain at the helm while the situation on the ground grows ever tenser.

*

While the full legacy of the ICTY remains to be written, its final legacy conference, held over three days in Sarajevo in June 2017, was intended as a showcase for its accomplishments during its near quarter century of existence. Ironically though, the conference was also an unwitting reflection of the tribunal's shortcomings. Despite the wide range of contributors from various institutions, and representatives from the ICTY itself, they did little, with a few exceptions, to address the ongoing issues confronting victims and survivors, some of which stem indirectly from ICTY procedures and practice.

The conference struck the wrong note from the start with the decision to invite the Croat member of the Bosnian presidency, Dragan Covic, to deliver a keynote speech, where he proceeded to dismiss one of the tribunal's declared achievements, the joint criminal enterprise. A further miscalculation was the balance between the time allocated to panellists and to contributions from the floor, where many panellists spoke at some length of their accomplishments, while just minutes remained for questions. When victim/survivors did manage to speak, the response from panellists was generally brief and inadequate, and the opportunity for a wider debate on the ICTY legacy, and for more transparency, was missed. And then there was the elephant in the room – the absence of an open discussion on the international role in the tribunal's establishment and work. While the initial almost insurmountable difficulties, financial, logistical and even existential, were frequently referred to, some of the main reasons underlying those difficulties were not.

This was all in marked contrast to an earlier ICTY legacy conference in Sarajevo in 2013 where, following the acquittals of several senior political and military figures, Bosnian survivors across the spectrum were given ample opportunity to air their grievances, resulting in fierce debate. ICTY President Theodor Meron, while not apologizing for his role in some of the acquittals, at least attempted an explanation, and Vice-president Carmel Agius expressed regret that there was no mechanism for compensation. Of course, had the ICJ found Serbia as a state responsible for genocide in Bosnia, the ruling would have provided an opening for the issue of compensation to victims to be addressed. As it was, the ICJ, despite not being bound by the same rules as the ICTY, simply echoed the *ad hoc* tribunal's findings, namely, that Serbia was not responsible other than, paradoxically, in failing to prevent the genocide.

Today, the international community, and especially the European Union, still fails to recognize the wrongs of the past in continuing to regard Serbia as a factor in stability between Russia and the West. Convicted war criminals are being rewarded with public platforms and influential positions in Serbia, denial of the Srebrenica genocide is the norm and, according to Amnesty, discrimination and threats against minorities are rife. A recently established Russian-run 'humanitarian' centre in Nis in southern Serbia is suspected of being used for Russian intelligence operations. The claim of the all-powerful Serbian president, Aleksandar Vucic, to support the integrity of Bosnia and Herzegovina must also be questioned. In March 2018, Serbia despatched some 2,500 automatic rifles to Republika Srpska (RS), where a new training centre has been set up, along with a heavily armed police unit. The former RS president, Milorad Dodik, currently chairs the Bosnian presidency, a position from which he is strongly placed to set in motion his goal of RS secession, and eventual unity with Serbia.

Bosnia underwent the first European war since World War II and became a symbol for national tragedy. In the meantime, there have been other wars and genocides, the fight against terrorism after 9/11 leading to invasions in Afghanistan and Iraq, and wars in Syria and Yemen, to mention just a few. During these years, key witnesses in Bosnia have died or become disillusioned in repeating their stories, often in the presence of the perpetrators to, at times, little or no apparent avail, while memories of the Bosnian genocide worldwide have dimmed.

At the time of writing, the Mladic and Karadzic appeal judgements, as well as the first-instance judgement in the Stanisic and Simatovic retrial, are still awaited. The Mechanism will, therefore, have the final word on whether there was a genocide in Srebrenica *and* in the other Bosnian municipalities in 1992, and also on the role of Serbia, both central questions in determining the nature of the Bosnian war. Recent developments at the Mechanism, however, including the refiguring of the appeals chamber panels, may risk challenging some of the main achievements of the ICTY.

While judicial institutions do not make history, the ICTY has made a substantial contribution to the establishment of a historical record for scholars and future generations. External pressure, and a lack of accountability at both tribunal and international level, however, have at times resulted in an outcome which has rendered less than justice to the victims and survivors of the (post) Yugoslav wars and may, if not adequately addressed even at this late stage, sow the seeds for further unrest in the region.

Afterword

The Karadžić Appeals Judgement on 20 March 2019 contained few surprises. Extending the 40-year sentence to life imprisonment was predictable, especially since Ratko Mladić and several of Karadžić's subordinates had already received life sentences. Similarly, the ruling that genocide was confined to Srebrenica in July 1995 mirrored previous judgements.

The new element was Judge Jose Ricardo de Prada Solaesa's robust dissenting opinion where he argued that sufficient evidence existed for genocide in the Bosnian Municipalities in 1992. Previous ICTY defendants indicted for genocide other than in Srebrenica had been acquitted, escaped genocide charges through plea bargaining, or died before judgement, although, in 2004, the judges in *Milosevic* did find a *prima facie* case for genocide in several municipalities, reflecting the UN Commission of Experts' Report and the *Jorgic* judgement (Dusseldorf, 1997), endorsed by the ECtHR a decade later.

Judge de Prada's conclusions, despite running counter to previous judgements, both at the ICTY and the International Court of Justice, represent a crucial contribution to the debate on the precise nature of the war in Bosnia and Herzegovina, and to interpreting the Genocide Convention. They also raise questions over the international role in Bosnia at the time.

The interpretation of 'beyond reasonable doubt' lay at the heart of Judge de Prada's criticism of the Majority ruling on Genocide Count 1, which he dismissed as 'a simplistic analysis of evidence that does not satisfy the reasonableness standard corresponding to professional judges, who have the obligation to justify why a concrete possible alternative inference can cause a reasonable doubt'.[1]

In fact, just 35 pages of the 380-page judgement were devoted to the Prosecution's Appeal compared with 270 pages for that of Karadžić, and only 12 pages on the issue of genocidal intent, where the Majority for the most part largely reiterated, rather than analysed, the Trial Chamber findings.

Significantly, de Prada was the only judge with direct court experience of the crimes against humanity in Bosnia, having served as an international judge at the Bosnian War Crimes Chamber, where he was involved in several appeals cases for crimes committed in some of the most notorious localities, including Foca, Visegrad and Sanski Most. Judge Batista Rosa was only appointed to the Appeals Chamber in October 2018, while the other judges were either previously based at the Rwanda court, or without international tribunal experience. The safe route, therefore, was to follow ICTY precedent on the genocide issue.

On the question of intent, or *dolus specialis*, the distinguishing feature of genocide, de Prada argued that the Trial Chamber lacked deep analysis, limiting itself to 'a formal approach' to the evidence, unsustained by sound argument.

> In my opinion, the legal, arguments provided regarding the *mens rea* for the crime of genocide are not correct, neither is the evidentiary assessment undertaken as it does not correspond with the required reasonableness standard.[2]

While neither the ICTY Statute nor the Genocide Convention provide a clear standard for genocidal intent, de Prada opined that a definition of genocide 'exclusively focused on the intent to destroy the group as such' made no sense. According to de Prada, 'The concept of the crime of genocide makes sense when understood as extreme criminal acts of discrimination against human groups, which can go as far as their physical destruction, but also includes all acts tending to this finality'.[3] In this context, he contended that 'thousands of Bosnian Muslims and Bosnian Croats, whom the Trial Chamber categorised as merely displaced, were in fact subjected to conditions of life aimed at their physical destruction'.[4]

Judge de Prada concluded:

> I do not intend to dwell on the reasons, of criminal politics among others, that according to my view could have influenced the development of an extraordinarily narrow concept of genocide, filling it with impossible requirements that make the concept almost inapplicable, losing all its sense and legal value for the correct protection of criminal attacks against human groups, thus gaining a mere symbolic character.[5]

*

The life sentence imposed on Karadžić was not unanimous; Judges Batista Rosa and de Prada dissented, the latter on grounds of human rights. This has opened up an avenue for Karadžić and his legal team to argue for review. Karadžić's request has already been lodged with the Mechanism which, if accepted, risks years of delay and legal obfuscation, possibly with eventual recourse to the European Court. Such prevarication could result in Karadžić managing to evade serving any of his sentence in a national prison – an ultimate travesty of justice.

There is currently a concerted move to rewrite the history of the Bosnian war, reviving misnomers such as the 'ancient ethnic hatreds' theory, and the 'civil war' argument where all parties are portrayed as equally culpable, calling for international humanitarian assistance but eschewing military intervention. The process of drawing a symmetry of guilt, evident in international peace plans during the war and regaining currency more recently, would no longer be feasible with a legal ruling that genocide occurred throughout the Bosnian municipalities as early as April 1992. Also, if genocide did begin in 1992, it may be asked why, with an international presence in the vicinity, there was a failure to act decisively to bring the slaughter to an end.

The only remaining opportunity for establishing genocide in the Municipalities rests with the Mladić Appeals judges. Does the divided judgement in *Karadžić* on Genocide Count 1 hold any significance for Mladić? Since the military and political leaders, Mladić and Karadžić, were both implicated in the same crimes from 1992 onwards, the Mladić Appeals Chamber will hopefully take Judge de Prada's arguments into consideration. As discussed earlier, however, the line-up of judges leaves room for some concern.

Glasgow, 31 March 2019

Notes

1 *Prosecutor v Radovan Karadzic*, Appeals Chamber Judgement, International Residual Mechanism for Criminal Tribunals, 20 March 2019, partially Dissenting Opinion of Judge de Prada, 808.
2 Ibid. 830.
3 Ibid. 837–838.
4 Ibid. 829.
5 Ibid. 838.

Index

For Product Safety Concerns and Information please contact our EU representative GPSR@taylorandfrancis.com
Taylor & Francis Verlag GmbH, Kaufingerstraße 24, 80331 München, Germany

www.ingramcontent.com/pod-product-compliance
Ingram Content Group UK Ltd.
Pitfield, Milton Keynes, MK11 3LW, UK
UKHW022010180926
475701UK00003B/290
9780367729134